Oct 2017

Dear Arlyn

Thanks for y
of support for t
life that contribu
this book coming to be.
the stories in this book
remind you of how to
do "slow medecine"

Much love
Patricia

# Warren Borgquist, MD

## Family, Friendship, and Rural Medicine

### A MEMORY BOOK

By Patricia Harrelson

Word Project Press, CA

WARREN BORGQUIST:
FAMILY, FRIENDS, AND RURAL MEDICINE

Copyright © 2017
By Patricia Harrelson

Published in the United States by Word Project Press, 2017

Requests for permission to make copies of any part of this work should be submitted to
info@wordprojectpress.com

This work includes bibliographic references.

Credits

Author Photo: Cindy Dixon
Cover Design: Melody Young

ISBN:  978-0-9970349-7-4
LIBRARY OF CONGRESS: 2017952761

*to Judy*

*with appreciation*

# CONTENTS

Prologue: The Day My Doctor Died     xi

### Part I: Little Warnie

Models & Glue     19
The Upper Dime     35
School Daze     47

### Part II: The Doctor

Mosey In     67
Picnic     77
TGH     87
Giraffe Clan     103
Mono Way     115
Birth Chair     131
Young Turks     141
Intrepid Friend     155

### Part III: The Papa

Fiddler     175
Considerable Attention     187
Chuck & Todd     203
Following the Stick     215
Alternative Birth Center     227
Midwives     237
Pavorotti Staying     253
The School of Life     263
A Beautiful Day in the Neighborhood     275
Mod Podge     287

Part IV: Gramps

Heaven for Kids                                          301
Plan B                                                  317
The Bigger Picture                                      329
Big-Hearted Doctoring                                   341
Holy Shit                                               351
Hospice                                                 365

Part V: Bald Guy For Peace

Circle of Life                                          383
The World                                               399
My Crazy People                                         413
Magic of the Night                                      427
Dammit, Warren                                          435


Acknowledgements                                        441
Bibliography                                            443

## Prologue

# THE DAY MY DOCTOR DIED

The day my doctor died, I sat in my garden plucking dried seedpods. Crushing the bulbous heads of spent love-in-a mist, I harvested seeds and worried that as the size of my family increased so did the chances exponentially increase for injury and death. I did not know my doctor was gone, but an encounter the day before had prompted this dire consideration. I'd attended a Roller Derby match to watch my daughter-in-law skate fiercely, wearing helmet, mouthpiece, knee and wrist guards to protect against the vigor of the sport. A woman, whom I hardly knew, sat beside me, and we spoke about cheering for family at sporting events. She grasped my arm when I said I had fourteen grandkids. "Do you have a favorite?" she asked.

"Yes," I demurred, "but the favored one changes frequently."

"My favorite is in coma," she said.

I sucked back alarm and listened as she told of a car accident, then a vigil that had been going on for several weeks.

The next day—the day my doctor died—I collected seeds and imagined my loved ones hurt or dying. A hot August breeze rushed about my bare shoulders. A plastic tub sat at my feet filled with tiny seeds and crumbled pods, the propagation of countless tender encounters with pollinating insects. On the other side of town, the man who had tended my family's ills for over thirty years had died in his sleep. He had treated pneumonia and earaches, rashes and whooping cough, broken arms and legs. He had caught my third baby in his Mono Way office and cared for my daughter when she hemorrhaged after a home birth. He made the call to have my three-day old grandson helicoptered to Children's Hospital in Oakland—a call that likely saved his life. When my mother lay hooked to a ventilator in ICU, he met with my siblings and me to tell us in a gentle, measured cadence, "You need to prepare for your mother's death."

The day my doctor died, I collected seeds to sow.

A week later, I sat with hundreds of people in the Family Worship Center. Dr. Warren Borgquist smiled down bigger than life from a projector screen at the front of the church—a bald man in his sixties with a closely cropped salt and pepper beard. Gazing at his brown eyes twinkling through wire rimmed glasses, I felt like he was looking directly at me. Currents of emotion roiled through my body. My 6-year-old granddaughter—a child Dr. Borgquist had delivered—sat on my lap. The church was so overflowing with mourners that many people were left standing. I spotted Judy Borgquist, Warren's widow, near the front of the church, encircled by four or five women. Her son Scott was on the dais. As he stepped to the podium, a hush descended. He introduced Lori Brandon who sang "I Can See Clearly Now."

My tears began to fall soon after when Scott faced the packed sanctuary and said, "If you've had a baby delivered by Dr. Borgquist or you yourself were delivered by him, please stand." More than half the room rose to their feet. I wasn't the only one crying. Sniffling was audible and tissues passed from hand to hand.

Over the next hour, we heard Warren's four children—biological, adopted and step—speak about this father figure. We heard twelve grandchildren tell stories about how Gramps challenged them to be the best person they could be. Four of his friends talked about jogging with him, about hiking and camping in Yosemite and Death Valley. Four colleagues described what it was like to work with him—moments in his medical practice that were mundane, commendable, or hilarious. The memorial was directed by David Purdy, Judy Borgquist's ex-husband.

Music and song—evocative and emotional—punctuated the

storytelling. "Sunrise, Sunset" floated over the crowd bringing to mind Warren playing the role of Tevye in a community theater production of Fiddler on the Roof. Two young women whose father Warren had cared for during the end stages of cancer sang "I'll Fly Away," filling the sanctuary with poignancy. Glimpses of Warren arrived in the lyrics of many songs—"Country Roads," "Sunshine on My Shoulder," "It's a Wonderful World" and "Amazing Grace"—conjuring memories of the rural family physician with a sunny disposition, who graced the community and made a playground of the world. A slideshow and three poster boards with pictures revealed a man with his family, often silly, usually beaming, and, my favorites, ones in which he leans in with a look of inane satisfaction— eyes half closed—for a blissful kiss on the cheek from Judy, or his daughter, or a grandchild. This was a fresh look at the doctor who had cared for my family, a look of delight and joy that differed from his generous, outgoing smile in the examination or delivery room.

David Purdy's daughter, Sarah, whom Warren had delivered, stood at the table that held the poster boards with pictures. She offered attendees cards that read "My favorite memory about Warren . . ." and invited us to write our memories to leave for the family. Nearly two hundred cards were deposited in a basket: stories from grateful patients that frequently mentioned his twinkling eyes, warm smiles, Birkenstocks, and colorful socks. After the service, people slowly—very, very slowly— left the auditorium, gathering outside the church in clusters to greet, hug, and reminisce, everyone reluctant to leave, for leaving signified another ending.

I thought about Warren Borgquist for days after the gathering. What was unusual about this man was the level of intimacy he had shared with those who attended his memorial. He had infiltrated lives with a style all his own: by telling a story or a joke, with deep abiding silence or belly laughter, by recalling a tiny detail or connecting a fact from one situation to another, by questioning and remembering, by reading and observing, by neglecting or choosing not to follow rules or protocol. Dr. Warren Borgquist found his way into our hearts, and we thought of him as a friend. His step-daughter Jennifer later told me: "We thought he was ours until we stood on the dais at the memorial looking at over 400 people who thought the same thing. They thought he was theirs."

Yes, each of his patients thought of Warren Borgquist as "my doctor." Like Jennifer, I saw something at the memorial that made an impression. Of all the pictures displayed, there was only one picture of Warren as a doctor. There were over a hundred pictures on the poster boards and probably as many in the slide show. They were pictures of a little boy, a son, a teenager; a brother, a boyfriend, a husband; a new father; a father-of-the-bride, an about-to-be grandfather; a buddy, an uncle, a man with lots of colorful socks. The pictures celebrated the life the man lived when he wasn't doctoring.

To be sure, we had heard stories from his life, for Dr. Warren Borgquist gave stories along with prescriptions and stitches. He treated streptococcus, retained placenta, or skin cancer with a mix of medical proficiency and his own experience. But when I heard one of his stories and understood how it applied to me and my situation, I didn't think about the life that contained the story. I didn't think about where the man who strolled in late from lunch had been while a reception room full of people waited to see him. I was prepared to wait because I wanted the kind of care I was sure he would provide, but I didn't think about him beyond the office. I didn't give a thought to where the doctor who had just delivered my baby was going next. At his memorial service, I suddenly saw the man beyond the examination room. This man had a life.

I couldn't shake an impulse to explore the giant footprint he had planted on the community. This wasn't a new sensation. The morning after I completed the final draft of my second book, I woke with an idea blooming in my mind: an impulse to write about Dr. Warren Borgquist. I wrote him a letter, and he called a few days later. I could tell he appreciated my interest, but he was reluctant. "I'm going on a trip. Why don't you call me again, and we'll talk. I'll keep your letter." We did talk again, a couple of times over several years. Each time, he smiled ruefully and said no one would want to read a book about him. But I didn't agree. I saw his life as large and entertaining and rich with story.

Then Warren died. But the idea to write a book did not.

A year late on closing night of *Tuesdays with Morrie* at Stage 3 Theater, I stood chatting with three women—Judy Borgquist, Ellen Stewart, and Kathleen Lorimer—about the play and mortality.

"Do you still want to write that book," asked Judy, redirecting the conversation to my now five-year-old query.

"Yes," I'd answered with a rush of anticipation.

"It won't be the same."

"I know," I said.

But I also knew a lot of people who would be eager to reminisce. And that's what I wanted to do: linger with those who fondly remembered Warren Borgquist.

# PART I

# LITTLE WARNIE

*Chapter 1*

# MODELS & GLUE

The family – that dear octopus, from whose tentacles we never quite escape, nor in our inmost hearts, ever quite wish to.

-Dodie Smith, *"Dear Octopus"*

If you were going to tell someone a story about your family—like this is where we came from—what would you say?"

"The Borgquists came from St. Paul, Minnesota as the Nelsons," said Marjorie Borgquist, launching into her family's narrative. Reminiscing with Warren's sister seemed like a good way to learn about the man who had been my doctor for thirty years. We were sitting at her dining room table before tall glasses of water and a box spilling with old photos. Marjorie answered my question with twinkling eyes and full-lips forming a smile so like Warren's that I was immediately enamored. She, however, had a curly head of grey-streaked hair that in no way resembled his balding dome.

"They were Swedish," continued Marjorie, "and there were four brothers who came to California. Three brothers went to King City, and my grandfather—my Dad's father—went to the Turlock area. There were so many Swedes named Nelson who migrated to California that the mail got mixed up, so they changed their name to Borgquist."

"Where did that name come from?"

"It's a common name in Sweden but not as common as Nelson. My grandma Sarah's family also changed their name when they came over. They were Alldren's with two L's, and they changed it to one L. Grandma used to tell about arriving in California on a train and seeing fields covered with lupine and poppies. She thought it was beautiful, but she also said it was sandy, which was worrisome because they intended to farm alfalfa and grains. She married David Borgquist, and they had four children: Gladys, LaVerne, Julius, and my dad, Clifford, who was born in 1923. Julius drowned in the canal when he was 5."

Marjorie paused, and we sat quietly with this part of the family story: the loss of a child. Another child would die in the next generation—a sibling to Marjorie and Warren—but that happened years later.

"My grandfather died when my father was 6 years old. He had what they called Bright's disease, which is a kidney disease. Later, when my uncle died of a liver ailment, I remember asking Warren if we had funky organs. He said, 'No that happened before penicillin. They probably had untreated infections that damaged those organs.' Since my father was so young when his father died, he didn't have too many memories about him, but later when he got Alzheimer's, he told the same stories over and over, and one was about his father getting a greyhound. Rabbits were a bane to farmers back then, but a greyhound could catch them. According to my dad, that dog had ninety-six pups. I have a picture of my dad with his father." Marjorie reached for the box of photos. "Here, it is," she said placing a small black and white photograph on the table of a man standing with two small boys before a horse-drawn wagon.

"What year was this photo taken?" I asked.

"Probably 1928. My dad looks like he's about 4 or 5. Grandma actually did very well for herself after my grandfather died. One of the neighboring farmers started growing peaches, so Grandma planted peaches too. Those ten acres of peaches made as much money at harvest time as the other thirty acres planted in grain. She learned to plant different varieties of peaches that came ripe at different times, so when the migrant workers arrived, she had a summer's worth of work for them. She was kind of a farmer-entrepreneur. Uncle Laverne was very astute too. He quit school in 6th or 7th grade and helped Grandma. He wound up making all kinds of money. There was some bitterness there because Uncle Laverne was very much the businessman. He had money. Dad was always broke. And Uncle

Laverne was instrumental in a lot of decisions that Grandma made, so she felt like she owed him more from the farm. That was a sore point between my uncle and my dad," added Marjorie.

"Mom and Dad met in high school. They were riding the school bus, and Dad was sitting with his best friend, Warren Appling—that's who my brother was named after. Dad spotted Mom and told Warren. 'That's the girl I'm going to marry.' So Warren got up and went over and introduced himself to Mom and then introduced her to Dad. Mom was not impressed with him at first, but they started dating. He used to take her for motorcycle rides in the peach orchards. They got married right out of high school. Grandma bought them a farm in Escalon, but it didn't do well financially. Dad always said the farm was a bad buy. 'The crops weren't right.'" Marjorie slapped the table for emphasis. "'The land wasn't right.'" She slapped the table again, and I got the picture. Cliff vigorously disclaiming any fault for the farm's failure. "He always swore she bought that place because it had a nice rose garden. And it did. But the truth was he didn't want to run a farm."

So there it was. Warren Borgquist's family history as told by his sister Marjorie, collapsed into a few significant stories, the kind of stories that become legendary in a family—greyhounds and peaches, love stories and financial woes, loss and survival. In the months to come, I would return several times to sit at this spacious dining room table and revisit these and other stories with her, and eventually with her sister Karma.

At first, I could see nothing of Warren, nor Marjorie, in Karma. She was elfin in size while her brother was large. Her nondescript brown hair was cut in a pixie, unlike Marjorie's curly froth, and she did not have the smiling eyes and mouth of her brother and sister. But I soon recognized Warren's wry sense of humor in her storytelling. Since Karma was the older sister, I expected her to have the better memory. However, she often turned to Marjorie to flesh out a memory. On the other hand, Karma often made summary pronouncements that nailed the significance of events. The more I talked with them, the more I could see that the sisters shared a common sensibility that came from being raised in the same home. For instance, they both agreed that theirs was the liberal branch of the family.

"Our Uncle Laverne's family were really nice people, but they were

so flaming fundamental," said Marjorie.

"What made your family more liberal?"

"We didn't go to church," blurted Karma, "Well, we did. Our parents sent us kids to the Lutheran Church, but they weren't church goers."

"They went on holidays," said Marjorie, adding, "Dad was disillusioned because the people in the church stole the farms from the Japanese. He was furious that they called themselves Christians."

"Mom was basically a nonjudgmental person," explained Karma returning to the question about what made them liberal. "She couldn't say anything bad about anyone, and she was obsessed with doing things for others."

"They were hardworking people," said Marjorie. "They laughed a lot, they cried, and they loved us. Uncle Laverne and Grandma were the cold Swedes," she concluded, shining a big-hearted smile my way. I felt the sisters' warmth as we poured over family photos and when we took a road trip to Escalon. From their reminiscing, I patched together a narrative of Warren's early life.

Cliff and Ruth married in August of 1941 as the country gazed east toward Europe and the escalating war. Because their families had cultivated crops, orchards, and livestock, Cliff's and Ruth's vision of the future centered around a working farm. By the time their son David Philip, named for his grandfather, was born in October 1942, they were getting settled on the little farm on Miller Avenue that Cliff's mother purchased for them. Cliff raised grapes, almonds, and turkeys while Ruth transformed the old farmhouse into a homey space, using her skills as a seamstress.

As demands of World War II blew across the central valley into the Borgquist home, Cliff took a deep breath, and headed toward the local recruiting office to enlist even though he was reluctant to leave his family and farm. He completed the paperwork and passed the physical, but when he stood before the recruitment officer, he was told that farmers were an exempt class, and he should go back to growing food for soldiers. Years later, Cliff embellished the story, claiming that the officer told him that farmers always had bad backs, and they couldn't have soldiers with bad backs, a condition that became linked in Cliff's mind to the reason he was deferred.

Though Cliff didn't leave his family, times were rough, so to help make ends meet, Ruth's older sister Wanona—called Aunt Noni by the kids—moved with her husband Doc and their two children to a second house on the farm. For the duration of the War, the families shared the work and expenses. Phil and his cousins, Eileen and Fred, thrived in the farmyard.

Phil was a sturdy little kid and gutsy to boot. At 3, he'd enter the turkey pen wielding a stick, and the big birds would scatter in his wake, a remarkable sight since even the adults feared the fury of these temperamental fowl. Phil loved the noisy farm machinery and clamored for ride-alongs on the tractor with his father. When Cliff bought a convertible, Phil commandeered the back seat where he could feel the wind in his face. One time the family was sailing down a country road when Cliff caught sight of 3-year-old Phil in his rearview mirror perched atop the retracted convertible roof. He didn't say anything to Ruth or Phil but slowed the car, and when he reached a slow enough speed, he hit the brakes hard so Phil fell forward off the seat. That, according to Karma, was her dad's method of teaching the boy a lesson.

On November 27, 1944, a second son, Warren Gregory was born. Warren wasn't as fearless as Phil. The almond shaker and the rumbling tractor startled him to tears, but mostly he was an easy going, smiling child, who was soon tagging cheerfully after his older brother. A picture of this family of four shows a smiling Ruth with baby Warren in her arms. Her dark hair is parted down the middle, her thick dark curls held back by barrettes. Cliff, a handsome blond in a white, freshly pressed shirt, stands beside his wife, squinting, his brow deeply furrowed. Three-year-old Phil stands in front of his parents clearly enthralled with the hefty pipe wrench he is holding. Perhaps Cliff's worried look was tied to the fact that there would soon be another baby, for daughter Karma Kay was born on February 13, 1946. Cliff and Ruth had heard the name Karma somewhere, and they both loved it. Of course, they had no idea how cool such a name would be for a young woman in the late '60s after flower power blossomed. Nor did they anticipate the reaction of the doctor who delivered Karma, who was appalled by its foreign—almost Japanese—sound and refused to put it on her birth certificate.

The summer after Karma was born, Phil's exuberance faded. He became cranky and complained of a headache. When he began to vomit each morning, Ruth took him to the family doctor who sent him to be assessed by an up-and-coming neurologist, Dr. Boldrey, at the University of California San Francisco Medical Center. Dr. Boldrey's diagnosis knocked the Borgquist family off kilter. The child had a brain tumor. That summer, Cliff and Ruth lost sight of the little farm in Escalon and their other two children as they took Phil for appointments at UCSF. While Aunt Noni or Grandma Sarah cared for Warren and Karma, their mother, who was also newly pregnant, sat holding her seriously ill 4 year old in waiting rooms full of suffering children. The sight of these sick children haunted her. That's why she consented to the surgery Dr. Borldrey said might save Phil. There were risks, including permanent disabilities or even death, but it was the only option offered for saving the boy. Though Phil survived the surgery, he never awoke. Twenty-five hours later he died. Cliff and Ruth returned to Escalon without their eldest son, burdened with the enormous grief carried by parents who lose a child.

If you are 2 years old and your older brother disappears from your home, trying to make sense of his disappearance is bound to occupy your mind. After Phil died, Cliff and Ruth found Warren in Phil's room. "Phil is never coming home, is he?" asked Warren.

"No," Ruth said, choking on her grief.

"I'm going to sleep in Phil's bed," said the younger brother. While some youngsters might view a missing brother as frightening, Warren was predisposed to a childlike fantasy that he could fix it, so the little guy climbed into his brother's bed confident that he could play the role of eldest. This leap of faith became family lore: the belief that after Phil's death, Warren knew he had to assume the position of the eldest son. The position of eldest but not first born—the surviving son—would define Warren's life.

The hand of fate, however, was not finished with this family. Deep in the throes of grief, Ruth suffered another loss. Her mother, who had been bedridden for years with rheumatoid arthritis, died of pneumonia. On May 13, 1947, three months after her mother died and six months after her son died, Ruth gave birth to another daughter, Marjorie. Ruth struggled to find her footing amidst sorrow. Meanwhile, mounting misfortune plagued Cliff. Grapes, which had sold for $125 a ton in 1945, dropped to a mere $8 a ton the year his first-born died. Cliff had been raising turkeys during the War when rationing was on, but after the War people didn't want turkeys anymore. They wanted beef. Cliff crashed financially and emotionally. He sold the farm and moved his family into town.

"We called it the stair house because it had two stories," said Karma describing the house to which they moved, a rarity among the single-level bungalows of Escalon. "I remember a big pine tree outside and Mom dressing us up in clothes she had made. It was like the three of us were dolls. She would stay up till two or three in the morning ironing the homemade clothing." While Ruth ironed her way through grief, Cliff opened a business with his friend, John Sutton, installing water pumps for the vast irrigation system in the Escalon area. They had a shop in a squat building in downtown Escalon. A hand-painted sign on the shop read "Sutton & Borgquist."

The family didn't stay long in the stair house but soon moved to a one-story place at 1333 San Joaquin Street. "You can't be triskaidekaphobia (fear of the number 13) in this family," joked Marjorie whose birthday falls on the 13th of the month as does that of her mother, father, sister and several children and grandchildren. Bad luck wasn't in numbers, nor was it even in the family's attitude. Ruth found her footing dressing her family while Cliff plunged into the pump business. The children played on quiet tree-lined streets in a square-block neighborhood that included the school, candy store, church, and canals.

In a family photo, minus Ruth who must have been the photographer, Cliff lies on the rug before a picture book with his children around him. He is a handsome man with thinning hair, full lips, and brooding eyes. Curly-headed Marjorie lies to his left. Her full lips, obviously inherited from her father, are set in a mischievous grin. Bright-eyed Karma, on her father's right, looks directly into the camera with a confident smile. Behind her is Warren, a chin resting on one hand, obscuring his mouth and drawing attention to his twinkling, earnest eyes. The three children are pictured in many scalloped-edged Kodak photos taken in the 1950s— Warren often centered between his smiling sisters. In photo after photo, Warren's wide-set eyes sparkle gaily or squint in a laugh. For his entire life, people would mention his eyes when describing him.

In 1956, the family got their first TV, and Ruth's dad, Guy Humphrey, came to the Borgquists every Friday night to watch the fights. "We always had to watch the fights with Grandpa and the other adults," recalled Marjorie, "even though we really wanted to go read. But 'No,' we had to stay there with Grandpa and be part of the family." The practice of sitting attentively in the presence of company—wanted or unwanted— was ingrained early on by Ruth and never lost sway. This rule of thumb reappears in many family stories, and it's conceivable that Dr. Warren Borgquist's unusual attentiveness to patients is rooted in his mother's insistence that her children sit, grin, and bear it.

Though Cliff failed at farming, he nevertheless came from farmer stock, so he planted a garden in an empty lot a few doors down from the house, where he grew beans, corn, and tomatoes. Warren helped in the garden. One of his chores was to pick the fat ugly worms off the tomato plants, but Warren hated picking worms. "They terrified his tender heart," said Marjorie. "I loved bugs and had shoe boxes with caterpillars and jars of grasshoppers. I was the one meant to be in the garden." Marjorie collected the worms on Warren's behalf, but sometimes she couldn't resist chasing him with them. "I wanted to be out in the garden with the bugs, but that was Warren's job, and he really wanted to be inside doing the vacuuming which was my chore."

Like most youngsters raised in the '50s, gender determined the assignment of household chores. Warren was willing to work hard, including doing most garden-related activities. Kentucky Wonder beans were a family favorite which Warren helped harvest. He also weighed and bagged the surplus, and along with zucchini and tomatoes, sold them in the neighborhood. Rewarded for his industry, he was allowed to keep the money, which he used to buy models.

Because Warren was the eldest and a male, Ruth believed in promoting him. Dr. Boldrey had grown iconic in Ruth Borgquist's mind, and she dreamed that some day Warren would meet the neurologist. Though Ruth didn't know much about formal education beyond high school, she expected her son to pursue a professional life, perhaps even become a doctor who would save people, especially children. Ruth didn't leave this possibility to chance. Instead, she investigated how to guide her son. When someone suggested dentistry, this became Ruth's vision for her son.

While his mother's hopes may have influenced Warren's career path, his sister Marjorie believes otherwise. Marjorie felt that the loss of his brother was what drove Warren's sense that he had to do something wonderful. He had to do something that would fulfill his mother's dreams and garner his father's love, which never seemed to solidify around Warren after Phil died. "Dad and Warren loved each other," says Marjorie, "but they were never a good fit."

Ruth, on the other hand, treasured Warren and decided that building models was a means to develop the manual dexterity he needed for dentistry. To prepare her son, Ruth bought him models of planes, cars, and ships, including the USS Monitor, a ship he later delighted in seeing on a cross-country trip with his own kids. Warren took to model building with pleasure, and he was soon purchasing his own models. The craft prefigured a life-long love for building things by hand. A special place was set aside in the Borgquist home for his projects. "He always had his glue and paints, and little boxes with airplanes and ships sitting on them to dry, and we couldn't touch anything," said Marjorie. "My parents did everything they could to encourage him. It's the way it was in our generation—the first generation to go to college. And they started at a young age with Warren."

Warren's early training regime included the position he was given in the back seat of the Ford Galaxy, where he perched to study Cliff's driving. Sitting directly behind Cliff by the window, while Marjorie and Karma took turns sitting on the hump in the middle of the back seat, Warren observed his father and learned when to shift and pass. " It was easy to study how to pass cars because Dad had to pass every car on the road," recalled Marjorie. "He was a maniac. There were moments of terror."

The Borgquist children's world widened during summer vacation car trips to Nebraska to visit Ruth's family—her brothers Kermit and Loren. Taking the scenic route was part of these vacations. Though the end goal was to visit family, they also aimed to see the country. The first trip was in 1955. Ruth's dad, Guy, traveled with them sharing the bench seat in front with Ruth and Cliff. They drove the southern route through Arizona and New Mexico before turning north toward Colorado. In Durango, Grandpa had a heart attack. The event was memorable enough for both Karma and Marjorie to recall the visit to the emergency room, but the attack must have been mild because they also remember stopping at the Museum of Natural History in nearby Denver where they saw a huge Tyrannosaurus Rex.

Eventually the family arrived in Nebraska at the homes of Uncle Kermit and Uncle Loren who were married to sisters, Gladys and Opal. "My mom's brother's wives were Lemons," said Marjorie. "That was their maiden name, and they were real lemons according to Mom and Dad," she added with a laugh. "But whether we liked them or not, Mom and Dad thought visiting them was something we had to do." Here again the message to grin and bear it was brought home to the Borgquist children.

Nebraska was a different world from their Escalon neighborhood. "They lived closer to the ground than we did," said Karma. "For one thing there was no indoor plumbing at Uncle Loren's." But the real difference was the family rifts that were a felt presence. "We always had to figure out who was on speaking terms," said Karma. "A mother might not be speaking to her daughter or two sisters might not be talking to each other. Everyone was in the same house along with a pile of anger and silence."

In one instance, ill-will was directed at Ruth. Aunt Opal said it was Ruth's fault Phil died earlier than he might have because she had consented to the brain surgery that ended his life. The pain of this accusation cut Ruth, but she abided by her own rule and kept quiet while in the woman's home. Later, on the way home in the car, Ruth let loose with her own opinion. "They should put Lyle in an institution. He'd be better off." As a toddler, Opal's son Lyle had contracted meningitis and encephalitis, which crippled him with palsy and caused him great difficulty when speaking. Unable to find ways to comfort one another in their personal tragedies, Ruth and Opal were accusing. Eventually, Karma would wonder if Opal had really blamed Ruth or if there had been a miscommunication.

Romping across the Nebraska countryside with his boy cousins, Warren had a different experience from his sisters, who had stayed inside with the women, eating cucumber sandwiches they didn't even want. Girls inside and boys outside—these were familiar practices to kids in the 50s. While the girls were stuck in the thick of their Nebraska family, Warren was more removed. That may have helped him be more discerning than his sisters, but Karma thinks it was just his way. "Warren was always on the lookout for great people." While Karma saw Uncle Loren as an adult for whom she needed to show respect, Warren looked at him and saw a poor farmer who was not very ambitious. He threw his garbage out the back door, and Warren thought this was uncool. On the other hand, he saw Aunt Gladys as a great person—unlike Aunt Opal. Warren thought Gladys was rich in spirit and full of acceptance and love. With hindsight Karma agreed that Aunt Gladys did not have a malicious bone in her body, and her laugh made people feel good all over. But on those vacations to Nebraska, most of the Borgquist family simply thought, "This is our family, and by god we're going to love 'em, like 'em or not."

While summer trips to Nebraska might have revealed the manner in which the family appraised the world, it had no bearing whatsoever on the children's sibling rivalry. Marjorie says she was a pain in the patoose. "I badgered Warren, and of course he got sick of it, but he was the big brother, and I was the pampered little sister, so he couldn't really do much about it." On occasion, Warren did manage to tease his adorable little sister. Once, he was outside working on his go-cart, and Marjorie was inside taking a bath. There had been a story about a peeping tom in the neighborhood, and Warren knew Marjorie was worried about this guy, so he decided to scare her. He sneaked up to the house and rattled the window over the bathtub. When she didn't respond, he brought it up a notch, sliding open the window. Marjorie froze. Warren reached his hand around the curtain, and Marjorie leapt from the tub and ran screaming out of the bathroom. Meanwhile, Warren ran back to his go-cart and continued working.

"Tell me what you saw," Cliff said to the sobbing Marjorie.

"A hand with a greasy finger coming through the window."

Cliff headed for the driveway where Warren was working? "Hold out your hands," he said.

Warren turned his hands palm up to reveal grease on one of his short stubby fingers.

"No! No! It's wasn't on that finger!" screamed Marjorie when she realized Warren was going to get in trouble. "It was on the third finger. That couldn't have been the hand I saw."

But Cliff saw right through her ploy, and Warren got a spanking. Cliff was a tough disciplinarian. "Our parents were quite the team," said Marjorie. "Dad was the enforcer, and with Mom, even if you were bummed out, you had to act happy. We couldn't be anything but polite, respectful, and cheerful. It was either be happy or die."

Only Phil had died, and in so doing, he became an omnipresent brother. "We didn't know him, but he was there," said Karma. "In pictures, he and Warren looked so much alike. But Warren was our big brother. Phil was forever foreign to us."

"They tucked the grief away," said Marjorie, "but it came out. Dad could be moody. He wasn't happy in his work, and he hated the valley fog."

"Mom got obsessed with things like ironing and sewing and helping others," said Karma, explaining her mother's way of dealing with her lost child.

On a field trip to Escalon, we bumped through a walnut orchard in Marjorie's sea green Prius, and the sisters revealed a fun-loving tendency I imagined permeated car trips with their family. Sitting in the front seat, they laughed with each bump while considering our whereabouts.

"I'm not sure where the house was," said Marjorie as she turned down yet another wide aisle of the orchard.

"I think we already passed the spot," said Karma. "Look, there's the elementary school. I can't believe it's that close. It seemed like such a long walk when we were little."

Marjorie maneuvered over several berms constructed for irrigating the orchard, and the bumpy ride had us all laughing as she made her way out onto the black top, where a trench for utility work extended the entire length of the street in front of the school.

"Remember when they tore up the whole street like this when were kids," said Marjorie as we drove past Dent Elementary School. "We played war in those trenches."

"We got in trouble for knocking in the dirt," said Karma, "but we'd be back the next day doing it again. Trench warfare. I loved it."

"We got the idea from old World War II footage on TV," said Marjorie, "and Warren Appling was a war hero because he came back wounded."

"So before you moved into town, you walked through that orchard to get to school?" I asked, redirecting their attention to our off-road adventure.

"Yes," said Marjorie, adding, "We all had the same kindergarten teacher: Mrs. Mummy. She came to Warren's performance of *Fiddler on the Roof* at Columbia College. Mom called her."

"Mom was always drumming up business for Warren," said Karma with a chuckle.

When we reached the corner after passing the elementary and high schools, Karma said, "That's the pool where Warren learned to swim. He was on the team— the Otters. He was really good at butterfly. I was too. But nobody noticed until I got to MJC." Sitting in the back seat, I smiled at this ancient sibling rivalry. "My dolphin kick was so good in college the coach used to have me demonstrate," she added to confirm expertise equal to that of her brother's.

"It helped to have a swimming pool so close to home," I said. By then we'd circled the block upon which the pool stood, and Marjorie was pulling up before the Lutheran Church.

"It's really a nice place,' said Karma with a trace of nostalgia as we looked at the red brink building with neatly trimmed rose bushes edging the walkway. "I remember a Christmas pageant where Warren and I were the co-narrators. Marjorie was an angel or shepherd or something."

"I got in trouble," confessed Marjorie, "because after I said my part, I walked down the aisle in front of everybody and kissed Timmy Dowleen. I got in trouble, and you guys were the stars," she said with her own touch of sibling rivalry.

Later, we stood on the street in front of the house at 1333 Joaquin, and the sisters reminisced about Christmases and a swing set and building forts in the back alley. The talked about the go-cart Cliff built with Warren and how Warren once stared down a cranky neighbor that the kids feared. After climbing back into the car, we headed to downtown, where we drove past the building that once posted the sign "Sutton & Borgquist," and the barbershop where Cliff and Warren got their hair cut. The women laughed as they told a story about a party at which Cliff and his friends passed out on lawn chairs after dinner and their wives tied their shoelaces together. Their memories of childhood in Escalon seemed to typify childhood in the 1950s when a neighborhood served as playground and parents held sway with rules and discipline. The sisters' memories were mostly sweet, so it was easy to conclude that Warren might have remembered some of it this way too.

We drove out of Escalon, wending our way on a curvaceous highway that forced travelers to slow down as they passed through this farm town that boasted a surprising variety of churches standing conspicuously on each bend of the meandering road. "We shouldn't have left," declared Karma.

But they did, because Cliff was not content, and the pump business failed.

# Chapter 2

# THE UPPER DIME

I will give you a new heart, and put a new spirit in you.

-Ezekiel 36:26 *New King James Version*

In a leap of faith, Cliff and Ruth bought the Sonora Variety Store in March 1959. Cliff had been looking east toward the foothills ever since he settled in Escalon because his friend, Warren Appling, had built a house in Sonora. Blue sky beckoned him to the rolling hills above the fog, so the couple made the move, dispatching them further still from the place where they had lost Phil, the place where a farm and business had failed. The Upper Dime, as it was called, was on Washington Street situated between the Timber Club and Muzio's Bakery. Taking on a retail business was a challenge for Cliff who had spent his life in outdoor occupations. Highly sociable Ruth was probably better equipped for the job, for even in Escalon she had kept her eyes and ears on neighborhood happenings, ever vigilant to a new born child, a sickly neighbor, or an acquaintance in need of company. In fact, Ruth had the bright idea of matchmaking a sweet widow she met at a Tupperware party with their dear friend Warren Appling. Ruth's match-making instincts were correct, for it wasn't long after meeting that the couple married, and the former widow moved with her two sons to Appling's chaparral-covered ranch. Ruth's neighborly nature would serve her well at the Upper Dime, but it took the Borgquist family a while to make the transition to becoming a Sonora institution.

When they purchased the Upper Dime, Warren was in his freshmen year of high school and Karma was in her final term before graduating eighth grade, so Cliff stayed in Escalon with the two older children while they finished the school year. As Cliff closed out life in Escalon, Ruth moved with Marjorie to Sonora to kick off the new adventure. At first, they stayed in a small apartment above the dime store where raucous noise and drunken revelry from the Timber Club rose to surround them far into the night. This was not the Sonora Ruth envisioned when moving from the church-filled streets of Escalon. It was disconcerting as she and Marjorie lay in their beds at night in their apartment above Washington Street, sleepless and scared, listening to the sounds of raised voices or breaking glass from the Timber Club.

They woke bleary-eyed each morning, and Ruth went to work figuring out how to run a variety store while her daughter went to sixth grade at Sonora Elementary in Mrs. McCormick's class—a woman the adult Marjorie would later describe as a "red-haired, yellow-fanged, terrifying individual." Marjorie had moved to a new school with a scary teacher and had to live in disturbing accommodations, so Ruth took her daughter and retreated to something more familiar, the Appling's ranch, where they partitioned off a room in the basement by hanging blankets from the ceiling. Cliff arrived each Friday night in his red pick-up with the other children and stayed until Sunday, making for crowded living but also diffusing some of the separation anxiety that everyone was feeling.

That summer, the Borgquists reunited and became residents of Sonora when they rented a house at 92 North Shepherd Street for $90 a month. The big cinderblock house was hot in the summer and cold in the winter. Ruth hung plastic drapes throughout the house—an item she sold at the Upper Dime.

"They look kind of nice, don't you think?" she asked the children. "They've got a liner to keep out the heat and cold."

"Oh, Mom they're so ugly," chimed Karma and Marjorie together.

"But Mother wouldn't hear it," said Karma years later. "She maintained a happy facade, and that's what she expected of us. Even if bummed, we had to act happy.

While the girls were advising their mother on home decorating, Warren was getting in condition to play football at Sonora High School in the fall. Warren's late November birthday made him one of the youngest in his class, plus he was on the small side. He nevertheless had athletic aspirations. In small towns, Friday night football games are the biggest show around. Warren sensed that football offered a chance to achieve something, and he was focused on achievement, so he headed out on county roads to run with other aspiring football players. He met John Burgess one hot summer morning, running on Shaws Flat Road with Butch Pastorini and Dave Croft. A few weeks later, John ran into Warren again at the Mother Lode Fair. "We hit it off," said John, "probably because we had the same nature—kind of easy going." As it turned out, John and Warren would be outliers, not football heroes, in high school, but that summer they ran with athletic hopes.

Meanwhile, Cliff and Ruth hired clerks to help at the store, Eunice

Crabtree and Louise Garrison. The Borgquist children also worked at the store, stocking bins and doing inventory. Merchandise was stored upstairs, so stocking involved a lot of stair climbing and descending, a chore Ruth delegated to the children. This was before packaging, when variety stores displayed merchandise in little bins formed by glass partitions. In those days, the Woolworth brothers had established the model for such stores— glass showcases, mahogany counters, and goods people could touch. The Upper Dime conformed to a small town version of this model—rows of shelves with different sized bins holding various items, for instance, two sizes of pink erasers. Everyone who worked at the variety store learned how to cut glass to construct the bins. Sometime in the early '60s, companies started packaging products. The cost of this packaging was passed on to the customer: five-cent items became ten cents and ten-cent items became fifteen cents, which meant they were now taxable because they were over thirteen cents. Customers were furious and so were Cliff and Ruth, but they had no choice. They had to change the way they did business. They got rid of the little bins and replaced them with pegboard to hang the products.

"We had to inventory everything in January," said Marjorie. "There we were on the first day of the new year, counting away." Cliff recruited the children's friends to help. "There was a lot of stock," recalled Bob Darling, one of Warren's high school buddies. "It took us a long time. Warren and I often got stuck working upstairs, counting the overstock— boxes and boxes of stuff." Cliff was a tough taskmaster, but he managed to make it fun.

"He charmed the socks off us kids," said Marjorie.

Bob Darling and John Burgess, who also helped with inventory, remember Cliff's off-color humor. "He always had a naughty joke to tell," recalled John. "Here's one he told more than once: This guy goes to church, and there's a woman in front of him in a coffee colored dress. When they stand to sing the hymns, the guy notices that dress is caught in the crack of her butt. So he just reaches over and pulls it down. She turns around and slaps him silly. So the next week when he goes to church, the same woman is in front of him. When she stands up, he notices her dress is just hanging loose. Knowing she doesn't like it that way, he reaches over and puts it back in her crack."

Obviously, this was humor that boys enjoyed given that the adult John recalled it verbatim. Marjorie's son Zac mentioned that he too found it appealing years later when returning from a camping trip with Cliff, he said, "I like Grandpa. He's funny, and everything's a little bit naughty."

"My father was defensive about not making it educationally or financially, and I think that's why he tended to use humor everywhere," explained Marjorie.

Like Cliff, Warren too employed humor. Bob Darling remembered that he first met Warren at the Appling home when the two were thirteen, before the family had moved to the county. "He was a funny guy, always cracking jokes. His comical expressions were as funny as his jokes. It was a blast to visit the Applings when the Borgquists were there because Warren made sure we had a good time."

Another task assigned to kids helping out was making bows for gift-wrapping at the Upper Dime. Bill Geiser, Warren Appling's step-son, remembered, "They had a little machine where you put a button-like stick pin, and then you'd crank this thing, and it would twist ribbons onto the button to make a bow to stick on a package. Ruth or Cliff would put us to work making a dozen or so bows whenever we came to the Upper Dime."

Ruth always sat at the front of the store, welcoming people. Betty Sinclair, who would one day be Judy and Warren Borgquist's neighbor, said, "Ruth was one of the first people I met when I moved to Sonora. I'd go into the Upper Dime with my three little kids, and she made me feel at home, like I was a part of the community. She'd rave about her son. She was so proud of him. It was a very comfortable place to shop."

Townspeople called the store the Upper Dime, because there was another dime store, Sprouse Reitz, owned by the Fisher family. Bob Fisher was a year ahead of Warren at Sonora High, and the two would one day be study partners at Modesto Junior College, but while in high school, what they had in common was parents who owned dime stores. Suzan Still, a contemporary of the Borgquist children, noted that many families owned downtown businesses: Tom Hobby, Bill Holman, Barbara Baer, Brian Curnow. The townspeople—as well as the county's loggers, ranchers, and miners—were rooted, connected, and tangled in an intricate history that Warren would one day take into account as he practiced medicine. "They were the town—and they cared about one another," said Suzan. When a customer couldn't find a product—say a particular brand of thread or a ballpoint pen— at the Lower Dime, Mrs. Fisher said, "I'm sorry we don't carry those, but you might try the Borgquists up the street at the Upper Dime." Ruth did the same, referring folks to the Lower Dime if she didn't have the merchandise a customer was seeking.

Cliff wasn't as happy in the store as Ruth. "He did what he had to do, and he did a good job," says Marjorie, "but he was often brusque and snappy. He was a farmer stuck indoors. I remember he came home exhausted, and he would have a few beers, and then he'd be okay. But on Sundays when we were unpacking or stocking, it was different. He was jolly and everything was funny. I felt like he painted the room a merry color. We'd unpack ceramic figurines wrapped in Chinese newspaper that we wanted to look at, and he always gave us time. Normally he was in a big hurry but not on Sunday." Thinking about this, Marjorie leaped back to Sundays in Escalon where the kids went to the Lutheran Church. "We had a wonderful, loving minister, but when we moved to Sonora, Mom didn't like the minister here. He was all about hellfire and brimstone."

Karma pointed out that this was exactly the aspect of religion her mother feared. "She'd been scared by Grandma's church—you know Armageddon, hell fire and damnation—that stuff scared the crap out of her, so we stopped going to church when we moved to Sonora. She wasn't going to send us to a place where the personality of the minister determined that God was scary."

That's when Marjorie remembered another message flowing through her family. "You can find spirituality in church, but there are other places you can find it."

Though they may not have been seeking spirituality, the Borgquists often headed back to the valley on Sundays to visit family. On one Sunday, they'd visit Dwayne and Gladys, on Cliff's side of the family, and on the next trip, they'd visit Ruth's sister Noni and her husband Doc. Road trips tempered the darkness of indoor life for Cliff and fed Ruth's pleasure in her family. Gradually the Borgquist family inhabited Sonora with Ruth and Cliff finding their niche through the Upper Dime as their children navigated adolescence.

Years later, sitting at her dining room table, Marjorie pulled a photo from the box and said, "Here's one of Big Warnie and Little Warnie."

"How long did you call him Warnie?"

"In high school we were advised to switch."

"Because of Horny Warnie and Corny Warnie," explained Karma.

"We were discouraged from using nicknames," Marjorie continued. "I didn't like being called Margie because of the song 'Margie, I'm always dreaming of Margie,' and Warren didn't like being called Warnie, so we got rid of the baby names." I made a note about the name changes, but later when interviewing Warren's friends—old and new—I would hear some of them use what Marjorie called the baby name—Warnie—as a term of endearment for their friend.

Looking at pictures of Warren from high school, I saw an average looking guy, somewhat slight of build, with a slick Brylcreem hairstyle. "He was not hip, swift, and cool," said Marjorie. "I was the cheerleader. He was more seriously inclined, and he was a band student. You know the social divisions in the '60s? He wasn't an athlete; he was a band guy, so that put him in the dork category." I'd also heard Karma call Warren a dork. I knew the word but looked it up to see if it was in use when Warren was in high school or if this was a descriptor the sisters were using after the fact. According to the Urban Dictionary, the term "dork" came into use in the 1960s to refer to someone who had odd interests, was silly at times, and who could be himself and not care what others thought. There were certainly parts of this definition that fit Warren. However, I doubt he was someone who didn't care what others thought.

"He played clarinet," continued Marjorie, "and he was good, but he and Bill Summers were always competing for first chair, so Warren decided to switch to tuba. Karma used to say he had garbage can lips. Give that man a tuba, and he became the life of the party. He and a group of friends—Stan Moe, Danny Ray, Bill Summers—formed a Dixieland band. When they played a tiger rag, Warren was something. He couldn't be on top with the clarinet, so he did something about it."

During Warren's sophomore year, 1960, the high school band was one of six that played in the Opening Ceremonies for the Winter Olympics at Squaw Valley. Karma was also in the band. "Two years later, we went to the World's Fair in Seattle. It was the year the Space Needle opened. Mom, Dad, and Marjorie drove up, and after the Fair, we traveled to Montana to see some of Dad's relatives. Warren looked at the map and said, 'If we take this road we'll get there faster.' So we got on the road, and it started deteriorating, turning into a dirt road, but we were committed. Eventually, the road dead-ended at a river, but there was a ferry—a very small ferry on cables across the river. This local guy had rigged it because people like us followed the map and ended up out there. We thought it was the end of the world, but it turned out to be the most fun part of the trip. It was thrilling crossing the river that way. Good call, Warren, even though you got us a little bit lost," said Karma with a skyward glance. That was the first of many stories friends and family would tell about Warren getting "a little bit lost."

Warren's years at Sonora High School in the '60s were pretty typical when described by classmates—Bob Darling, Linda DuTemple, John Burgess— and a bit tamer than the scene described by another classmate, David Carkeet, in a memoir entitled *Campus Sexpot*. The book contains a novel within the memoir, a "sleazy take" on Sonora, in which a high school teacher has an affair with a co-ed and many of the characters are modeled after Sonora citizens. The thing is, at the heart of Carkeet's hilariously piercing work, is the truth about the romantic fumbling of hormone-saturated young men as well as what it was like to come of age in a small town. Like most teens, Warren was focused on achieving a bit of social status, hanging out with friends, and, to use Carkeet's language, "getting some action" with the opposite sex. Thumbing through musty Sonora High School yearbooks with Linda DuTemple, she pointed out black and white pictures of Warren with the band and as an officer in student government, and Marjorie pointed to pictures of the girls he dated, Bridgett Matthews and Carolyn Morse. There was a picture of him with the Drama Club. "I remember him being in a school play," said Marjorie. "I have no idea what play, but I remember he had one line. He was supposed to come out and say forcefully, 'Where are my shoes?' He was supposed to be mad, but he said it softly with a grin on his face. Anger wasn't something he could fake."

Ross Carkeet went to high school with Warren. "He was a few years behind me, so we didn't hang out, but I remember one of my high school cronies telling me about this time when Warren and some of the other band guys took the rotor out of his distributor while he was on a date.

42

He was pretty upset when he went to get in his car, and it wouldn't start. Warren had a kind of a prankster, playful side to him."

"Warren used to say we were nerds," said John Burgess by way of describing their place in the high school pecking order. "We were over-achievers, dedicated guys. When we were juniors, he was dating Judy [not to be confused with his eventual wife], and I was dating Bridget. We used to double date, and for reasons I can't quite remember, when we were seniors, we switched that around. I dated Judy, and he dated Bridget. But before that happened, I remember once when Warren and Judy had some kind of tiff. Warren was upset, so we cut school and went down to Peppermint Falls, driving Cliff's truck. We hung out down there talking and commiserating about girls, and by the time we got back, the whole school knew we were missing, and we got called into the vice-principal's office. He threatened to expel us. I guess he called my dad, who was a Sonora High alum, and somehow my dad talked the VP into backing down because we were basically good guys and had never missed school, and also it would be embarrassing to my dad and Cliff to have their boys expelled. The funny part is that Cliff's truck had the phone number of the store on it, and somehow Warren and I never put together that was the reason everyone knew what we were up to. Anytime we goofed off, a report got back to Cliff."

Warren and Bob Darling had Lambretta scooters that they drove all over the county. Bob recalled one day when they were riding on Lime Kiln Road. "There was this girl who lived out that way, and we were going to stop and say hello. We didn't know she had a boyfriend, but he was there when we stopped. This big guy came out the door after we pulled in the driveway. I was parked closest to him. The guy didn't say a word. He just came over and pushed me over on top of Warren. There we were in a heap, and Warren said quietly, 'It's okay. Let's just come back another time.' So we picked ourselves up and rode away. He was that way about everything. Just took it in stride."

He may have taken some things in stride, but at home his little sister could be annoying. "We used to have this Formica dining room table at the Shepherd Street house," recalled Marjorie. "I still have it upstairs in my sewing room. One time when we were teenagers, I was in a state about something, totally badgering Warren, just asking for it, and suddenly he decked me. I flew across the table, hit the chair, then the floor. Warren was aghast and I was hysterical. Dad took him back to his bedroom and said, 'Son, you're getting big. You could hurt a woman and you can't do that. You have to be gentle.' Warren used to say that talk with Dad was of the proudest moments of his life because it made him feel like a man," added Marjorie.

The man Warren became was a doctor, but he originally planned to be a dentist. John Burgess remembered Warren working with models to improve his dexterity because he intended to be a dentist. "I'm not sure when he decided to become a doctor instead."

By way of explanation, Marjorie offered a bit of family lore that blazes with a teen's hope of getting some action with girls. "One of the stories he liked to tell is about being on a double date and the other guy was Mr. Super Cool. This guy said he was going to be a doctor. Up until then Warren had always said he was going to be a dentist, but he heard this guy Eddie say he was going to be a doctor, and Warren saw that girls just moved in on him. Right then and there he switched over: he was going to be a doctor. I think he might have been dating Carolyn Morse then."

"Carolyn was our favorite," said Karma.

"She was two years behind him," Marjorie said. "He shouldn't have let her go. But he went to Modesto Junior College and met Nancy."

"I never thought of Warren as nerdy guy," said Carolyn Morse McGinty, when I spoke with her. After college, Carolyn left the county but then returned for a time, only to retire and move to Washington State, where I caught up with her by phone. "Before I dated him, I used to watch him. I was attracted to him. He was not exactly a clown, but funny. He joked around a lot. He always made me laugh. That was one of the things I liked about him. And he flirted. He was dating a girl named Bridget. He was always with Bridget. Years later, when my sister-in-law told me that Warren dated all kinds girls, including her, it was news to me. The only other girl I ever saw him with in high school was Bridget. When they broke up, we started dating. I was a junior, and I think by that time, he was already at Modesto Junior College (MJC), but he came home every weekend, or maybe it was every other weekend.

"Stan Moe's family had a ski boat, and we would double date with Stan and his girlfriend, Judy Godfrey. The four of us would go out on the boat and ski. Warren's family was wonderful to me, especially his mother. I was very fond of her. The Upper Dime was on my path to and from school. When I was seeing him and even after, I stopped in frequently. I discovered that they had sheet music. There was no other place in town where you could buy sheet music with popular songs. I played the piano and sang, and I liked to play more popular stuff instead of the old classics my teachers made me practice. I found out that Mrs. Borgquist could order anything, so I started ordering sheet music from her. She was the nicest, friendliest person who just brightened your day. His sisters were around a lot, and they were nice to me, and the father was nice but kind of quiet. I didn't get into any long conversations with him. Warren used to invite me to his house for dinner. He came to my house a few times too, but my parents were not as easy-going and open as his. I think they made most of my friends uncomfortable. They didn't draw people into conversations like Mrs. Borgquist did. She made you feel at home immediately.

"One time, Warren invited me to go with his family on a picnic up in the Immigrant Basin. I remember we walked on the trail to this place where you could look out over a huge canyon and see clear across to the other side. It was a gorgeous view. I was standing there with Warren, thinking about my whole life ahead of me, and it's kind of sad, but I knew he wasn't the right person for me for the long haul even though I was really crazy about him. He had that twinkle in his eye, and he was so funny, and he made me happy, but when we stood there and I saw that view, I thought, 'I can't commit to him because there's a whole life ahead of me, and he's not the right person.'

"Actually, he was the one who broke up with me sometime after that hike. One weekend when he came home from MJC, he said we needed to talk. 'I met someone at school,' he said, 'and I'm in love with her.' And I said, 'Thank you for being honest.' It was so brave of him to tell me. He probably expected me to fall apart. All my friends said, 'Why aren't you more hurt? Why aren't you angry? Why aren't you jealous?' It was because I knew I was going to do something else—I was going to meet other guys, go to college, and have a career. I truly wasn't angry with him. The thing is most guys wouldn't have been that honest.

"After we stopped dating, he transferred to UC Davis, and I also went to Davis. You would think we would see each other, but it was a big school. I only saw him once. I'm going to tell you something that's really weird. After I graduated from UC Davis, I went to law school in Sacramento and then practiced in Fresno for twenty years. When I married my second husband, we decided to move back to Sonora in 2000. My Aunt Lena lived in Sonora in the house next door to Warren and Judy. By the time we moved back, she was in assisted living, so her house was empty, and we stayed there for four months while we were looking for a house to buy.

"In all the years I used to visit my aunt, I never saw Warren. Even though I knew he lived there, I didn't go knock on his door. But one day I saw a young man who was the spitting image of Warren, and I thought it must be his son. Finally, I ran into Warren. We met by the mailbox and had the nicest talk. It was interesting to see how his life had gone and what kind of person he'd become. I knew him as a goof-off—always joking around. I didn't think he was a serious student, so I was as surprised as anybody to hear he was pre-med at Davis, and then when he got into medical school, I thought he must've really cracked down."

Hanging up the phone after talking with Carolyn, I understood why Marjorie and Karma particularly liked this gracious woman whom their brother once dated. However, these young people were not destined to be together, for as Carolyn explained, Warren had fallen in love at MJC. Simultaneously he got serious about being a student.

*Chapter 3*

# SCHOOL DAZE

It wasn't easy becoming a physician.

—Arne Vaino, *The Country Doctor Revisited*

I went to Modesto JC because anything farther away from home made me nervous." So wrote Warren on a questionnaire sheet for his 20th high school reunion. In describing what had happened since graduation, he continued, "I started in pre-dentistry, but then I thought about it. Thought was a new concept for me, but when I did it, I decided looking in peoples' mouths was gross. So I switched majors, and considering the things I look down now, it's clear that thought was not one of my strong points. Actually, the reason I switched to medicine is because the guy sitting next to me in zoology lab (Ed Harris) was going into medicine, and since all the cute girls I wanted to look at me were always looking at him, I decided to go into medicine too."

Warren's self-deprecating humor belied the serious, more determined part of the young man who headed to Modesto Junior College, sixty miles west of Sonora—but it also established that testosterone played a role in directing his future, so much so that his sisters recalled Warren's change of professional direction as having taken place on a date rather than in the classroom.

"Warren was on the water polo team," explained Marjorie. "He hadn't done athletics in high school, but he'd always been a good swimmer. At first, he was on the lowest string, but he kept working and working to build himself up. He had these massive strong legs. My dad's legs were like that too. Huge thighs. The coach made him goalie, and he was the game-saver several times. He used to say that water polo saved his life because it made him believe he could do something. It gave him confidence to succeed in college."

Bob Fisher also recalled Warren playing water polo. "People were amazed at how well he treaded water. He could kick himself out of the water up to his waist. It was phenomenal and intimidated the other team. It was interesting to see him in that vein because I didn't remember him being like that in high school."

Bob and Warren were in the same Economics class at MJC. "We sat in the back, and we'd swap homework. We had to create a portfolio and chart the progress of our stocks. My father subscribed to the *Wall Street Journal*, so I used to get tips and pass them along to Warren. I don't know what his final grade was, but we both excelled during class. Warren worked hard all through school. I also remember chatting back and forth across the aisle about a young lady named Nancy. I had a fencing class with her, and we agreed she was a foxy girl. Warren obviously had his eye on her."

"The other thing that stands out in my memory about Warren is our study group for zoology. We met at Don Moore's place—a house he rented close to the school. Warren wasn't part of the group initially, but I remember the first time he showed up. Zoology is full of factoids and requires an incredible amount of memorization. We'd pick a phylum and start rattling off all this stuff about genus and species and so on. Warren was sitting there with his mouth wide open, and after maybe fifteen or twenty minutes, he said, 'Jesus Christ, how do you guys remember all this crap?' We told him he had to make a memory tool—like the acronym Roy G. Biv to remember the colors of the rainbow. He knew about mnemonics from music—Every Good Boy Does Fine—but he never thought about using it in zoology. He latched onto it. I think that was a key to his success, at least in that class. I never really did anything socially with him. He was a bookworm. He did a lot of studying, other than the time he spent with Miss Nancy."

I knew that Warren's first wife, Nancy, was the one who knew the most about Warren's life from his time at MJC through his internship in Panama, so I made arrangements for a phone interview. When Nancy answered, I imagined a blond teenager with a sun-burned nose. It was an image formed from a picture I'd studied at Marjorie's dining room table. Though the woman I was speaking to was probably near seventy, I nevertheless heard the pretty blond in the picture respond to my questions: "Let's start with describing how you met Warren and what your romantic attraction was like?"

"We met in a lifeguard class. He was a water polo player, and I taught swimming lessons. Water sports are my thing, so that's where we met."

"Were you immediately attracted to one another or did your relationship develop gradually?"

"We were friends at first. We studied together, but then it turned romantic, and I got pregnant, so we got married."

Since we didn't know one another, Nancy's incredibly abbreviated version of her early days with Warren didn't surprise me, but her statement was surely a huge simplification of a life-changing moment in this young couple's lives. I decided to keep my questions equally superficial, so I said, "Tell me about that. According to Marjorie. you went out of state to get married."

"Yes, we eloped, because in California girls couldn't legally marry at eighteen, and boys had to have their parents' consent. So we went to Glenn Falls, Idaho. They had different rules there. It was a fast trip. We just drove there and turned around and came back."

"Just the two of you?" Again I was imagining the happy young couple in a photo in which Warren held Nancy possessively, one arm pulling her close and the other wrapped around her upper arm, snuggling it against his chest. He leans his head against hers and broadcasts his broad, buoyant smile.

"Yes," said Nancy. "At a justice of the peace."

"So you got married and came back and lived in Modesto"" I said.

"Right," she said.

"And somewhere along the way Marjorie came and lived with you.

Is that right?" I asked.

"Actually, during our marriage, a lot of people lived with us. My sister lived with us, and Karma, and a friend of his from medical school, and we had a foster child. This was all later in San Francisco when Warren was going to medical school. No one lived with us in Davis because we lived in a single-wide mobile home."

"And you had a baby by then. Was Greg born when you were still in Modesto?"

"No, not until we were in Davis."

"So talk about Greg's arrival."

"We moved in September, and he was born in December. I had toxemia the last three months, so I was bedridden in this trailer in a mobile home park in the winter. I didn't know anyone, so it was pretty lonely. My grandmother was good about writing and calling, and actually his grandma came right before Greg was born to stay because I wasn't supposed to get out of bed except go to the bathroom."

"Would that be Grandma Sarah?"

"Yes, Sarah. She was a wonderful lady. She cooked. Warren had been cooking, but he really didn't know how. He'd just make a big pot of goulash with whatever he could find, so I really appreciated when Sarah arrived."

"Marjorie also told me it was a difficult birth," I said which was true, though actually I'd heard Warren tell the story of his son's birth on several occasions, usually accompanied with this cautionary comment: "Birth is 99 percent pure joy and 1 percent pure terror."

"Greg was breech. And he was nine pounds, three ounces. It was a natural birth because we couldn't afford any complications. In those days, you paid or you didn't have a baby. In the hospital, anyway. So we saved enough just for a natural birth. They x-rayed me at the last minute because he was big, and they could feel things weren't right. They thought maybe I had twins. It was an old hospital, and the x-ray machine was in the basement. The elevator didn't meet the floor, so I remember going over this huge bump on a gurney while I was in labor. It was not fun. When they saw he was breech, they called in a specialist, because my doctor was just a family doctor. I was closing my eyes and relaxing—well trying to anyway. And they were talking about doing a Caesarean, and my eyes popped open. I said, 'You can't do a Caesarean. We can't afford it.' I was the boss because that's what determined it: money. I knew I didn't want to yell or anything because they might go ahead and do one, so I didn't make a peep the whole time."

"Was Warren there for the birth?" I asked.

"Yes. He was interested in all the details. We named him Gregory Guy," continued Nancy. "Guy is Ruth's father's name, and Gregory is Warren's middle name."

Marjorie has a picture of Warren holding baby Greg at about three months. The baby sits on his forearms, a foot or so from his body. The two look into each other's eyes, studying one another. Warren is smiling, and Greg has an expression of fascination. The most striking thing about the photo is Warren's youth. Though he turned twenty shortly before Greg was born, in this picture, he looks much younger. Thin, bespectacled, and wearing a white T-shirt, he looks less like a father and more like an older brother to the child in his arms.

"So now you have this little baby and a husband in pre-med. What was that like?"

"The trailer park was across the highway from the university, and it was pretty rural. The first winter was hard because our heater only had two settings—all the way on or off—so until Greg was six months old, he had ear infections and so did I. I remember sitting in the doctor's office with Greg, crying and asking the doctor if I was ever going to be normal again. I'd been bedridden during the pregnancy, and then we were both sick for months. I didn't have family or friends around, so I had no opportunity to get out. No students lived in our park. It was mostly older people. There was one couple across the street who were nice and visited sometimes."

"I suppose Warren was at school and probably working too."

"He wasn't home much. He even studied away from home with study groups."

"What kind of student was he?"

"School wasn't easy for him, but he worked hard, so he excelled." Nancy's words echoed those of Bob Fisher describing Warren at MJC.

"He was pretty young to be a father. How did he do with that?"

"He was very proud of Greg, especially when we went any place. He was very attentive then, but day-to-day, he was less involved. He was busy studying. The second year we were in Davis, I babysat another child, and I had my own business. I made art items that I sold in gift stores, and I taught art classes through the recreation department and adult education. We didn't have money to do anything, so our big treat was to go visit my family or his. Here's a little tid-bit. When he finished school, he had less school debt than his single friends."

"Why is that?" I asked, feeling like Nancy was beginning to warm to speaking about her long-ago marriage to Warren.

"Because I'm a good manager. We owned the trailer, which his parents helped us buy, so we only had to pay space rent. We actually ate K-rations, and I supplemented our income by babysitting, and he worked for the railroad; he was a flagman. His summer jobs were always in a different town. One summer, when my dad got him a job, we stayed with my parents. Another summer, he worked in Hughson—a little town near Modesto—for a family doctor, and we lived in the middle of a peach orchard in a one-bedroom house. We ended up getting a grant towards the end of medical school, but mostly we just managed."

"Did you get along well with Ruth and Cliff?"

"I got along with the whole family. Ruth and Cliff enjoyed being grandparents. Once, when we were first married, we went to Thanksgiving dinner, and Grandma Sarah asked me to serve coffee. She had this beautiful china—the kind that when held to the light you could see through. I didn't realize that I needed to keep my hand on the lid, and it fell off and broke a cup. Sarah was so gracious. She mended that cup, and it was just as good as new. And the next time I served, she made a point to show me how. She was a very special lady."

This was a different view of Grandma Sarah than what I'd heard from Marjorie, who had told of Sarah belittling Ruth. I wondered if this was an instance of elders finding it easier to be sympathetic to the next generation. In a photo dated April 1965, Warren sits at the dinner table between Grandma Sarah and his mother. The occasion appears to be Easter because three decorated sugar eggs serve as the centerpiece. The eggs are set so that the peepholes—windows into miniature, idyllic scenes—point in different directions around the table. The dioramas inside such eggs usually depict a blue-sky world of Victorian gentility. Warren is leaning back in his chair, gazing upward, smoking a cigar in his own version of after-dinner genteel behavior. Grandma Sarah and his mother are smiling delightedly at him. His father is looking at him too, but his expression is much more difficult to decipher—a tight-lipped smile with perhaps a hint of displeasure. The expression may have been evidence of Marjorie's comments about the lack of connection between Warren and Cliff. Ruth, on the other hand, always spoke glowingly about her son and proudly noted his achievements. She sent notices to the *Union Democrat* announcing his educational progress, for example, when he became a member of the National Junior College Honor Society and when he earned his Bachelor's degree. Then she taped these newspaper announcements to a display near the cash register at the Upper Dime.

"After graduating from Davis, he went to the University of California at San Francisco. Do you know why he chose UCSF?" I asked Nancy.

"I don't remember. I know it was a good school, but I don't know beyond that."

Nancy may not have remembered, but Judy Borgquist told a story, presumably the way Warren told her. "UC med school in San Francisco was the only school he wanted to go to because of his brother. At first, he was put on the waiting list, but he was determined, so he made himself known. Once a week for the whole summer, he went to San Francisco and talked to the secretary at the medical school office. He kept asking what he could do to move up on the list. Sometimes he took her flowers. Then suddenly, he was third on the waiting list, and then magically he was in. He was the last person accepted to medical school for that term. It was the week before, so he and Nancy had to scramble to get a place. He was so naïve. He wore a suit and tie the first day. He took his microscope and his *Grey's Anatomy* with him on the "N" Streetcar and barely made it on time."

"First we lived in San Francisco on 19th Avenue at Noriega in a top-floor flat," said Nancy. "We could see the ocean out the back, but everything had to be carried up three stories."

"Including a baby," I added.

"Greg was high energy, so he was able to walk it," said Nancy

"How long did you stay there?"

"Six months. A friend of Warren's from high school, who was

working for city transportation, found us a place in Daly City. They had taken out all the houses except one on a block where they were going to build a Bart Station. The city ran out of money, and there was this one house left standing that we were able to rent at a very good price. It was three bedrooms and two baths, with another bedroom and bath downstairs. We had a foster son when we lived there . . . Frank."

"Marjorie told me about Frank. She said Warren was tutoring him."

"That's right. We knew his grandmother. She was raising him, and as he got to be a pre-teen, he needed a different kind of supervision, someone who was younger. We didn't apply for it or anything. It was informal. Weekends at first and then he was just staying with us all the time."

"So you were helping the boy's grandmother by taking him in," I said to confirm what I thought she was saying.

"Right. We had Frank, and I was babysitting another little boy, and then in '66, we adopted Mimi."

"That's a big decision for a young couple to make," I said.

"It was my idea. When I was younger, I wanted to have a large family. I wanted to have two or more of my own, and then I wanted to adopt the rest. I was the oldest of four children, and my mother worked, so I grew up like junior mother. Warren wasn't into family much at that point. I think he caught on to it as a grandfather. But at that point, he wasn't, so I modified my idea. I wanted a girl because we had a boy, so we decided to adopt. Warren was fine with it. Well, maybe not totally in agreement, but he was willing to cooperate."

"Sounds like you were into being a mom, and he was focused on med school."

"Right. I know we started prematurely, but the project had begun, and I really wanted a girl. There were a lot of children available. Mimi was in a foster home with seven other babies. When we got her, she had diaper rash all up her back and her weight was declining. She was seven pounds at birth, but when we adopted her at seven months, she was only fourteen pounds. She didn't smile, and she hadn't tried to crawl. They said she was a finicky eater, but she never was with us. I think she was starving for love. They've done studies of children in orphanages who didn't get enough love."

54

"I believe it's called failure to thrive," I said.

"Yes, infants can actually die from not getting enough love and touch. Mimi always ate well, and she sat up and started to crawl in the first month. She also became very demanding because she learned that she loved to be held, so she wanted to be held 24/7. That was a challenge because I still had Greg, and the little boy I babysat, and Frank, but I never felt like it was too much. I took it in stride."

"So could we back up a little? Did you get to choose Mimi?"

"No, not really. We told them we were looking for a girl, and we didn't care about nationality or race. It's like when you're pregnant. You don't choose the baby you get."

"Did you have to go through home visits and all that?"

"Oh, yeah. They went through our closets and everything. We were totally checked out."

"Karma said that the day you went to get Mimi, she went with, so she could hold Mimi during the ride home, and you could hold Greg, so he wouldn't be jealous."

"That's right. Karma was living with us then and taking classes at San Francisco State. She's Mimi's godmother. I picked Mimi's name when I was a little girl. I named her after my parents. My mother is Mimi and my father is Gale, so she's Mimi Gale."

When asked what he recalled about his younger sister's arrival, Greg had said, "Mimi was just part of my reality growing up. From early on, I knew she was adopted. I remember camping when I was a kid," he added, turning to the kind of memory an active boy was more likely to retain. "Dad and Mom bought a boat. It was before he started his internship. I was about 4. I remember the boat breaking down, and my dad tinkering with it. He didn't get it running, but we got towed back to our camp. I remember this because he didn't panic. He was so reassuring, telling us everything would be okay.

"I remember my foster brother— Frank. He was black. We lived by this huge vacant block in Daly City. I think it's a terminal for BART now. But back then, there was only one house on the block—a cool, two-story Victorian. The house was built on a slope and half of the garage was encased in earth and the other half was exposed. I remember one time Frank and I found a big can of balls—like big bowling balls with holes to put your finger in. We turned them into wrecking balls and had all kinds of fun breaking things in the garage—things my parents had in storage. My mom really gave it to me, and I was nervous because she was going to tell my dad. At first, my dad was like 'What the . . .?' but then he was OK. His attitude was like no-use-crying-over-it. But he did revisit that vandalism story a few times in my childhood, making sure I remembered the moral to not break things people are trying to keep. Having Frank as part of our family was another cool thing about my pops. He was truly a humanitarian. He could see beyond ethnicities and cultural differences."

Marjorie told a story about Warren and Nancy going with the children to a family gathering in Turlock. "There was blond Greg, and Mimi—a beautiful Puerto Rican baby—and this black boy, Frank, all sitting at Grandma's dinner table. The relatives weren't that accepting, so it was pretty tense. I remember Warren going for a walk with the kids down Grandma's street, and she looked out the window and said, 'There goes the United Nations.'"

There is a picture of Warren's young family in Daly City. Frank is not in the photo, but sisters Karma and Marjorie are affectionately flanking the family. Warren is holding a jubilant Greg. Nancy—a California blond with big hoop earrings and a black-and-white print shirt—holds dark-haired, dark-eyed Mimi, who looks a bit stunned and is the only one in the photo not smiling. Karma recalls, "We could hardly change Mimi's diaper because she just wanted to cling to someone. She had a death grip."

"So now you've got a house full," I said to Nancy, "and your husband is in medical school, and I assume he still wasn't around much."

"No, he wasn't, but I was raised to be independent, so I kept busy. I had my art business, and when I taught classes at night, if Warren wasn't home, I'd get a high school, neighbor girl to babysit. I had a couple of shows at the Stonestown Shopping Mall, and I did consignment. I painted seascapes, landscapes, still lifes, portraits. I called it my therapy time. During Mimi's nap, I would say to myself, 'What do you want to do today? Paint or take a nap?' I had a workshop in our garage, and the bench was up high, so the kids could play and ride their bikes while I worked, and we had a backyard with play equipment. I once painted a scene right out our front window—a field of wildflowers in the vacant lot that grew taller than me —blue and pink and white and yellow flowers growing on fertile land. It was gorgeous. Across that field, you could see the skyscape of San Francisco with Mount Tamalpais in the background. I kept busy painting. I remember this old lady who would walk by our house every day with her dog. She wore a long dress and a hat and looked quite ethnic. She actually ended up staying in our guest room for a while when she was homeless or transitioning. That room got a lot of use."

Jim Makol, Warren's classmate from medical school, stayed in the spare room, and he too has colorful memories of San Francisco in the late '60s. "The Haight/Ashbury was in full bloom. Every day, the sound of Congo drums permeated the east end of Golden Gate Park. The Fillmore Auditorium was at its peak, and concerts by the Grateful Dead and

Jefferson Airplane filled Speedway Meadows in the park on weekends. The drug culture, with an acceptance of experimentation, was on the upswing and the Black Power movement was evident in Oakland. All of that was a stark contrast to the need to study and exhibit discipline to succeed in learning medicine.

"I was from Massachusetts," explained Jim, "and went to college in New Hampshire. During the winter in New England, the snow gets over your head. I was watching TV and seeing all the beaches out west, so I applied to UCLA and UCSF. I didn't know anybody in California. I don't think I even knew anybody who'd been to California. I just had a TV image in my mind. When it came time, I got on a plane to someplace I'd never visited.

"I remember getting up in the morning and walking up that hill to Mt. Parnassus. It was a hundred-odd steps up from Irving Street to the medical school. I'm sure it was intimidating to everybody who walked through those doors. You don't know anybody and you don't know how you are going to stack up. It's a very competitive environment with smart people from all over, very ambitious people. It was a big place high on a hill, lit up over the city. Heck, it was a city unto itself, and you had to find your way through a maze of hallways, stairs, buildings. I think for us, coming to San Francisco and the University —Warren from a small town in California and me from Springfield—was a big step. It was high-powered.

"I often got to class sort of late—and so did Warren, so we sat in the back of the room, the last row or two. That's how we met—because we sat in close proximity in the back of the class for most of that first year. I don't remember specifically how I came to live at Warren and Nancy's, but I think it was summer, and they were going someplace. I don't know where, but I was in transition with roommates, so somehow we agreed that I would live in their basement. I believe Warren's sister lived there just before me. They had this cat, and I was in charge of feeding him. One day, I went upstairs, and he was lying on the floor stiff as could be. So I dug a grave and buried the cat, and when they came home, I had to explain to them that the cat was gone.

"By the time I lived at Warren's place, I knew Nancy and the family. I remember they had taken in an African-American boy. How can I put this delicately? He had some problems that caused him to be difficult to take care of—hygiene-related problems, and he was a teenager. I remember them trying to deal with this. In retrospect, I realize it was an unusual situation for a relatively young Caucasian family to take in a black, teenaged male who didn't have parents. But at the time, I had no experience. I just remember thinking it was odd.

"There were very few married students in medical school, and those who were lived a different life from the rest of us. They went home to wives, and the rest of us hung around our apartments studying. I had three roommates, and one of them was gay, which I didn't know until after he moved out. That's another thing that was going on in San Francisco—a gay community all around us. I only mention this because people get into their own space with roommates or whatever, and Warren and Nancy were off someplace else from the rest of us."

"Talk about the decision to go to Panama for Warren's internship," I said to Nancy.

"I don't know if they still do this, but back then there was a matching program where the students put in their top three choices for internship, and the hospitals did the same thing, ranking their top choices. Warren's first choice was Stockton Hospital because it paid the most, and he let me decide the second choice. I chose Panama because I thought it would be exciting to go to a foreign country. He got his second choice, and we went to Panama."

"We traveled by ship, driving to New Orleans first. Then they shipped our car and all of us and the dog."

"You had a dog, too," I said.

"I got the dog when I was pregnant with Greg—a poodle, who had belonged to my sister. He was my main companion back then. I had him well trained and everybody loved him. He was great with the kids, and he went to Panama with us."

"What was his name?"

"Zeke. Warren named him."

"Why Zeke?

"He was reading the Bible—so it was like Ezekiel."

"Did you guys go to church?"

"I came from a church background, but his family didn't. Except for his Grandma Sarah. Warren wasn't really interested in church. I went with the kids sometimes, but it never became a part of our life. When we got the dog, Warren was reading the Bible like an investigation."

Nancy was describing an early example of Warren's habit of reading for information. Later in life, he would spew forth facts acquired this way, in a style that could be entertaining or annoying, depending how often you were subjected to listening. Apparently at this point, however, his exposure to new information simply translated to a name for his dog.

"There was a pool on the ship," said Nancy. "It didn't have a shallow end. In three days, Greg learned how to swim."

"Sounds like the swimmer gene found its way to Greg."

"Yes, I guess it did," she said. "When we lived in the Canal Zone, all the interns lived in fourplexes with one garage underneath for all four places. They weren't big, but it was more than adequate for the four of us. We were down to four because Frank had returned to his grandmother. The complex was for employees of the Panama Canal Company, not just interns. I'm not even sure if that's the right name, but Gorgas Hospital employees were included."

Gorgas Army Community Hospital, like UCSF, was built on Ancon Hill, overlooking Panama City. Built on the site of a former French Hospital in 1904, it is named for Army Surgeon General Samuel C. Gorgas, who expanded and modernized the facility to help with medical care during the canal construction. By the time 26-year-old Warren arrived in 1970, the hospital complex was large and rambling like UCSF—a mix of old architecture and new—a setting the young intern probably found vaguely familiar and surely engaging. By the mid-1980s, as the Panama crisis heated up, Gorgas Hospital became a tumultuous place, experiencing regular bomb threats, and protestors camping in the parking lots, and, on the night of the US invasion, an attack by the Panama Defense Forces. However, pictures taken during the '70s show a bucolic hospital in a tropical setting. A picture of Warren holding Mimi on a hill above a secluded beach is likewise tranquil. In the faded image, Mimi is almost laughing as her father dips his head toward her. Warren is gaunt and has a mustache. His big smile is absent, replaced with a tender expression.

"Most of the interns didn't have children," continued Nancy, "so again, I was kind of out of the loop. In fact, the only time I went to a party was after the med students found out where they were going to intern."

"Do you mean back in San Francisco?"

"Yes, in San Francisco. They had just graduated and someone had a party."

"Were many of the interns married?"

"Not very many. Some had just gotten married, and there was one family with older children. And some of the wives were pregnant with their first babies. They were more into planning than us," said Nancy, after which she was quiet for a moment.

"What were the pressures?" I asked, knowing that it was in Panama that things fell apart for the couple. "In Davis, you were isolated because you had health issues and then you were a new mom. And then in Daly City, you were incredibly busy with a young family, and then you get to Panama. I imagine there were cultural issues there."

"Not really, because we were all Americans living in one area. And everybody had a maid. We paid them well, which made the other Americans mad. We paid them more than they were used to being paid, which still wasn't very much. So we had a maid, but she didn't live in the building. She came to help during the day. I had mixed emotions about her because Mimi learned how to boss her around. She was 2, and she would tell the maid 'Put on my shoes,' and Cecilia would do what she asked. I didn't like that. Greg started kindergarten while we were there, so he was always out doing something. He was very high energy. In fact, a lot of people labeled him hyperactive, and maybe he tests that way, but my attitude was that he was who he was, and he'd have to learn to deal with it. I used to tell him, 'When you learn to work the way you play, you're going to light the world on fire.'

"You asked about the pressures," continued Nancy. "Warren was very busy because of his work. I didn't have any comparisons, so I thought that was the way it was in medical school, but it also seemed like he was choosing to be busy rather than be part of the family. One of neighbors—a medical student with older kids—would play ball in the street with his son, but Warren didn't have time for that. Greg used to say, 'He never threw the ball with me.' Greg was a natural athlete, so we got him in swimming lessons, and pretty soon he was on the swim team and making records. It was a big deal, but Warren never had time to watch him. He just wasn't around that much. He even volunteered to take shifts for other interns. He did more at the hospital than he had to. Honestly, being a doctor was the most important thing to him. He ate, slept, and thought about it."

As Nancy told this story from her perspective, I wondered how Warren would have told it. The experience of internship is so unique that Dr. Robert Marion, a professor of pediatrics and obstetrics at Albert Einstein College of Medicine, wrote a book called *The Intern Blues*. The book is a compilation of diaries kept by three interns—Mark, Andy, and Amy—describing the day-to-day exhausting, frightening, frustrating entryway doctors are required to navigate and endure as part of their training. Dr. Marion reports that the three were afraid they would "lose touch with their non-physician friends who had no understanding of what it was like to work a hundred hours a week." In the Preface to the second edition, he writes that the book "should be read by the parents, other family members, and loved ones of interns prior to the start of the training years. That's the only way they'll truly understand what hell their loved ones' life is likely to become." This book was written years after Warren's internship in Panama, so it's potential insights were unavailable Nancy, who was living the experience from the position of wife to a doctor-in-training.

"So what happened next?" I asked Nancy

"When we came home, we divorced, and he moved to Sonora and started his practice."

Again, Nancy was abbreviating as she had at the beginning of our conversation. Though others reported that Nancy's involvement with Greg's swim coach was pivotal in the couple's separation, a failed marriage usually has many contributing factors, none of which are comfortably revisited. Warren, too, touched only lightly on this part of his life when completing the questionnaire for his twenty-year high school reunion. He gives only three short sentences of a two-page narrative to his time in Panama: "Internship was in an American hospital in the Panama Canal Zone. It was a good experience to be someplace so different. It was a bad experience when working so hard, losing all reasonable perspective, and losing a wife and kids to divorce at the end of it all." So the end of Warren's schooling coincided with the end of his first marriage, which significantly defined how and where he would start practicing medicine.

# PART II

# THE DOCTOR

*Chapter 4*

# MOSEY IN

I wanted to run away from everything
but I wanted to run towards something too.

-Sherwood Anderson, Winesburg, Ohio

"Warren came to Sonora in August 1971 with his 6-year-old son Gregory," said Judy plunging into the story at her entry into Warren's life. "He was 27 years old and in the process of getting a divorce, and he had custody of his son. At the time, there was no ER at Tuolumne General Hospital, so Chip Chiapelli, who was on the Board of Supervisors, made an arrangement with Warren to run a private practice out of TGH in exchange for being on-call for emergencies. When Ken Trout's baby was badly burned, Warren was the one who took care of him."

Judy assumed I knew Ken Trout and the fact that his baby had been burned. I did know Ken as he'd been my boss on a summer job in Twain Harte, but I didn't know about his baby being burned. I soon realized that Judy assumed I knew many of the people who appeared in her stories, and sometimes I did, but I also learned that I needed to ask if I didn't. When she veered back to Warren's arrival in Sonora by mentioning another name, it was a person with whom I was vaguely familiar, but I had not yet gotten the knack of asking for more information.

"Frank Smart wrote a snarky letter to the editor of the paper about Warren because his draft status changed from 1A," Judy continued. "Warren had custody of Greg, and he didn't want to be drafted. He'd written a request to be a conscientious objector but hadn't submitted it. Chip was able to get Warren's draft status changed when he came to work at the hospital. In 2001, Warren marched in the Peace March with a peace symbol drawn on his bald head," Judy added, leaping to a future point to illustrate Warren's position on war. This was another thing, I would learn to expect, leaps through time among related events. After the 2003 Peace March reference, Judy dropped back to 1971.

"I was working on my teaching credential and got hired as an intern to teach first grade at Sonora Elementary School. On the first day of school, I looked up and there was a skinny guy in white pants and a purple shirt standing in the doorway of my classroom with this grin on his face. There was a little blond boy at his side and the two just stood there. They were late. Class had already started. I still have Warren freeze-framed in the doorway in those white pants and purple shirt. To this day, I think white pants on a guy are sexy.

"He and Gregory came in, and we got him situated. When Warren left, I heard this big roar from the street because his car at time was a green dune buggy. So he roared off and left Gregory, who is ADHD, with me. The hyper part is intense, and Gregory and Warren had been through a difficult period. They were living in Panama, where Warren was finishing his internship at Gorgas Army Community Hospital, when his wife ran away with Gregory's swimming instructor and moved to Colorado. She took their daughter, Mimi, who was a sweet, easy little girl. But Gregory was difficult. He got kicked out of kindergarten. So she left him with Warren. They were both pretty traumatized by the time I met them. Greg had been through a lot. His mom was gone, and he'd moved to a strange place. If Warren had to go to the hospital in the middle of the night, he had to take Greg to his grandparents, who lived right here in town. So there was a lot of new stuff coming at him."

"Is ADHD the term you would have used back then?" I asked.

"I might have said hyper. Greg was difficult in class, and he had a great deal of trouble learning to read, so Warren came for a lot parent conferences, and he told me the story about why he and Greg moved back to Tuolumne County to help me understand what was going on with his son. He was the most incredible father and later grandfather. It was paramount in his psyche to be good parent. He was 'the Papa' —the role he played in Fiddler on the Roof.

"I think the turning point with Greg was . . ." Judy paused before offering, "Mr. Goodbar candy bars were popular back then, and I decorated a little round paper badge that said Mr. Goodbar. Whenever Greg had a good day, I gave him the badge. Warren helped a lot. When Greg got the badge, he had to go home and tell his dad how he earned it, and then Warren gave him some kind of reward too—like a trip to the park or time playing catch. I eventually made Warren a badge that said Mr. Goodbar Senior. I still have it somewhere. That went on until Christmas vacation, but then Gregory didn't show up the day after vacation. But Warren did. He told me that the other grandmother had insisted her daughter get Greg back. She said, 'You're a terrible mom. You can't do this.' So she took Gregory back. In those days there weren't any formal custody agreements, so he went back to live with his mother, Nancy. Without Greg, we didn't have parent conferences, so we said good-bye."

The story pouring out of Judy was one I'd heard Warren tell again and again, albeit somewhat differently. During visits for annual check ups, he had related—eyes twinkling with mirth—how he'd fallen in love with his son's teacher during parent teacher conferences. One of the things I'd always loved about Warren as a physician was the way he used stories from his own life as illustrations and examples in his medical practice. I'd heard this story about him going to parent-teacher conferences and meeting Judy when I was worried about my daughter's set-back in reading in the summer between first and second grades and when I couldn't make it to my youngest child's parent teacher conferences because of a heavy work load and his father went without me. Warren had made his story applicable to my own, calming and reassuring me with stories about his struggles as a parent and a partner. The repetition and forthright disclosures were an appealing aspect of my doctor.

"Warren was an iconoclast in Sonora," said Judy. "He was everything the other docs were not. He wore jeans and Birkenstocks with weird socks, and he never wore a white coat, nor did he wear a tie. 'Ties carry germs,' he said. He listened; he cared. That was his gift. Which also made him late—always. He really could've picked up the pace," said Judy. "It drove me crazy. It was unconscionable. But he got a lot of patients very quickly, and his practice was soon full. He was very generous, especially when it came to caring for his parents. He paid their back debt, and he bought them a house. He worked his way through medical school doing odd jobs. Like at Davis he was a night watchman. He'd walk around the buildings and study while walking. He also worked on the railroads and in the peach orchards. He didn't pay off his loans until the '80s."

In the first half hour of our first meeting, Judy rattled off a ton of information, much of which provoked additional questions. I assumed Warren had planned to come back to Sonora after medical school, and maybe he had, but the opportunity to get a draft deferment by practicing medicine in a county hospital certainly dressed up the choice. To learn more about Warren's arrival at Tuolumne General Hospital—or TGH as it is usually called—I would need to talk to people who had worked beside him, but I also wanted to clarify the details about the job offer.

After Judy mentioned the deferment, I searched the Internet to see if I could learn more about what kind of deferment he may have had. I discovered something called a 2A draft classification: a status designated for occupational hardship situations. While the 2A status was generally reserved for young men in agricultural occupations, rural draft boards granted this status to entice or retain professionals, like doctors and lawyers, to serve their communities. Apparently local draft boards had considerable discretionary power in making classification decisions, and I discovered another interesting thing about draft boards. In rural communities, a county board of supervisors often doubled as a draft board, so it was plausible that Supervisor Chip Chiapelli could have arranged this option for Warren if he agreed to work at TGH—the county hospital which served the poor and uninsured.

My next stop was the Carlo M. De Ferrari Archives—the repository of all official records for Tuolumne County. The Archives are located in a cement-block, two-story building on the side of a hill behind the county library. To get there, I had to drive past Heaven for Kids playground—which houses a turret-like structure that I knew Warren had helped build when service clubs were creating the park. Charley Dyer, Records and

Archive Coordinator, was expecting me as I'd requested an appointment via email, explaining the purpose of my visit: to examine the minutes from the Tuolumne County Board of Supervisors meetings for 1971.

"So you want to look at minutes from the Supervisor's Meetings," said Charley.

"Yes. I'm working on a biography about Warren Borgquist. He was a local family doctor who died a few years ago."

"Warren was my doctor," said Charley, which didn't surprise me. Almost every person to whom I mentioned the project seemed to have some connection to the man.

"I'm hoping to find historical documentation in the minutes about him being hired on staff at TGH," I explained.

Charley led me to a beautiful oak table at the center of the Research Room, upon which lay two oversized blue volumes. "These books include all of the Board minutes from 1971," said Charley as I settled myself in one of several heavy, old-fashioned office chairs set around the table. "I went to Warren for about thirty years," he continued, leaning against a gorgeous but outmoded card catalog. "A lot of doctors act like they are above you—kinda God-like—but Warren was just a hometown doc." Charley had my attention, for I could feel a story coming. "Back in the late '90s, I started getting real bad pains in my gut. He sent me for all kinds of tests: barium studies, x-rays, endoscopy, colonoscopy. But he couldn't figure it out, so he referred me to a gastroenterologist at Stanford. She diagnosed me with a mild form of Crohn's disease and two or three years later, I had surgery."

When Warren's name came up, people seemed to move to a place where intimate health details were readily shared, a behavior that I found as mysterious as it was useful. This middle-aged professional was detailing a health crisis that Warren himself would have been prohibited from telling me because of confidentiality laws.

"I couldn't have asked for better treatment at Stanford," continued Charley, "but here's the thing. When I went back to see Warren and explained all this, he said, 'I'm sorry I couldn't find it.' That's what I liked about him. He was genuinely disappointed that he couldn't figure it out. But he referred me, and that was great. Anyway, that's my Borgquist story. Now I'll let you get to work." Charley smiled.

"Is it OK if I make note of that story?" I asked. I had my notebook and pen ready.

"Sure, but no pen," he said.

"Excuse me?

"Only pencil in the Archives."

"Oh, right!" I said, putting the pen away and getting out my mechanical pencil. I was sitting before a ledger of historical documents that he was responsible for preserving, and he was reminding me how to treat the material.

I opened one of the books dated February 1971 to September 1971. The pages of thick acid-free, archival paper noted the Tuolumne County Board of Supervisors Minutes for six months—twenty or more pages for each meeting—typed and signed by Carlo M. De Ferrari, who had been County Clerk for thirty-three years. This was going to take a while. The minutes were full of routine information like status reports by the auditor, resolutions related to obtaining Federal Assistance, and personnel appointments, but buried in the notations were tiny nuggets that were relevant to Warren Borgquist's story. For example, I discovered that Supervisors Tilio "Chip" Chiapelli and Ralph Thiel constituted the Hospital Committee. One or both of these men's names were associated with resolutions about Emergency Services Plans and proposed contracts with medical professionals working at TGH, confirming that it was likely that Chip was involved in Warren's appointment at TGH.

As I made notes, Charley returned to see how I was doing. "It's slow going," I said. "I haven't found what I'm looking for yet—confirmation that Warren got a draft deferment in exchange for going to work at TGH. Would you happen to know if the Board of Supervisors was also the Draft Board back then? I've read that was often the case in rural counties."

"I'll dig around and see what I can find," said Charley. "In the meantime, here's another story about Borgquist that I think you'll like. I used to work for the Sheriff's office. Bob Wolfganger, a guy I worked with, told me about taking an inmate from the jail to the ER. Borgquist was on duty, and he demanded that Wolfganger take off the handcuffs. I guess he was being the liberal doc. Wolfganger warned him, but Borgquist insisted As soon as he removed the handcuffs, the inmate cold-cocked Borgquist."

I wasn't finding confirmation of the draft deferment story, but Charley was making sure I had something to record in my notebook. Warren's trusting attitude toward the inmate had a "peacenik" flavor. Maybe he was simply concerned about the inmate's dignity, but ignoring the officer's warning had consequences. I wondered what he took away from the incident besides a bruised face.

Charley was still reminiscing. "Warren had this sign in his office about buying drugs from Canada. Actually it was a cartoon, so I asked him why he had it. 'That's for the drug salesmen who come in there,' he said. 'But why do you have it?' I asked again. 'Because it pisses 'em off.'" Charley grinned as he repeated Borgquist's answer. Then he explained that Warren encouraged him to order pharmaceuticals from Canada as a cost-saving measure for the medications he was required to take.

The Archivist headed back to his office while I continued to look for evidence that Chip offered Warren a job that came with a draft deferment. I studied the Board minutes from June 8 to September 7—the Tuesday after Labor Day and the first day of school at Sonora Elementary, the day Warren had delivered Greg to Judy's class, and still there was no record of the Board hiring him or anything about a special draft deferment. About that time, a large man with a shock of white hair, moving slowly with walker, emerged from a door leading to the main archive area. Charley came out of his office behind the man. "Where are you headed, Carlo?" he asked.

"Just going out for a breath of air," said the gentlemen.

"Before you go, could you speak with this woman? She has some questions about the local draft board in the 1970s."

Charley lead Carlo De Ferrari to the table, his respect and affection clear in his tone of deference and ready assistance to the man with the walker. Carlo took a seat in an upholstered office chair situated at the end of the table. I knew Carlo by reputation as a third generation Tuolumne County native and notable local historian. He was frequently quoted in the Sonora Union Democrat on matters related to history, and the Archives were named for him. His signature appeared again and again on the records I'd been reading for over an hour. After introductions, I asked Mr. De Ferrari a few questions. Carlo did not recall if the Board of Supervisors had doubled as the county draft board, but he was certain that there were no draft records in the Archives. "Chip is dead, so you can't ask him," said Carlo.

While we were chatting, Charley buzzed open the door for attractive brunette, carrying a basket. Charley introduced his wife Theresa, who had brought lunch for the two men. After hearing what I was working on, Theresa said, "When Warren died, we wondered what we were going to do without him. We liked him as a doctor, but he was also a great person." The core of Theresa's statement—a sense of loss followed by a positive assessment— would become a frequent preamble to a Borgquist story. Theresa continued, "I worked over in Mariposa County, and for some reason they always gave me a 3:30 appointment which was crazy because I didn't get off work until 3:00. So I would call and ask, 'Is he running behind?' And of course he was always at least an hour or more behind, so I'd say, 'That's good because it'll take me that long to get there.' And even when I got there, I'd have to wait. Everyone waited, but once you got in, he was all yours."

Charley was waiting for Theresa, and I had more pages to examine. Carlo had crossed his arms on his chest and closed his eyes. While he rested and Theresa and Charley talked in the office, I opened the second tome of minutes. In the October 5, 1971 minutes, I found an item that reported three new additions to the staff at TGH: James B. Huchinson, MD, Pierre Marquis, DDS, and Warren G. Borgquist, MD in Family Practice, confirming that he was hired to work at TGH in the fall of 1971. What was not clear was if or how the draft deferment happened.

The next step was to look at the newspaper archives. I found two pertinent articles. One, dated October 12, 1971, pictured a very young man with no glasses, no beard, and a broad toothy grin—certainly not a visage that called to mind the notion of a physician. The article announced that this man had opened a family practice at TGH and explained that following medical school at the University of California, San Francisco, Borgquist completed an internship at Gorgas Hospital in Panama. Warren is quoted describing one of the problems he noted while in Panama. "In Latin American cities, it is hard for doctors to set up a practice in the city, but that is where they go. The rural areas are neglected." I wondered if this observation played a part in his decision to open a small town practice.

The byline on the second article, dated September 26, 1996, was Kathe Waterbury, then a staff writer for the Democrat. In the picture accompanying this article, Warren has a thick, dark beard, he is bald, and his smile is as large as ever, but his face seemed to have grown into the toothy smile visible in the earlier picture. Waterbury wrote, "Dr. B, as he is called by much of the county, celebrated 25 years as a physician on September 13. It was a date noted by his mother, he said, because mothers keep track of such things." So there it was! The date he opened his practice. While that clarified one fact about Warren's history, the next paragraph tangled the threads. "When I left Sonora, it was the last place I wanted to return to," Borgquist was quoted as saying. "It was small-minded and I couldn't get far enough away." Next Dr. B said Tilio Chiapelli, the father of his high school friend, Jerry, told him, "Warnie, we need doctors here." According to the article, Warren told Chip he was a poor risk because he was classified 1A, but Chip told him not to worry about that. The last line in the paragraph read: "A year or so later, Borgquist found his draft records had been burned."

Judy had mentioned a letter to the editor in which Frank Smart criticized Warren for draft dodging. That letter was printed on October 10, 1996. Frank Smart, who founded Chapter 391 of Vietnam Veterans of America in Tuolumne County, had helped establish war memorials at the Tuolumne County Library and in downtown Sonora. He took exception to how Borgquist "avoided the draft." Smart wrote: "I don't care what his views were on the war then or now. I don't even care how his draft records were damaged. What I care about is his apparent gloating over the fact."

While I would not have described Warren's statements as gloating, his words were characteristically blunt during the interview with Waterbury. They had stung Smart, who was equally blunt, calling for Warren's "public apology to all who were drafted and honorably served their country and especially to those who were drafted and wound up in Viet Nam." Borgquist and Smart stood on either side of a line drawn, and felt, by an entire generation in the late '60s and early '70s. On one side were those who did what they could to avoid going to Viet Nam for reasons ranging from moral objection to personal safety or just plain fear. On the other side were the men who were drafted, fought, and survived Viet Nam. They came home to suffer in silence, rage vehemently, or crusade for respect and acknowledgement for veterans. Whether a young man went to Viet Nam or not colored the rest of his life experience and ongoing worldview. Here, twenty-five years after the fact, Borgquist and Smart stood firm declaring their positions.

Reading Warren's words in 1996, I didn't doubt the truth of his report that he had not wanted to return to Sonora when he was 27 years old, but I couldn't help but wonder if he had embellished the story by saying the draft records were burned. Chip wasn't around to tell his part in the story, so I would have to locate the archive of draft records if I wanted to know for sure. And what about Warren's comment about Panamanian doctors neglecting rural areas as he'd said in the article. Where did that observation fit into the mix? All I knew for sure was that Warren had returned to Sonora from an internship in Panama with a young son after separating from his wife. His mother had marked his start date as a doctor in Tuolumne County, and his draft classification appeared to be a factor in opening a family practice at Tuolumne General Hospital. The decision to return to Sonora looked like a turning point in Warren Borgquist's life, complex and complicated like such moments are, tinctured with values about family and politics—full of the friction that shapes a life.

Over the next few months, I would learn that the only way to tell Warren Borgquist's story was through the stories others told about him, for the man left little in the way of written documentation. He did not keep a diary or write letters. There were no research papers. Of course, he dictated patient notes, but those were confidential. The only way I'd hear about his work as a family physician was from patients, like Charley Dyer, who chose to tell their stories. Nurses, office workers, and professional colleagues would describe the man they worked with. And family and friends would tell about the brother, father, step-father, or grandfather; about the guy who loved to swim, hike and bicycle; to eat, sing, joke, and build things. As Judy said, it would not be the story he would have told, but person-by-person, a picture of the man emerged.

# Chapter 5

# PICNIC

The bond that links your true family is not one of blood,
but of respect and joy in each other's life. Rarely do members of one
family grow up under the same roof.
-Richard Bach, *Illusions: Adventures of a Reluctant Messiah*

"The year I got divorced," said Judy Borgquist, "I took thirty units, and it was my first year of teaching in an internship. And I had to go to class two nights a week plus two summer school semesters at UC Davis. It was bad. The poor kids. Some nights, I fell asleep at 6:30 p.m. We had scrambled eggs and mac and cheese most nights."

It was a chilly November day, so Judy positioned us in wingback chairs before the fire, sipping tea. Four or five books were piled on her ottoman. To my left, stood the piano with a huge array of pictures of the Borgquist family.

"Was that the year you had Greg in your class?"

"Yes," said Judy. "Greg left to live with his mother in December '71 after the first semester. After Dave and I split up, he and Ellen left town, and I lived in that house for a year-and-a-half. Warren and I started dating the summer of '72. He proposed in November, and I moved in with him during the following Christmas vacation.

"The first time Warren met my mother," Judy continued, "he took her for a ride in the dune buggy. My mother was kind of a hoity-toity

person. I thought she was going to die. She advised me against marrying him. But she liked the fact that he was a doctor. When we married, she didn't want me to work because it would look bad for a doctor to have a working wife."

"Talk about how you and Warren connected after Greg went back to his mom," I said.

"I was walking down Washington Street one day early the next summer, and I saw him. 'Do you want to get a cup of coffee?' he asked. So we did. And then he started asking me out. He had a motorcycle by then in addition to the dune buggy. In November, he took me for a ride on the motorcycle. At the time, you could get up the backside of Bald Mountain. On the top of the mountain, he got down on his knee and asked me to marry him. Isn't that the cutest?"

From where I sat in Judy's front room, Bald Mountain was visible as a backdrop through the wall of windows, and I thought it perfect that the mountain where he proposed served for years as a guardian to the place where this couple made a home.

"I lived way out Phoenix Lake Road," Judy continued, "near where Sullivan Creek School is now, and Warren would stay over a few nights a week when we were dating. In the morning, he would coast his motorcycle out before the kids got up. One night, Scott said, 'Warren, you might as well stay and have breakfast with us.'

"Not long after that Warren said, 'This is crazy. Let's just move in together.' He had this tiny house behind the county schools office. It had two bedrooms and was much closer to the hospital than my place. So Scott and Jennifer and I moved in there. But when I went back to school after Christmas vacation, I got called into the principal's office. A woman had called the School Board and said, 'Are you aware that Judy Purdy is living with Warren Borgquist without benefit of marriage?' The principal told me this was inappropriate. That was the second or third of January, and when I told Warren about it, he said, 'I guess we are going to get married this week.'"

"So we got married January 7, 1973. He chose this hippy-dippy shirt. It was a flowered shirt with bright colors. JoAn Martin and I went down to Lerner's in Modesto, and I bought a cheap Gunny Sack dress. A picture that Marjorie took of us at the wedding hangs in our bathroom. Actually, we weren't concerned about clothes. It was more: *Can we pull this off in a week and get our families here?* And we did. My mother and brother came and his family. I don't remember if Karma was here. I think just Marge and Craig, and a couple of friends and the kids. My cousin Kathy might have come. We had no invitations. We called people because it was such short notice. That worked for us. It was at the Gunn House in a little sitting room that later became a bar. Anyway, Judge Carkeet, the father of one of Warren's high school friends, performed the ceremony. Warren wrote a poem. All I remember is that it was something about this rolling ball of our love. Jeeze, it was corny, but he was so proud and excited to say it to me. I don't recall if I wrote something too, but it was mostly that he had to say this piece about how much we loved each other. He was so cute."

"I met Judy at their little place—this cute little hippy pad," said Marjorie.

79

"I really liked her. She was funny, smart, and clever. But the marriage surprised me. It happened so suddenly. What I remember was that she was told at work that she couldn't live with him and keep her job. Something about being an example in the community. So they decided to get married in a matter of a week. The wedding was at the Gunn House, and Judy wore this beautiful velvet dress."

"It was a Gunny Sack," said Karma. "That's a brand that mixed fabrics— prints, and stripes, and they were old fashioned and were finely made, well crafted, and comfortable."

"So were you at the wedding, Karma?"

"Yes. Our parents were there, and her mom and the kids and maybe Aunt Noni. I'm not sure. The wedding was small, tasteful—very sweet. Appropriate for a second marriage."

"I remember Greg had on a white tie," said Marjorie. "They got married in January of '73, and Craig and I married in May of the same year. Judy wore her wedding dress to our wedding."

When I asked Shelley Andrews, a friend who taught with Judy, what she recalled about Judy's marriage to Warren, she said, " I think it was almost a done deal by the time we knew what was going on. I have to tell you back in those days shacking up could be a real problem. I'll never forget one morning after I'd spent the night at Don's house when we were dating. We were full-on adults, Don teaching at the college and me at Curtis Creek. I was an early riser. One morning, I was coming from Don's house on the Columbia side of town and my principal was at the stoplight coming from the other direction. There we were at 6:30 a.m. looking at each other. We never said a word about it. But that was in the early '80s. Judy and Warren got caught in the early '70s. I don't think she talked about it for obvious reasons. It would've been much worse for them in '73."

That November day in Judy's front room with a huge collection of family photos peering from the piano, she continued the story about how she and Warren made a family after their hasty marriage.

"By then we had this Suburban. It had two bench seats, and you could put a queen-sized mattress in the back. His mother was a seamstress, and she made a cover for the mattress and curtains. We had reservations in Carmel after the wedding, but we got a late start, so we got to some walnut orchard between here and there and stopped. We had candles and champagne and that was where we spent our wedding night. It was wonderful and the start of our thing for picnics. We always took picnics. We would even have picnics on the floor in the winter. For wedding presents, we always gave a picnic basket that had plates, knives, cutting board and napkins and a card that said: 'Make your life together a picnic.' We finally made it to Carmel, and we had a few days there before we came back to work. I must've taken Monday off. We took many trips like that—weekend jaunts. That was thirty-nine years ago!" Judy paused and took a sip of her tea.

"Then we had to deal with blended families," Judy continued, diverging into the reality of what happens when two divorcées with children marry. "When we first got married, Greg and Mimi came every other weekend. It was hard because Warren wanted to lavish love and attention on them, and at first Scott and Jennifer, who had him all the time, didn't get it when he dropped them all of a sudden to put his focus on Mimi and Greg. That caused some strife. Mimi and Greg were like, 'These guys get you all the time.' So they clung to him. When we'd go out, Jennifer said, 'It's them and us.' Because Warren, Mimi, and Greg would walk together and . . . well obviously six people can't all walk together down the street anyway, but 'them and us' became a bit of a theme in those first years. Scott and Jennifer had a real advantage because they didn't have an every other weekend arrangement with their dad. It's so disruptive. So it wasn't easy the first year or so trying to make sure everyone was happy and getting along."

The impression I had as a patient was that Dr. Borgquist took pride in his blended family, so much so that I was never sure which kids were his biological children since he referred to each as "my son" or "my daughter." Judy's admission that it took some doing to make sure everyone got along wasn't a surprise, but I was curious about how they'd managed this challenge, and she was about to offer their particular solution.

"In the summer of 1975," continued Judy, "we decided to take a family trip for five weeks across the country. He outfitted the Mustard Monster—the Suburban—building a wooden platform behind the back seat for the queen-sized mattress. We could store camping gear and suitcases underneath the platform, and we had a big rack on the top. That was before seatbelt laws. I mean we never even thought about what a projectile a child lying on a mattress could be. Now I don't even go out of my driveway without my seatbelt on.

"So we set out to build a family. The kids were 8, 10, 12, 14—two years apart—and we were going to do a lot of camping." Judy laughs aloud. "We did some camping, but it was summer, and motels had swimming pools, so mostly we stayed in motels and tried to become a unit. It wasn't easy, but that trip made our family. We had books and music on tape, and we played games—like all these vocabulary games. Scott would try to get Mimi to say big words, and the two of them would tell jokes. When we reached St. Louis, we were going to go see the Arch, which we did, but we were checking into this hotel, and we had a rack on the car. There were two garage attendants standing right at the entrance, and they just stood there watching us drive in and lose the rack because the Suburban was too tall. They didn't say 'Stop.' They just stood there thinking, 'There go the fools.' And we were. We had to buy a new rack.

"We went all the way to the East Coast. We camped one night in Jamestown, Virginia. In the middle of the night we were swatting mosquitoes because they were so bad, and the kids were crying. They couldn't stand it, so we got up at 3:00 a.m. and found a place where we could have breakfast. Warren loved Monticello. Jefferson was always one of his big heroes, so going there was a thrill for him. He believed in Jefferson's intellect and his way of looking at religion. Jefferson and Franklin were deists. They believed in God or some higher power, but they weren't Christian in the 'Jesus is my savior' sense. Warren thought Jesus was a great guy, a great teacher, but he didn't believe he was divine. Warren wasn't a Christian. He believed there was something, but it wasn't Jesus."

Judy took a sip of her tea before continuing with the story about their first blended family summer vacation. "We traveled up the eastern seaboard to Washington, D.C. and on to New York City to visit our friend, Sandy Dorman, and her family. Then we headed to Maine, which the children loved. We had a hotel right on the beach and a room with a balcony. Warren and I were on the balcony, and they were all on the beach throwing rocks into the water and running and having such a good time together. At that moment, we looked at each other and said, 'Mission accomplished.' That trip formed the basis for our belief that trips are life changing and transformative. You learn so much about yourself on a trip. You always bring back many more psychic gifts than the ones in your suitcase."

As I interviewed Judy and later others in the Borgquist family, I would become familiar with their family lore: stories that are told again and again and become emblematic of a point in time or a major transformation. That cross-country trip became part of Borgquist family lore. When I asked Judy's daughter Jennifer about the trip she said, "That's when we became a family. I remember when we started off, it was 'us and them.' Warren and Mimi and Greg would be walking together, and Mom and Scott and I would be together, and by the end, we were all mixed up. We spent a lot of time inside the car driving. Nobody cared about seatbelts back then. Usually it was two kids in the seat and two lying down in the way back on the mattress with all kinds of pillows. It was all quite cozy. One of the things we liked to do was write messages to travelers who were driving along side and see if we could get them to honk and wave. One time we were writing all these positive affirmations, 'You're special!' 'We like you!' People would hang out of their cars and wave and honk, and we'd wave, and Warren would honk.

"We'd been camping a lot, so it was fun to go to Howard Johnson's. We thought it was a fancy motel because it had a restaurant. We all developed a love for their deep fried shrimp, and it was super fun to play in the pools. It was going to be a good night when we got to stop at a Howard Johnson's. We also learned a bunch of history stuff. In fact, my love of American history started on that trip. I've taught eighth and fifth grades, and both are American history years. Getting to see Monticello, going to Williamsburg, and battling mosquitoes in Jamestown, along with Warren's love of trivia, definitely made history come alive because it wasn't just boring statistics. It was fun, life moments, and that's what makes history exciting."

Mimi repeated much of what Judy and Jennifer remembered, but with her own twist. "One of my best childhood memories was when we traveled cross-country. We were in our Suburban that Dad had finagled. He put a riser in and a pad on top with our luggage underneath. Of course, back then you didn't have to wear seatbelts, so we would all take turns, the four of us kids, lying in the very back and then sitting in the middle. I remember everywhere we went, he had some type of story to tell. Back then when he started, we'd go, 'Here he goes again.' And he would always quiz us, like if we were in a certain area, he would say, 'Do you know what tree this leaf comes from or this pine cone?' He'd always have some magical story to go with whatever he was showing us. When we made it back East to the museums, he had something to say about everything. It was from years of reading *National Geographic*, which was his favorite magazine, and the Smithsonian was his favorite museum. I remember his stories and him singing.

"And he gave the sex talk on those summer trips. We were all two years apart, so when Scott got his talk, he had to have been 14 and I was 8, so I don't really remember it, or Jennifer's either, but I do remember when Greg was getting the talk. Dad had Judy drive, and he sat in the back seat with us, and he drew it out all out on paper. He drew the girl and the boy and described the ovaries, the fallopian tubes, and how the egg comes down, and how the little sperm comes out. That whole thing: how the egg and sperm meet. He just drew it. I really appreciate that about him because I don't think any of us kids were ever embarrassed to talk to him about sex."

Greg's memory of the trip veered off into thoughts about doctors. "I remember long hours in the car and looking for license plates from every state, and I remember when we found Hawaii in the Midwest and everybody celebrating. I think it was in Nebraska. I remember going on the USS Constitution. My dad had built a model of the ship. It was a doctor thing to put models together. Later, I was like 'How come you don't play with models anymore?' and he said, 'I was just trying to prove something to myself.' But I've paid attention going into doctor's homes and being around a couple of doctors' offices, and they had models, too. It symbolizes 'If I can put this together, I can put you back together.' The first year he was practicing medicine, when I was living with him, he would take me to the ER. I spent a lot of weekends, a lot of hours kicking back at the hospital— the old red brick one, Tuolumne General. And he had an office that looked over the train tracks, and I remember having the run of the whole hospital—being in places I probably shouldn't have been. People used to say, 'Oh, that's Dr. Borgquist's son.'"

"I remember being in the back of the Travel-All," said Scott, "lying on the mattress and playing games. I'd whisper the answers in Mimi's ear, so they thought she was a very smart little girl. I think I read six or seven Tarzan books in that back seat. I remember stopping in Kansas and meeting Ethel Mary who was some friend of theirs— a girl my age, and we were out in the hammock, and there were fireflies. It was very romantic. I remember New York was a pretty scary place, and Greg got freaked out by this black bum. There was a big deal over that. We ate lobsters in Maine, which was quite fun, and I remember driving under an awning somewhere and taking off the whole travel rack."

The more I learned about the early days of Warren and Judy and their family, the more curious I got about how family life fit with his burgeoning medical practice. Greg's story about going to the ER suggested the two occasionally blurred. Just exactly how did it work to have an office for private practice in the hospital and also be an ER doctor? Judy said he was everything the other docs weren't. What did that mean? Was it just her own bias or did his youth and color add vitality or rancor to the medical community? I expected the stories would twist and fold on themselves between the personal and the professional. For instance, when I eventually got in touch with his early office staff and colleagues, I discovered that Warren's bookkeeper at the office, Gail Bonavia, had a story to tell about that cross country trip.

"Being a family doctor took a lot of his time," said Gail, "but he was not going to deny his own family. He spent a lot of time with them. I imagine Judy would say 'not enough,' but he made sure they took a long vacation every summer. I remember one summer. He had this big International or whatever they called those great big vans, and he had a bunch of kids. Judy had two and he had two, and they were going to take a trip across the United States. So they took off, and did some camping, and they were going everywhere and having a wonderful time. Then he called and said, 'They won't take my credit card.'

"'What?' I asked.

"'They won't take my credit card,' he said again. So I got his number, and I went right to the bank. It was Mother Lode Bank, but it had changed hands, and they had canceled the credit cards. I was furious. 'Look,' I said, 'He's back East with a carload of kids on vacation. Don't tell me you're canceling his credit card.' So they said they'd honor what came in while he was gone. God! The poor guy out in the middle of nowhere with no money."

Gail's story was a small indication of how Dr. Borgquist's medical practice intertwined with his family life. I knew he injected personal stories during appointments as a means of illustration and reassurance. However, just as he selectively chose parts of a story to tell a patient, each storyteller I spoke with had his or her own take on the stories. The girls and Judy, for instance, mentioned the lack of seatbelts on the trip, while the boys headed in other directions. Warren's life was a saga, a long involved story full of many small incidents propelling it forward. As Judy and I closed an early interview in her front room, she added her own take on how the two were related. "Warren was the same kind of father that he was doctor. Always present."

How was that possible? To always be present at home *and* at work?

*Chapter 6*

# TGH

The secret in the care of the patient is in caring for the patient.

-Dr. Francis Peabody, Lecture at Harvard 1925

One afternoon, wanting to get a feel for the place in which Warren started his practice, I stopped by Tuolumne General Hospital, which had closed in 2006. I parked on Hospital Road in front of two buildings that sat on the south side of a short spur of crooked, rolling road. The older building—a two-story structure with a stucco facade, heavy architraves above each window, and a recessed door—conveyed a stately image, suitable to a hospital that served the community for 158 years. After a new brick facility was built in 1966, the older building was used for hospital administration and auxiliary health services. An interior causeway joined the two.

A long cement ramp ran along one side of the newer three-story hospital, serving as access in lieu of a staircase. Four black lampposts topped with large white globes edged the walkway leading to large sliding glass doors. I walked up the ramp and pressed my face to the glass of the locked doors. The wide linoleum-tiled entryway was flanked by what had once been the Emergency Room on the right and an information window on the left. Blue upholstered chairs lined the walls. At the end of the broad, spacious lobby, a pastoral mural decorated the wall from which two hallways extended, one going left and the other right. Staring through the window, I thought about the hurting people who once came here.

"It was April or May of 1972," said Charlene Ingalls when I asked how she came to be a patient of Dr. Borgquist. "I was six or seven weeks pregnant with my first child and very ill. For weeks, I couldn't keep anything down. I was sick 100 percent of the time. I got so dehydrated that Dr. Coombes, who I was seeing at the time, put me in the hospital—Tuolumne General. For some reason, they kept me isolated for a week and wouldn't let me see any of my family. She put me on IVs, and the nurses wouldn't let me go to the bathroom without help, so I had to use a bedpan. I was a naive, 23 year old, doing what my doctor told me to do. Her premise was that I didn't want to be pregnant. She kept coming up with reasons why my body was trying to get rid of the baby. On top of being miserable, I thought something was wrong with me mentally. Every night, when my husband called, I begged him, 'Please come and get me.' And the whole time I was lying there—day and night— I heard the PA system in the background: 'Dr. Borgquist. Paging Dr. Borgquist.'

"On the seventh day, they unhooked the IVs and let me go to the bathroom. I remember using the toilet and throwing up at the same time, but I didn't tell anybody. I just wanted to go home, but I vomited all the way home, and my husband kept saying 'Oh my god,' and I kept saying, 'I am not going back to that hospital or to Dr. Coombes. I won't do it. I can't.' I felt like I was going crazy. Guy, who is this very honorable, honest man, said, 'You're going to have to let her know,' and I said, 'I'm never talking to that lady again.' So he called her. I don't know if it was that day, but he told her, 'This is not working.' It was very honorable of him. However, I was still in bed, still vomiting and dizzy, thinking, what am I going to do? And then I remembered the PA announcements, and I told Guy, 'I want to see Dr. Borgquist.' We called for an appointment. When he walked into the examining room with that big smile, I just felt … "

A huge, audible sigh filled the room. It was forty years later, and we were sitting in Charlene's spacious family room on an early summer morning. That enormous sigh punctuated her story with the relief she felt when she came under Warren's care. "I remember him sitting on his stool, leaning against the wall and saying, 'I don't believe this is in your head.'

After he said that, I would've stayed with him even if I'd lost the baby. It was such a relief. Don't ask me how I stayed pregnant because I ended up losing thirty-two pounds, though I gradually gained them back, so that by the time I had Tara, I was five pounds over my average weight. He tried a bunch of things. I remember him prescribing suppositories, but nothing really seemed to help, except staying in bed, so that's what I did. After a while, Warren consulted doctors at Stanford and learned about a syndrome with a big long name in which morning sickness goes on forever and ever."

I knew of the condition, for coincidentally I'd just read about this syndrome in Atul Gawande's book *Complications: A Surgeon's Notes on an Imperfect Science*. I wrote *hyperemeisis gravidarum* in my notebook from memory because I had carefully copied the words the day before when reading the book. For me, the book was a page-turner because Gawande writes with candor about the uncertainties and perplexities of medicine, including a whole chapter on nausea as "the most frequent complaint for which patients consult physicians." In that chapter, Gawande tells the story of a woman with *hyperemeisis* that is so similar to Charlene's that I was bursting with the impulse to tell her about the book, but I refrained as she continued.

"I remember one appointment when Guy was with me," Charlene continued. "Warren said, 'We're going to try Thorazine.' So I ended up on a medication they used with mental patients to keep them sedated. But that didn't even work. I was vomiting on the delivery table, and I remember Warren saying, 'This is going to be over soon. I promise.' And he wasn't talking about delivering the baby. He was talking about the vomiting. And I'm not kidding, seconds after Tara was born, the nausea went away. She was a healthy baby which was a miracle, but I didn't realize how much of a miracle. By the time I was pregnant with my second child, Warren said, 'We don't use Thorazine anymore.' Of course, that made me worry about Tara. Not only was I sick the whole time I was pregnant with her and on Thorazine, I was smoking back then. None of us is perfect," Charlene added with an apologetic look. "But Tara has had a serious weight problem most of her life, and I wonder if it's connected with what went on during pregnancy. She was starved and drugged when she was in my uterus."

Gawande's book explains that despite trying various drugs over the years, at the time of publication in 2002, nearly thirty years after Charlene's pregnancy with Tara, physicians had not yet determined a successful treatment to relieve the suffering of the five in one thousand women who have severe "pregnancy sickness." Given what Charlene said next, Warren had kept abreast of the changing practices.

"The day I realized I was pregnant with Todd," Charlene continued, "I called Dr. Borgquist's office for an appointment. As soon as he walked in, I asked, 'What can we do before it starts?' That's when he told me things had changed. By then, Bendectin was the only drug they would prescribe for pregnant women with serious nausea. As it turned out, I was able to control the sickness better during that pregnancy—crackers when I first woke up and then a little water. I still threw up—just not as much. But even so, Warren was my mental salvation—physical salvation too, but truly my mental salvation—because I couldn't keep from thinking, 'Maybe Dr. Coombes was right. Maybe I don't want to do this.' Warren would not let me go there. He listened, and he didn't judge." To Charlene, Warren's approach did not feel judgmental. It probably hadn't occurred to her that she was critically appraising him just as others had when he first arrived at TGH.

When I asked Ruth Weston, a nurse who worked at TGH, to talk about her impression of the new doctor, she said, "TGH was as laid back as medicine in this community was in those days. Warren was, nevertheless, a breath of fresh air. I remember the first time I saw him. He was a young guy who didn't have on a lab coat. He didn't even have on long pants, and he wanted a chart. 'Who the heck are you?' I asked. "His dress—wild shirts, shorts and sandals—caused friction with the older doctors who looked at him and said, 'Where the hell did you come from?'

"He was very casual. He wanted us to call him by his first name. But Millie Thomason and I would not allow that. We had some young nurses who would have felt that was totally appropriate, but it wouldn't have worked to have some do it and not the others. He called all the nurses by their first name. The older doctors never did. They would say Mrs. Weston or Mrs. Thomason, or they called us by our last name with nothing preceding. 'Hey Weston! Hey Smith!' Dr. B did not do that. He looked you in the face, and if he had time, he would sit down and talk to you—go over a patient's chart or whatever. He told patients what was the matter with them, what medications they were getting and why. He was as casual in manner as he was in his dress. That was not commonly done here. I mean it was done. Don't misunderstand me."

"Just not to that extent," I said to let Ruth know I understood she was maintaining her professionalism.

"There were some physicians who did something like that, but he was a new breed."

"Was this how new doctors were being trained or was it a personal style?"

"When I first began nursing, we could not tell a patient what they were taking, but shortly after Dr. B got here, we began to see a change. We were allowed to do more of that type of thing. You had to know your physician before you crossed that line. But we were seeing a different way to do things. Medicine became more patient-involved in the '70s. We also had clinics and in-service training that brought fresh ideas. Dr. B was one of the doctors who were big on in-service training, and he loved medicine. He loved the science of it, but he adored the art of it. He was a people person. Sometimes to his detriment. I think his empathy took a toll emotionally. As it does with someone who loves the art of medicine. They are the ones who become involved with their patients and their families. He had a lot of compassion, but he also had empathy, and not all doctors do—nor nurses, for that matter. They may have compassion, but they don't have empathy. Warren was fun to work with, but he was also problematic. Sometimes he would see a problem, and he would not investigate enough before he charged in. He was eventually able to temper that trait, but in his early days, he lacked the maturity to finesse some things."

"Can you give an example?"

"No."

"Because of confidentiality?" I asked.

"Yes. It would divulge too much. He learned from his mistakes," said Ruth, continuing with generalities that felt professionally appropriate. "And from the nurses and some of the physicians he became close to, especially when some of the younger ones started coming in. He knew when to refer and defer. He wasn't a neurosurgeon or an orthopedist or an OB-GYN, and he knew it, so he would consult with other doctors and refer patients. He would also defer to nurses he respected and trusted. He had a crusader complex. He would go to bat for the nurses if we had problems that needed to be addressed. Another strength was his acceptance that death is inevitable. He understood a person's need for respect and dignity in those last hours."

"When I first came to Tuolumne County," said Shelley Andrews, a teacher friend of Judy Borgquist's, "I went to Dr. Farris because he was my first husband's Tom's family doctor. I changed to Warren after Tom's mother had her second stroke. She had gone to Dr. Farris because she had these horrible headaches, and he gave her Valium, saying she was just stressed. But she had high blood pressure, and a few months later she had a stroke that paralyzed her. I don't want to blame Farris. Maybe medicine up here was not up on the symptoms that precede a stroke. Two years later, when she was 46 years old, she had another stroke. She was at TGH, and Warren was caring for her, maybe because she was in the ER. I don't remember why, but I know I never saw Farris during that time. Warren said, 'I can give her something to slow the bleeding,' and Tom and I asked, "Will it save her life?" And he said, 'No.' Warren was like that— very frank. He handled things directly. She died the next day on Valentine's Day. After my mother-in-law died, I started going to Warren.

"I already knew Judy because she and I were in the same intern program. I was young, and Judy was older and had these kids. I was impressed that she had orchestrated getting an intern job at Sonora Elementary while she was getting her degree because she needed to leave Dave and she had these two kids she had to take care of. Later when I started teaching at Curtis Creek, Judy's son Scott ended up in my class. By then Judy and I had already hit it off, but my friendship with Warren and her as a couple didn't really take off until after I was married to Don Andrews. Then I was the one dragging my new husband to my family doctor."

When reading the sympathy cards Judy received after Warren's death, I found one from Shelley. Though she and her husband had moved away, her note to Judy expressed an enduring friendship and also referenced the fact that she was a patient of Warren's from the early days. That's why I had called her. In her estimation, she was an uncommon patient for Warren at the start of his practice. "He didn't know what to do with me. I was always a feminist. I was Ms., never Miss or Mrs., and that was pretty radical at the time. I didn't think it was important for anybody to know whether or not I was married. All they needed to know was that I was a woman. So that's the frame of mind I had when I went to see Warren for an annual pap smear. I told him that I wanted my husband, Tom, to come in with us when I was having my exam, and he said, 'I don't know about that.' I parried with, 'It's pretty uncomfortable, and I want him to know what I'm going through.' Warren said, 'Let's ask your husband.' Which was the perfect thing to say because Tom said, 'Oh no, I don't need to do that.' But then during the exam when Warren had the speculum in, I said, 'I want to see what I look like inside,' and he said 'Okay.' He had the nurse set up a mirror, so I could see what he was looking at— all the way up my vagina to my cervix. He was pretty unflappable. I think he was a little taken aback, but he didn't miss a beat when it came down to it."

BZ Smith had this recollection from when she first met Warren. "I came up to visit my brother in 1972. Warren had come from somewhere in Central America and was friends with my brother. It was strange because I came from Southern California where you didn't have personal relationships with physicians. So I was impressed that my brother had invited this young guy, who was a doctor, to a party at his house. That was the first time I met him. Then I moved to Sonora in January of 1973.

Before I left Los Angeles I'd gone to the health clinic at Cal Poly Pamona. The doctor did my very first breast exam, and he freaked me out when he said, 'I feel some lumps. You need to get them checked out.' I told him I was moving to Sonora, so he said 'Make sure you get a doctor as soon as you get there.' So I did. I went to the clinic at TGH, and there was this young doctor who knew my brother. I was so nervous having this guy, who wasn't very much older than me, giving me a breast exam. He said, 'You're fine. You just have lumpy breasts.' I remember a great sense of relief and then thinking, 'Well that's interesting. I have lumpy breasts. From that day on the phrase 'You've got lumpy breasts' rings in my ear when I think about Warren. It makes me laugh and go phew. I'm good."

As Ruth Weston had asserted, Warren was more patient-centered than the other doctors who took an authoritarian approach. Warren listened. He was honest and direct. He was in the process of building a practice, and it appeared that his style and approach were attracting attention. He was also acquiring an office staff, many of whom would stay with him as long as his early patients.

The first member of his staff I located was Marge Hutchins, Warren's first nurse. During a phone conversation with her, she related her initial impression of the young doctor. "He was a very happy guy, but his dress was hippie style. I remember him coming down the hallway on his way to the Emergency Room wearing Birkenstocks and two different socks, a pair of scruffy jeans, and a scrunched T-shirt. He didn't care what he looked like. To me, he no more represented a physician than I did."

"You were already working at TGH when Warren came. Is that correct?"

"Yes. He inherited me. I was working for Dr. Buschard and Dr.

Comiso. Buschard left, and Warren took his place. So yes, he inherited the nurse who was assigned to that position, which was me. I started with him in 1971 as an LVN, and I worked for him until 1977 when I left to go to Modesto Junior College to get my RN when I was 49 years old.

"What was the office like then?" I asked, calculating that Marge Hutchins was now in her early eighties.

"When you came in the front door of the hospital, there was an open office to the left, and then on the other side of that, there were two rooms. Dr. Borgquist had one of the rooms, and Dr. Comiso had the other. I worked for both of them. I had a small workspace in the back with a door on each side, and I would run from one side to the other, keeping up with them. The girls who did the billing and transcription worked down the way in another hall. Gail Bonavia was the bookkeeper. Somewhere along the line Monique Tomasovich came on as receptionist. My daughter actually worked for Borgquist for a while, too. Eventually, he became our family doctor. He took care of all of us: my brother, my kids, myself."

"What kind of doctor was he?"

"He took a lot of time with his patients and had good rapport even though he frustrated me because we always had a room full of patients waiting for him. But I learned to deal with it. When he came out of the examining room, he didn't waste time getting to the next person. He'd say, 'Okay, who's next?' I'd tell him, and he'd start toward the door, and I'd say, 'Hey wait! I've got a question, and he'd say 'Later.' So I'd grab him by the belt loop, and say 'No, we've got to talk about this now.' And he would stop and listen. He was always kind and gracious and very helpful. If I had a question, he'd answer it, and if I said 'You need to explain that,' he would.

"I also worked the Emergency Room with him when he was on call. One time, a man brought his wife to the hospital in an automobile. She was a cardiac case. I was headed down the ramp with a wheelchair to get her, and here comes Dr. Borgquist trotting ahead of me. He lifted the woman out of the car and carried her to the lobby where he put her on a gurney. I think he even started CPR. I mean that's how conscientious he was. Oh, and here's another story: My brother was a highway patrolman. He called me one day from the scene of an accident. Some kid had literally wrapped his car around a tree, and the crew couldn't get him out because of his injuries. They needed to use the jaws-of-life, but the kid was traumatized and so broken up that every time they moved the car, he screamed in pain. So my brother called and asked, 'Do you suppose Warren could come out and give him some morphine?' When I asked Warren, he grabbed his bag and said, 'Let's go.' He had this dune buggy, and we got in that car, and honest to god, I've never driven so fast in my life. We tore down Lime Kiln Road. When we got to the accident, he talked calmly to the boy as he gave him the injection. Then we got back in his car, drove back to the office, and went back to our regular routine. When something came up like that, he just jumped on it."

"That's a precious story," I said.

"And a very uncommon response in my experience," added Marge.

Gail Bonavia was part of Warren's office staff for many years. "I originally worked for Dr. Buschard and Dr. Comiso. They rented offices from the hospital and worked the ER. Today, they have hospitalists, but in those days, they didn't. Buschard went back to Sacramento, and that's when Warren came. He didn't hire me; he got stuck with me. I don't think I ever had an official title, but I did all of his bookkeeping, paid all of his bills, and talked to patients about collections and so forth. There was another girl who did the insurance and the reception work. He called me the office manager, but I was really what PG&E calls a grunt.

"I'd worked for doctors for twenty years," said Gail, "and here came Warren with his tie-dyed T-shirt, purple socks, and pea coat. I was used to professional doctors with suits and ties and the whole works. He was so casual, and I thought, oh god, now what do we have? But of course, he was so outgoing and actually a breath of fresh air after the stuffy doctors who dressed up. I remember going to a Christmas party shortly after Warren came, and Dr. Thompson was there. He said, 'How do you like your new hippie doctor?' I said, 'It takes a little getting used to having tie-dye in my office, but as an individual, he is outstanding.'

"He was somebody who cared, and he didn't look at a patient as a dollar sign," explained Gail. "He never knew who owed him money, or who didn't pay their bills. He left that up to me. And he didn't want to know because he wanted to practice medicine. He didn't want to be a policeman. But he could be in some cases. I remember there was this gal on the front desk, and she had a drinking problem. I could smell booze on her every morning when she came in. But I never said a word to him because I thought it was up to him to determine what should be done. Then one day, he said he'd fired her. And I said 'You did?' And he said 'Yeah, I had several complaints from patients, so I fired her.' After that, we hired Monique Tomasovich. We stole her from the health department. She was wonderful—worth a million bucks. I don't know how she did it. She was always pleasant. I never heard her be rude, short, or curt with a patient."

Monique Tomasovich met Warren as a doctor before she went to work for him. "My first mother-in-law was dying of cancer at TGH, and Warren was her doctor," Monique explained as we sat in her cozy kitchen—a room that was as pleasant and agreeable as she. "The first time I met him, he was wearing jeans, a tie-dyed T-shirt, and Birkenstocks. I can't remember if his socks matched that day. But of course, I came to know him as the sock man. He was at the nurse's station writing something, and I walked up and asked the nurse if I could I talk to the doctor, and lo and behold, it was him. He introduced himself and shook my hand. I thought this guy is pretty down to earth. That was when he first started at Tuolumne General. I worked at the health department right next door, so I was able to see my mother-in-law every day. I ran into him many times. He was fabulous with her. And with us. He was so honest in explaining things, and he was perfect at gauging when it was time. 'She doesn't have long,' he told us one day. He did that again and again over the years— with my mom, my dad, my sister. He was great at those critical times.

"As I said, I worked at the health department, and he became the doctor for the birth control clinic, which was initially looked down upon in this county. I assisted him in the clinic, typed his notes, and transcribed everything for him. We had this old-fashioned transcription machine with a big thick belt that slid into the machine, and after you erased the belt you slid it out. One time I was doing his transcription, and I didn't know I had two belts in there, one with a stack of charts he'd dictated. The minute I pulled out the belt, I knew I'd erased his dictation. I had two thoughts: I can just pretend it didn't happen, or I can go over and tell him what I did.

Because it was Warren, I decided to tell him. So I went over with the stack of charts and the belt, and told him I'd done a terrible thing. He started laughing. 'What's so goddamn funny?' I asked. He smiled that big smile and said, 'You're so honest. Why didn't you just feed me a line of bullshit?' Then he told me not to worry. He'd dictate them again. As I was leaving, he thanked me for my honesty. A short time after, he called me at home. It was a Sunday, and he asked me to come to the hospital. 'I'm on call,' he said, 'so I can't leave.' I thought, oh god, what have I done? When I got there, he told me he needed a receptionist/transcriptionist and asked if I was interested. Of course, I said yes.

"His staff included Gail, Marge, me, and a young gal, Julie, who helped Gail with some of the billing and typing. We were a small office, and at lunch we'd hide in Gail's office or in the back of the lab with Marge. We'd close the window from 12:00 to 2:00, but we couldn't close off the hallway. People would just come and go. There wasn't a real door; just an opening with this little wooden plank that dropped down. It was really funky. The exam rooms were awkward, too. It was kind of a one-direction thing. Let me have a piece of paper, and I'll sketch a floor plan."

I tore a page from my notebook and handed it to her with a mechanical pencil, and she went to work. "He would go into one room here," she said pointing, "and when he finished, he'd go through a door here, into the next room. He had to be sure to open the door in such a way that the person in one room couldn't see who was in the other room. It was kind of like that shells and pea game. Marge was really good at keeping track of who was where, but I know that crazy space was one of the reasons he was glad to move to Mono Way.

"He wanted us to create an office manual, so everybody was on the same page about what instructions to give patients and when the holidays were and stuff like that. We all had a part in creating it. We met once a month to work on it until it was done. And he was always teaching us things. He taught us about blood pressure and birthing. Once, he invited me to see a childbirth, which was fabulous, and I got to see a total hysterectomy performed by Chris Mills, which was amazing. He included us in the whole picture. And it was a crazy picture. Sometimes we'd hear him paged when a trauma came into the ER, and off he'd fly, running down the hall, and we'd have to keep everyone calm.

His patients sat in the lobby in chairs right beside the people visiting the emergency room. They were one big mix. Depending on what was going on, he'd let me know if he was going to be awhile. Then I'd have to inform his patients. I'd ask if they could wait or if they wanted to go get coffee or something."

"Did people typically stay or leave?" I asked.

"They brought a book or magazines and were willing to wait. Others had errands to do, so they left but came back. Some would get mad and reschedule. But people got to know what to expect."

Not everyone knew what to expect, especially his contemporaries from high school. When Ross Carkeet returned to Sonora after attending college at Humboldt he discovered his former doctor had retired. "I'd heard Warren was here," said Ross, "so I signed up with him. That was in '71 just before Peggy and I got married. He drove this old pickup truck. I saw him going through town one day and thought, he's a doctor and he's driving that old beater. I remember one of our first conversations after I returned to town. I had a beard—a red beard—and he liked it. He always called me Corky from back in our high school days, so he said, 'Corky I've got to tell you that when I was an intern, I grew a beard, and this doctor in charge said, 'Dr. Barklist, there has never been a beard on this floor.'

"'What'd you do?' I asked.

"'I went home and shaved it off.' It was his first year as an intern. A few years later," Ross continued, "I had a skin lesion. He looked at it, and I could hear his breath. 'Sheesh! It's deep, Buddy. You waited a long time on this. We're going to have to do a biopsy.' So he did the biopsy, and it came back as squamous cell carcinoma. Risky—it could move fast. And he said, 'We've got to excise that. I'll get Jim Hongola to do the surgery.' I didn't know Hongola, so I wanted Warren to do it. He said, 'It might leave a scar. Hongola's the expert.'

"'Warren,' I said, 'I've known you a long time, and I trust you.' So I went in shortly after, and he came in all prepped for in-office surgery, and it went well. After it was over, the nurse handed me a mirror. And I said, "Jesus, Warren, I look like Captain Ahab in Moby Dick!'

"'God dammit Corky,' he said, 'I told you there was going to be a scar!'

"'I'm just kidding Warren,' I said. 'It's a Robert Redford scar.'"

"My first meeting with Warren was in 1973 when I worked with Judy," said Ann Leonard. "She and I shared a classroom, and she and Warren had just married. I became his patient immediately. He gave me a 20 percent discount as a courtesy. I was not making a lot of money, and my husband wasn't working, and I had a baby, so the discount was very nice. The thing that impressed me immediately was that he was willing to consult another doctor if he didn't know what was going on. Right in front of you. He'd call and say, 'I've got a patient here, and I'm not sure about this. Can you give me some advice?' He wasn't pretentious.

"One of the problems I had as a young woman was horrible PMS. Every month things would be going fine and all of a sudden—charuung! Incapacitating. I started doing a lot of research. It was before much was known about PMS. I went down to San Francisco Medical Center and used their books to find out everything I could. I learned that a hormone shot—progesterone—might help it. So he gave me shots of progesterone. He would listen and do the research too, and he said that what I was telling was helping him with his wife. On occasion, he called me at home and said he had a patient who was suffering from PMS, and he asked if she could call me. And I said of course. On the professional level, it was always him drawing his little diagrams and telling little jokes. When my daughter was 7, we lived on the ranch out on Italian Bar Road, and she stepped on a pitchfork and had to have a tetanus shot. He gave her the shot, and then he said, 'Here's a prescription.' He handed me the slip, and it said, 'Take her to get an ice cream cone on the way home.'"

Some Tuolumne County folks didn't even seem to know they were seeking change in medical providers until they ran into Warren Borgquist. My neighbor Lynne Brown was another early patient. She first met him during an Emergency Room visit. "I took a spill in my front yard, and my ankle swelled up, so my husband took me to the ER at Tuolumne General. Warren was on call. He examined my ankle thoroughly, and told me it wasn't broken, but it was badly sprained. He wrapped it in an

Ace bandage, gave me a pair of crutches, and told me to stay off it for a couple weeks. Then he said, 'Go home and drink a Mai Tai.' I liked him immensely.

"A few months later, I decided to take my daughter to see him. She was 2, and I had been taking her to a local pediatrician. She had a cold that went into her chest, and this doctor prescribed amoxicillin. I told him she was allergic to penicillin, and he asked me how I knew that. I explained that she had taken it when she was five months old and had broken out in a rash, and I was told she was allergic to penicillin. He insisted it would be fine because this was a derivative—a distant cousin—of penicillin. So I gave her two or three doses but that little mommy voice in me kept saying, 'This isn't right.' Then the skin on her palms and the bottom of her feet began peeling. So I called Warren's office, and they got her in pretty fast. After he examined her, he looked at me and said, 'You need to teach this baby to say I'm allergic to penicillin.' He picked up the phone to make a call, and I said, "Who are you calling?' When he answered with the pediatrician's name, I said, 'Hang up. We've already been there, and that's why we're here now, and you're our new family doctor.'"

Hippie iconoclast Bob Dylan declared that times were a-changin'. In the early 1970s, the changes he intoned reached the foothills of California in the form of Dr. Warren Borgquist. As Judy said, "He got a lot of patients very quickly."

# Borgquist Blended Family

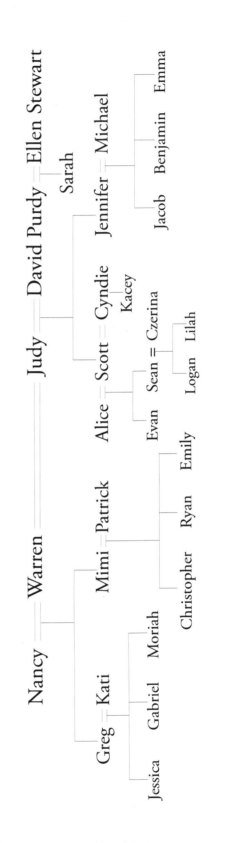

# Chapter 7

# GIRAFFE CLAN

As giraffes say, you don't get no leaves unless you stick your neck out.

-Sid Waddell

The Borgquists lived on the corner of Calaveras and Alpine. I had driven past the corner numerous times, admiring the creamy adobe-like walls set upon a hillside that created a sense of privacy, but I didn't realize it was their home until Judy first gave me the address. A mailbox painted with a giraffe motif stood at the base of a steep cement driveway that led to the front door. A wooden giraffe was poised to the left of the door. Giraffes were positioned throughout the home—on the small shelf around the huge day bed in the TV room, on the floor beside the door to the sunroom, hanging in a potted fern, and on the pencil with which Judy noted our appointments. Judy would eventually explain the significance of giraffes, but first I heard about the formation of this family from the players.

Warren's first wife, Nancy, told me during our long phone conversation that she hadn't realized how divorce would affect her children. "I thought they'd be fine, but it was hard on them. Warren had them every other weekend, and we took turns having them on the holidays. Actually we got along pretty well until… I'll just be frank…until Judy came into the picture. The trouble was my kids were younger than hers, so they were always second fiddle in that family. I have a mother's heart, so it hurt me to see that. And again, I think Warren was preoccupied with work."

Judy actually saw the problem, especially after her 10-year-old daughter, Jennifer, pointed out the "us and them" fissure that happened each weekend when Warren brought Greg and Mimi into the mix. Many a divorced family is beleaguered by the confusion of continual reconfiguration, but Judy listened to her daughter's clear-sighted appraisal and decided to do something. She and Warren fashioned a vacation remedy to soothe the breach.

"Warren consciously set out to be an outstanding father," said Judy. "It was of paramount importance to him. After our first family vacation across the country in 1975, Warren always took three-to-five weeks every summer."

"Were you already in this house by then?" I asked, referring to the home in which we were sitting, curious about how the blended family shaped up beyond vacation time.

"Yes. With Mimi and Greg staying every other weekend, there were six people in the two-bedroom house at the Cassinetto's property where we first lived. We'd purchased property out on Racetrack Road, where we intended to build a house, but we needed a bigger place right away. It was raining the day we went house hunting. We walked into this living room," said Judy, gesturing to the spacious room with vaulted ceilings, opening onto the kitchen area. "Well, not exactly like this. The ceiling beams were gouged, and the builder, Stewart Hatler, had painted them black, and there was this cheap paneling. It was pretty ugly, but the room was essentially the same, and the location was good—close to downtown, the high school, and Community Hospital—so we said, 'OK! We'll live here for a year or two.' We bought it in March of '73, and Warren set to work remodeling two of the bedrooms for the kids. In the boys' room, he built twin beds, one high up with drawers underneath it. That was for Greg. And for Scott, he built another bed, and he lined the walls with redwood paneling—very boyish. And we had two twin beds and girly stuff in the girls' room. He was so proud of what he did to this piece-of-shit-house. He spent the next two years fixing those bedrooms. That was before we took off cross country and became a real family."

Each of the four children had their own stories about how their re-configured family emerged and what it looked like. "When my mom and dad got divorced," said Greg, "I went with my dad at first, and my sister went with my mom to Fort Collins, Colorado. I remember crying myself to sleep every night because I was used to being with my mom. My dad worked eighteen-to-twenty hours a day their whole marriage. That was smack in the middle of the women's rights movement—the National Organization for Women, Title IX, and that whole thing—and my mom was a feminist. They got divorced as he finished his internship. So he became a doctor, and she went off to be independent. I think the reason I cried so much was because my mom had been my caretaker. But what I remember about my dad is running to him and getting swooped up and kissed. I wouldn't go to sleep until he told me my bedtime story. He was the best storyteller. He was solid like that.

"My pops was, as my mother says, very sensitive to the fact that I was pretty miserable without him. And that was one of the reasons I was lashing out in school. I think that was how Judy met my dad because he came for a parent-teacher conference up at the old school at the Dome. I remember he came to pick me up after school, and it wasn't the greatest feel-good moment because he had to talk to the teacher about me."

"We lived with my grandparents on Shepherd Street most of that semester. I remember my grandparents were really proud of their son, the doctor. Did anyone tell you the story about him and the MJC counselor? He told the counselor he wanted to be a doctor and the counselor said, 'Don't you think you might want to be something like a police officer?' The guy totally tried to discourage him. My dad used to say one of the things that drove him when he went to Davis was that someday he was going to go back and tell that counselor, 'Hey, I'm a doctor.' Of course, he never did because by the time he was a doctor, he was more humble. He was always very casual about being a doctor, and he had a very casual office. Did you know he had the highest paid staff in all of Tuolumne County, including federal and state agencies?"

Greg's admiration for his father seemed as big as that of his grandparents, but I wanted to know more about what his family was like when he was young, so I reigned him back. "I understand you went to stay with your mom after one semester in first grade with Judy."

"Yep," said Greg. "And after that, my father religiously came and got us every two weeks. My mom had moved to Lake Port near Clear Lake. It was a crazy long way, and my father came without fail every other week. It was sixteen hours of driving in a forty-eight hour weekend," said Greg. "My childhood was broken into those little segments, and I craved being with him. As soon as he dropped me off, I started missing him. I could call my dad on his direct line at work anytime, and if he couldn't talk, he would say, 'I'm in a procedure right now. Call me back in fifteen minutes.' He gave his staff instructions that he was available whenever his family called. For my first ten years in Sonora, I was the doctor's kid. It was a very small town, so I felt like I got special recognition everywhere I went. People would say, 'That's Dr. Borgquist's son.' Some of the recognition had to do with my grandmother having the Upper Dime. She knew a lot of people too. I was known everywhere. When I got my driver's license, if I did a California stop, it was relayed to my parent's before I even got home."

Gail Bonavia was one of those people who had her eye on Greg. "He had more broken bones than any kid I knew. Breaking his leg, breaking his arm, breaking this, breaking that. I was always paying doctor bills for Greg. I teased him about being in pieces most of the time."

"One time," said Greg, "I crashed my bicycle, in front of the Seventh-day Adventist Church on the road between our house and my dad's office. I was knocked out. No helmets back then. Some lady scooped me up in her car and drove me home. I broke my collarbone and had a concussion. I liked football, and I got into fights when I was a kid. My dad wasn't into that stuff, not even when he was a child. He used to say, 'I don't know where you came from.' My grandfather Cliff, his daddy, was more like me. I was attention deficit and hyper-active to 'nth degree," said Greg, "always going faster and more furiously than anyone else, but my Pops, he put up with me. 'Slow down,' he'd say. 'Don't play with that. But I would. Every truck my dad ever owned I managed to smash the bumper. As a kid, I always wanted a motorcycle because my dad had one. When I was an adult, I asked him why he didn't get me one. 'Because you broke fourteen bones before you were thirteen years old.' And he was right. I might have killed myself.

"One time, he took me to the hospital and showed me this graphic example. 'This is what happens when you drink and drive, son. If you touch alcohol, don't touch the steering wheel of a car.' I probably got twenty-five of those messages from him: 'This is what happens if you drink and drive.' He had a saying: 'Greg's not stupid. He gets it. It just takes a million-and-one times for him to hear it.' And that was true."

"My earliest memory of my dad," said Mimi, "was when I was about 6 or 7, after he married Judy. We visited them every other weekend in Sonora. I don't remember the name of the street, but there was a little driveway that went down a hill to the house. I remember that house when I was super-young, but mostly I remember the house on Calaveras.

"Dad and Judy always had us kids do chores, and I wasn't used to that because at my mom's house, she did everything. I remember one time when I was about 8, I had to do the dishes. I was complaining because I had a stomachache, and they were like 'Just do the dishes.' They thought I was trying to get out of it because I was kind of a dramatic child. I finished the job, even though my tummy hurt, but then I woke up during the night in a lot of pain. I called to Dad and Judy and pounded on their bedroom door. I remember Dad asking me where it hurt and pushing and prodding my belly. I might've had a fever. I'm not sure. He took me to the hospital—the old one over by the park. He didn't think there was a surgeon who could do the job, so he drove me to Modesto. The next thing I remember was waking up in a hospital bed with a tube coming out of my body. My appendix had burst, and that's how they drained the fluid back then. I remember my poor father felt so bad because he was a doctor, and he felt like he'd let me down. But I was a difficult kid who complained and tried to get out of chores. My mom, Nancy, kept saying, 'You're a doctor; you should've known better.' But he was human, and he was being a father not the doctor."

"Mimi never mentioned a bellyache until she stood on the stool to do the dishes," said Judy, remembering the incident, "so we told her to stop whining. Then in the middle of the night, she convinced us it was more than just having to do dishes. Her appendix burst. It was bad— really bad— and Warren felt awful."

"I was the drama queen," said Mimi. "Now that I look back, I can laugh, but growing up, everyone teased me, and I couldn't stand it. I thought they were all mean. Judy did this thing I hated. She'd say, 'What kind of ice cream do you want for dessert?' If you said vanilla, she'd come and kiss you on the forehead or the cheek or nose or somewhere on your face that was the spot for that flavor. It just sent me over the edge, and I'd storm off to my room and pout. I wanted real vanilla ice cream. They loved to tease me because I was so dramatic."

"I remember when my mom first started dating Warren," said Scott. "He always came up with fun things to do. Like we'd go to Lake Tulloch and jump off the bridge. They have a sign now that prohibits jumping, but not in those days. The big thing with Warren was to go to the river and do things like inner tube trips down the Stanislaus. I remember the first time I got in trouble. We were moving from the small house to Calaveras, and I was poking along. Warren basically threw me in the back of his old truck to get me going." Looking at the tall, urbane man who was telling the story, it was hard to imagine anyone throwing him in the back of a pickup, but there was a flicker of mischief in his smile that revealed the child who would have loved jumping off a bridge but could also move slowly in the face of work.

"Another time— just after I started high school—Mom and Warren left me alone for the first time. They were doing a motorcycle trip over the pass. And as soon as they left, I had a party with kids in the neighborhood and some friends. We were having a great time, and we ran out of beer, and someone had a driver's license, so a few of us drove to get more beer. When we got back, we were walking up the driveway and someone goes, 'There's a bald guy in the room.' I looked through the window, and there was Warren sitting there with some of the kids. I was like, 'Aw, shit!' Warren was really disappointed in me."

"I also remember Warren giving the official sex talk, which wasn't normal in any way. It was very detailed. He pointed out all the little parts on a model and used all the medical terms. He gave that talk to all of us, even the grandkids. We were very sophisticated in our knowledge of sex."

Kris Danz Scott, Jennifer's childhood friend, recalled an invitation to visit Jennifer at her new house after Judy and the children moved to Sonora. "Jennifer was giving me a tour of the house. 'Here is the kitchen, and this is my room, and this is where Mom and Warren sleep,' she said as we waltzed through the house. Judy nearly choked since they weren't married at the time, but it went right over my head. All I got was they had a waterbed that we got to play on, which was very cool."

Jennifer reminisced about how she had connected with Warren on the cross-country trip through their shared love of history. "I liked historical novels and stuff like that before that trip, but getting to see places I'd read about was definitely big. Warren was very engaging. He didn't worry about what anybody else thought, and that was a big influence in my life. I'm a teacher after my mom but also through Warren because teaching was a lot about performance and being goofy. During that trip, we got these fabulous pewter goblets because everybody drank out of pewter in the colonial days. The next Halloween, Warren came up with a costume—a car wreck victim or something like that. He affixed one of those pewter goblets into a plaster cast on his arm, so that he never had to set his cup down. It turned out the pewter was so cold it froze his hand, and he kept having to fill it with warm drinks."

Besides bonding through trivia and silly moments during the cross-country trip in 1975, Judy recalled that they made a major family decision when the kids said, "We don't want to move. We like our house. We can walk everywhere. Let's just build a swimming pool. We'd rather have that than a new house."

"So we built the pool," said Judy. Behind her, on the other side of the full-length windows, the pool sat, surrounded by caramel colored Mexican style walls, glittering a serene aqua invitation. "It's heavily engineered," added Judy, "because there was just a little dirt hill going down to the street on that side of the house, so they had to build this steel structure to support the pool, the deck, and the walls. Of course, it cost a gazillion dollars, but Warren didn't care. Sure, it was for the kids, but it was for Warren too. He was in that pool four or five times a day."

"You should've seen him do the butterfly," said Jennifer. "Oh my god, it was gorgeous, just amazing. When we were little, he could do the butterfly all the way across the pool with all four of us hanging on to him. He was very strong, and that brings up family wrestling matches. We used to do a lot of full-contact wrestling. Mom would stand there saying,

'Someone's going to start crying,' and we all knew it was true, but it was so much fun. Warren was into horse-play—all kinds of physical, goofy, pick-you-up-and-rocket-you-around kinds of things."

"I remember one Easter," continued Jennifer. "Mom and Warren took us to a sunrise service. They were checking out the Unitarians because they kept thinking they should provide some sort of religion for us. So we went to the service, which was not interesting at all, but there were all these animals to represent the fertility of spring, and we got to hang out with the animals. I remember afterward Warren said, 'So what did you think?' I said, 'It was horrible except for the animals.' I was always pretty pragmatic." Then Jennifer veered, as these conversations tended to. "The other day I was talking to somebody about him and said, 'We were always smarter and better looking and more compassionate, wonderful people because he thought of us that way.'"

Jennifer's comment echoed one I'd heard Karma and Marjorie speak about their father. They described how he would look out at the world during family trips and declare: "We're special. That's just us; we're special." Perhaps I was conjuring a resemblance between Cliff and Warren Borgquist, seeking attributes the father had passed on to the son.

For Greg, Mimi, Scott, and Jennifer, early memories of their father or step-father ran the gamut from a rough-housing dad who could be irritable and unsympathetic to kids who were whining or pokey, to a more unique father who drove miles and miles to be with them, initiated sophisticated, unreserved sex talks, and swam a fierce butterfly that held them aloft. While Nancy recalled a husband and father who was mostly absent and preoccupied, Judy described him as intent on being an outstanding father. By his own admission, he had lost reasonable perspective during his first marriage when he was training to become a doctor. But as he and Judy blended a family, Warren seemed to heed lessons learned from the fallout of divorce. Greg felt his devotion; Mimi recognized his humanity; Scott welcomed his good opinion, and Jennifer absorbed his gifts as a teacher. Of course, he surfed the waves of parenting with Judy, who splashed on her own version of teasing love.

"Talk about parenting two to four kids when both of you were cultivating professional lives," I said, sitting across from Judy on a cool February morning. We'd developed a routine during our meetings of sitting opposite one another in wing-backed chairs sipping tea. Sitting in an inglenook, the chairs faced the fireplace with our backs to the rest of the room. My chair sat near a piano upon which sat twenty or more pictures of children and grandchildren. Judy was framed by the light from the huge windows behind her that looked onto the pool and toward the mountain where Warren had proposed. Glimmers of reflected light shown through her champagne colored hair.

"We were always extremely busy," said Judy. "We both loved our jobs, so it was a joy to work, even when I became principal at Sonora El and there were difficult times. We worked long days—twelve hours were the norm. I once came across an article that reported school teachers worked harder than physicians," said Judy with a burst of laughter, adding, "I taped it to the refrigerator door." Judy's face flushed warmly with the memory of convivial competition with her husband.

"What grounded us was that we met every morning of our married life at 5 a.m. for coffee. Early on, Warren decided that would be the glue that kept us together. I wanted to wake up, have my coffee, and read the *Chronicle*," said Judy with a sigh. "'Warren,' I said, 'this is the only time I have to myself. Do I have to give that up?' and he said 'Yes, you do.' Of course, now I have coffee and read the *Chronicle* every morning, and I'd really like to have him here," she added wistfully. " We got up at 4:45," she continued, "until we got a digital clock, and I decided it was much cuter to get up at 4:44. He always called me 'the 4:40 whore.' We'd get our coffee and sit and talk—about our schedules or what needed to be done or what we were feeling."

"How do you do that?" I asked, imagining Warren in my seat, chatting with Judy in the predawn. "Keep that kind of schedule, I mean."

"It didn't seem that difficult. Warren was very easy going, and he tried to make sure he was home every night for dinner.

"What was a dinner at the Borgquist's like?"

"We'd eat between seven and eight—never before seven. That was what the kids always expected. I still don't eat until at least seven. I can't imagine eating earlier than that."

"Who did the cooking? You?"

"Always. Warren could only make a quesadilla in the microwave. He never cooked. One Valentine's Day, Warren, Jim Wilson, and Doug Lorimer cooked Valentine's Dinner. That's the only time he ever cooked. He was good at cleanup. I never did dishes. I didn't do laundry, dishes, vacuuming, cleaning. I did nothing except cooking, and he did everything else. That's why I have a cleaning lady every two weeks because Warren isn't here."

"What did you talk about at the dinner table?"

"We talked about what happened during the day. About the world or politics and religion and what we believed. When the kids were teens, we did a lot of what ifs. What if someone offers you marijuana? What if you're at a party and you're drunk?"

"Sounds like a permissive dialogue," I said.

"Yes, they were who they were, and that was fine. We have this darling picture in the hall of Jennifer and Greg that says it all." Judy retrieved the framed photo, in which a smiling Jenn is in a blue T-shirt that reads "Support Your Local Draft Resister." She's holding a guitar and a celery stalk. "Because she was a vegetarian," said Judy. Greg is grinning too, blond hair poking from his ball cap. In one hand he holds a plate with huge steak and in the other a gun. "Must've been a bee-bee gun," said

Judy, "because we never had guns.

"It wasn't easy to be awakened in the middle of the night, which was the norm for doctors who did OB, so that wasn't great, but that's the way it was," said Judy, returning to my question about what it was like for two professionals raising a family. "I think we both accepted that we were dedicated to our professions and to our family life. I'd like to tell you it was more complicated than that, but it wasn't. It might have been difficult if I'd been a housewife who didn't have a sense of self, and he didn't get home until 7 o'clock. Since I didn't get home much before him, it was never a problem. We balanced it with a good social life. We had great friends, and we loved to go to San Francisco for the weekend. We would go down Friday night and have a nice meal. We liked to stay on Lombard Street in the Marina. On Saturday, we would get up and walk all along the Marina Green and over the Golden Gate Bridge and down into Sausalito. We'd have a really lovely lunch in Sausalito and take the Ferry back and walk to the hotel. Warren loved pissing off bridges," said Judy laughing. "He had a science for peeing off the Golden Gate Bridge, which is hard because a lot of people are walking by, and you have to time it just right with the wind and all that. When we had our Swiss foreign exchange student, Nicolas, he taught him how to pee off the Golden Gate Bridge."

Now we were both laughing. "What is it about guys and peeing?" I asked.

"It's because they can," said Judy. We each reached for our cups of tea to regain composure.

"One more question, and we'll wrap this up for the day. Why do you call yourself the Giraffe Clan?" I asked, having heard her use that moniker a couple of times.

"We are the Giraffe Clan because Warren always made us stick our necks out and try something new. 'Try, try, try … You can do it,' he said anytime the kids were afraid. And he made me do things when I was afraid —shoot the rapids in a kayak or leap on boulders across a river. One day, I said, 'Dammit, Warren! You're always making me stick my neck out. It's driving me crazy. Are you trying to make me into a giraffe?' We had a good laugh and that's when we became the Giraffe Clan." So that explained the highly visible giraffe motif, which seemed a bit like coat-of-arms heraldry in the Borgquist home.

A photo taken of the family—before the clan name originated—reveals the kinship growing in the disparate family of birth children, adoptee, and steps. Six broad smiles exhibit straight white teeth. Everyone has a thick mane of hair except Warren who has a deeply receding hairline. Greg is the only blond, Jennifer and Judy have a touch of auburn, and Warren, Scott and Mimi are solid brunettes. They are all dressed in jeans sitting on a hillside of dry grass—maybe on the slope where the pool now stands. A spray of red Pyracantha berries arches over their heads. Warren and Judy flank the brood. Mimi sits between and slightly uphill of Warren and Jennifer. Her forearms rest on their shoulders. Judy holds Greg in a light embrace. Jennifer is at the center of the grouping, the pragmatism she claims is evident in her fresh, straightforward gaze. Scott sits to the back of the group with a slight forward lean, his arms resting on his knees. He is the only one who displays an air of caution, which is most likely a part of his nature as much as reticence about this new-formed family. The photo confirms they were all trying—sticking their necks out—to become a family. However, with the exception of cautious, sensible Scott, this picture precedes the children's teen years and the arrival of Greg and Mimi to live full time with their father and Judy.

*Chapter 8*

# MONO WAY

I'm not the smartest fellow in the world,
but I can sure pick smart colleagues.

—Franklin D. Roosevelt

As Judy Borgquist noted, the work of a physician—especially a family physician with obstetrics as part of his practice—has demands that intrude upon family life. The stories I'd heard from colleagues and patients about his early days at Tuolumne General Hospital described a dedicated doctor who spent long hours at work.

My sister, Anne Stock, saw Dr. Borgquist while he was at TGH and told a story that describes the doctoring style he was developing. "My first visit to Dr. Borgquist was in 1972. My hands were covered with bleeding eczema from the harsh chemicals I used working as a maid and housecleaner. I remember sitting on the examining table as Dr. B looked at my hands and then looked up and asked my husband's profession. I explained that Charles was taking time off from school and working as a surveyor's helper to save money, so he could finish his education. Dr. B wrote a prescription, which he handed to me, and then he left the room, saying he'd be back in a minute. As I looked at the script, I doubted I'd be able to afford the medicine, considering the cost of the appointment was beyond our budget. A few minutes later, I heard a knock at the door, and he re-entered, holding twelve sample boxes of the prescription he'd just given me—a miracle cream. I sparingly treasured each drop of those samples. With each application, I thought of the small kindness—actually a huge gift. Dr. B had discretely identified our poverty. My first visit launched a long association with this discerning doctor, who would deliver my babies, relocate a dislocated elbow, diagnose spinal meningitis, provide emergency care for our dying mother, and enough other adventures to write a TV mini series."

Most of my sister's time with Dr. Borgquist took place at his second office on Mono Way, where indeed a mini-series as good as the PBS program *Doc Martin* unfolded. Like Doc Martin, the socially misfit physician unceremoniously plopped in a small English fishing village, Dr. Borgquist found himself in a small, conservative town where he appeared tieless and in Birkenstocks, a doctor whose slow, seemingly casual medicine was strange to many. Like Doc Martin, Dr. Borgquist didn't plan to be a small town doctor. Circumstances drove both of them to the hinterlands where oddity stood out like a sore thumb.

Gail Bonavia, Dr. B's office manager, expressed a viewpoint that showed not only how perplexing she found him, but also revealed some of the biases he faced. "Nine out of ten of the ER patients were on welfare—people who'd bring a kid in on Friday night, even though the child had been sick for weeks, and suddenly want him cured. It didn't bother Dr. B at all. He was very altruistic. Sometimes I'd have to get after him because he was just too easy. He ignored his paying patients and gave all his time to the poor patients. I'd say, 'Look, they're eating out of your pocket. Let's balance things out a little.' Not that my cajoling made a difference. But he knew the ER was tiring him out."

"He got called to the emergency room because he was so convenient," said Monique Tomasovich, his receptionist. "Even if he wasn't on call, he got called all the time because he was right there. It became quite difficult for him. He wanted his own space. Our offices were small and cramped and full of noise from the hospital and ER intervention. One day he said, 'I've found a place' and he took us to see it—up the hill away from town and the ER. He wanted ideas about what we wanted and needed. He designed everything and hired John Roberson, a terrific cabinetmaker. The space was big and bright, and we loved it. There were four exam rooms, including one we used as a delivery room. His office was in the back, and he brought in a desk and put up a wallpaper mural of a redwood forest. Once a month, we'd all go back there and spread a blanket on the floor and eat a picnic lunch in front of this beautiful mural."

"I remember the waiting room was really cramped," I said, envisioning the office where I'd become Dr. Borgquist's patient.

"Yes, and there was only the main door—no back door. People always knew when he was late. Or that he was leaving. He had to face the music. He couldn't fake it. Either way, he'd have to apologize and scoot."

Almost every patient I talked to commented on Dr. Borgquist's habitual lateness. Lynne Brown, one of the patients who first saw him at TGH said, "I remember waiting as long as three hours. But it was no big deal because once he came through the exam room door he was yours until you didn't need him anymore. He never, ever made us feel pushed for time. Whatever we needed he had, and if he didn't have it, he picked up the phone and called a specialist. I appreciated his philosophy that mothers know their children better than anybody else. If a mom thought there was a problem, he'd take a look because there probably was. He never brushed me off."

"We moved up here in 1976," said Susan Russel, "and opened Mountain Bookshop in 1977. Gail Bonavia, his bookkeeper, was a customer of ours, and that's how we ended up getting to see him. The image I always have about Warren was that no matter how long you were in the waiting room—and you sat for a long time—you knew when you got in the exam room he was going to be there for you. He would come in like a teddy bear, and he would sit on that little stool next to the counter, and he would always wear these crazy socks and have a smile on his face, and you could tell him anything."

Patients may have resigned themselves to waiting for Dr. B, but his staff was less tolerant. Marge Hutchins, his nurse at TGH, moved with him to the Mono Way office. "I started at seven in the morning. If we had a minor surgery, I'd set things up. He'd lollygag in an hour later. One afternoon, he was due back at one, but he didn't show. I started looking for him about 1:20. I put in calls, thinking he might be at one of the hospitals, but I couldn't find him anywhere. At two, I finally reached him. Do you know where he was? At home in the swimming pool. He had four patients sitting there waiting. When he came in, I said, 'You devil,' and all I got was that big grin. He needed time for himself and that was his way of doing it. Swimming!"

"But," Marge continued, "he was probably the most caring physician I ever worked for. If he didn't know something, he would say, 'I need to research that,' and he would either call somebody or get one of his reference books. He did a lot of research, especially to identify things that weren't commonplace. That's one thing that took a lot of time because he was much more involved than the average physician."

As Marge talked about Dr. B's inclination for research, I recalled a story his sister Marjorie told about her grandson. "When Cooper was four, he got very sick. His skin was grey and his eyes were yellow and red-rimmed. The palms of his hands and the bottoms of his feet were blistered and burned because of fever. He was the worst looking thing we'd ever seen. We had our doctors, but we called Warren when we were really worried, so Cooper's parents called him. Warren said, 'I think it's Kawasaki Disease. I was just reading about it the other day.' Cooper's mom said, 'OK we'll take him to our regular doctor tomorrow.' And Warren said, 'Oh no! You're going to Children's Hospital in Oakland right now.'"

Kawasaki is a childhood disease that causes inflammation of the arteries and lymph nodes causing all the symptoms Marjorie described. There had never been a case of Kawasaki in the county, but as it happened, Dr. Borgquist had read about it only days before being presented with Cooper's symptoms. This was a good example of how a doctor's education never ends. Most doctors regularly peruse medical journals and take part in continuing education, necessary to maintain Board Certification every seven years. Since Warren entered general practice after a one-year internship, there was plenty he had to learn on the job. His thirst for knowledge served him well professionally, though it became a point of teasing, especially among his grandchildren, who would tell hilarious stories about "the useless crap" Gramps frequently espoused. Nevertheless, I would hear countless stories in which Dr. B had just read about a medical condition or leaped to research a constellation of symptoms either in medical books or among his colleagues who were specialists.

After Marge left to go back to school, Warren hired two nurses: Billie Morrison and Reese Coffer. According to Billie, Reese asked her if she wanted to split a job. "I was interested in part time work because I had a lot of dairy stuff going on at home," said Billie, "so I agreed, and Reese said, 'Let's go talk to Warren.' He interviewed us, and we told him we wanted to split the job. Even though he thought it was an unusual idea, he said it might work.

"The day I started, I was sitting at my desk looking at some charts when he came in, slammed the door, and walked down the hall. So I went down the hall behind him and said, 'Fuck you, Borgquist.'

"'What did you say?' he asked, swinging around.

"'That got your attention didn't it,' I said. 'A simple good morning would've been nice.'"

Billie's coarse language with her new employer didn't surprise me. I already knew she was a salty gal, for she'd been Dr. B's nurse when I became his patient. Catching up with Billie to find out more about nursing with him wasn't easy, and when I did locate her, I had to set aside all my preconceived notions about nurses. She told me it would be hard for her to get away for an interview because by then she was a sheep rancher and had to tend her sheep every day. I said I'd come to her. When I arrived at her home in San Andreas, Billie was standing in the driveway beside an ATV. She climbed on and beckoned me to sit behind her. Then we bounced over rutted roads that dropped into a brush-ridden canyon where her sheep were corralled. Dust moats floated in the morning sun all around us as I wondered what I'd gotten myself into.

Deep in the ravine, she parked the ATV, and three huge dogs greeted us. These were the nighttime guards. She freed the herd from their pen, and with the help of the dogs, drove the sheep to a grazing spot. Finally, she set up two folding chairs in shade cast by giant buckeye bushes and scrub oaks. The ancient webbed lawn chairs gave a rusty squeal as she opened them, thus setting the stage from which she'd tell her story about serving as Warren Borgquist's nurse.

By the time Billie told the story of her first morning at work with Borgquist, I'd been surprised by so many things that I was growing immune to astonishment. First, there was the fact that, after more than thirty years, she had remembered me as a former patient and also remembered the name of my son, whose birth she had attended. Then, there was the fact that she was now a sheep rancher. Finally, there was the wild ride on an ATV clinging to the waist of the solidly built dynamo. Sitting opposite this woman in her seventies, who had just settled herself in an ancient chair amidst weeds tramped down by her sheep, I felt as unhurried as she had once made me feel when I was in labor. She had an aura that was commanding and tender, earthy and irreverent.

"I wanted to work for Warren because he practiced the kind of medicine I like," said Billie. "He had a sixth sense about diagnosing unusual conditions. He was a master. I'm sure you remember him getting out his books or calling people at UC San Francisco and asking questions while you were right there in the office. It was one of the things that made him stand out.

"We had a birth room at the Mono Way office. That was a thrilling part of the job. We had lots and lots of mothers, and I related well with them. Obstetrics was my favorite part of nursing. Before I went to college, I worked at Community Hospital as an orderly. I was there two years, earning almost nothing, working night shifts, but that's what made me want to get my nursing license. The best doctor back then was Dr. Margolis. You've probably never heard of him, but my OB background began with him. He used to stick around after a birth and talk to me while I was cleaning up. I got a feel for obstetrics from him and also from a head nurse who was at Community, so that's why I decided to get my license and also why OB was my favorite."

Billie had been present when I delivered my third child in 1977 in the Mono Way office. I also knew several other women who had delivered in the birthing chair that Dr. Borgquist had built, which was designed after a model he'd studied at the Smithsonian Institute during the cross-country vacation with his family. Billie was not alone in appreciating Dr. Borgquist's approach to birth, for tales about births and babies would soon fill my notebooks. However, sitting beside her in a foothill ravine fragrant with dusty chaparral, I was privy to another flavor of story. The feisty former nurse shared her point of view from the back rooms of Warren Borgquist's medical office—stories most nurses would not likely confide.

"You can put this in your book because it's so funny, and he's dead and I'll be dead," said Billie. "Warren always said it wasn't a sin to get a social disease, but it was a sin to keep it. One day, he called me because he was preparing to do a pelvic exam. A nurse always had to be present when a doctor did pelvics. I got the woman set up with the light and a drape. He was sitting there with the speculum when he motioned me to come take a look. Somewhere along the way I'd told him I'd never seen crabs. I wasn't Miss Goody Two-Shoes. I'd just never seen those babies. As I moved around to his side, he put his finger to his lips, gesturing "SSHH" because he knew I had a big mouth. After pointing out the infestation, he asked, 'How should we treat this?'

'Raid,' I whispered. It was all he could do to keep from laughing out loud. Later the same day, a pest control guy was in the office to deal with an ant problem, which got bad in that office every summer. The guy had on a mask, and he was spraying the room where we'd examined the woman. We were in the lunchroom, and I pinched Warren's shoulder and pointed toward the guy in the other room. We had a really good laugh. He said he never forgot the Raid moment."

"Sometimes I identified things in our patients that I'd actually learned because of ranching. One time, this boy came in with an earache. He'd been to Arizona visiting his grandfather, and flying home, he'd started screaming with ear pain. The kid was in such pain. Earaches are a common occurrence in children, and we saw a lot of them. When Warren looked in this boy's ear, he said, 'The tympanic membrane is cloudy and grey.' Something stirred in the back of my mind. I asked if I could look, and he said, 'Sure.'

After looking in the boy's ear, I said, 'He has an ear tick. They go down and swell up across the membrane. You can't see the legs. All you can see is the grey thing.'

'How the hell did you know that?' he asked.

'Because I ranch. Cattle get ear ticks all the time. They shake their heads madly because it's so painful.'

'What next?" he asked.

"Irrigate with a lavage.'

"God, I don't know what I would do without you,' he said."

Pausing to smile, Billie patted the big head of the sheep dog leaning against her leg. Lost in the moment, she was oblivious to the fact that her anecdote illustrated yet another way in which Dr. Borgquist was willing to learn, not just from books and specialists but also from his staff. Still stroking the head of the big animal at her side, Billie veered in another direction. "Warren had a temper."

"Really," I said. "I haven't heard anything about that. What made him mad?"

"I called it doctor's syndrome," said Billie. "Did you ever see Doc Martin? He's such a grump. Sometimes Borgquist acted crappy like Martin, but not that often. If he was in a bad mood, we'd just leave him alone for a while. Nobody's happy all the time. When we got mad at him, we'd give him a cactus. And we did get mad at him. We had shit sessions about once a week. That's what he called them. He said, 'If you've got a gripe, let's work it out. I don't want anybody holding a grudge.' It was a good way to work," said Billie. "I think his temper came out more at home with Judy. One morning, he came in saying, 'Everything is such a mess at home. I was in a bad mood all night and all morning. When I left, Judy gave me this list of things to pick up on the way home. See this?' he asked, pointing to the sheet of paper. At the top of the list Judy had written 'socks for shithead.'"

Billie chuckled at the memory. She was fully into reminiscing, one memory flowing to another as we sat in the shade, three big dogs stretched out before us and insects flitting lazily here and there.

"Warren taught me to never panic. I'm energetic—a type-A personality—and I had to learn to keep that under control. He always kept his cool, and I learned from him. I can't think of anybody who died on my watch, so there really wasn't any reason to get worked up.

"My father was one of my worst patients," Billie continued, her stream of retrospection rolling on. "He'd come into Warren's office demanding attention. He was 94, very tiny, and really cute, but he would walk right through the waiting room door, and say 'I want to see Warren.' And he meant right then, which would piss off Monique. Patients had to wait and wait. But they got over it because they wanted to see him. Warren had a personality that made you love him."

"Did Monique tell you about the time we got high on pot?" asked Billie, heading off on another trajectory. "I wanted to see what it was like. I don't remember who supplied it, but after work one evening, we all had a go at it. We opened the window, so the smoke would go out. Then I heard the front door. 'Oh, crap,' I thought. 'It's Warren.' He came into the room, saying, 'Do I smell pot?' By then I was trying to climb out the window. Everyone was laughing madly. Warren too. It wasn't like he said, 'You're fired, you drug addicts.' I mean, we had a serious medical practice, but he took the whole thing in stride, just like he did everything."

"He was always open about things most of us don't like to talk about. One time we were having one of our staff sessions and talking about birth control. And I said, 'Just don't anybody talk to me about diaphragms. I don't want to hear it.' He asked why, and I said because there's nothing worse than pulling out your diaphragm and having it pop out of your hand and stick on the ceiling. Everybody died laughing, but I didn't think it was funny. At the time, my son was in the sex ed class at the high school, and Warren visited the class as a guest speaker. My son came home one night and said, 'Warren is so funny. He told this story about a woman who got her diaphragm stuck on the ceiling.' The next day at work I said, 'Did you tell that story about my diaphragm to the high school kids?'

"'I didn't mention any names,' he said.

"We were like a family in that office. We all had kids, and if our kids got sick, we put them in Warren's office where we could keep an eye on them. He used to say, 'I don't want anybody to say they're sick if they're not. If you need to take a day off, don't lie to me and say you don't feel good.' So we had diddle days. That's what he called them. It was a relaxed atmosphere. That's what I liked about working with him," said Billie.

The rest of the office staff spoke similarly about working for Dr. Borgquist. Monique, as the receptionist, had plenty to say about his time issues. "I'd get pissed off because he was late and everybody had to wait."

"Is that the main thing that made you mad?" I asked.

"It was the only thing. And when he didn't tell me he was going to be late. Most people were wonderful as long as I could tell them he was running late. But we had one young man who owned his own business. He had an appointment for a physical. He arrived on the dot, and he expected to be seen on the dot. He had been waiting about twenty-five minutes—which was nothing—when he came to the window and said,

'You tell him I'm sending him a bill for my time. My time is as valuable as his.' I apologized, but he left angry. I told Dr. B about the man leaving and asked what he wanted me to do.

"'He's right,' he said. 'His time is as valuable as mine.'

"So I called the guy and told him Warren was very sorry, and it would never happen again. We made him a special appointment and got him in within ten minutes after his arrival. Warren was good at soothing others. But over and over when two o'clock came, I'd think 'Where the hell is he?' One time, he said 'Monique, you intimidate me.'

"'What the hell do you mean by that?' I asked.

"He said I made him feel guilty about being late. He said I was like his office wife. I tried to explain that I wanted to keep his patients happy and sometimes it was very hard. I was there to make his business run smoothly, and I was committed to keeping patients happy and returning. We talked things out and cleared the air. Later, we had a meeting with all the staff to go over the schedule and make it more workable for him and the patients. He outlined his needs in terms of the time needed for each appointment and when to schedule physicals and procedures that take longer. It seemed to help, but as you know, waiting to see Dr. Borgquist was an everyday thing.

"We had one patient, this wonderful lady who absolutely loved him. Whenever she called, she said, 'I need to see Smiley.' One time, she called and said, 'I've got to see him right away.' I tried to put her off, but she demanded to be seen. I said, 'He's booked out the ass,' and she laughed. Finally I said, 'Why don't you come in at six o'clock. His last scheduled patient is at five, and he's usually an hour behind, so come at six, and I'll make him stay. You can bring us dinner.' I meant it as a joke, but she arrived with salad in a cut glass bowl, bread and butter, and a table cloth."

According to Gail Bonavia, his business manager, honesty was his greatest power, but she saw also the flaw in this so-called power. "I almost fell off my chair one time," said Gail. "This patient, an older woman in her sixties, had a pap smear that came back indicating the possibility of cancer. Apparently, he had not looked at the lab slip carefully, or he was thinking about something else and misread it, so somehow she'd been informed all was well. He had to have her come in so he could tell her what the report really said. You have to understand that Borgquist was very outspoken. He said what he thought, regardless of how it sounded. This woman walked in, and he said, 'I screwed up your diagnosis.' Actually, he said, 'I fucked up.' I was horrified. I hate that word in the first place. Everybody in the waiting room could hear. I'm thinking, 'Get her in an exam room where nobody can hear you. Don't tell the world.' But he blurted it right there in the hall. He continued to explain the situation, and it turned out fine. We talked about it after—the girls in the office. We concluded that if we had heard him say that as a patient, sitting in the waiting room, we would think he was honest. Even though the way he did it was definitely a no-no, the woman appreciated his honesty. She wasn't upset at all. Instead of Mickey Mousing around and making excuses for his error, he was straightforward. His honesty and a certain boyish innocence—those were his strengths."

When I related Gail's story to Marjorie Borgquist, she said, "That's very much my brother. He admitted his mistakes. Not always, but most of the time. That incident is typical of Warren. There are other ways to be direct, better approaches that are more discreet, but for Warren, discretion did not always factor in."

"Another thing I liked about Warren," said Gail, "was that he was very good about explaining things. He would do in-service trainings for us. He'd say, 'I think you girls should know about diabetes, and he'd set aside a time to teach us. We had a whiteboard that he used for drawing pictures or other teaching lessons. One time, he wrote KYAC on the board and said 'Figure that out.' He gave us a week, but no one figured it out. Finally, he said, 'It means Keep Your Act Clean.' That goes for all of us,' he said.

"There were times when I would get after him," said Gail. keep an office going on air. He was quite a spender, but sometimes he really couldn't afford it. When we moved to Mono Way, I started stashing money. I don't even remember where I got it. I mean you have to account for every penny that comes in, but I got it from somewhere. Creative funding. I remember the first time he came to me saying, 'I really wanna …'

"'Oh, quit whining,' I said. 'I've got some money.'

"'Wonderful,' he said. "Where'd you get it?'

"'I stashed it so when you came whining I'd have something.'

"After that, every once in a while he would come crying. I'd have a couple hundred dollars, and he'd be thrilled."

When Gail mentioned that the office had a very low percentage of people who didn't pay their bills, I recalled sending monthly payments of $20 to Dr. Borgquist's office for my family's medical care. My husband was a seasonal worker, and we didn't have insurance, so we budgeted every cent, and it helped to pay medical costs in installments. Gail said Dr. B once asked her why they had such a low percentage of non-payments when other doctors in the community were struggling with this issue. "I told him it was because I prayed over the bills before I sent them out," said Gail. Her sincerity, along with a detail Monique provided, convinced me that something unique was working in Dr. Warren Borgquist's office when it came to payment for services.

"Gail had a form," said Monique, "a letter she had created with little characters and a checklist that patients completed and sent back. It read like this: Dear Dr. Borgquist, I haven't paid my bill because ... Four or five reasons were listed, each with a funny little face. One of them said, 'I just don't feel like it.' One was 'I can't afford it; I've got kids to feed.' People really responded to the form because we weren't sending them to a collection agency."

Though I didn't recall this letter, I know I paid $10 a month on the bill for my third child until he was close to 3 years old. As Monique continued, I realized we hadn't been alone. "We had patients who were seasonal workers, and they couldn't pay during the winter. They didn't have anything but unemployment. They could hardly buy food. But come spring, either when they got back to work or when they got their tax returns, they could pay. I remember one kid was up here from the Bay Area skiing, and he broke his leg—a really bad break. Warren was on call. Anyway, long story short, the guy was temporarily disabled, couldn't work, and didn't have any income. He called the office and said, 'I know I owe this bill, and I'm so grateful for what Dr. Borgquist did for me. Maybe I can pay a dollar a month.' I told him to send whatever he could, and I mailed him a bunch of pre-stamped envelopes. I'd get one of those envelopes with a dollar and then $3 or $5, and then one time he sent $10. I was so excited. Then when he had about two hundred bucks left, he sent it all with the nicest letter. 'Thank the doctor for his patience. I appreciate him so much. You will never know what it did for me.'

"Warren's patience was one of his strengths," continued Monique. "If it took ten minutes or forty-five minutes to hear someone out, he gave his time. He didn't let anything get in the way nor did he allow us to get in his way. He said, 'If it's life or death call me, but otherwise don't.' We didn't have a paging system, but we had a buzzer for emergencies, like if somebody came in threatening us or a patient collapsed in the waiting room or there was an altercation. One time, this guy, Bobby Cale, came in raving, ranting, and screaming. Billie hollered, 'Push the button!' So I hit the buzzer. Warren came out of the exam room like a shot. Bobby saw him and said, 'I'm sorry, I'm sorry.' And Warren said, 'Get out of my office. I'm not going to be your doctor anymore. You can't come in here and scare my staff.' Bobby sent cards to all of us, apologizing. He brought flowers. He brought candy. He would come in to say hello, how are you, and thanks again. I mean he was just so sweet. Warren's anger really affected him."

"Another time there was a salesman from a drug company. He always looked neat and clean in a suit and tie, but he would corner Marge in the back office and say lewd things to her. When she told me, I said, 'The next time he comes, you can meet him here in front, so I can protect you.' When I wouldn't let him past the front desk, he got snippy, saying, 'I'm here to see the doctor or Marge.' I repeated, 'They're not available,' so he got more intense. I said, 'I'll see what I can do,' and I buzzed Warren. He came out and said, 'You can't treat my staff like this. Get out of my office and don't ever come back.' So that was the end of him."

"Once a lady came in," continued Monique. "I thought she was having a heart attack, so I hit the buzzer. It wasn't a false alarm, and Warren thanked me. I had another lady who had come from Groveland. She didn't sound good. She was having trouble catching her breath. That one turned out to be a heart attack, too. Then there was a lady from Twain Harte. It was winter and snowing. Her husband called and said, 'She's not feeling good. I don't know what's wrong.' She was a nice gal—not one of those alarmists. So I said, 'Bring her down, and we'll work her in. It might take a few minutes, but I'll get her seen. He brought her down, and she had aortic cancer. Later, Warren said 'You saved her life.' I didn't think that was true. 'No' I said, 'You're the doctor. I just stand guard.'"

"But Monique," I countered, "You seem to have some kind of intuition—an ability to know if a person is crying wolf or not."

"Dr. B gave us triggers to look for. Shortness of breath, for example. If they reported it or we could hear it. When someone came in blue around the lips, it meant they weren't getting enough air. Abdominal pain, he said, could be anything, but possibly serious. Babies and ears were a big thing. 'I know a screaming earache can seem like a nuisance,' he said, 'but we've got to see them that day. Not that minute, but that day.' Burns, no question. Depending on how much of the body is burned, the person might need to go directly to the emergency room. Fractures—if it was an arm, we might bring them to the office; otherwise we sent them to the hospital. If they needed x-rays, we'd say go get the x-ray and then come to the office. We'll set your bone, that type of thing. Uncontrollable bleeding—we always sent them to the hospital. We knew what was important, what was an emergency. I also learned a lot by typing his notes. He recited the patients' complaints, and then he'd go through how he came to his diagnosis. I got points from transcribing those notes.

"We had one female patient who was very dramatic. She had all these emotional problems and would throw herself at me. 'I've got to see him right now.' Everything was an emergency to her. One day, she said 'I'm going to faint.' I went into the waiting room and sat her down in a chair beside her. I said, 'It's so hard for Dr. Borgquist to see everybody who needs him. He has so many patients pulling on him. If you have an emergency, maybe you should go to the emergency room.' She didn't want to do that. I talked to her for thirty or forty minutes, trying to show his side, and she finally got it and said, 'I want to thank you for spending time with me,' and she never did that again."

The staff that worked with Warren Borgquist at the Mono Way office—Monique, Gail, Billie—spent time with me too, sharing stories from beyond what I'd been able to see as a patient in the waiting room. These were the people who had helped to make his practice work— sometimes in unique ways. Dr. Borgquist had found a professional family who worked with and for him at Mono Way. Gail Bonavia, for instance, worked Warren's life into her prayers.

"Nancy was taking him to court," said Gail. "She had primary custody of the kids, and she wanted more money. I didn't think that was right. She had a boyfriend who made lots of money, and they lived together. I remember Warren saying, 'She's got more money than I do.' He was buying his parents a house, and he was buying his own house. He was extremely generous. So I said, 'That's not right. I'm going to call down all of our power,' and I got to praying that she would not get any more money, and she didn't."

*Chapter 9*

# BIRTH CHAIR

When you change the way you view birth,
the way you birth will change.

-Marie F. Mongan, *Hypnobirthing*

Since Warren was a general practitioner who opted to include obstetrics in his practice, birth had a way of interrupting his and Judy's life. "Once, we were in Los Angeles visiting our newborn grandson," said Judy, "and a woman called to say her baby was coming. It was already dark, and there was snow on the grapevine, and we were racing back to Sonora. We made it in time for him to deliver that baby. There was another time—also in the winter—when we'd gone to Bear Valley on the motorcycle. We'd just had the best dinner and were happily ensconced in our little room, and he got the call that a baby was on the way. We hopped on the motorcycle and drove home on that freezing night."

I doubt if many moms thought about Judy when making the call to Warren's exchange to say their labor had started. I hadn't, but I now knew I had interrupted one of Warren and Judy's morning coffee dates because he delivered my third child at 6:25 a.m. Those of us who delivered in his Mono Way office in the late 1970s were simply grateful he'd made an alternative birth option available. Twenty-seven women took advantage of the opportunity. Here are the stories of three of those births.

"I showed up in Sonora five months pregnant," said Julia Rhodes. "I was 19 years old, not married, and having a hard time living in New Mexico. I called my friend Karen. We'd met in Old Mexico in the gambling casinos but had since moved back to the States. 'What's it like in California?' I asked her.

"'You could get a job right on main street in Sonora with all your gambling experience,' she said.

"At the time, there were card rooms on Washington Street—places like the Silver Dollar and the Gay Nineties Club. So I jumped on a bus and came to California. I got a place in a little red trailer at the top of Big Hill—one of Hatler's places." Julia was referring to a local developer, who rented sub-standard trailers and cabins to low-income tenants on the mountainside that loomed over the Northeast side of Sonora. He was also the man who had built Warren and Judy's Calaveras Street home.

"I roomed with this other girl who was also pregnant. She was sixteen, and we were both called Julie. We called our place the trailer for wayward girls. We pooled our money to buy a Ford Fairlane for $175. Neither one of us knew how to drive, but we needed a way to get to town, so we figured it out. I spent most of my time skinny dipping at the river and playing cards downtown."

"I wanted to have a home birth, but I was looking for a doctor, because even though I was pretty healthy, I'd had high blood pressure back in New Mexico, and someone told me I could be at risk for edema. I don't remember how I heard about Borgquist, but he took me as one of his patients, and I was thrilled, because he seemed to get that birth needed to focus on the woman. He did my prenatal care, gave me basic information, and suggested I take a Lamaze class, which is where I met you," said Julia, beaming her infectious smile, just as she had done at the first meeting of our Lamaze class.

"Right," I said, recalling that in the class of six couples, we were the only women there without husbands. Instead, we each had friends as our birth coaches. That's what allied us from the beginning.

"My Lamaze coach was the wife or girlfriend of my yoga teacher," said Julia. "I can't remember which," she said, admitting that her memory was a little fuzzy some thirty years later.

"And my coach was Connie," I said, referring to my brother's girlfriend, whom I'd asked to go to class with me because my husband was going to be working out of town on my due date.

"I was just looking at the reunion picture of that Lamaze class," said Julia. "We lined all the babies on a couch and stood behind them."

"Help me remember who was in the class."

"There were six of us: you, me, Earlene, Sue, the Dunkard lady, and I can't remember the sixth woman's name. She moved away, but the rest of us stayed in the county."

"And we all gave birth in Warren's office, except for Earlene. She ended up being the first delivery Ellie did in the county." Ellie was a local midwife who continued to serve the county more than thirty years after that first birth.

"But my birthing coach was out of town when I went into labor," said Julia, "so I called you. I wasn't totally sure it was labor, but you'd already had two kids, so I figured you'd know." There was that smile again. Julia had not changed much in the intervening years. She had cut her waist length blond hair to shoulder length, and it was a different shade now that it was mixed with gray, but she was still as lithe, fit, and energetic as she'd been at 19.

"You were living in MiWuk with Karen by then," I said, naming the tiny mountain village five miles up the road from where I lived.

"Yep. I called and you came."

"In my Mercedes."

"In your Mercedes, because I didn't have a Mercedes," she said, and we both laughed. Back then, the make of our old cars was a joke between us about our relative socio-economic status. Moreover, the Mercedes story was tied to my birth story, but Julia was telling her story now.

"I'd kept the Fairlane when I moved in with Karen. The other Julie had moved in with her boyfriend, and two weeks before I went into labor, I got a call from her saying she was in labor and was going to do it by herself. She was adamant. Then I got a call in the middle of the night from a nurse at the hospital, who said Julie wanted me to come help her.

So I jumped in the car—pregnant as could be—and drove down. By the time I got there, she was delivering. It was fast and her cervix ripped. She had a different doctor than me, and I was so grateful I had Dr. Borgquist because her doctor had a terrible bedside manner. He was really rude. He shoved her baby into my arms without saying a word of greeting. Julie was so out of it she couldn't do anything, so I just sat there holding her baby while he sewed her up. I was pretty sure that if the doctor had just been patient like Warren and better understood birthing and the body, things would've been different for her."

"So I went home and two weeks later, I went into labor, and you came and drove me to Dr. Borgquist's office and his birthing chair. We were all so impressed with that chair," she said. The story we'd heard was that Warren had gone to the Smithsonian in Washington D.C. and measured an old-fashioned birthing chair, which he built and then installed it in his office. "I'd seen the chair, and I knew what to expect," added Julia. "Unlike my friend Julie, I understood what was going to happen because Dr. B had explained all that. She hadn't even gone to a Lamaze class. My son was either the 22nd or the 24th baby born in the chair. Sean came so fast that he left skid marks. That's what Warren called them, but I had no tears, because of the way he assisted the birth. I didn't have any drugs. They weren't necessary. After the birth, Billie kept an eye on me for a couple hours. Then you took me home and dropped me off."

"Yes, that was weird. I remember driving away and thinking I shouldn't just leave you and Sean there with Karen, who knew nothing about newborns or new mothers."

"But you were pregnant too," said Julia.

"And two weeks later, I was sitting in that chair," I said.

My due date had been October 16. As it turned out, I was standing beside Julia that day, directing her to pant during her contractions. After Sean was born, wrapped in a blanket, and settled in Julia's arms to nurse, Dr. Borgquist reached over and laid a hand on my belly. "You won't be delivering this baby until Raymond gets home," he predicted. He was right about that. Ten days later when my husband arrived home, I was still pregnant, and the huge rambling house where we lived in Twain Harte, east of Sonora, was beginning to fill with out-of-town guests who were coming for my brother Andy's wedding. When he and his girlfriend, Connie, had decided on a wedding date of October 29, they asked if I thought my baby would come by the due date because I'd already asked Connie to be my birth coach.

"Oh yes!" I said with total certainty.

On Friday October 28, the house was overflowing with guests, and I was still pregnant. At 11:30 p.m., most of the household was asleep, including our two young children. Raymond was building a bookcase in the corner of the dining room, and I was on the couch, recording the extremely erratic contractions I'd been having for days. "They're getting a little longer and little closer," I said, "but there's still no pattern." We were both hyped and not the slightest bit sleepy. By 2:00 a.m., I was confident I was in active labor, so I called Dr. Borgquist. After I described how things were progressing, he told me to call him again in two hours. I took a shower and donned a giant cotton caftan my mom had made. By 4:00 a.m, I'd had a bloody show—one of the indicators of a progressing labor—so Dr. B told me to go to the office where Billie would meet us. Raymond woke Connie and Andy to see what they wanted to do. They were to be married later that day at noon in a high mountain meadow an hour's drive away. They leaped from bed, saying they were coming.

Connie and I climbed into the back seat of the Mercedes, which Raymond drove. Andy, who was to be the photographer for the birth, followed in his car. The ticking diesel engine and the soft leather seats of the Mercedes were a comfort as we drove down the highway from our mountain village. I'd had an outrageous dream of owning a Mercedes since I was a teen, so after I miscarried a baby, Raymond gifted me with the 1962 model to soothe my sorrow. Amazingly, the baby I was about to deliver was conceived the day he purchased the car. Many of the birth stories I heard were full of colorful strands like this one, or Julia's gambling-skinny-dipping experiences, all of which got woven into the twenty-seven tales about Warren and his birth chair.

What I remember about the drive to Warren Borgquist's office was Connie's quiet reassuring voice and a huge swath of white glow from a full moon. We arrived at 5:00 a.m., and Billie checked me. I was six centimeters dilated. I spent the next hour walking up and down the hallway, stopping to lean against doorjambs, as the contractions got steadily more intense. At

5:30, Dr. B arrived. After talking to Billie for a minute, he came out into the hall to speak to Connie and me. He probably offered some niceties, which I've forgotten, but I remember he said, "This baby needs to be born by 6:30 a.m. because I have a date to go hiking Half Dome in Yosemite with my buddies." We laughed, and I said I'd do my best.

By 6:00 a.m., I was in transition—the most intense stage of labor—and Dr. B and Billie were setting up the birth chair. They lifted the back segment of the exam to form an oblique angle that sloped back for the comfort of the laboring mom. Dr. B had designed the structure to transform the exam table into a birth chair. The main feature of the structure was a seat attached over the short part of the table which supported the woman's bottom, but which also had a cut away to accommodate the birth of the baby. Dr. B's structure also had footrests, so that laboring women could brace their feet while pushing. Once assembled, the chair allowed the birthing woman to sit upright with her legs splayed, so that the doctor could easily move in to catch her baby.

The practice of situating women in an upright position, which allowed gravity to assist in the birth of the baby, was old and universal, an historical tidbit of which Dr. B was no doubt aware. Birthing chairs were pictured in wall paintings in Egypt dating back to 1450 BCE and in sculptures from 200 BCE in Greece. In some cultures, women sat in an attendant's lap to give birth, a position quite similar to that of sitting in these chairs. In modern times, physicians began to have women lie flat to give birth, but in the 1980s, birth chairs made a bit of comeback. During that time, studies showed the use of birth chairs speeded up the time of delivery and increased the comfort of expecting mothers.

Billie and Dr. B had to help me into the chair, not only because I was in the throes of labor but also because the structure was elevated to allow the doctor to roll a stool into position for delivery. The seat was padded and comfortable, and the oblique angle allowed me to lean back and rest between contractions. There were no arm rests, so Connie and Raymond stood on either side of me, lending their shoulders, arms, and hands for support as needed. Other than the chair, I noticed nothing different about the exam room. There was probably an oxygen tank, and Billie pulled blue Chux pads from cabinets to place under me and on the floor beneath the chair, but because women wanted a natural birth with

minimal intervention, there was no need for much more. Once settled in the chair, I recall holding fast to Connie's and Raymond's forearms during the transition contractions, panting to ride their powerful waves.

After that, two distinct images have stayed with me. First, during a brief twilight interlude—a yawning surreal pause in the intensity of birth experienced after transition and before pushing—I remember Dr. B standing across from me at eye level. He was leaning against the counter, arms folded, completely at ease as if he had all the time in the world. It was one of those stop-time moments. The other image is not really a memory, but rather a photo my brother took. I'm in the chair, leaning back, looking as though I'm sleeping. Connie is peering over one thigh and Raymond over the other—each with an expression of awe—and Dr. Borgquist is sitting between my legs supporting my baby's head before he is fully born. One push later, and he fully arrived at 6:25 a.m.

At my first post-natal visit a week later, Dr. Borgquist said to my nine-and-half-pound son as he cradled him in his arms, "You know, we had to hike off the trail with headlamps because of you. Good thing there was a full moon."

My sister, Anne Stock, was one of Warren's early patients at Tuolumne General Hospital, and one of the last mothers to give birth in his office. "We left in 1973, so Charles could finish his Divinity degree, and our first child was delivered by a midwife in Santa Cruz. In 1976, we returned, and there weren't any midwives practicing in Tuolumne County, but I discovered that Dr. Borgquist was doing office deliveries, and I thought that was the next best thing. I was amazed he was willing to take a risk. It was a true need because there was no birth center and no midwives, and there were a lot of us—most of the young women in my church—who wanted alternatives.

"Anastasia was born four weeks early, and she didn't breathe right away. In that moment, I felt like I got to watch Dr. Borgquist go into action to save a life. You know how upbeat he always was? Well, in this situation, he became very quiet and a little bit pale and highly focused. I remember he was frustrated with his nurse because she hadn't set up the oxygen machine. I think he realized he was in danger. He was risking malpractice. But he was really quick and resuscitated her. He got my baby to breathe. I saw the same thing another time, later at the birthing center. I was coaching a friend, and she started bleeding out. I'm actually still a bit traumatized by how quickly and how much blood—it was a river—and Dr. Borgquist did the same thing. He was suddenly uncharacteristically silent and pale. He started administering Pitocin until he got the bleeding under control. His nonchalant manner disappeared, and he went into extreme focused action.

"He used to say birth is 99 percent pure joy and 1 percent pure terror," I said. "You're describing how he faced the 1 percent."

"I know the joy too," said Anne. "I was delighted with Anastasia's birth—a four-hour event with no cleanup. We took her right home from the office, and everything felt right. Three days later, however, I became very concerned because she was jaundiced. We were living in a tiny mobile home and made only $6,000 a year. I was so worried about an expensive hospital visit, but when I called him, he offered to check her at his home. It was a sunny December day, and we drove to his house. Right there at the bottom of his driveway, he looked at her in the sunlight— you need to check jaundice in natural light. He declared her within the acceptable range and said to give her sunbaths every day, and the situation would resolve itself. He made it easy on us—saving us financially as well as the time and crazy energy we didn't need to be expending under the circumstances.

"In that very short window when he was doing office deliveries, I got to attend several births to coach friends," added Anne. "One of my favorite stories was my friend Pam's birth. I called Dr. Borgquist from her house at midnight, saying she was definitely in good, strong labor. Though he didn't ever hurry women to come in, his wait-and-see attitude didn't seem appropriate in this situation. Shortly after the call, her labor got really intense. It was her second baby, so I just made an executive decision and said, 'We're going now.' When we arrived at the office, I realized the reason for his hesitation. There was another woman who had just delivered. He moved her off the birthing chair—barely having delivered the placenta—onto the couch in his office with her husband and baby boy, just in time for Pam to climb on the chair and push her baby out. It was Easter morning. After things calmed down, I knocked on the door to his office to congratulate the other family. They were so happy to show off their new baby. That was my first encounter with Gay Wolf who has been my friend for thirty-eight years.

"Here's a funny thing. All of my girlfriends and I would fix our hair and get dressed in our nicest clothes when we went to see Dr. Borgquist because we were crushing on our doctor. He had hero status. I know it's normal to bond with those present when you give birth, and some of that hero status was deserved, but our imaginations were at work too," said Anne. She followed this with a divergent comment made by her husband. "Charles used to say, 'I think Dr. B really enjoys coming out smelling like a rose.'"

I wasn't sure what Charles meant by "smelling like a rose"—which commonly refers to something ending positively which could have been deemed bad or dishonest. Did Charles view Warren as toying with the potential risks of office births in order to enjoy the hero status Anne described? If that was true, Warren Borgquist had found a pretty nifty way to smell like a rose. Powerful hormones drive the birth process, and Warren had placed himself square in the middle of the oxytocin-induced euphoria that accompanies the birth of baby. The entire office felt the effect. "It was thrilling to be that close," said Monique Tomasovich.

"The delivery room was right next to the kitchen, so Billie could keep a close eye on the moms. It was exciting; we were all tuned in when it was daytime birth."

"How many deliveries took place during the day?" I asked.

"There were several, and a few that started during the day, but we left before the baby arrived. We realized the gravity of what was going on. We knew there could be problems, but he was on it. So careful, so cautious, and I think it was a wonderful thing for many women."

"I only remember one birth in the office where the mother had to be taken to the hospital in an ambulance," said Gail Bonavia. "She was bleeding a little too much after the delivery, and he didn't want to take a chance. But other than that one time, there was never anything scary about it. Back then, Warren was always fighting the rest of the community, pushing for more humane, more natural births with the fathers involved."

"One of the pleasures about office deliveries," said Billie, "was that everybody was expectant. There was the mom in the delivery room and everybody else waiting for something wonderful. The cops even stopped by one night. 'What's going on up here?'

"'We're having a baby' I said. 'Get out of here.'

"'Can we wait?' they asked.

"It was an exciting time," Billie concluded. "But the other doctors weren't happy. One day Dr. B came in and said, 'I've got to move it down to the labor and delivery at the hospital.'

"'Why?' I asked.

"'They're on my butt about doing office deliveries.' Warren and I did so many OB's together," said Billie. "It was what I loved most about the job."

Warren too might have loved obstetrics the most. Not all general practice doctors performed the branch of medicine that dealt with pregnancy and childbirth, but he had from his first year at TGH. And then he took it one step further into office deliveries. Whether seen as the act of a renegade or a guy who wanted to come out smelling like a rose or simply a physician who believed women needed more options in the birthing arena, the birth chair was an artifact particular to Warren Borgquist's medical practice.

# *Chapter 10*

# YOUNG TURKS

Change is the law of life. And those who only
look to the past or the present are sure to miss the future.

-John F. Kennedy

"Dr. Borgquist, Dr. Dorman, Dr. Wilson, Dr. Hall, I think those were the major ones," said Ruth Weston, when listing a string of young doctors who arrived in Tuolumne County in the 1970s. "Oh, and Dr. Mills. They wanted to bring this community up to date. They wanted to get good equipment and make sure the Sonora medical community was top notch, and they all worked hard at it." Ruth added that Dr. Mills was the first OB-GYN to come to the county, and he had trained at UCSF Medical School where Warren studied. I put a star next to his name in my notebook. I wanted to interview him not only about Warren as a colleague but also about the relationship between general practice and the specialty of obstetrics.

"Sure, I'll talk to you about Warren," said Chris Mills when I called. "Come to my place. Make it after seven because I like to watch the news."

Though I had never actually met Dr. Mills, he was, as he would soon describe himself, an "institution" in the community. Because it was a small town, I knew about him from various sources. He and his first wife,

Claire Mills, had divorced years ago. Claire was the nurse-practitioner I had gone to since Warren's retirement. His daughters, Megan and Emily, had grown up in Sonora, and Megan and I both swam with the local Masters Swim team. I also knew his second wife, Arlene, who'd been my colleague at the college. This familiarity with his family led me to think of him as Chris rather than Dr. Mills. His second wife had also moved on, so the man lived alone. His home was easy to find near downtown Sonora, not far from where old Columbia Way Hospital once stood. The house was a much newer construction than the other homes on the street, but the design was not out of sync.

When I knocked on the heavy door, a raucous barking arose. A minute later, I heard dead bolts sliding noisily before the door opened to Chris holding onto the collar of a dog that surely had pit bull in his heritage. We greeted one another over the clamor of the dog that quickly revealed himself to be more needy than ferocious. I followed the man and his dog through a front room and dining room into the kitchen where he invited me to sit at a little table tucked into a bay window. Books were piled everywhere—absolutely everywhere—on end tables, the pool table, the dining room table, and a bar top in the kitchen. Plus there were ceiling high bookshelves packed to overflowing in every room. For the next two hours, this doctor—dressed in blue jeans and a flannel shirt and resembling Woody Allen in stature and acerbity—regaled me with stories, punctuated by Dino's barking.

"I understand that you were in medical school with Warren," I began, after I'd opened my notebook and started the recorder.

"There were five of us from UC San Francisco who ended up in Sonora: Ralph Retherford, Jim Hongola, Borgquist, Michael Fitzpatrick, and myself. We were all in the same class. I knew Warren was in the class and that he was married and had small children, but that was about it. There were a 106 people in that class—only four or five women and no minorities that I recall. UCSF med school was very popular, and it was hard to get in. Everybody wanted to go there because it was San Francisco, but we never saw much of the city because we were busting our butts. And the married guys, you never saw them. It was old school. The teachers wore bow-ties. And by today's standards, it was cheap. My tuition was $244 a quarter. I worked summers as a research assistant, so

I didn't have to borrow any money."

Nancy, Warren's first wife, had said Warren had completed school with less debt than his single friends because she was a good money manager. And Chris too was claiming that going to medical school was relatively inexpensive compared to today's costs. According to the American Association of Medical Colleges, the average cost of attending a public medical school for one year in 2015 was close to $33,000. Talking to Chris and other doctors, I would discover that costs were just one facet of medical education that had changed significantly since Warren's time.

"I did my residency at San Joaquin General Hospital, and one day Warren called. I was a junior resident in my second year, and he asked if any of the senior residents—there were only two—would be interested in coming to Sonora. I said, 'No, they've already got their spots picked out, but if you still need somebody in a year, give me a call, and I'll come talk to you.' So that's what he did.

"Back in those days, you came up with your wife to meet with some of the docs. We met at John Dorman's house. He used to live by the high school. Borgquist, Dorman, and Ron Goldman, the pediatrician, were there. We all sat down at the kitchen table, and it wasn't so much about whether the doc wanted to come. It was more like, does it look like his wife will be happy here because there's no Macy's. That's what they were checking out, because if the wife wasn't satisfied with the situation, they knew you weren't going to be staying."

"What year was this?" I asked.

"1974. If it hadn't been for Warren, I wouldn't have considered this place. I figured it was a drive-through town, population 2,500, with nothing going on. But really, Sonora is the center for the whole county, and I was the first one here, so I was going to be an instant success. Warren wanted somebody because he didn't like dealing with obstetrical problems. "I was pretty concerned when I first got here. The place was totally in the dark ages. There were leather restraints on the delivery table. I'll show you."

"You have them?" I said, as he got up from the table and set Dino into a barking frenzy.

"Yeah, I've got them in here," he said, heading toward the front part of the house, the dog skittering behind on the hardwood floors, barking all the way. Apparently there was more than books archived in this house. He returned, holding thick leather straps that were stiff with age and disuse. "See these got stuck in slots on the table," explained Chris. "You put the lady's wrist in here, and you closed it, so she couldn't go thrashing around raising hell no matter what you did. I was horrified," said Chris. "I told those guys, 'Take those off the fucking table. What are you guys doing?' And babies who were premature back then were simply put in the bassinet, and they either made it or they didn't. No neonatal resuscitation. No transport to Children's Hospital in Oakland. I set up all of that: arranged for neonatal transport and got undelivered mothers who were in trouble down to UC. I did the first laparoscopies for tubal ligation and started the outpatient abortion clinic in Stockton. I was bringing a whole new thing to Sonora, and it was cool."

Without prompting, Chris returned to the topic of Warren Borgquist. "Warren was fresh out of his training, having done his internship in Panama—one of the old rotating internships."

"What does that mean?" I asked.

"When you get out of medical school, you go to a hospital for one year and rotate through the different services; pediatrics, internal medicine, obstetrics, emergency room, surgery. You spend a couple months in each one, and then you're done. You've got a license to kill!" said Chris with a wry grimace. "How much training do you get in two months, say in obstetrics?" he asked rhetorically. "Not much. Instead you get your real training on-the-job after you finish your internship. I always had a lot of respect for Warren because he had to learn on the job and from the old fellows who, back in those days, did everything. They pinned hips, dealt with bleeding ulcers, and everything else. There weren't any specialists up here. We were the new wave, the specialists, and also the family practitioners—guys like Warren. But really he wasn't a family practitioner. He was a general practitioner."

Having only recently learned the distinction between these two kinds of clinical practice, I picked up my pen to note what Chris had to say on the matter. I knew the difference had to do with training. Early on, Judy had corrected me when I referred to Warren's time in a Panama as a residency. "He did his internship in Panama," she said. "He didn't do a residency." I was under the mistaken assumption that all doctors did both an internship and a residency, but Judy explained that when Warren trained, a doctor could finish an internship and immediately begin working as a general-practice doctor. This training option ended shortly after Warren went to work in Sonora, so the guys who came later, like Waldman, Stolp, and Runte, were family practitioners.

"Warren had common sense, " continued Chris, "and he wasn't cavalier. Over the years, he gained a lot of experience. I used to call and ask him, 'What the hell should I do about this?' Or 'Who can I send this person to?' Because he knew. He had his little circle of specialists, and he was kind of opinionated. He could be a little stubborn about how he thought things should be, but he wasn't out of line. He was reasonable."

"That feels like a good segue to ask about the office deliveries he did," I said, for I was fairly sure Dr. Mills had something to do with shutting down that operation.

"Yeah, he had his birthing chair and the office delivery thing, but that was bullshit," said Chris, expressing his own strong opinion. "We weren't going to put up with that, and we ended up clamping down on him. About the time we clamped down on his office deliveries, they also closed the birthing room at Tuolumne General."

"Why do you think he did it—offer to deliver babies in his office?" I asked, recalling Gail Bonavia's take: "he was fighting the rest of the medical community. He wanted it to be more humane, more natural, with fathers involved."

"He believed that was the way to go," answered Chris, "and probably because he could do things there the hospital wouldn't allow him to do, but he stayed out of trouble. He wasn't doing stupid things. I used to sign out to Borgquist because I was comfortable with him doing my deliveries," he said, referring to the need to identify a physician to be called when he was on vacation and a woman went into labor. "One time, I went up to Beardsley fishing, and he did two deliveries for me. I paid him $250 each. I caught two trout, so they cost me two hundred fifty bucks apiece, but I didn't leave very often. If somebody needed a C-section, he couldn't do that. He'd have to call a surgeon because they used to do all that stuff before I got here, but they didn't like doing it.

"I never made any money. Warren had trouble making money too. He used to get in so much trouble with his wood shop thing because he'd buy stuff he shouldn't be buying, but he'd buy it anyway. If I needed to see him about something or borrow a tool, he'd always be down in his shop doing his thing. He was always broke. He wasn't a very good businessman. He was like me. He didn't give a shit about the money. Doctors are greedy and selfish as a general rule. Now Warren, he had a kind heart. He just did!

"We used to socialize with Warren and Judy. They had a Christmas sing-along every year, and we always went to that. We did these wine trips to Napa on a bus. I'd rent a party boat down at Berkeley or sign up a bunch of the guys to go sports fishing. I had a big Christmas party at my office every year with champagne, catered by Tom Bender from City Hotel. I remember partying, drinking, and raising hell. It seems like when you're younger that's what you want to do. Now I'm not much inclined. I'd rather stay home and read a book."

Dr. Mills and his team—wife Claire, nurse, and Jan Dunn, nurse-midwife—had served many of my friends back when I was new to the community. Eventually, the small town rumor mill churned news that Chris and Claire had split up. I didn't know the whole story or probably even much that was true. But I did know that after the divorce, Claire set up her own practice as a nurse practitioner, specializing in women's health. She garnered a reputation for superb diagnostics as she had made the first call of cancer in several of my friends, including once walking me through a breast cancer scare. It seemed prudent to get Claire's perspective on the decision to come to Sonora, since Chris had explicitly said that what the wife thought mattered to those who were enlisting new physicians to come to the community in the 1970s.

We met on Claire's lunch break, for like Chris, she was still working as a medical professional. For a meeting place, we chose Schnoogs, the same coffee shop where I'd first met Judy Borgquist and where Warren and his cronies met weekly later in his life. Claire and I sat outside at the same table the doctors once occupied.

"Tell the story of how you and Chris came to Sonora and what role Warren played."

"Chris's senior resident had gone to Oregon to open a practice, and he had offered Chris a position, so that's what we planned to do.

Then Warren called. We told him we had other plans pending, but right before we decided for sure, my father was diagnosed with lung cancer. He and my mother had recently divorced, and it was apparent that I needed to hang around, so Chris came up and talked to Warren. And the other thing that happened was that Doreen Goldman ... Do you remember Ron Goldman?"

"The pediatrician?" I said.

"Yes, his wife Doreen called me, and she said, 'You don't know me and that doesn't matter because I'm just going to tell you all the reasons you have to move to Sonora.' She just went on and on and on. It was delightful. She really wanted us to move here."

"Why was that?"

"Because there were no OB-GYNs across the three mountain counties. I don't think any of the old guys were doing deliveries anymore. I think Warren was doing all of them. They had a pediatrician, but no OB. It didn't make sense to not have one."

"Were you already an RN?"

"Yes."

"And you worked in Chris' office."

"I set up his practice. He finished his residency, and we moved here in June of '74. It was obvious they needed more doctors. So they started recruiting others from their class at UCSF. Jim Hongola, Mike Fitzpatrick, and I think Gordie Davis came along shortly thereafter, but he wasn't part of the initial wave. Oh, and Jim Wilson."

"Did you guys socialize?"

"Oh, my god, yes. It was such a small group that the entire medical community socialized."

"What did medical practice look like in the '70s and '80s?"

"It was very different. Much more personal. It wasn't go-to-work-and-take-care-of-patients. Our patients were our friends and neighbors— the storekeeper down the street and the bank manager. We were able to provide care within the context of a community. It wasn't as fragmented as it is now. But the workload was tremendous because there weren't enough primary care providers."

Claire was buoyant as she went on to talk about the early days in Chris Mills' OB-GYN practice and eventually training to become a nurse practitioner. I could see that their practice had something of the same heart that Warren brought to his pregnant mothers, but it was more concentrated and focused in a specialty office, and they were better prepared to deal with the contingencies that might arise. Warren had recruited Mills because he knew the community needed an OB-GYN specialist who would develop services for women and babies. It looked like his hopes and concerns extended beyond the image I held dear—an unhurried practitioner waiting patiently for my baby to arrive, a doctor who had gently, almost reverently delivered my child while we were surrounded by loved ones. I was beginning to see the bigger picture he must have had in mind when inviting specialists to come to Tuolumne County.

I knew that radiologist Jim Wilson was a big part of Warren's life because almost everyone I'd talked to thus far had asked if I'd talked to him. Wilson was less visible as a major player in the medical community. But anyone who knew Warren, knew that he and Jim were the best of friends, and after talking to Chris Mills, I suspected Wilson was also probably another one of the change agents who transformed old-style medical practices in Tuolumne County.

So one fall morning, I drove out a winding road to the Wilson home, which was perched on a knoll looking southwest. The home was so different from the Borgquist's. Instead of a steep narrow driveway climbing from a Sonora side street to smallish home with compact rooms, the Wilson's home had a broad driveway with ample parking and a sprawling interior with wide spacious hallways. Wilson's tanned athletic body and full head of short-cropped hair also contrasted with Warren's thick physique and bald pate. One thing I knew they had in common was wives who bore the name Judy. I'd actually known Judy Wilson for years, having frequented the same aerobics classes, gyms, and swimming pools. Back in my running days, we were often in the same age group at 10K street races, but I'd never actually met Jim. I knew him by appearance from the days when I passed the table of doctors deep in conversation at Schnoogs and before that at the Pie Tin.

Jim led me out to a patio with a grand view of the foothills, the terrain upon which he and a whole crop of doctors had decided to establish medical practices in the 1970s. After a few preliminaries, I asked him to tell me how he and Warren had met and what brought him to Tuolumne County.

"During my residency training, one of my supervising doctors said, 'I have a friend who works out of Sonora part-time. He drives up from Sacramento to read films once a week, but he's getting ready to leave. You mentioned you wanted to move to the country. You ought to go take a look.' So I came up and looked around, and then I brought my family to see how they liked it. That was the summer of 1974. We spent a week here, and I worked at Tuolumne General Hospital where I bumped into Warren. He invited Judy and me to dinner. We had a nice dinner together, and about 9 o'clock Warren goes, 'You guys can stay as long as you want, but I'm going to bed.' And I thought, 'With this guy, there's no beating around the bush.' The other funny thing was the method he used to get doctors to come to work here. He'd say, 'It's kind of a crummy little community. We don't have much going on here.' It was a negative sales pitch, and it worked. I saw him do it with a lot of folks.

"I was about six months from completing a dual therapeutic and diagnostic radiology residency. There was a woman administrator at Tuolumne General Hospital. I talked to her about coming here. 'But you're going to have to wait six months,' I said, 'and you're going to have to upgrade the equipment.' The technology was antiquated. On my first day at TGH during that summer visit, I walked into radiology and the technician said, 'Put these goggles on.'

"'What are these for?' I asked

"'They're to get your eyes dark adapted.'

"The equipment was out of the '40s. It was so archaic. I'd never seen anything like it, so I told the administrator I'd come to TGH if she got the place upgraded. I was young and wanted to move to the country. Actually, I would've mowed lawns to be here. With Judy it was a different matter. She was less enthusiastic. She'd grown up in La Jolla, which was miles away from Sonora in many ways. But the hospital upgraded, and we moved here at the end of 1974."

"Warren and I got along great. His office was right off the lobby at TGH, and mine was just next door. We were always fooling around and playing jokes on one another. I had a Morgan motorcar, a wide-open little thing. One day, I came out, and he had parked his bicycle in it. So I took his bike up to the third floor where the hospital had storage, and somehow I put the bike out on the roof. We goofed around like that all the time.

"There were a group of us who had just gotten out of residency programs, people like John Dorman, who was a neurologist, and Chris Mills, who is still practicing OB-GYN. And Mike Fitzpatrick, who's a pathologist. They were here before I got here, but not by much. Who else? Chuck Waldman came after me. Waldman was a GP like Warren. So there were half a dozen new guys, and since we were younger than the old fellows, we referred to ourselves as the Young Turks. The old guys—some of them—were not good in their standards of practice. So some of that Young Turk business reflected the fact that we were beginning to clean up the operation."

Judy Borgquist was proud of Warren's role in changing the face of medicine in Tuolumne County. "Those early years were exciting," she said. "Warren set out to cultivate a well-rounded, fabulous medical community that other doctors would want to join. Things changed because he brought in the specialists. When he got here, there was not one specialist. He'd call doctors he knew or had some kind of connection with. First, he brought in a pediatrician because he'd had a kid with meningitis, and it scared the hell out of him. So he brought Ron Goldman, who was only here for about five years because Doreen, his wife, said they couldn't raise their kids here. They're Jewish, and there was no temple here, so they moved to Modesto. Then he brought Chris Mills.

"We'd have like a salon, if you will," said Judy. "We had the doctor and his wife for dinner, and that was the interview. If we liked them, they got to come and be doctors here," Judy added, laughing at the audacity of this near-truth. "If he didn't like somebody, he would discourage them from coming. There were a few he didn't think would fit in. We had people like John Dorman, Chris Mills, and Jim Wilson to dinner with their wives. I don't think people know how purposefully Warren set about building a rich medical community. If a doctor came and inquired at the hospital about working here, Warren was notified, and we invited them to dinner.

"He and that group of newer doctors used to meet once a week for coffee. He really made that happen, because he thought it gave them a chance to talk about how they were going to do medical care around here. It was how they were going to stay connected. Those weekly coffee dates were just like our morning coffee time," added Judy, connecting Warren's professional style to the way he managed his personal life.

"Did the fact that you were both docs influence your relationship with Warren?" I asked Jim Wilson, pointing the conversation toward the friendship I'd heard these men shared.

"Absolutely. Because we could talk about our failures."

"That's an interesting way to say it."

"It's sort of like going down to the local bartender to tell him your miseries. When you're a doctor, you don't have anybody except a fellow physician to whom you can say, 'I really screwed up. I made a horrible mistake.' You need someone you respect and trust to talk to—to lay out the situation, and say, 'This was my thinking and this is what I did, and it was a mistake.' Warren had a unique capacity to lay himself bare. For us, being fellow physicians and best friends was like being Catholic and going to confession. We could lay it all out."

"Talk about Death Valley," I said. "I know you guys went there every year. What was the attraction?"

"Warren and I had another good friend, Doug Lorimer. The three of us were best buddies. Doug and I were climbing partners at first, and one year, he and I planned to climb in Yosemite around Easter. We met at my house, and it was raining like crazy. It was inconceivable to climb in the rain, but I'd taken the week off work, so we decided to head south. We took our cross-country skis and threw our packs in the car. We went to Mammoth and cross-country skied out to Hot Creek. There was snow everywhere. We had to spend the night in the creek just to stay warm. So then we said, 'Hell, let's go to Death Valley.' We basically spent the week running around the desert. We'd drive out some deserted road until we found what looked like a good spot, and we'd put on our running gear and run through the hills and come back to the car at night and throw our bed rolls on the ground. We had a ball. That was the beginning of what turned out to be forty years of week-long experiences in Death Valley. The following year, we took Warren, and the three of us went every year after that, almost without exception. One year, my wife blew out her knee skiing and had an operation, so I stayed home. That was maybe '83 or '84. Doug missed one year, and Warren the first, but I don't think he missed any others. The three of us spent forty weeks of our lives over there fooling around."

"Most of our time was spent running up canyons and peaks. On the spur of the moment we'd decide, 'Let's do this or do that.' It was all spontaneous. I was pretty much the fastest of the three, and Doug was right behind me. Warren was a little slower. Warren was like a diesel. It took him a while to get going, but then he'd just kind of motor on in his own fashion. We spent all those years running at different paces but keeping an eye out for each other and nobody ever died. It just seemed to work. We did have to watch out for Warren. He was not exactly absent-minded, but he would get a notion that he was going to do something, and it was almost like everything else would go out of his head. He'd be cruising along and see something off in the distance, and he'd forget about everything else and just amble off toward his new goal, even if we'd decided in advance that we were doing something else. So we had to keep an eye on him. He'd get this look: his mouth would drop open, he'd get a far off look in his eye, and he'd take off for parts unknown. 'There he goes,' we'd say."

As Jim talked, I recalled Karma talking about the "Duh-Borgquist-look," which she had demonstrated. I was sure that was the look Jim was describing.

"Warren and I flew down to El Salvador to see Doug when he was in the Peace Corps. We were in this crowded market place in the town of Usulutan. We didn't have our bearings at all. The three of us were walking through the marketplace, and I saw this look in Warren's eye. All of a sudden he got slack jawed and headed off through the marketplace. Doug and I looked at each other and nodded. 'Yeah, there he goes.' We had to be like referees kicking the soccer ball back in the field of play with him. The three of us spent a lot of good times together.

"I have images of Warren in different circumstances, getting scared shitless on rock climbs and stuff like that. It's hard to describe some of his expressions, but when he got himself into trouble, you could see it in his face. You could tell when he was scared, when he made a mistake, or when he was gleeful. Like I can see him on the Grand Canyon trip, trying to herd a turkey up the trail on the Colorado River. That was one of his gleeful looks. I've got a picture I'd show you, except I gave it to Judy for the photo board at his memorial."

"There was only one picture of him as a doctor on those photo boards," I said. "I think that says a lot."

"People didn't view Warren as human first and doctor second," said Jim, looking thoughtful.

Guilt washed over me. I had certainly pigeonholed Warren into his professional role, which was evident in the surprise I felt studying the one hundred seventy pictures on display at the memorial. People like Jim Wilson and Judy Borgquist didn't find it surprising there was only one picture of him doctoring, for they knew the man beyond the doctor.

"But his patients knew he viewed them as human beings," Jim continued, "and that's what made him so special."

Before I left Jim's home, I asked to use the restroom. On the bathroom wall was a photo of Warren and Jim. The two men were standing on the side of the road facing the desert with their backs to the camera, urinating.

*Chapter 11*

# INTREPID FRIEND

The proper office of a friend is to side with you when you are in the wrong. Nearly anybody will side with you when you are in the right.

-Mark Twain- Notebook, 1898

Scanning house numbers, I drove slowly along one of the hilly, crooked back streets of Sonora, searching for the address Doug Lorimer had given me. I didn't need a number to find his home, for I recognized it immediately by the rock work in progress on the steep slope beside the house. Doug was a stonemason, and I knew his work from examples at the Borgquist's, his former home with ex-wife Kathleen, and a memorial he'd constructed at the college. Doug and I had shared acquaintances, but we had rarely socialized.

As I climbed the steps to his front door, he came around the corner of the first landing to greet me—a deeply tanned man in a tank top and shorts. Thick gray hair was the only indicator that this trim, muscled man was in his seventies. Just as I'd done with Jim Wilson, I couldn't help but compare his appearance to the rotund, bespectacled Warren. On the surface, the only thing the two had in common was a bright engaging smile. We settled in his sunny front room where rattan furniture and bookcases were surrounded by South and Central American artifacts. After chatting about a few of our shared friends, I asked Doug to tell me how he met Warren.

"I'm a Sonora High grad," said Doug. "I've lived here my entire life."

"Were you in his class?"

"No, I'm older. I don't really remember Warren in high school. I remember his folks and the dime store. I lifeguarded at Columbia pool and remember young Warren coming to the pool. That's the first time I knew who he was, but we weren't friends or anything." Doug had an expressive voice, full of changing cadences. I felt myself being drawn in. "Years went by. I went to college, got drafted, got married, and came back here to settle down. Then I became friends with Jim Wilson. My wife Kathleen knew his wife Judy from San Diego. Jim and I hooked up because we had the same interests, rock climbing in particular. One day, he brought Warren over to the house. So after that, the three of us would take off and do things together."

"Like the Death Valley trips," I said. "Would you talk about those?"

"Sure. One year Kathleen and I were going to San Diego down Highway 395, and I talked her into ducking into Death Valley. We drove through, not stopping to explore, but I was really intrigued by that quick look. A few months later, Jim and I were going climbing, and the weather turned dark and ugly, so I said, 'Let's just throw all our gear in the truck and go look at Death Valley.' So that was the first time."

"Thereafter, we set the trip around Easter because Jim and Warren could get a little window of time. You know, doctors are on call, and they have to make arrangements. I was a stonemason, so I said, 'I don't care. You guys organize the dates and that's when we'll go.' We'd done other trips, like to Tuolumne Meadows and Half Dome, for a bit of climbing and running around, so we were comfortable with each other, and it just went from there. Then Judy Borgquist and my wife Kathleen bonded, so that was good too."

"Did your families do stuff together?"

"Always. The Borgquists had this big ol' extended family—kids all over the place. We just tumbled along with them. Plus a bunch of smart people came to Sonora at that time which made for a great social scene."

"Who for instance?" I asked

"Jim Hastings, and Jim brought along a lot of the guys from the college—Doug Koterek, Jon Hagstrom. Dean Colli was also a very dear friend of Warren's. But Dean was a little different from Hastings, Hagstrom, and Koterek. All those guys liked to drink and smoke, and Dean was a straight-arrow guy, so he didn't mesh so much. Warren and Dean used to go to Knight's Ferry, like once a month. They had this little routine. That's the thing about Warren. He liked routines, and he compartmentalized friendships. He had this mob of relationships, and I was a part of that. But I was just one part."

"I understand you did some work at the Borgquist's house."

"Warren and his house," said Doug, shaking his head. "He had house dreams. They bought property, and he was going to build a house. He'd wade through all these magazines, thinking he was going to do this, that, and the other. He would get so wrapped up in his ideas."

"Can you give an example?"

"Have you been to Jim's house?"

"Yes," I said.

"Did you see all that rock work? A bazillion tons of granite. Jim has great vision. He knows what he wants to do, but he turns it over to a specialist. Not Warren. He was a do-it-yourself guy. One time he called and said, 'I need a little help at the house. I want to change out some fixtures.' When I got there, I asked, 'Is the power off, Warren?' He says, 'Yeah, sure, Doug.' So I stick in my screwdriver and ZZZZAP.

"'Wow, I didn't think that was going to happen,' he said.

"If there was a solution for something that needed fixing, he'd want to do something else—make it a little more complicated, a little more decorative, add something because he'd been pouring through these magazines. He would subscribe to magazines and research, research, research. Instead of doing the direct and least complicated approach, he was all over the place. It was a hobby for him. A hobby—because work was another thing. There's no question the man was devoted when it came to his work."

"Was he your doctor?"

"I never really had a doctor. I've never been sick. But if I had any doctor, it was Warren, and he took care of Kathleen and the kids. He was always willing. Do you know where Sardine Falls is?"

I nodded, envisioning the short hike to a waterfall near the summit of Sonora Pass.

"When the kids were little, we were hiking at Sardine Falls. We had our dogs with us, and it was a great day. On the hike back to the car, there was a little patch of snow on the trail. Kathleen hit the snow, and she shot down, falling into a rock pile, which tore up her legs. There was blood everywhere. I got everyone to the car, and we drove back to Sonora and called Warren. It was 7:30 at night. He met us at the ER and patched her up. There is just no end to those kind of stories." Admiration soaked into Doug's resonant voice.

"When I signed up for the Peace Corps, I had to have a full physical. Warren goes, 'I'll do it for you.' I said, 'What's it going to cost?' He didn't charge me. When I decided to get a vasectomy, Warren says, 'Just drop by my office. I'll knock it out for you.' He took care of my parents, too. My mom had a heart attack, and my sisters were unhappy with her care, so I said, 'Let's turn it over to Warren.' He'd drive out to the house and sit with her. I don't think he ever billed. Hours and hours of making sure Millie was OK until she passed on. My dad had a life-time of health issues, and Warren took care of him. He saw both my parents to their deaths. He was right there with the family grieving and helping everybody get through. He was always there. There's no way to count the hours he spent with a lap full of babies, making up stories. He was Uncle Warnie to the kids. That's who he was."

After a brief pause, Doug added, "And we had no end of adventures. We got stuck everywhere. I mean that's why we went to Death Valley. We'd take our bicycles and just drive out one of those roads and say, 'OK, let's go." And we'd get way up high and realize nobody had brought water. We're two hours from the truck, and we had to just get tough and suck it up. Warren was a burly guy, and he was intrepid. He just put one foot in front of the other."

"From what I understand he didn't have good sense of direction," I said.

"Or time," said Doug. "He and Jim came to visit me in El Salvador when I was a Peace Corps volunteer. I wanted to entertain my boys, so I said, 'Let's go climb this volcano.' It was an active volcano and an incredible hike. We were heading up and the track was getting steeper and steeper. Warren says, 'You guys go ahead. I'm going back.' So Jim and I climbed to the summit and started back down. I was having blister problems, so Jim took off, saying, 'I'll see you down the trail.' I was pacing myself, taking care of my foot, and I saw Jim coming up the trail with two policemen. He was beat to shit—bleeding on his face and knees. Turned out these hoodlums with guns assaulted him and stole his camera. Actually, he just threw his pack at them and took off running. He got away, but they'd already knocked him down and banged him up. Meanwhile, nobody knew where Warren was. We got to the police station, but they weren't moving, so I got on the phone to Peace Corps security and said, 'We've got an issue here. We have a couple of Americans. One's been assaulted and one's missing. I need help right now.' So they came, and the police got involved again, and all of a sudden here comes Warren, strolling down the road.

"We lost him four or five times like that. Over and over, we'd finish a hike and have to go back out and prowl around to find him. He'd always have some little story to tell. 'I just decided to take a rest,' or he wanted to go look at something. We got to a point where we said, 'We're not letting you out of our sight. You either keep up or we'll chain you to the truck.' That was another thing. He had these monstrous trucks—big ol' giant four-wheelers. He'd rig out his truck so he could sleep in it. Jim and I camped, but Warren sprawled in total comfort in the back of his truck."

"Was it odd to be a group of three friends?" I asked, wondering if things ever got dicey with these guys.

"It's not supposed to work," said Doug "But we bounced off each other."

"You and Jim seemed more athletic," I said. "You had that in common. In what way did you and Warren connect?"

"I just loved Warren, his gentle soul. He was a part of my family. He nourished my kids, and our wives got along. It wasn't hard to like Warren."

Meanwhile, I was falling under Doug's quixotic spell. He was charming. "What do you think he would have said about you?" I asked.

"I was the crazy one. For both of them. I did things with them that they probably would never have done otherwise. Stuff that was a little off the charts. But they didn't want a steady diet of it. That wasn't the way they lived. But Death Valley was always our joy—simple and uncomplicated. We camped. We didn't spend money. We just played. We were like little boys. We'd get on top of a sand dune and slide off—go rolling and tumbling down. We challenged ourselves too. It was brilliant."

The little boy in Doug peeked through as he talked about Death Valley, but then he lapsed into thoughtful repose, so I asked, "Is there anything else you want to say about Warren?"

He sat quietly for a moment and then spoke slowly, almost hesitantly, his sonorous voice dropping a decibel. "Warren was as decent a person as you'd ever want to meet,"

He paused, and I waited.

"But he was troubled, too. Doug shook his head in puzzlement. "He was bedeviled by alcohol," he said very slowly. "Until he said, 'I can't do this. It's bad for me.' Then he just dropped it. 'Good for you Warren.' I said 'I don't care if you don't, if you don't care if I do.' That was the way we settled it. He could drop things like a rock, but something chewed at him," Again there was a long pause.

"I think his weight said something about that," I noted.

"Food! Ice cream!" Doug intoned. "He could not leave the ice cream alone." Doug emphasized each word. "Jim and I worried about him. 'Jesus, Warren, stop!' we'd say. 'Look what's happening to you.' But he had appetites. From a young age he thought that he could handle it— that he could keep all the balls in the air. That he could be on call at the hospital, and all that, until he realized he didn't have the stamina any more. But you couldn't ask for a better friend or a nicer person. And the way he was with the kids and grandkids. Rare guy, but he was a hick. I'd say, 'Warren, you need to tune into current culture. Let's listen to rock 'n roll. Let's listen to reggae. He had a player in the truck, so I'd bring my music, but Warren would turn on his hokie country western. Look at the way he dressed—mismatched socks and big ol' pants. Completely unpretentious. But you could have these great conversations with him. Jesus the stuff that guy contained in his brain."

I drove away from Doug's house, chewing on a few things. He had mentioned a troubled Warren. As a patient, I'd seen no sign of these traits but rather a forthrightness that was particularly appealing in a doctor. Of course, his close friends were likely to have a different view of the man than I. Occasionally, they seemed to be skirting an issue, no doubt obliged to

maintain the confidentiality of friendship. In their telling, Warren seemed to have a fools-rush-in side—taking off mindlessly on the desert. They admitted to worrying about and admonishing him. Jim said that he and Warren were able to talk about their failures, and Doug had called him "intrepid," which I took to mean that Warren lacked the kind of fear that causes one to hesitate, a trait valued by these outdoorsmen.

Doug brought up Warren's friendships with the men at the college—men I'd worked with, and one of whom had been my friend and professional mentor—Jim Hastings. I knew these men—Hastings, Hagstrom, and Koterek—had wrestled with their appetites—especially drinking and smoking—the latter of which had killed all three by way of cancer. The one friend from Columbia College, about whom I hadn't been aware, was Dean Colli, at least not until he spoke at Warren's memorial and told stories about their friendship. Doug was right when he said Dean didn't mesh with the other guys, and I found his statement that Warren compartmentalized his friendships to be astute and a new slant to understanding the man.

Dean Colli was appointed an administrator at the college in the early 1980s, shortly after I started to work there. His jurisdiction crossed into some of the areas I worked, and we became acquainted. He was warm and personable, and I have to admit that I found him much less intimidating than the group that was often called the moss-backs—the old guard at the college who were not all that old but who seemed to leak testosterone and intellectual power that made me wary. The guys Doug Lorimer had mentioned—Hastings, Koterek, and Hagstrom—were among this group. Being both female and newly qualified with the degrees that allowed me into their ranks, I tended to be guarded during interactions with them. But Dean Colli was different. Blond, somewhat slight of build, with an engaging manner, he was quite approachable. That's why I was eager to call him and request an interview. Because Colli lived in Southern California, we decided on a phone interview.

After I called Dean to schedule an interview, he emailed a written version of what he had said at the memorial service, so the following stories are a mix of his written words and our telephone conversation. Here's the part of the eulogy that answers the first question I asked everyone: Tell me about the first time you met Warren.

Warren's and my first encounter was a chance one—in 1976, a year after Sharon and I had come to Sonora and put in our front landscaping up the street from Warren & Judy's home. Warren used to meet his doctor buddies for a weekday morning run ... John Dorman most regularly, often with their dogs in tow ... right in front of our house about 6:30 a.m. They used to stretch out, leaning on our lamppost, and, I'm sorry to report, dogs Mandy and Lalo used to regularly relieve themselves on our new lawn. Well, you just don't do that to this Type A, left-brained, fussbudget without some critical intervention.

When after a few days I came out the front door to confront the situation, Warren quickly disarmed me, in that soft resonant doctor voice. He expressed concern for my spotted lawn, which he attributed to "silver dollar fungus," and an invitation to join in their morning run. I just wasn't quick enough to effectively spar, and the rest was history. I should add that a week or so later, Warren owned up to the misdiagnosis of my spotted lawn with a grin on his face and apologized for Mandy's and Lalo's un-neighborly canine behavior.

At the memorial, Dean talked about Warren serving as his family doctor, including being present at the births of his children. In the eulogy, he told of Warren picking asphalt from his daughter's leg after it was accidentally run over by a boat trailer, and he emphasized the frequency with which Warren came to their home to treat ailments "with a flashlight and a spoon rather than in the office with a lamp and a tongue depressor." Then he added: "He did my vasectomy. That by itself was not so special, except that he entered the office operatory with an eight-pound splitting mall on his shoulder."

Like most patients, Dean was also familiar with the effects of Warren's peculiar sense of time on his practice of medicine. "More than one person walked out of his office after waiting an hour for an appointment," said Dean. "Warren spent too darn much time with his patients, but he felt it was important to take whatever time was necessary. Jon Hagstrom was one who walked out saying, 'Tell Warren he's a technician just like me. My students don't wait an hour for me to show up for class, and I'm not waiting an hour for him.'"

"That's pretty funny," I said, realizing that this was an example of what had intimidated me about the college guys. They had the attitude that they were owed attention, not that Jon was alone in his frustration with Warren's lack of timeliness. It was more that Jon called attention to himself by walking out. The thing is, I was pretty certain, this moment didn't change how the two men related. They could maintain a friendship despite Jon's frustration. I knew this because I had watched Warren tenderly care for Jon at the end of his life.

Dean's summation of the incident was also pertinent. "It didn't matter that people pushed Warren, whether it was Judy pushing him or the nurses pushing him, he had his own pace and that was the pace he went." But Dean also connected this story to the way Warren handled friendship, though the way he veered did not predict where he was going. "I'm sure you've had conversations with his kids and grandkids about Warren being a master of trivia."

"Oh, yes," I said, " except they referred to it as 'useless crap.'"

"Oh, very good! Those would've been his words. You see, Warren felt it was important as friends, not just with me but with all of his friends, to be both interest*ed* and interest*ing*." Dean inflected the pronunciation of the suffix of each word for emphasis. "We all have relationships with people that are painful because it's pretty much one person talking. Warren felt we have to have something interesting to say, but we also have to be interested in what the other person brings to the conversation. He was into the *con* part of conversations—*con* meaning with," said Dean, and I could almost hear him smiling through the phone at the potential misunderstanding in the double meaning of the prefix. "Not pontifications, but discussions and conversations make friendships. He felt strongly about that," concluded Dean.

Like Doug, Dean talked about how Warren supported the Colli family beyond doctoring, especially how he connected with the Colli children. In his eulogy, he offered an example of Warren working with his son:

At a Borgquist Halloween party, Warren was the only adult brave enough and patient enough to give four-year-old Brian a knife to carve a pumpkin just like the older kids. It was too easy for Brian's parents to say, as he pouted, "Brian, you're too little!" Instead, Warren was so great with Brian, who he knew was often a challenge to his young and inexperienced parents. Warren patiently guided Brian's hands, as together they wrestled to carve the requisite eyes, nose, and smile, so Brian would have a pumpkin just like the big kids. The picture we have of that outcome, with broad grins across both Brian's and Warren's faces, is truly a treasure.

During our phone conversation, Dean described another treasured image of Warren. "They invited us to Mimi's wedding, and the song for the father-daughter dance was a country-western song called, 'That's My Job.' It's about a dad taking care of the child even when it's hard. In the lyrics, the dad says, 'That's my job. That's what I do. Everything I do is because of you, to keep you safe with me.' It was special for Warren and Mimi, and we watched them get teary-eyed as they danced—a real hanky moment." So that was Dean's take on Warren and country western music—this image of him dancing to a Conway Twitty tune with his daughter. Musical tastes are very personal, and so while Doug viewed country-western as the hick genre, Dean and Warren were drawn to its sentimental side.

"There was another country western song that Warren and I totally got," said Dean "—about doing right by your woman. It's called 'Take It Like a Man' by Suzy Bogguss. The refrain from the female singer's perspective goes like this: 'If I give my love to you, like a woman can, will you take it like a man?' When it came to spousal discourse, we were guys. We were still in seventh-grade when it came to saying something without thinking and getting ourselves into trouble with the wife. The female gender has a much better way of turning a phrase. So we used to laugh about that." Clearly, country western lyrics could hit the nail on the head for these two men.

"After you moved to Modesto," I said, "one of the ways you maintained your friendship was to get together at Knight's Ferry to walk."

"That's something we did regularly. By that time, neither one of us was running anymore, but we would cycle or hike along the river. Those were great times, just the two of us, talking about everything under the sun. Maybe every fourth or fifth time, my wife Sharon and Judy would join us—not to do the activity—but for breakfast afterward out on the deck at the River's Edge Restaurant. I remember one time Warren asked if Mimi could join us. I don't know if you know this, but Mimi sometimes lacked confidence. Down by the river, there are these piers on which a small bridge had once stood, but the bridge is gone now. Warren would jump from pier to pier, just maintaining his walking stride. At that stage in his life, he was pretty large, but he took those piers without stopping. Mimi however balked. I remember him coaxing her, telling her to stick her neck out and do it. It was a 'giraffe clan' story," Dean added.

"Exactly," I said.

"He got me to do things I wouldn't normally do, too. Warren used to say, 'Every tight ass like you needs to have a friend like me.' And he was absolutely right. And it was the same for Mimi. He got people to do things that were beyond their comfort zone."

"And what did you do for Warren? What was your side of this friendship?"

"I thought you were going to ask me how did I push Warren out of his comfort zone," said Dean laughing, "and I can't think of a thing. Let's see—early on we had common interests, running, biking, and later hiking. Our wives were similar. They were both in education, outspoken women of the '60s, and there wasn't anything they let Warren or me get away with."

"I bet he would know what you brought to the friendship," I said.

"The chemistry was good," said Dean. "We were good at opening up to each other without being afraid. You have to have confidence in a person when you confide in them. That comes after you take a leap of faith and find out you can count on someone. Warren found out he could do that with me. We were both willing to cultivate and maintain a buddy-ship. Many of Warren's close male buddies were doctors, but not all. Maybe hanging out with me was a way of getting away from that. I'm not sure. Whatever it was, it worked."

"I remember Warren talking about a mutual friend," said Dean, still thinking about the question. "He had done something that disappointed

Warren and Judy. It was a marital thing and some of our friends were saying, what he did was wrong and they weren't going to be friends with him anymore. But Warren wouldn't do that. He said, 'We all have our bumps.' I know it's easy to make a generalization about a given profession, but doctors more than other professions are not very open to admitting their mistakes. Maybe their egos keep them from getting there, but Warren wasn't like that. He was a regular guy, and it was important to him to be a regular guy."

"Once we were running down by the Seventh-day Adventist Church, right near where we both lived in Sonora," said Dean, setting the context for his next story. "We were just trotting along, and Warren said, 'I need to share something important. I'm an alcoholic. I'm recovering, and I'm going to AA meetings. And I want you to know what moved me to make this decision. I have two very good friends who have babies on the way. You and Sharon, and Chuck and Janet Waldman. I'm tired of wrestling with the fear that I'll fail miserably or have to call somebody in to take over a birth. I actually had a nightmare about having drank heavily one night and not hearing the phone when Sharon called to say she was in labor. So I'm going to AA.'"

According to Dean's story Warren Borgquist's decision to quit drinking was connected to fear of failure as a doctor, and especially fear of failing a friend. I wondered if this was a place where Warren had taken a leap of faith to confide in his friend. Or was he simply following the guidelines of Alcoholics Anonymous to admit powerlessness and make amends?

Judy tells a slightly different version of the story. "Warren's parents were both alcoholics, and his sisters are alcoholics. He had the gene. You can't drink too much at night if you are a doctor," said Judy, "because you might have to get up and go somewhere. That's when it became difficult. One night, he couldn't come to the phone, and that's when I said, 'That's it!' I told him I wouldn't stay with him if he didn't stop drinking. 'I love you beyond anything, but I can't live like this. You can't live like this!' That was five years into our marriage, and he knew I was serious. He wanted to keep me, so he went to AA. And it wasn't hard for him. I mean, I would be very upset if you told me I could never have another drink, but he had a good sponsor, this old guy who said, 'It's real simple. You just don't drink the al-kee-hol.' And so he didn't."

"How does a doctor go to AA?" I asked.

"He just marched in there. It didn't bother him. I got hysterical. I said, 'Warren, you have to go to Modesto for AA. You cannot go here. All of your patients will find out. Your whole practice will be in jeopardy. You must drive to Modesto once a week where you'll be anonymous.'

"'Like Hell!' he said. 'If my patients find out, the majority will admire me, and if I lose some patients over something like this, oh well.'

"I was all for hiding, and he was all for being open. I think he helped a lot of alcoholics in this community because of that. Here is my doctor admitting he is powerless. Maybe I can do it too. He felt it was his duty to go to meetings here."

"All three of us Borgquist children are alcoholics and in the program," said Marjorie Borgquist." Mom was not real thrilled about it because she felt like a failure. Dad was an alcoholic but not like we were. He might have just been a heavy drinker. Alcohol was always part of his life. It was his coping mechanism and a way to medicate. In that generation, they just didn't get touchy feely. I knew something was wrong with us, but I had no idea we were alcoholics for a long time. I just knew something wasn't right."

Then Marjorie explained how AA—the program—helped to make it right. "You can find spirituality in church, but there are other places you can find it as well. And the spiritual component of Alcoholics Anonymous is the thing that keeps us good, keeps us sober because it gives us grace. But in order to maintain that grace you have to keep in fit spiritual condition. You have to be mindful of your actions and your words and your thinking."

Warren was open about going to AA, so stories of how and when he told people cropped up again and again. He announced his sobriety to friends and professional colleagues alike.

"He took the entire office staff to lunch at the City Hotel in Columbia," said Monique. "That's where he told us. 'I'm an alcoholic, and I'm sorry for any problems I've caused in the office or to any of you personally. I'm in AA. I'm getting my life together. I'm doing the right thing, and I want you all to know what's happening.' I was totally shocked. I couldn't believe it because he did everything he was supposed to do on a daily basis. He was a functioning alcoholic. I don't know how long he had been clean and sober when he told us."

"I remember so many dinner parties where he would go to bed at 8:30," said Kathleen Lorimer, Doug's wife and Judy's good friend. "Everyone else would be around the table, and he'd just get up and go to bed. But I never saw him sloshy, so I was shocked when one day he said, 'I'm an alcoholic, and I'm going to AA.' He never made Judy and me feel bad about our drinking, and sometimes we'd get pretty silly. He was never judgmental. He just knew he couldn't because he had a very addictive personality. He went from alcohol to food. And then he'd try so hard to exercise. I loved that about him. He'd be a hundred pounds overweight and get out and ride his bicycle. He was a very complex human being. He let you in on some things, and other things he didn't. I think that's why he broadcast the alcoholism— because that's what he wanted you to know."

"When Warren went in to recovery," said Dean Colli, "he'd have tall club sodas with lime while Judy and I enjoyed our cocktails. He used to say, 'Go ahead and enjoy your evening. Don't do anything different because I'm here.' I can't imagine it's easy to be in the company of people who are drinking when you are recovering, but I guess Warren thought this was his pill to swallow."

Another of Judy's friends, Shelley Andrews, also recalls Warren at a dinner party. "They came to dinner one night, and we were serving wine. Warren said, 'I don't care for any. I'm not drinking.' But Don kept trying to push it on him. Then Warren said, 'I can't drink anything because I'm an alcoholic.' Warren was the first person we knew who came out and said those words. It shook us deeply because he never seemed like the kind of person who was out of control and that was our definition of an alcoholic. At some point, Warren told me it was dangerous for him to drink. It was sure eye-opening when he defined himself as an alcoholic. When I asked where he was going to AA, he said, 'Here—in Sonora.' I think that was part of his mission—to de-stigmatize it if he could."

Pat Valkenberg, who was Warren's nurse after Billie, said, "He was clean when I worked for him. I was in AA at the time, and I ran a meeting at the Alano Club on Thursday nights. One time, I was at the podium, and when I looked up, there he was in one of the chairs. I thought, Oh Lord. I'd heard rumors, but I'd never run into him. After the meeting, he came to greet me, and he grabbed me in a hug that almost broke my ribs. I was stunned, but I could tell he came because he needed to hear what I said.

"People go to those meetings because they need to hear someone tell them how terrible it can be, but that you don't have to stay in that place. The whole alcohol thing is about denying feelings, and we do that in a lot of ways. Some people shop. Some people gamble. Some drink. Some use drugs. Some have sex. Look at the Hollywood people. Look what they do to try and push down their feelings. But you've got to peek from under the rock and examine your life. The truth is people who lead unexamined lives are not that interesting. Warren was not exactly humble, like say Friar Tuck. He just kind of shuffled around, but he didn't consider himself above others. He didn't consider himself to be anything more than he was—a C student."

While talking to people about Warren, they would suddenly make a statement like this: "Warren saved my life. He got me to AA." Or sometimes people spoke of a loved one he had helped. His receptionist Monique spoke about his work at a local treatment facility. "When Maynard's opened, he did all their incoming physicals. He would stay late one night a week after hours to do all the physicals and get the labs taken care of. We kept track of who was seen and when. He went up to the facility to help too," added Monique.

The rules about anonymity in AA make it a challenge to tell the stories of Warren helping fellow alcoholics, but here are a few from people who said I could include their stories and names.

"He was my sponsor," said John Gleason, a local real estate agent.

"Warren came here in the middle of the night," said his wife Barb, "and did a little intervention with John, right here," she said, gesturing to the front room in which we the three of were sitting.

"Yep," said John.

"A friend said we should call Warren. She knew him from AA. So we called, and he was here in half an hour."

Ruth Hagstrom was the Columbia College Nurse, and she had enlisted Warren to help her with a weekly clinic on campus. "It was during the time when venereal disease was pandemic, the early '70s. I knew we needed a doctor on campus to treat these kids because they weren't going for treatment. He did the clinics with me for about six years."

The Borgquists and the Hagstroms were also friends who socialized, so at this point, Ruth turned to her husband's relationship with Warren. "Jon and Warren had a real nice deal going. They both liked working with wood. So they shared lumber," explained Ruth, giving substance to the story of Warren's friendship with the guy who walked out of his office because he had to wait an hour. "He was our personal physician," added Ruth and then she said this: "He set up an intervention when Jon and I needed it. He probably saved our lives, because our drinking was totally out of hand."

Charlene Ingalls, one of Warren's patients during his first year at TGH, had an interesting perspective. "My mother, who died shortly after Warren delivered my first baby, was alcoholic. It was easy to talk to Warren about my mom because he understood. We talked about the genetics of alcoholism and about role models and how the adult you become is affected when you have an alcoholic parent. I read a lot of books about children of alcoholics, but I learned more from him than any book. Warren was fascinated with my family because there are five of us children and not one is alcoholic. We each decided as children that we weren't going to do the alcohol thing. We didn't care what it took. Still, I remember sitting in Warren's office with my husband as he described the chances that our children could become alcoholics. He called it 'the gene,' and he gave us percentages. He was nonjudgmental, and he believed people could get past things if they understood them."

With this pronouncement, Charlene summed up a significant part Warren's outlook, a perspective that endeared him to others and most likely carried him over some of his own stumbling blocks.

# PART III

# THE PAPA

# *Chapter 12*

# FIDDLER

Tevye hauls his horseless milk cart, lifting it with a warm smile,
a gentle humor and an open heart as he and his fellow exiles
continue their universal search for a more promising land.

-Frank Rizzo, *Variety* December 2015

After hearing Judy Borgquist's version of the blending of her family with Warren's, I thought it would be interesting to talk to her ex-husband Dave Purdy and his second wife Ellen Stewart to see how the blending looked from their perspective. Ellen and Dave received me at the house where they had now lived for nearly forty years. We sat around a wrought iron table on a wooden deck near the pool, where shade fell from a large oak and sunlight glinted from the many windows of their home. I could see the roof of a large barn on the other side of a fence east of the driveway, and behind me the aquamarine pool shimmered. Though this house was more rambling and disjointed in its architecture than the Borgquist's, there were small noticeable similarities—the windows, the pool, a huge dining table, and a kitchen with a signature design.

"I'd left San Francisco State," said Dave, "and was working at Columbia College. Judy and I were ending our marriage of twelve years, which was pretty hard. Warren remained pretty much in the background, which I think was considerate, all things considered."

"I was going to Fresno State for my master's degree," said Ellen, "and a friend of mine lived on a horse ranch with her parents in Clovis.

They had a stable that had been made into an apartment. That's where we stayed."

"I had the fall semester off from Columbia in exchange for working the summer," explained Dave, "so I went to Fresno with her."

"And Judy and Warren lived here," said Ellen, gesturing to the house before us.

"But he decided that living up here was problematic for a doctor on call," added Dave, which was certainly true since the house is eight miles from Sonora on a winding road with a speed limit of twenty-five miles per hour, in part because of deer that regularly cross.

"The point at which Warren and I began to have a relationship had to do with Scott's first experience with alcohol," said Dave. "Judy and Warren went someplace on a trip, and Scott, along with his friends, managed to drink most of Warren's liquor cabinet. Several of his friends puked on the front porch. Warren came home and found them. He figured the hangover was sufficient punishment, but that we should have a family conference, so they invited us over. That became a fairly standard thing that we continued as part of sharing kids.

"And the second bit of a breakthrough had to do with Cliff, Warren's dad. Cliff took Scott hunting out on the outskirts of Modesto. But fishing and duck and pheasant hunting were the basis of my relationship with Scott. My thought was that Warren was beginning to overstep. He sensed how I felt about that trip, or maybe Scott told him. Anyway, Warren said, 'I'll look for other ways to relate with Scott.'

"I'm going to tell one more story because it was the third thing that got the four of us into some sort of relationship. Jennifer had always wanted a kitty. I was allergic to cats and didn't want one. We had dogs. One day, when Judy and I were still together and living in Half Moon Bay, there were great tears from Jen's bedroom. I ran in and asked, 'What's happened?' She said, 'My kitty Sassafras has run away.' The kitty had been living there a month without my knowledge. So we went out and beat the bushes and checked all the streets until we found Sassafras. After Warren came on the scene, the cat went with Jennifer to the new house. For some reason, Sassafras didn't much like Warren. The young doc was busy furnishing his new place, and there were new leather couches the cat took to shredding. This did not set well. And then the cat would spray his doctor bag with absolute malevolence."

"It was a bad cat," said Ellen.

"No, it was a great cat," said Dave with a chuckle. "Eventually, Warren had the cat's claws pulled and that left only the ability to spray on the doctor's bag. Then the cat apparently snuck into the car and ended up at the hospital which really had Warren up in arms."

"I always like to preface this story," said Ellen. "Because it was 1973 or '74, and Nixon was about to be impeached, essentially for lying and covering up. So that was the backdrop. We had been pretty much on the moral low ground," said Ellen, referring to the fact that her relationship with David began during his marriage to Judy and implying that lies and cover-up had tinged their family status.

"Anyway" said Dave, continuing his story, which would explain Ellen's preface, for this time it was Warren who did the lying. "One night, the cat stowed away in Warren's car and ended up at the ER, and they had to chase it up and down the corridors ..."

"The important thing is," interrupted Ellen, "that the kids were here because it was summer, and there was a phone call one morning while Jennifer and I were busy making pancakes. It was Judy and Warren, each speaking on different extensions of their home phone. Warren said, 'I am sorry to have to tell you, but there's been an accident. Sassafras was run over. We hung up and there were some tears, and then we all had pancakes.

Later that day, Jennifer and I went downtown for something, and she was really sad about Sassafras, so I got this idea to go to the pound—I've never been to the pound before or since. I just had a magnetic draw to the pound. We walked up to the runs, and Jennifer started screaming, 'Oh my god, it's Sassafras' and I said, 'Oh no, honey, Sassafras bit the bullet,' but she wouldn't stop. 'No, that's really Sassafras. Look, she doesn't have any claws,' and I thought, oh, shit, it is Sassafras. But it was Sunday, so we couldn't bail her out, so we went home and called Judy and Warren, and I said, 'We've got the greatest news. We found Sassafras at the pound.' Long pause. We were oblivious. And Jennifer was on the phone crying, 'We've got to go get her on Monday as soon as the pound opens.'"

"The jig was up," said Dave, "and about forty-five minutes later,

Warren called. 'I've got to come up and confess to Jennifer because I think it's important that we have an honest relationship.' And I said, 'Oh, for god's sakes Warren, you can carry this crap too far. I'm not going to say anything. You don't need to either.' He said, 'I'm coming.' So I walked down to the bridge to intercept him. 'Don't do it,' I said. 'You don't need to.' But he wouldn't hear it, so we drove to the house, and he talked to Jen. On Monday, we went to pick up the cat, and it had distemper."

"It had been there long enough," said Ellen, "to have gotten every disease that comes with cats."

"By the time it was all over, Warren had paid a fortune … almost $700."

"And not too long after that something really bad did happened to Sassafras—a fatal injection," said Ellen with droll humor.

"Yeah, this time Warren really put the cat down, and the coda is that years later …"

"Many years later," affirmed Ellen, "out here on the patio, we started telling this story because the kids all seemed old enough—I don't think Jennifer knew the whole story—and everybody was full of wine at that point, and those three children—our Sarah too, who usually didn't give either of us too much of a nod—were falling out of their chairs laughing. We'd been worried that they might not want to hear that Warren wasn't the saint, but they were rolling on the ground."

After a bit of chortling about this less visible side of Warren, I said, "You just mentioned Sarah. Would you tell the story of her birth and how Warren fit in?"

"We were going to Dr. Gary Johnson. He was newer to the community than Warren, just a young doc starting out."

"We were pretty tight with Gary," said Dave. "We were one of his first patients, and we asked him to do a home delivery. He hemmed and hawed and wasn't sure if that would be something he could do, and finally, he said 'I can't. I'm too vulnerable. There are some new OB-GYN's, and there's a big political thing coming.' Not just here in this county, as it turned out, but I guess they were going to limit the number of births that could be part of a GP's practice, and Warren had been overstepping that. But when he heard Ellen was pregnant, he said, 'Don't worry. I'll do it.'"

"We were at opening night of Dale Bunse's gallery down at the Smoke," said Ellen. Bunse was an art instructor at the College where Ellen and Dave worked. "The first signs of labor started," said Ellen launching into the birth story.

"Ellen was walking around in circles," interjected Dave. "So I asked why she was doing that, and she said, 'I saw my cat do it.'"

"Anyhow," said Ellen, "Warren came about ten o'clock that night, and Jennifer was already here because it was summer. And Warren had a nurse named Billie."

"We had very carefully put together the music we wanted," said Dave. "Everything was going according to … "

"We had lots of music," interrupted Ellen. "We had a magnum of champagne."

"The dilation was taking place right on time … "

"Not really," said Ellen. "We had our birth crew—Jennifer and Billie and Warren and Dave. By six o'clock in the morning, despite everyone's best effort, Warren said, 'This isn't happening. We need to go downtown.' Then he quickly explained the difficulty he was in politically with the OB/GYN doctors. Various docs had been actively taking him on, but Mills was his pal."

"The closest that might be called a pal," I said, thinking about Mills calling Borgquist a renegade.

"So Warren said he'd meet us downtown at the hospital," said Dave. "The plan was we were going to drive to the emergency entrance."

"We had a Pinto, a horrifying ugly Pinto that Dave's mother bought us, and some form of truck. So there was nothing to do but load me into the back of the Pinto. I'm not sure how I got in there. The seat folded down or something. I remember lying down in the back of the Pinto and going down the rutted dirt road which isn't even as good as it is now. It took like an hour because we had to stop for labor and go slow on the bumps. So we get to the hospital … "

"Warren was going to park in the back, and we were to park in front. Then he'd come in through the back door, and we were going to feign meeting each other for the first time," said Dave, laughing a guttural guffaw at the lunacy of it all.

"I don't think anyone was fooled … " said Ellen as Dave said, "I think most of the staff knew."

"Warren was threatening me with a Caesarean," continued Ellen, "and I didn't want one. Actually, I hadn't even wanted to go to a hospital, but you know when there's a baby stuck in you and you're on a pot-holed road in a Pinto, you think again. At the last moment, rather than do a Caesarean, he put some sort of egg tongs in and went slurp and out comes this poor little baby, her head squished down to a point."

"Warren cut the umbilical cord, and the baby was fine," pronounced Dave.

"And shortly thereafter," said Ellen. "Warren gave me fine words of advice when I told him how worried I was about sudden infant crib death. 'I'm terrified,' I said, and he said, 'Wait till she's driving.' And another thing he said that was really good. 'Make sure you have a date with your mate once a week. You don't want to become mom and dad and that's all.'"

"So by this time we've obviously integrated our family," said Dave.

"With the birth of Sarah," I said.

"And then Judy became her fairy godmother," said Ellen. "Warren and Judy always treated Sarah very well—made her part of their family. In fact, Sarah much preferred them to us. We weren't nearly as fun."

"So that all serves as background for the *Fiddler* story," said Dave, having arrived at the part of the story about Warren Borgquist that was mentioned as many times as his colorful socks and beaming smile. "We were holding auditions, and it had become fairly apparent after a couple of sessions, that we didn't have anybody in Tevye's age range. During a conversation, Warren indicated he had seen and loved the character. It was a role with which he identified."

"The Papa," said Ellen.

"When Warren indicated his interest," Dave continued, "I suggested he audition. It was the first time he'd ever auditioned for anything, and he couldn't sing."

"Not at all," said Ellen.

"At all," repeated Davie. "He had an absolute tin ear. Madeline Young coached him. Not successfully, but the point was the degree to which the character of Tevye inhabited his most desirable self that was enough to get him over the hump. He never sang it well, but he did sell it."

"I didn't want him to do it," said Judy Borgquist. "Jim Wilson didn't want him to do it. Because we'd heard him sing, and he wasn't the best singer in the world. But he practiced. He had to do it. Plus Dave was the director. I thought that was weird. We didn't have any hard feelings by then, but still ... Anyway Warren was determined. I thought, oh, my god, this is going to be terrible. Just terrible because he can't sing." Judy punctuated this remembrance with a disgruntled sigh that probably replicated her feelings at the time.

In 1980, Warren Borgquist stepped wholeheartedly into the role of Tevye in the Columbia College production of the musical *Fiddler on the Roof.* "Tradition!" sings Tevye—the milkman, long-suffering husband, and adoring father who tries to make good matches for his daughters while staying true to tradition. Throughout the play, Tevye talks to God about his daughters' romances, about his desire to be a rich man, about persecution by the Russians. Tevye likens his people's precarious position to that of a fiddler on the roof, and just as the fiddler teeters, so too does the play between comedy and tragedy—the poignancy played out in song. "Do you love, me?" sings the prayer-shawled peasant to his wife Golde. Then slowly, reluctantly, with formidable resistance the realization of an imperfect reality dawns on him.

"The first time I met Warren was in his doctor's office," said Don Andrews, the Musical Director of *Fiddler on the Roof.* "I had a fragment of glass in my thumb. It had been bothering me for two days, and I was kind of desperate. Warren said, 'I have a new set of knives. I ordered them from Germany, and they're brand new. I can't wait to try them.' He had to use a magnifying glass to actually find the piece of glass, but he was so excited to try his new knives. I was relieved to get it out. It was serendipitous that right after that appointment, he tried out for the musical and got the part of Tevye. I spent a lot of time with him rehearsing and watching the phenomenon of Warren.

"We cast a lot of families on purpose," continued Don, "because we needed an ensemble of all ages, and we wanted be able to rehearse efficiently without separating parents from kids too much. The rehearsal period was probably over a month. We were together almost every night, sometimes with only the leads, but Warren was always there. I don't know how he arranged his schedule. I think he might have left a couple of times for emergencies, probably delivering babies. He had a fascinating relationship with the cast as a father figure to the younger ones and a friend and colleague of the older members. Some of them were his patients, so he was called on to doctor during rehearsal. During a break, someone would mention that they had a bad cough or were coming down with something, and he would take care of it.

"I loved working with him because he was receptive and open and very dedicated. He saw himself as Tevye—like the role was a life long goal. He was committed to getting it right," said Don. "He grew his beard a certain way. He started wearing a little cap like Tevye's in the show. He already looked and acted like Tevye, but once he was cast, he started perfecting it to an amazing blend of his own personality and a stage personality. He perfected an accent. He must have listened to a lot of recordings because he seemed to know the show very well before we started rehearsing, so it was mainly a matter of helping him with diction and expressions of the voice. He wanted to be bolder on stage than he was in person. Tevye is such a father figure—a judgmental man in some ways. I don't think that was part of Warren's personality, so he had to work on that."

"Were you responsible for helping him with the singing?" I asked. "What was your impression of him in that department?"

"He had a basic talent, but his voice was somewhat coarse. The character generally has a smooth, rich voice, sustained like an opera singer who delivers some of the characterization through pitch, but I mainly encouraged him to be himself. At first, I thought it was going to be weird telling my doctor what to do. But then I figured it would work because I could tell he wanted me to shepherd him without taming his instincts. I might say, 'Warren that's not quite right. You've learned it wrong,' and then I'd explain what he needed to do, and we'd practice it about seven times until he relearned. Sometimes I'd say, 'That's close enough,' and he'd say, 'No, I want to get this right.' I thought he was a busy guy, he was tired and had a long day. Why should I beat him over the head and try to change two notes or one when he's got it close enough? It wasn't going ruin the show. But he'd say, 'No, Don, we're going to do it again.'"

Dave Purdy and his crew built a stage for the production in a basin-like setting on the campus. Shelley Andrews, Don's wife and Judy Borgquist's teaching friend from the early days, said, "I remember sitting out there watching them build the sets. I would bring snacks and sit back and watch the rehearsals. It was just an amazing production because it was a great weaving together of the community, people from all walks of life—medicine, real estate, teaching—plus all the kids and students from the college. Molly Cunningham, the college President's wife, was in that production. There is a great story about somebody cursing in front of her and everybody freaking out. Molly said, 'I can handle it.' Years later, she partnered with Warren in developing Hospice of the Sierra," said Shelley, pointing out the ways in which *Fiddler on the Roof* was a nexus of small town talent and diversity as well as a springboard to further community development.

"I remember working late one night," said Ross Carkeet, who was by then an instructor at the college. "I was headed to my car in the faculty parking lot just as the rehearsal for *Fiddler* was ending, and I saw Warren on the way to his car. 'Hey, Corky,' he said, "as he kind of stumbled up to me. He looked totally exhausted. 'How's it going?' I asked. 'I'm a total basket case,' he said.

"We hugged. 'You're doing fine.' I said. 'Hang in there.' I tried to encourage him, but he looked totally worn out. He put his heart and soul into that play. We were both pluggers, local yokels. We struggled in college, and he always said he was an overachiever."

"The rehearsal schedule was huge," said Monique. "Every afternoon, he had to leave early, except maybe one day a week. He could not sing at all when he started. He could not carry a tune, period. But his goal was to do this thing and with Dave as the Director of all people. He'd come up the back stairs of the Forest Road office singing. At first, we'd cringe. Then all of a sudden one day we realized, 'Damn he sounds good.' We were so proud of him, but it took a lot of time and energy. His call group was not very happy because he had to take time off. Whenever he left to go to rehearsals, they had to cover for him, so they were not pleased. I think it was hard on him too."

"I was just roped into the whole deal," said John Gleason about the production of *Fiddler on the Roof.* Warren was the Gleason family doctor, and John also came to know Warren through AA. " First, Barb said, 'The girls and I are going try out for *Fiddler.*' And I said, 'Oh great. I can be carpool dad when it gets late, and throw everyone in the car and drive them home.' So I got down there, and, you know, Dave Purdy could sell refrigerators to Eskimos. He said, 'You ought to be in the chorus. You've got a beautiful voice, and you're here anyway. No pressure, but it's just a stand-up thing,' So I said okay. We got to the point after a few weeks where the rehearsals were going longer and longer. Dave was never good at cutting it off when he was supposed to. First, we were done at 9:00 and then 10:00, but pretty soon it was 11:00, 11:30, 12:00. We had an old Volvo station wagon, and we packed it with sleeping bags and food for dinner. We'd rehearse until nine o'clock, and then we'd tell Dave, "No more kid stuff.' We parked the car on the lawn right next to the stage, and the girls would go to sleep in the car.

"About a week before opening night, the guy who was playing the Russian constable got a real job in Hollywood. Dave tapped me on the shoulder and said, 'We've got to fit you for a costume.' I went from Jewish to Russian overnight. I was in this big Army costume with heavy boots. The problem was I wore glasses. Dave said, 'You can't wear those eyeglasses. You've got to take those off.'

"'I won't be able to find the stage, Dave, and I don't wear contacts.'

"Then I hear Wally Flynn, a local eye doctor who was playing a rabbi say, 'Would a pair of little wire spectacles work if I could get the right prescription done in a hurry?'

"'Sure,' said Dave. 'That's what they wore in those days.'

"So the next day I was down at Wally Flynn's office, and he was fitting me for the glasses. It took two tries to get it right and everything was fine which brings me to my Borgquist story. It was during the third performance. I had my lines down pat."

"You didn't have a whole lot," said Barb.

"No, but they were important lines because they showed the audience that the Russians were about to kick the Jews out of their village. There's this scene early in the play. It's the first time I meet Tevye on stage. I'm strolling down the street, and when I reach him, he says, 'Good evening, Your Honor,' and I reply, "Good evening, Reb Tevye." He responds, and when it's time for my next line, I draw a complete blank. I have total stage fright, but Warren never missed a beat. He looked me in the eye and started talking into my speech, and I picked it right up. Dave knew, but no one else. Later back stage, I hugged him and said, 'Thank you, thank you.' Unflappable is the word I would use to describe Warren Borgquist."

Almost everyone I interviewed had something to say about Warren Borgquist in *Fiddler on the Roof.* Patty Patton, who would eventually be his nurse, remembered seeing the play. "It was the second or third night of the show," sad Patty. "In the bedroom scene, he flashed the audience, so he bought new underwear, and he took it to his mother. He had her sew up the fly, so he wouldn't flash anyone after that."

His buddy from medical school, Jim Makol, said, "One day I heard Warren was going to appear in this play. I had no idea he could sing. My wife and I drove up from Sacramento to see him perform. The theater was outside, and we nearly froze to death, but I must say, I was impressed with his ability."

"There's one special thing I remember," said Monique. "One of our wonderful patients for many, many years was an elderly man who was dying. He said, 'I'm not going until I see Warren in the play.' We were going to get him a front row seat and help him get to the performance, but he was too ill. He was at the old Sierra Hospital in the section they'd turned into a convalescent unit. There was this big room with a fireplace, and Warren arranged for the whole cast to come in costume and perform some of the songs for him. It was unbelievable."

Sometimes when looking at a man's life, a theme emerges, a comet tail trailing in his wake. Warren Borgquist's theme was family. Leaping into theater and music, he landed squarely in a role that fit his sense of family as neatly as the yarmulke on his slowly balding head. There was intention behind the leap, despite the considerable doubt of others. Just like the MJC counselor who thought Warren was not doctor material, many thought he was not cut out for musical theater, but they did not take into account the power of the plugger, nor did they see the underscore on the adjective of his professional title: *family* doctor.

"It was interesting to see him relate on a whole different plane," said Dave Purdy. "He was very good at using his personal skills to become part of the cast."

"Warren was really the father of the whole cast of eighty," said Barbara Gleason.

When Dr. Warren Borgquist embodied the role of Tevye, he revealed a large part of himself to the community. BZ Smith summed it up when she said, "I think the whole town fell in love with him in a completely different way when they saw him as Tevye."

"He did a great job," said Judy, who went to every performance. "I remember when I saw him after the first performance, I was just sobbing, mostly out of relief. He was hugging me, and I was sobbing because it wasn't as embarrassing as I thought it would be. He loved the whole experience. He loved being the Papa. He took food to the cast. He built the cart that he pulled as the milkman—got wheels from a foundry and built it. We had the cast party at our house after closing night. Warren liked the fact that our house was not fancy and people felt comfortable here. He loved having everybody here. He liked being the star. He loved being the Papa," said Judy. "That's who he was at the core."

# *Chapter 13*

# CONSIDERABLE ATTENTION

"If you are careful," Garp wrote,
"if you use good ingredients,
and you don't take any shortcuts,
then you can usually cook something very good.

-John Irving, *The World According to Garp*

Over and over on the memory cards and during interviews and casual encounters, people mentioned seeing Warren as the Papa in *Fiddler on the Roof*. The years from 1977 through the early '80s teemed for the man who identified with Tevye, the milkman who addresses God when his daughters get minds of their own and his little village no longer feels safe. In real life, Warren was juggling as many variables as the character he had played. He moved his practice from Mono Way to Forest Road near Community Hospital; the Birth Center opened at the old Sierra Hospital; and he had a house full of teenagers, including an exchange student from Switzerland. Warren was a family doctor, and for him the adjective "family" preceding "doctor" signified more than basic grammatical order. The order reflected his priorities, which had shifted since his first moments as a young parent. As his family grew, both in size and maturity, the attention he gave to them also grew exponentially.

Like Tevye, in *Fiddler on the Roof*, Warren had to figure out how to parent teenagers. Dave Purdy's story of Scott's experimentation with alcohol in the absence of parental supervision is not novel. But as the eldest child in the Judy and Warren Borgquist household, Scott's caper was the first time Warren dealt with teen-age foolishness. As reported by both Scott and Dave, Warren had an easy-going approach, and he trusted the power of natural consequence. Another incident with Scott turned out to be more of a lesson for Warren than for the teen he helped parent.

"Warren always had a motorcycle," said Judy, who had already told several motorcycle stories, including one about a freezing nighttime ride from Bear Valley after Warren was summoned to a birth. But this story involved a ride with his stepson that changed his affinity for this mode of transportation. "One time when Scott was a teen," continued Judy, "he and Warren were riding on Racetrack Road, and a car pushed them off the road toward a barbed wire fence. Warren lost control momentarily and then managed to lay the motorcycle down. He was scared, and that was the end of that. No more motorcycles."

"The advantage of being the oldest," said Scott, "was that mine was the first trip." He was referring to a practice Judy and Warren initiated with Scott and continued with the other children and eventually the grandkids: a trip somewhere in the world to expand their horizons beyond Tuolumne County. "We took my trip shortly after I graduated high school," said Scott. "First, we went to visit Warren's sister Karma in Hawaii. You can drink at 18 in Hawaii."

"Never mind that you were only 17," interrupted Judy, "but who was counting?"

"Close enough," said Scott. "I remember being slightly hung over flying to Australia.

Then we continued to Alice Springs with barely a stop, so it felt like forever." A few quick calculations confirmed that this trip took place in 1978, which meant Warren was likely newly sober. I wondered what he thought about Scott's imbibing alcohol. Given reports of his particular tolerance of others drinking, including Scott's early experimentation with liquor, I concluded that he might have merely maintained a watchful eye.

"We went to Alice Springs because the story was that my grandfather—mom's dad— had been stationed there. The whole story was that he and his platoon had traded a tank to get drinks." This was Judy's father who she reported drank to assuage unhappiness. "I remember waking up in Alice Springs and being out of it and walking down the street and seeing the aboriginal people and drunks, and that was kind of crazy, but it was really fun going out to Ayers Rock. Driving through the outback was pretty neat and then up the Gold Coast on the east side of Australia was spectacular. I remember having Passion Fruit Pavlova …"

"Yes," said Judy, clapping gleefully. "I was just thinking about that." The memory of the decadent meringue dessert clearly thrilled her.

"And we met someone who took us to a club in Cairns—a casino, where we won sixty dollars, and I got drunk off my rear-end. You really let me drink a lot on that trip," said Scott to Judy with a chiding tone, and we all laughed, having dropped into the merry abandon of a far-away adventure.

"He was mature for his age," Judy said by way of excuse.

"We went to Green Island," continued Scott, "and snorkeled in the Great Barrier Reef. After Australia, we flew to Christ Church, New Zealand and did the Shotover River. The guide drove up the river really fast and almost ran into the rocks. There was a bungee-jump too, which I wouldn't do. We went fishing, and I caught rainbow trout, and that was a lot of fun. I was collecting beer bottles through that whole trip and had quite a few by the end."

"Yeah, we had two suitcases," said Judy, chiding good-naturedly as she recalled the long ago trip with her first born. "But you forgot our last stop," added Judy, just as I noticed that Warren was absent from much of the recollection.

"Right, we stopped in Fiji. I remember when we landed and got into a taxi, and we drove what seemed like forever. I was getting my pocket knife ready."

"We thought the driver was going to kidnap us," said Judy, with a hint of serious anxiety.

"But suddenly, there we were at the Regent Hotel, right on the water. It was really beautiful. And I said that was where I was going to get married. I kind of failed you on that one, honey," said Scott, patting his

wife Cyndie's thigh. As Judy and Scott enjoyed recalling this adventure, their spouses momentarily faded to supporting roles. Cyndie and Warren were essential in their lives but not central to this story. Clearly, Warren had not failed Scott by taking part in the trip—filled as it was with a view of an exotic world far away from Tuolumne County. "That was a great trip," said Scott, "It really got my travel bug going."

Nicolas Milliet barely spoke English when he came to live with the Borgquists as an exchange student from Switzerland through the American Field Services (AFS). By the time I spoke with him on Skype more than thirty years later, he spoke not only French and English but also German and Spanish. I needn't have worried about understanding his stories about living with the Borgquists, for his English was as clear as the picture of him on my computer screen, speaking from his dining room in Nice, France.

"I was living with another family at first, and things didn't go well," said Nicolas. "They lived out of town, and they weren't interesting, so it was difficult for me. I stayed maybe two months with these people, but they wanted me to change families. A lady in Sonora said she knew a family, and I could have a dinner with them. She didn't say anything else, just 'Have dinner. Get to know each other.' These guys were Warren and Judy, and I went to their little house for dinner, and I never left. There was no, 'OK, nice meeting you, Nicolas. Let us talk it over, and we'll call you in two days.' It was just straightforward. You're staying with us."

Judy remembers it a little differently. "Scott had just gone to college, and Jennifer was a junior. AFS contacted us to see if we'd take a student. We said we were too busy, but we'd be liaisons for students who had problems. We agreed that they could call us or we'd have them over for dinner once a month and be their welfare check. We got a call from someone in charge saying Nicolas was going to come to dinner because he was unhappy, and he wanted to talk. I think it was the first of September, and he'd been here since July. So I answered the door, and there he was with his bags. He was not going back. So it was a bit of a controversy because his host family was upset. It was the year that Mork and Mindy came on television, and these people ate dinner in front of the television. It wasn't intellectual enough for Nicolas, so he wasn't going back. We said we'd take him. He played the dang piano all the time—jazz piano—and Jennifer would yell at him to stop."

"I was barely 17," said Nicolas. "It was 1978, and there was no Skype. Today, if you travel overseas, you see the same brand names in the stores as you do at home. Things were completely different then. I think there was only one person in Sonora who could speak French. It wasn't easy because I'm not an outgoing guy. I wasn't a soccer or football hero. I tried football. I think I played fifteen seconds before being knocked down on the field, and that was the end of my football career. As a result, I spent a lot of time with Warren, Judy, and Jennifer."

"My first impression of Warren was that he was very young. I was 17, and he must've been 33. The guy already had children, divorced, and was a doctor, so he was young when everything happened in his life. I think his first son was born when he was 20. He got out of medical school when he was 24. He did an internship in Panama, and suddenly he was in Sonora doing lots of things. Nowadays, you couldn't be a gynecologist, GP, surgeon, emergency room physician, all at the same time. It would be impossible, but those patients—they had the same diseases and the same problems as they do now, so he had a lot of responsibility."

"Judy and Warren were half a generation away from me—not the same age as my parents or my classmates or friends, more like a big brother and sister, although Warren introduced me as his son—just as he spoke of his daughter Jennifer, who was not really his daughter. Scott was in junior college. Warren's two younger kids were still coming only on the weekends or during vacation. I remember going to Watsonville to get them. Actually, we flew down there with a friend of Warren's. That was very cool. We'd fly down and then hop in a car to go get them. Warren and his ex-wife didn't communicate, so we'd immediately fly back to Sonora. People didn't divorce in my family, and all of a sudden I was thrown in with a couple and children who lived with their other parent. Everything was so different: the country, the culture, the food. And our relationship was different. Not really father and son. He was kind of my mentor and definitely a very important person in my life, no doubt about that."

A picture of Warren and Nicolas taken during his year in California reveals something like a big-brother relationship. Both guys are bespectacled—Nicolas in smallish wire-rimmed glasses and Warren in the huge owlish frames that were popular at the time. Warren has a full, dense black beard and a deeply receding hairline though he was not yet bald. Nicolas' dark hair is close cropped with a slight feathering across his forehead. Both are wearing polo shirts—Warren's is burgundy, navy, and white striped, Nicolas' is red. They are both in shorts. Nicolas is holding a gray long-haired cat around the shoulders with its back legs dangling, and Warren has hold of the tip of the cat's tail. Neither is smiling but there appears to be mischief afoot. The most striking thing about the photo is that Nicolas had not changed much in the thirty-year interim. The man I faced on Skype was smooth skinned and handsome like the teen. The only sign of aging was a touch of gray in his hair.

"We would hang out in his shop. He'd do carpentry work, and we'd talk. I took up English only one year before coming there, so I would ask him about idiomatic expressions and American slang. He was very good at answering. He was always remodeling the house, a never-ending process. We used to go jogging together. One day he said, 'Next Sunday, we're doing a 10K race.' I'd never run in my life, except maybe 100 meters in high school, but I took part, and I finished. So our main activities were jogging in the morning on the ditch and doing carpentry work in the shop. Maybe you've heard the story about old farts," said Nicolas.

"No," I said, "tell me."

"At first I didn't understand much, just a few words and phrases like, 'running' or 'working tonight.' Warren used to say, 'You know, Nicolas, when you're an old fart like me, you'll do this or you'll do that.' So a few months after I got there, I was invited to the Soroptimist Club to talk about Switzerland and do a slideshow. The ladies were very friendly, and after my presentation, the leader asked, 'Do you have any questions for Nicolas Milliet?' And one of the ladies said, 'What do you want to do later on in life?' So I said, 'When I'm an old fart ...' and there was this big silence and puzzled faces staring at me. The next evening, I asked Warren, 'What does fart actually mean?' So it's a family joke. Now that I'm actually getting old, when Judy telephones, she says, 'How are you doing, old fart?'

"I read the books Warren was reading. He gave them to me. I remember he was reading this book about flower power and hippies. He used to work near the Haight-Ashbury, and he'd see all these naked hippies, zonked on LSD with flowers in their hair coming for treatment, so he was reading this book about illicit drugs. I'd read books from the 19th century in New England and now this. One book he really liked was *The World According to Garp,* and I read that."

"What did you learn about the world according to Warren?' I asked.

"We'd speak about—what's his name? Murphy's Law. In his office, he had a poster about Murphy's Law. We'd go to this place in San Francisco to buy funny posters because he liked to put them on the ceiling. I asked, 'Why do you put them on the ceiling?' and he said, 'The patient is lying on the examination bed. I want him to have something to read.'"

"Did you go to the hospital with him or to his medical practice?"

"Yes, he showed me his office. And one day he said, 'Do you want to see a delivery?' I was very young, but I said, 'Yes,' so one time, he woke me up at four, and he said, 'Nicolas this is the day.' He had asked this lady who had four or five children if it was OK. He didn't choose a difficult case. I watched him deliver the baby, and it was just amazing. I remember he was very emotional, and I thought this was special, you know? But other than that we didn't talk that much about medicine back then. It was later when I saw him on subsequent trips.

"One week before I left—I had been at Warren and Judy's for a year— he came to my room one morning. He was very nervous, and he said, 'Nicolas I have to tell you something. I'm an alcoholic.' I was this very naive 18 year-old boy, so I said, 'Why don't you explain this to me.' And he said, "Once I start drinking, I drink myself to unconsciousness.' He said he had been doing this frequently at night, and so he couldn't drink any more. I said, 'I don't care. It doesn't make a difference to me.' Then Nicolas veered to a question. "Did you know the Borgquists cry at good-byes? They don't like to say good-bye. The first time I cried when I left someone was when I left the Borgquist house."

"In December of Jennifer's senior year," said Judy, "Dave and Ellen were in England. Sarah was a baby, and they asked Jennifer to come be their nanny, so she left her mother," said Judy, imitating a dejected sob. "Jennifer and I are very close, but she went off to another country. I didn't get to see her graduate from high school because she didn't get back until after that."

"I took a test and got out of high school early," said Jennifer. "My dad and Ellen were on sabbatical, traveling around the world, and they had reached England, so I went to help with Sarah. My mom wasn't happy, but then she and Warren came, and we did my trip to France, Italy, and the Netherlands, and I got to stay with our exchange student Nicolas in Switzerland. It was fabulous to travel like that."

Gregory Borgquist had traveled to and from his mother's and his father's homes since he was 6 years old, but that ended during his teen years. "My mom told me that when I turned 16, I could go live with my dad," said Greg. "So the day I turned 16, I headed to Sonora, and I never went back to my mom's house."

The stories Judy, Nancy, and others had told about the impulsivity of the blond child magnified when he hit his teen years. Greg's behavior wasn't always something Warren could handle. His sister Karma recalled him "losing it" with Greg when he was about 15. "We were on vacation at Strawberry. The two of them were outside, and we were all inside the cabin watching Warren rage at poor Greg, who was trying to be courageous, though he was crying. I don't know what it was that set Warren off."

"Special needs children, like Greg, don't understand cause and effect, said Marjorie Borgquist. "All teenagers suffer from having a powerful brain with faulty brakes, but it's worse in these kids. My son Joaquin had some of those issues. The frustration you feel with that kind of kid can drive you crazy."

Betty Sinclair, one of the Borgquist's neighbors, told a story about Greg not understanding cause and effect. "It was winter time, and my husband Denny and I were going out to dinner. We headed down the hill past the Borgquists, and suddenly Denny backed up, saying, 'Oh, my god, their house is going to catch on fire.' There was a tin bucket sitting beside the wooden support post to the carport and flames were shooting out of it. Denny ran up to the front door and told Warren. It turned out Greg, who was in high school at the time, had taken out the can with ashes from the fireplace and put it right by that post."

"After Greg came to live with us," said Judy, "he was home alone until we returned from work, and that was not the best thing. Everything came to a head during his senior year," said Judy. "By that time, he was nineteen because he'd been held back a year, so he was two years older than most of the kids in his class. He wasn't doing well in school. He was ditching and would come home and get the notices out of the mailbox before we got home. Finally the principal called and said, 'This isn't working.'"

"When I got in trouble at Sonora High School," said Greg, "the counselor took out all the notes I had written. Judy couldn't tell the difference between my handwriting and my dad's. I could copy it so well. I'd steal one of his prescription pads to write the note, so it looked official, and I wouldn't be questioned. That was one of my ploys. No one is going to bother a busy doctor."

"We also realized Greg was smoking dope," said Judy, "so we talked to him. 'These are the rules in our house. You can't live here if you are going to ditch school, flunk out, and smoke dope. We love having you here, but this is not going to work unless you follow the rules.' He said he would comply, but he didn't. Then he said, 'I'm going to join the Army.'"

"I know Warren could get frustrated with Greg," said Marjorie, "but depending on who you talk to, he was also guilty of giving him another chance more often than not. He enabled Greg ridiculously. Warren was like one of those punching clowns that bounces back. It was the ultimate in parental forgiveness, which was totally different from the standard he held for everyone else. He used to get this look in his eye, didn't he?" said Marjorie to Karma. "It was like hold it. I expect you to do this." Marjorie had described Warren behaving this way during family trips to Nebraska, but with Greg, it seemed his standards were wobbly. "Warren held all of us to the standard he held for himself," emphasized Marjorie, "Whether or not it could happen, he held the standard. But it was difficult with Greg, and he didn't have much sway over Mimi when she was younger either. He had more over Jennifer, but Jennifer was born wonderful."

"I had this metatarsal deformity," said Jennifer, "so when I was 18, I had surgery on my foot. Warren said, 'Just do the surgery, and it will be all better.' But it wasn't. I had to go for a second surgery when I was in college. I had just gotten the cast off following that surgery and was waiting for the doctor. The x-rays were sitting there. I already had them up on the light when the doctor came in, and I was in tears because I could see it was not right. 'Why are you crying?' asked the doctor. 'You don't know how to read an x-ray.' 'Yes, I do.' I said. 'I'm a doctor's daughter.' He wanted to schedule another surgery, so I went home terribly depressed. I was supposed to start a cool job at an organic coffee house in Santa Barbara. When I talked to my friends at the coffee house, they said, 'There are other things you can do.' My boyfriend's ex-girlfriend was very smart about alternative medicine, and she started working on my foot and basically fixed it.

I believe that was the first time Warren saw that Western medicine wasn't necessarily the be-all-end-all. He always wanted to grapple with and exchange ideas. The fact that I was showing him more options fit with his learning style. He didn't give medication that wasn't needed, and he tried to find other alternatives to pharmaceuticals. He took the time to figure out things, and sometimes that scared people. He was compassionate too. I could ask questions and not necessarily doctor questions but just grown-up questions. That's how it was. My friends had their own relationships with him. All my friends would hang out with him when they came through the house."

Kris Danz Scott, Jennifer's friend, talked about communication in the Borgquist household. "As teenagers growing up, they were the parents you could talk to when you were having trouble with your own parents. They were so understanding. I'm the fifth of six kids, so my parents had lost their enthusiasm for decorating kids' rooms by the time it came to me. I wanted shutters on my bedroom window in the worst way. My mom ordered them from J.C. Penny—unfinished because they were cheaper—and we were going to paint them, but they sat there for a really long time, and finally Warren said, 'Bring them over.' And he spray-painted them. He and Judy always looked after me like that."

"Warren was the one who convinced the high school that sex education needed to be part of the senior Health and Safety class," said Jennifer. "It was an all encompassing class where we learned how to brush our teeth and drive a car. He thought we needed to learn about birth control, so he came to the high school to give the sex ed lectures," said Jennifer. "That was a bit difficult. Having me in the room actually made my classmates ask fewer questions. After he left, they'd asked me their questions because they knew I was up on birth control and reproductive health. Later, I applied to be the birth control advisor at the local high school in Santa Barbara. While I was waiting to hear if I got the job,

I actually had a dream that I was Margaret Sanger," said the animated woman.

"Jennifer and I became friends in high school," said Dolora Dossi. "Our fun had to do with boys and getting stoned and going down to the river and swimming naked. We were all about crystals and Birkenstocks. I didn't hang out at the Borgquist home. Well, I did, but more so when we were in college. We would swim in the pool and have a dinner around the table. When you're younger, some friends have families who socialize well. You know an evening at their house is going to be full of food and stories and wine, and the Borgquists was one of those places—one where the young people felt like they could be seen and heard and no subject was off the table. It was very different from my family. At the Borgquists', kids brought up sex and drugs. We would openly discuss it all, so that was a strange shift for me. I didn't know there were parents like that. I also watched the Borgquist and the Purdy clan when Sarah was born as everyone mingled, taking care of Ellen and Sarah. It was an interesting way to be with your ex—to combine families—and that was unusual for the times. But it made sense to me. I thought it was beautiful to see their interaction beyond the hurt feelings and lingering wounds."

"I came to live with my father when I was 16," said Mimi, "the summer before my junior year of high school. There was some stuff going on with my stepfather, and I needed to leave. I never went back to my mom's after that. Judy and my dad wanted people to express themselves. Judy was huge on talking, and my mom didn't raise me that way. Her version was: 'You're a child. You're to be seen and not heard.' So when I got to my dad's, I would act out and do things that I couldn't or wouldn't do at my mom's. I thank Judy every day that she got me to communicate and not be afraid of my feelings."

"It sounds like you could throw a fit every now and then at your dad's, and you knew you would still be loved," I said, speculating about Warren's and Judy's permissive style of parenting.

"Yes, exactly. If I had a fit, it wasn't the end of the world. Also they encouraged us to talk and to make our own decisions. When I was ready to have sex—I was 17 or 18—I went to my dad and said, 'I'm ready to try this.' That was the whole point of his sex talks. He wanted us to feel comfortable coming to him. He wanted us to know that we needed to take precautions and protect ourselves. For me, it was easier to talk to my dad than my mom. He had a non-judgmental persona. His dad was hard on him when he was growing up and a poor communicator, so my dad figured that part out for himself.

"When I was a senior in high school," said Mimi, "I was dating an older guy who was out of high school. Judy and Warren didn't want me to date him. My dad said he wasn't a good influence, but I was 18, so I said, 'Screw you. I'm moving out.' I moved in with the guy before I graduated. Being a parent myself now, I know Dad was trying to lead me in the right direction, but he really had a hard time being stern. It was hard for him to put his foot down. When he did, we'd go, 'You're kidding, right Dad?' because he was so laid back. On the flip side, he'd say, 'You guys have to learn from your mistakes.'

"When I graduated high school, they threw a party for me at the house, so they kind of accepted my boyfriend. They weren't thrilled with him, but they kind of accepted him. It turned out that they were right. Our relationship was touch and go. He was bad for me, but I was afraid to go home because I thought they'd say, 'I told you so.' When I was 20, I went home and said, 'I can't do this. He's verbally abusive,' and of course they opened their arms. They didn't judge or even say 'We told you so.' They just welcomed me back."

"Judy was always outspoken. For a long time, she and I did not get along. I always thought she didn't let my dad have an opinion on anything, and it was really hard for me. I didn't find out how Dad and Judy's relationship really worked until I took my trip with them when I was 21. Because I'd moved out, they didn't offer the trip until I got my act together. We went to Spain and Portugal, and during that trip, I remember yelling at my dad saying, 'You never stand up to her. You never talk back or tell her what you think.' He then offered these words of wisdom. 'Mimi, I pick and choose what I think is important to fight about, and if I don't think it's a big deal, it's not worth my time and effort. She can have her way. But when it comes down to it, I speak up and hold my ground. Of course, two days later, I saw him speak up. I didn't live with my dad until I was 16. I had a weekend relationship with him, so

I didn't really understand his relationship with Judy. Judy and I got our differences figured out on that trip too. It was a huge transformation for all of us."

Judy admitted to struggles and biases in dealing with Warren's kids. "Greg's first girlfriend was my friend Madeline Sharp's daughter," said Judy. "There is an infamous family story about how I made Mimi's boyfriend get out of a family picture, but I let Greg's girlfriend stay." Dealing with Greg was an effort for Judy from their first encounter when he was in first grade. She wanted him to succeed, but as Marjorie noted, hopes for kids like him are fraught with frustration.

"Greg did very well in the Army," said Judy. "We were so proud of him. He was going to get $25,000 for college. He was in for two years, and the second year he was in Korea, and then finally, he was coming home. We were at SFO waiting for him when we got a call to go to the white courtesy telephone. An Army officer was on the line, and he said, 'Your son is not coming home. He is going directly to federal prison in Leavenworth, Kansas.' He sold drugs," said Judy, glumly recalling the call. "The officer on the phone said, 'If you want to see him, you can have ten minutes with him if you get to the Oakland airport where we're touching down. So we raced to Oakland Airport and had ten minutes with Greg before he went to Kansas."

"I was in South Korea," said Greg, "counting down the days—three hundred sixty-three and wake up, three hundred sixty-two and wake up. Then I woke up and tomorrow was the day. I was getting out of there. There was a guy in my company who had failed a urine drug test. He wanted out of the Army, so he became what the military called a registered informant. He had to give the criminal investigation division of the Army three people they could bust. Ronald Reagan had been in the White House for five years, and Nancy Reagan was going hard with 'Just say no to drugs.' I had partied with this guy earlier in my tour, and he'd tried to get me to buy some illegal drugs off base, but I told him no. I was on track. I was totally on track. Long story short, I succumbed to peer pressure. This guy came to see me about eighteen hours before I was going to get on the airplane for home. I mean, I was checked out of the Army. I was wearing civilian clothes. My hair was past my ears. I was going home. But my roommates persuaded me to go off base and come back with some speed. We called it 'go' or 'crank.' Those MPs had a party when I came back. There were like twelve guys, and they used me like a training exercise. I had purple indentations, purple bruises, where the muzzle of .38 slammed into me. I had a weak constitution, and I succumbed to peer pressure. I knew better. I didn't want to do it, but I did. That's a recipe for disaster: Doing something you don't really want to do."

"He lost his scholarship," said Judy, "and got a bad conduct discharge. We offered to pay for a lawyer to try to get the charge reduced, but he wouldn't do it. Of course, we visited him in Kansas. If you ask the other kids," said Judy, "or even if you asked Warren—Greg got three-fourths of our time, attention, and money."

# *Chapter 14*

## CHUCK & TODD

> Whenever a doctor expressed an interest in setting up shop,
> we'd have them to dinner.
>
> —Deborah Lee Luskin, *The Country Doctor Revisited*

Walking on a trail near Columbia College one morning, I ran into Dr. Chuck Waldman, who was the first family physician to come to the county following Warren. I introduced myself, and explained my project. "Could we meet sometime to talk about Warren and general practice back when you first arrived in the county?" I asked. We exchanged contact information, and a week later I was headed down the Waldman's driveway toward a rustic two-story country home set far off the main road in a sun-dappled glen of oaks, mountain mahogany, and manzanita. Chuck met me in the driveway and escorted me through a distinctive assembly of flowerbeds filled with columbine, poppies, and herbs, to a covered porch that wrapped around his home. "How do you manage to keep the deer out of this lovely garden?" I asked.

"They'll find it come fall when their usual fare grows sparse. They're grazing creatures, so we try to plant things at various levels to keep them from taking all of one variety of plant during a pass through the yard."

We stepped into Chuck's studio, where piles of frames were stacked against the walls and a lovely array of his paintings hung—scenes from the streets of Sonora and Columbia as well as the mountains and European lanes. Chuck was a plein air painter who sometimes stood on a corner in downtown Sonora early in the morning when the light shined obliquely down Washington Street. His easel rested before a bank of windows looking out on the woods behind the house. Chuck introduced me to his wife Janet and their Great Dane. While Janet went to get tea, we took seats in comfortable chairs around a coffee table. Chuck explained that Janet had recently had carotid artery surgery and was still recovering which led to a discussion that ambled through opinions about the advances and limitations of modern medicine. Then Chuck made an intriguing statement: "It might be the end of the golden way."

Janet returned at that moment and served the tea while I studied the couple. They shared a calm demeanor and rarefied country warmth. I recalled Chris Mills describing Chuck as humble. I could see humility in both Chuck and Janet in the modest, unassuming sense of the word.

Once Janet had served the tea, I said, "I love that phrase: 'the golden way.'"

"We were lucky to have had that for a number of years," said Chuck. "You kind of assume it's going to last forever."

"Yes, but nothing lasts forever," I said, and Chuck nodded, murmuring agreement. "I know Warren did a lot to encourage people to come here," I said, "and the other day, when we met on the trail, you spoke to that."

"Warren was one of the first young docs in Sonora. When he came back to Tuolumne County, all the others were old: Dr. George Farris, Dr. Gillis, and Dr. Hutchinson. Warren was looking for younger folks to come up here. Family practice was a new thing, and the training programs were new too—just spittin' folks like myself out. It started in late '60s-early '70s, a resurgence of family practice, getting GPs a little more training. Warren didn't have that; he came in before, so he slipped through and missed that stuff, but he got training, luckily, from doctors like Farris and Hutchinson. Dr. Bob Thompson was a mentor of his. When we first visited Sonora, I still had a year of residency to finish, and we were living in Merced. I was doing a UC Davis family practice residency at the hospital there. They wanted us to get out at the beginning of our last year to find a mentor to work with, to see what was happening outside academia, even though Merced wasn't really academia. It was a county hospital, so we were seeing and doing things that were much more intense than we would be doing once we were on our own establishing practices.

"I'd been to school at Davis, did an internship in Bakersfield, and then spent two years in Merced, and I couldn't stand the valley fog anymore. So we made a big trek through Northern California, Oregon, Idaho looking for a place to land. After making the trip, we knew we were not ready to leave California, nor did we want to be too rural. I wanted to have some colleagues. We met docs in places like Quincy and Hayfork who were *it*, and we met Warren who was kind of *it* too. There really wasn't much back-up for him. He had to turn his patients over to doctors who were doing 1940s-style medicine. He was desperate for help. So I came up here and took over his practice for a few weeks while he ran off on some trip."

"We stayed at his house," said Janet.

"He was so desperate to get someone that he bent over backwards to make us feel welcome. This felt rural enough to us. Tuolumne General was a nice little county hospital, and by that time, there were other doctors in town, specialists: Jim Wilson, Jim Hongola, Chris Mills, Ron Goldman.

"You guys were the young Turks," said Janet. "They were the nonreligious group," she added, laughing.

"Yeah, more like the young infidels," said Chuck, hitting the nomenclature a little harder. "So after residency, I came back, but first I wanted to build a house."

"Warren had that idea too," I said, struck by this similarity.

"He probably encouraged me in my foolish efforts, but I'd built a lot of stuff already, a lot more than Warren—some boats, a garage, and things like that. Warren was a great dreamer.

"Anyway, I worked a couple shifts a week at TGH and started building this house, and I'd occasionally cover for him while he was gone. Before we were done building this place, Warren said, 'I can't wait anymore.' So that fall, I decided I could do it. It was going to be easy. Finish the house, start a practice, no big deal. So we started the practice in October 1979, and it *was* a big deal. I basically had no time after that. I can see why he was so desperate for help. For the next twenty plus years, no time. It was just the two of us for a number of years ... sort of like

Huck Finn and Tom Sawyer.

"Then the Stolps came in the '80s. They stayed here with us for a few weeks until they found a place to live. That was partly Warren's influence—he'd been good to us when we arrived, but it was also how we were. There were a lot of pay-it-forwards. When anybody new came to town, we wanted to encourage them."

"We had Steve Jensen here too," said Janet, referring to a podiatrist who had also been here since the early eighties.

"We needed someone interested in sports medicine," said Chuck, adding to Janet's comment about Steve Jensen. "Warren had been the Sonora High team doctor, and I inherited that job from him. Warren started great projects, but someone had to finish them." Chuck laughed gently. "The job involved organizing free physicals for high school athletes and going to all the games, so when Steve Jensen showed up, I thought, Oh, good. Someone who actually knows about sports injuries. Steve was a good athlete and very interested in injury prevention.

"For quite a while, Warren, Todd, and I shared call. We were like full service family practice because we did OB. One time, Warren went on one of those Christmas getaways out of the country. I was just a few years into practice, and we had sixteen deliveries in a week, and most of them were Warren's. I was on call for all those new babies, all those moms, plus ICU and assisting in surgery.

"So much learning takes place after you get out of school, especially back in the days when it was General Practice. Those guys finished medical school, took Part One of the national boards, did their internship, and then took the clinical part of the boards. That got them their license, and they started practicing medicine. Many ended up in the military —WWII or Korea and even Vietnam to some degree. They got more experience in the military, and when they got out of the service, they were doing obstetrics and surgery—gall bladders and stuff like that— because they'd been in the field hospitals doing everything. Maybe they shouldn't have, but they did. A lot of medicine isn't trauma though. It's just general medicine."

"But then there was all this fragmentation in the '50s and early '60s as medicine went from general to specialization," said Chuck. "You had to see your baby doctor, your OB, your gynecologist, your skin doctor, your allergist. It was just ridiculous. No one was overseeing it all," said

Chuck, describing part of the rationale for creating the specialty of Family Practice. By beefing up the training programs to include a three-year residency, the family physician gained credibility. Moreover, as Chuck went on to explain, their training let them weave a lot of the pieces together in a way that didn't happen in the specialization practices. "In Family Practice training, we learned to do pediatrics, obstetrics, a lot of terminal medicine, and a lot of psychiatry that presents more like general medicine. A lot of it is behavioral medicine—for depression, anxiety, and disorders that people don't want to see a psychiatrist about because of the stigma with mental health. As it turns out, a lot of mental health is general medicine."

"What would a patient present with?" I asked.

"You name it," said Chuck. "Pains that won't go away. They'd come in and say, 'I've been to all these doctors, and my stomach still hurts.' Or 'I've been to the cardiologist. I've had a heart cath. But my heart still races. It's pounding out of my chest, and I feel like I'm going to die.' The problem is, they've been told what it isn't, but they don't know what it is. They're throwing symptoms at you like crazy, and you're trying to sort it out. What's real and what's emotional? Is this someone with cancer or Crohn's disease? Is this guy suffering from panic attacks? I think family practitioners are the best place to go because we see so much variety.

"I saw a lot of plain old depression—caused by grief or normal postpartum depression, before it was called that. We called it the baby blues. But it wasn't serious. Most of it was just seeing and talking to people. Being present—that's what was needed. That's the thing though, you can't talk to someone for ten minutes. It takes an hour minimum once a hurting person finds someone he can talk to because the floodgates open. And then there's the part about seeing the whole family. It's not just the person in front of you. There are generations—grandparents and so on. This is the first person asking for help. I think family practice is very good at identifying generational issues, especially mental health stuff."

"So can you talk about the issue of time?" I asked. "Because whenever Warren's name comes up, you hear about his time issues, and you've just described a reason why that could have been happening."

"I wasn't good at time either, but Warren was the worst or the best, depending on how you look at it."

"Exactly, because it takes time to sort out stuff, and you guys were willing to give the time."

"If your intent is to find out what's wrong with the person, there's no way to know unless you hear their story. They have no barcode on them that you can scan. Everybody thinks medicine is so simple. You can find out what's wrong on the Internet. People don't come in with a diagnosis; they come in with a fear and hurt and a story. And they aren't necessarily good at telling the story. They wander all over. They'll come in and tell you, 'I noticed this on February 1 and then on February 9, I had this, and then I thought it went away, and then it came back, and by then my blood pressure had dropped.' They don't give you a clinical story. They say, 'I don't feel well' or 'I can't sleep' or 'I'm sad' or 'I have headaches.' And you say, 'Tell me about it.' Sometimes nothing makes sense for weeks, for months, or even years because the story isn't finished. Because they don't know the story or aren't willing to tell it yet.

"There's a lot of that, and it takes a lot of time. Warren was good at it. I think Warren and I were kindred spirits there, and that's one of the reasons we moved here. I was already getting hounded during my residency for taking too long with people. There were the guys who were the stars, who were running people through. But that was in Merced, and there were language issues, cultural issues. I don't speak much Spanish. The patients didn't trust me. I was a white guy. So I was trying to break through that barrier and assure them that I wanted to help. I felt like I needed time to get through. Plus, I'm a slow thinker. I was decent—just slow. That's the way I am; I can't change it. I tried to keep up, stay on the schedule, but there were times when it was hopeless. I liked that about Warren. He was good at plugging along.

"We had breakfast meetings every week, and that was Warren's doing. Warren liked to be the leader of the club, unofficially, but it meant so much to him to bring us together. We met Thursday mornings at the Country Kitchen in Jamestown for years. We had to pick a day when no one was off. We'd talk about stuff and gossip about other crappy doctors and how good we were—boost ourselves up. We needed that. No agenda. Oh, sometimes there'd be an agenda when we talked about the call schedule. We'd rotate weekends. For a long time it was just Todd, Warren, and me. And then Erik Runte came. Eric was mostly at the Primary Care

Clinic at Tuolumne General. He was doing everything we did, plus he was doing all kinds of stuff beyond our skills. He was the only guy taking care of AIDS patients. No one else would see them.

"For a number of years—it seemed like very a long time, ten or fifteen years—there was just the four of us. There were so many fantastic things that Warren started and encouraged us to do, like taking house calls for hospice. I probably would not have done certain things if not for him. He liked to be the leader, liked to be in charge—the Papa. That's how he saw himself."

Todd Stolp was three months into retirement when I interviewed him. Actually, he was only retired from doctoring, for he was fully engaged in a project called Innovations Lab and Maker Space, which was coincidentally situated on the third floor of the closed Tuolumne General Hospital. Stolp was one of several private individuals who had partnered with the county Economic Development Authority to create a space and services for people to collaborate on and create projects related to science and technology. I'd followed stories about the opening of the lab in the newspaper, and I heard my grandson describe a field trip to the lab, but until Todd suggested we meet there, I did not know he was affiliated with the project.

I parked at the front of the hospital even though Todd had asked me to meet him at the back door. Months before, I'd visited TGH, peering through the locked glass doors into the lobby, trying to get a feel for the busy days when Warren, Chuck, and Todd too, as I would soon learn, had worked the Emergency Room. The dim, empty corridor was a dismal reminder of the changes that had taken place since that heyday. I took another peek through those front doors, and then made my way around the building to a door where I pushed a button that would summon Todd to let me in. I watched through a window as an elevator door opened, and a youthfully handsome man with grey hair stepped out. Todd unlocked the door and invited me in. We spent a moment talking about the old days, stepping briefly around orange caution cones and yellow tape to look down a few hallways on the first floor. I saw an area where I had once sat awaiting a sonogram for excruciating belly pain on my right side. I remember seeing Warren after he got the results.

"Mittleschmerz," said my doctor.

"What?" I asked.

"It's a German word for one-sided abdominal pain that sometimes accompanies ovulation. It translates, 'middle pain' because it happens midway through the menstrual cycle. Great word, isn't it?" he asked, with a broad grin, clearly enjoying this explanation of the pain that had plagued me regularly for about a year. "Just take ibuprofen. It'll go away with menopause," he concluded.

I smiled at the memory as Todd led me to the elevator. We ascended to the third floor, formerly the psych ward of the hospital, and weaved our way through rooms loaded with spiffy equipment—computers with 3-D printers and software to assist in gaming and application development. We went through an electronics lab and a metal and wood shop where a man was working on a prototype. When we reached a brightly lit conference room with a large table, Todd and I took seats. As was my custom, my first question was, "Tell me about the first time you met Warren."

"That's a funny tale," he said, his blue eyes flashing behind wire-rimmed glasses. "It was Easter break, and I was in my last year of family practice residency. It was time to start thinking about what comes after residency, so my wife and I took several weeks off to drive up and down the west coast in our old Volkswagen van."

"What year was that?" I asked.

"1983. We drove into Sonora—actually Martha drove in as I had fallen asleep in the back of the van—and I woke up in this delightful little town. We camped someplace, and the next morning I started asking around at TGH if anyone knew of a doctor interested in having a partner. And someone directed me to Jim Mosson. He was the new internist in town, working hard because that was the hottest new thing at the time. When I found Jim, he said, "I think my friend, Warren Borgquist, is looking for a partner. Why don't you give him a call?"

"I called Warren, and he said, 'Let's meet in the parking lot by Payless." The drugstore Todd mentioned, along with a market, was in a shopping center built in the late '70s, replacing what had been a horse pasture when Warren was a boy. "When I arrived and got out of the van, there was Tevye." The role was history by 1983, but that was exactly the point—Tevye would forever be part of Warren's history. "We introduced ourselves and shook hands, and then my wife came up and said, 'I have a hunch this is going to be a good relationship.' And we said, 'Why do you say that?' And she said, 'Well you both have your flies open.'" Martha had identified an auspicious sign for the first meeting of these two men, for openness is integral to forming a partnership.

"After we talked for a while, Warren said, 'I'd be interested. Maybe the way to do this would be for you to come work in the county and get a sense of the place. Then we can talk more about what arrangement you might be interested in.' So before Martha and I left town, I went back to the hospital and spoke to the hospital administrator at TGH. He explained that they had a contract for the emergency room with a group run by Ron Deckman—he later became quite well-known as a pediatrics emergency physician—and Deckman ended up being the one to hire me to join the group. In fact, they were short a couple of doctors and needed immediate help. I was in residency down in Ventura, so I would fly into the Bay Area and go to Ron's house to get his car to drive here to work a 24-hour cycle. I must've done that five times between March and June while I finished my residency.

"It was intense but a great way to get to know the medical system here. Each time I was up, I would stop by and get to know Warren and Judy a little bit better. I brought Martha one time too. So that's how it started. I worked in the emergency room for the first year and a half I was here, and about six months into that run, Warren and I worked out an arrangement where I would pay him to work in his office. He had some extra exam rooms, so that's how that came to be."

"Did you pay rent?" I asked, unclear how such an arrangement would work.

"You know how Warren was about business. I was the same way. So it was more like. 'How does this sound?' 'Oh, that sounds fine.' We never had a contract. We just talked it out, figured X amount of money and some details about staff and supplies. There wasn't a piece of paper between us. It was all done with a handshake."

"I imagine your styles differed. How did you complement each other?"

"For me, Warren was invaluable for all of the practical stuff—how to make decisions in this environment. I was fresh out of residency, so I often crossed the hallway to say, 'Could you take a look at this?' Or 'What do you think about this?'

Curious about what the younger doctor brought to the relationship, I prompted him. "When I was a fresh, new professional, those more senior in my department liked to talk to me about cutting-edge information I'd gleaned during graduate school. Did you offer that to Warren?"

"I imagine so, but then there's the other side of that. Did you see the movie *Doc Hollywood*?"

"Yeah," I said recalling the comedy with Michael J. Fox.

"Remember when the young doc starts going on about the kid having mitral valve regurgitation leading to cyanosis, and the old doc treats him with Coca-Cola because he recognizes that the kid has chewed some of his dad's tobacco. That was classic. Perhaps a little bit over the top, but there was some of that in my early days with Warren."

"What did you see as his strengths?" I asked, acknowledging Todd's respect for his senior partner.

"His honesty—absolute on-the-table honesty in all subjects in terms of dealing with emotions. Patients appreciated that. His generosity and caring for his patients. He was old school in that regard—described himself as a dinosaur. He would make house calls—care for folks in their home even though he didn't wave that flag. He just did it because he did it. That was certainly one of his biggest pluses. Our friendship is what led me to ask him and Judy to be godparents for my son."

Then Todd launched into a story about doctors and the people they serve. "One of my heroes is Sir William Osler, a guy in the late 1800s who really was the father of American clinical medicine. He talks extensively about the practice of medicine as it looked when I started in Tuolumne County and the vision that I think Warren had. One of the vignettes that Osler describes is the door of the primary care physician's office in a small town. He says you'll notice if you look closely that there is worn place at the top of the door from somebody knocking who is quite tall. That belongs to the husband, the head of the family, knocking in the middle of the night to reach the doctor to help someone in his household. If you look again, you'll see an area near the middle of the door. That's from the knock of an adolescent whose parents are ill, so they have sent him to come and get supplies in the middle of the night. Then there's another worn spot where someone in a wheel chair—someone who can't even stand—has knocked. That was the image of medicine we held—a story about the people's reliance upon that door. Our vision wasn't practical; it was idealistic."

Todd turned in another direction after relating this fable-like tale. "I'll never forget the celebration at the end of my residency," said Todd. "One of the big practice physicians in southern California had invited us to his farm, and he said, 'There's a change on the horizon. It's what they call managed care. It'll be a different world.'"

In 1984, when Todd joined Warren Borgquist and Chuck Waldman as a family physician serving Tuolumne County, the three men were focusing on a shared conviction: when a patient knocked upon their door, they would be there to give the care that was needed. Each doctor added his own particular style to his approach. Chuck was thoughtful, gentle, and regarded as "humble" by colleagues and patients; Todd was effective, efficient, and described as "brilliant" by many. The most frequent word used to describe Warren was "compassionate."

Dr. Warren Borgquist welcomed physicians to the community who had something he didn't have, and something he apparently wanted— Board Certification in the specialty of Family Practice. I remember seeing him at the gym most mornings, walking on the treadmill with his Walkman. I knew he was studying for his Boards by listening to lectures on audiocassettes because we had talked about this method of study. At the time, I was working with learning disabled adults, helping them identify their learning styles and developing strategies by which they could deal with challenging college material. During one of my annual appointments with Warren, we talked at length about my work. I was delighted with his interest. After talking with Dr. Chuck Waldman, I saw how this kind of interest was a feature of family practice doctoring—that is, eliciting the whole story about a patient. During that appointment with Warren, he told me about using the Walkman to make the best use of his time while preparing for the Board examination. I remarked that he must be a good auditory learner, and he agreed that he was. I was more interested in his methods of study than I was in what and why he was studying. To glean more understanding about Board Certification,

I asked my friend, Dr. Ken Renwick, a Family Practice physician, "Why do you think Warren wanted to get Board Certified after fifteen years in practice?"

"GPs weren't thought of as quality physicians," said Ken. "A GP did an internship and then hung up a shingle and started treating patients. That was the pathway Warren took, and it actually closed shortly after he opened his practice. There was an initiative in the late '60s to improve the status and skills of GPs by establishing the specialty of Family Practice. That pathway wasn't even available to him because he was training as the requirements for the specialty were being developed. But he board certified after being in practice for many years, and it was a big deal—to go through all the bells and whistles and pass this extremely comprehensive exam—because by the time he took the exam, he was competing with people who had training he didn't get."

Chuck said Warren had learned a lot on the job from the older doctors who were still practicing when he arrived, and Todd talked about how he had learned from Warren. But the practical experience one gets on the job—the Coca Cola trick of the *Doc Hollywood* movie—is not what a comprehensive examination assesses, so Warren had to put in hours studying to learn what younger docs just coming out of their residencies knew. What I had seen as his patient, however, was my doctor relating to my work and me by sharing a tidbit about how he studied. I simply enjoyed his interest in me—his method of practicing family medicine—not realizing he was deep in the throes of learning material necessary to bump his professional status up a notch.

# Chapter 15

# FOLLOWING THE STICK

> As rural docs, we'll always live with our people.
>
> -Tom Bibey, *The Country Doctor Revisited*

"We couldn't do any more office deliveries, and the Mono Way office was too far from the hospital and Emergency Room," said Monique Tomasovich. "That worried Warren, so he started planning a new space," she said, explaining the move to the office at 193 Fairview Road. The complex with the Fairview address was generally accessed from Forest Road. After passing the office complex, Forest Road then wound past Community Hospital and through Seventh-day Adventist property to connect with Bonanza Road. Speed bumps slowed traffic on this short curvaceous passage to Calaveras Way, where the Borgquists lived.

"When he moved to the Forest Road office," said Judy, "it was a much better location. He could ride his bike or walk and be there in minutes."

As Judy spoke, I recalled a Soroptimist luncheon during which Dr. Borgquist became the topic of conversation. Luanne Lupo leaned across the table and said, "Dr. B delivered me. The story is that one of his kids had the car, so he rode his bike to the hospital for the delivery."

"That's why we never moved from this house," continued Judy, "because it was so convenient for him when leaving in the middle of the night."

"He was excited about the move," said Monique, "because he was going to have six exam rooms, which meant he could have a partner."

"Can you sketch the layout of the office?" I asked passing a tablet to her.

"There was a big waiting room with a counter and window opening to my desk," she explained as she drew the floor plan. "The bathrooms were just inside the door from the waiting room and cockeyed to another counter where patients checked out. There was a kitchen with a built-in counter along here," said Monique, drawing a skinny rectangle segment to represent the counter. "It served as desk for two nurses. John Roberson built all the cupboards for this office, just like he did for Mono Way. There was a narrow room for files and sample medications here, and three exam rooms on one side of this hallway and three more on the other. We turned one of these rooms into his office and later another one became Todd Stolp's office. I remember this room right here," said Monique, tapping her pencil on one of the rectangular squares.

"One night after everybody had gone and the lights were off, I was pulling charts for the next morning, when I heard a voice. 'Hello. Is anybody out there?' We had forgotten a patient in this last room. I apologized, and she said, 'It's all right. I fell asleep.' I was mortified that no one had caught this, but I rescheduled her, and she was real nice about it." Monique gazed at her drawing for a moment more and then continued. "Off the kitchen there was a deck and a stairway, like this." She drew boxes representing each. "Now he had a back door to come through. We had a table on the deck, where we'd eat lunch or sit for our breaks. I remember him coming up those stairs singing, 'If I Were a Rich Man.'"

"I was at the Forest Road office for a year or two," said Billie, Warren's nurse at the Mono Way office. "I left to go to work at Sandbar—a dam project up in the mountains by Beardsley Reservoir. I was ready for something different. I'd worked doctors' offices because of my kids, so I could have weekends off. But it was on my bucket list to do ER nursing. Another girl conned me into the job. She said the money was real good. I started off at thirty-two dollars an hour, and I worked twelve-hour shifts from 7:30 at night to 7:30 in the morning. My friend told me that nobody stayed up there because of the drive. Warren gave me Sorel boots as a going away present."

Beardsley Reservoir, created by building an earthen dam on the Stanislaus River in 1957, lies about fifty miles East of Sonora off of Highway 108, down a winding road into the steep river canyon. In 1980, work began on an afterbay dam, including a point of diversion to create the Sandbar Power plant. This is the project for which Billie was hired as a medic.

"Warren had to supervise me. I was the safety engineer on site, but I had to have a doctor overseeing me. One time, he drove out to Sandbar in his little red truck to check on me, and he blew a tire. He was pissed. He wanted to know what the hell I was doing down there. I said, 'I'm saving lives.' They were digging an underground tunnel two and a half miles through granite. These were Mormons from Utah, and the outfit was paying well. It wasn't union. They were working the guys long hours, so they were taking drugs to keep going, and that meant accidents. It was really cold, and it snowed a ton that year. It was a hard job because I had to do everything, even drive the ambulance. I wasn't a licensed ambulance driver, so I could only drive up to the highway, where another ambulance met me to drive the patient down to Sonora. I saw stuff I'd never seen anywhere else. Once, we had a decapitation. That was awful. But a lot of the time, it was a nothing job. Just cold! I put Warren's name down as the doctor. I didn't give him any choice. I said, 'You have to.'"

"Billie had gone to work on the dam project," said Pat Valkenberg, the nurse who replaced her in Warren's office. "They had some bad accidents up there. She called Warren when there was a problem. He'd tell her what to do or what medications to administer. She was still working under him. Not for him, but under his tax ID number or something like that. Warren called me at home and offered me Billie's job for more money than I was making at the time," said Pat. "So I put in my notice. Eventually he partnered with Todd Stolp, and my dear friend Maureen Wertz worked for Todd. We worked the back office side-by-side for years."

"What do you mean when you say back office?" I asked.

"We didn't have anything to do with the front. We nursed. We ran the patients through and did all of the instruments. We made up the surgical packs and sterilized them. When Todd came on board, we did all kinds of lab work too, drew blood, spun it down. We had urinalysis on site. Our back office was really busy after they partnered. When Billy was there, Warren had five exam rooms and his office, and they saw eighteen patients a day. When Todd came into the practice, they divvied up the rooms. They each had two exam rooms and their own offices. Warren and I saw thirty patients a day.

"I don't know how many Todd was doing, but that meant that Monique, who was in the front office, went from eighteen to maybe fifty or sixty patients a day. We had charts. There were no computers, so you're talking about long-hand note-taking. Maureen and I started early and worked late. We did things like take care of refills or prescribe for an ear infection over the phone, but they couldn't get a prescription over the phone unless they scheduled an appointment for a check-up in five days. The practice exploded exponentially. I work better under pressure. The more things I have going on the better. Going fast was what I did.

"Each room had a little cubby thing attached to the door where we put the patient's chart. After we put a patient in room, we'd put this stick—a wooden dowel—into the cubby, indicating this is the room with the next person to be seen. The stick meant he needed to go there next. Warren would just shuffle along like an Umpaloompa following the stick. Sometimes, he forgot to look for the stick, and he'd go in the wrong room, and the entire schedule was harpooned. I was ready to beat him with that stick. He had one speed. It was either go or stop. It's not like we could hurry him. He'd be in an exam room talking to somebody for twenty minutes. I'd say, 'You can't talk to somebody for twenty minutes when we've got fifteen people waiting. Move your ass.'

"Our back office was everything: break room, kitchen, lab. We had this little nurses' station with stools in front of the counter and our phones and cupboards with everything we needed. We knew all the pharmacists by first name, and they recognized our voices because we called in the prescriptions. I was connected with so many professionals. Everyone knew Warren's office. We were amazing. People felt better just coming in because we were laughing. We laughed all day. We were flipping people through there, and people would be stacked up in the waiting room, and Monique would stand there with her eyes literally fixed and staring, dilated pupils. But we laughed all the time, and sometimes we cried.

"We were doing everything from vasectomies to circumcisions, many, many circumcisions. He always tried to talk the parents out of it, but not so intensely that if they decided to go ahead, they would feel guilty. That's a fine line to walk with a new mom. The procedure didn't take long. I would set everything up, and then put my hands under the sterile field to hold the little legs apart. My hands were committed. I couldn't move, so it was all up to him. Our faces were three inches apart—him on one side of the table and me on the other—both of us tearing up. That baby lying there as innocent and as trusting as he could be and in a split second, he was screaming. Warren was quick—one, two, three, and he was done. I couldn't get that baby into my arms fast enough. I'd just scoop him up. Warren would look at me and say, 'You know these boys are all going to be waiting for us at the pearly gates, don't you?' I said, 'Yeah, we'll need to wear a disguise." That's how we got through—with humor. I'd say, 'Disguise your voice, for gosh sakes." We laughed, but it wasn't funny. We dreaded it. You can't tell me that there isn't some memory of pain in that area.

"Once this girl came in. She was young, maybe fifteen, and her periods had been terrible. She'd been bleeding heavily. The only difference between a heavy menstrual flow and a hemorrhage is the length of time. After forty-eight hours, you need get yourself to the ER because you're hemorrhaging, and you can't exactly put pressure on it. Sometimes teenagers are shy. They wait a long time to call. It's tricky. This girl's mom got her in, and she was white as a sheet. Then she fainted in the hallway. Warren carried her to an exam room. We did a blood draw and waited for the results, which indicated she absolutely needed blood. He saved her life. If she'd seen somebody who couldn't do the blood work on the spot, she might have died. I witnessed things like that all the time—Warren's particular kind of concern.

"I remember in the early '80s when he used to get letters from Delta Blood bank about transfusions that might have been contaminated with HIV because they didn't have safety measures in place back then. He had to call people and tell them they needed to get tested. Then one of his patients, who had a transfusion, came back positive, and as it turned out the guy had given the virus to his wife in the interim. That wasn't Warren's fault. It wasn't anyone's fault. They just didn't know enough back then. That was one of the crises of the heart he had to suffer through.

"We were a team—a special kind of a team," said Pat, affirming her loyalty to her boss. "I got the patient prepared. I set up what he needed, and then he'd breeze in and do what he did. Then I would come back to finish up and get the room ready for the next person. I made sure I didn't forget anything because it was a waste of time if he had to call me for something. You never know for sure what will be needed because patients don't tell you everything. You have an idea if they want a mole checked that you should have a surgical kit ready. But I couldn't always know what he was going to do once he got in there. I'd think it was going to be ten minutes, and it turned into forty-five, and I'd want to slap him with that stick.

"One day a nurse called who had cut her hand while washing a glass. 'It won't stop bleeding. It's been four hours,' she said. Keep in mind this is a nurse I'm talking to. And I said, 'It sounds like you need to come in.' Her husband brought her, and it turned out the reason she didn't come sooner was because she was terrified of needles. I'm thinking, 'What kind of nursing do you do?' I realized I was going to have to baby her like a 5 year old. Her cut was terrible, into her knuckle on the back of her hand. So I got her all set up and applied topical anesthetic— actually a liquid cocaine. My pain plan for this woman was that she not experience a millisecond of hurt. I treated her with kid gloves and got it numb everywhere he might want to go in with the needle. Her husband was at her side holding her other hand. I got her all squared away, and Warren came in. She turned her head away. She couldn't watch. He had the injector, and she had her head buried in her husband's chest. Warren was doing fine; she couldn't feel a thing. Then she said, 'Is it in yet?' And I said 'Oh honey, never ask a man that.' Warren never missed a beat. He just kept working. She started laughing and her husband couldn't believe what I'd said. Heck, I couldn't believe it, but she'd given me a perfect opening.

"I remember one Halloween when we all costumed up. He dressed as a priest and was giving absolution all day to everybody up and down the halls. It was hysterical. Here's this man with his collar turned around, playing a priest. I was Groucho. I had my hair slicked back, a big painted mustache and eyebrows, glasses, the baggy pants, and my voice is pretty deep anyway. Late in the afternoon, I took a patient—a little old lady—back to the exam room and said, 'Take off your clothes and put on this gown, dear.' And she said, 'I haven't had a man ask me to do that in years.' Those were the days. We were always laughing.

"Warren was an affable guy, never taken with himself. He was like that character in Sesame Street—Snuffleupagus. That's who he was, schlepping down the hall. He never took personal pressures from work or home into the patient's room. Here is one thing about Warren you might want to get down. He had an absolute heartfelt feeling that eating was sacred and reading should not be interrupted. If he was doing them together, God help you if you nudged him. We tiptoed around him. We didn't bug him, touch him, or give him a little squeeze of encouragement because it was sacred. And another thing: he thought the second most amazing physical thing anyone could experience was an incredibly good sneeze. The man enjoyed certain pleasures and laughing was way up there. One time, he took us to this conference in Modesto, so we could get continuing education credit. We were in this lecture where a doctor was talking about fiber. The man said, 'You should eat enough fiber every day to produce a ten-inch floater.' I thought Warren was going to break his pencil. We laughed about ten-inch floaters for months.

"Our office was friendly, on a first name basis, loving, and affectionate. Warren, Monique, and I had November birthdays, so we always had an office birthday party. We were close. It wasn't like we had time to talk about our problems, but you knew when someone was having a bad day, when their kid was doing something crazy. You knew by their face. You could tell they were only going through the motions that day. And we would rally around and do our best to be supportive.

"When I left, it wasn't because of Warren. It was because my kids and I were in danger. This was before the movie *Fatal Attraction,* before people understood stalking. But things happened to me, like high-speed chases through town. This man loosened the lug nuts on the front wheels of my truck, and I lived on a hill. It was terrible. He was following us. He sent me a fifteen-page, typed edict, stating that Elijah had come to the foot of his bed and told him to kill me. People laughed at me. The DA laughed. But when I gave it to Warren, he said, 'You have to leave.' And so I did because he was right. There was no other way."

"I had a terrible first marriage," said Monique, introducing a story about another time when Warren was a sympathetic boss. "One day I went home from work and my husband was in a blind rage. I got my clothes, deodorant and toothbrush, and I went back to the office. It was eight or nine o'clock at night, and everybody was gone. I slept on the couch in the back, and in the morning Gail was the first one to come in. She'd seen my clothes in the car, and she said, 'You're going to stay with me until you're safe, and you have a better place to go. I don't want to hear any crap about it.' Meanwhile she had contacted Warren, and when he came in, he handed me a check made out to an attorney for three hundred dollars. 'Go get a divorce. This will pay for it in full,' he said. 'You have an appointment at ten o'clock with this guy.' He and Gail set up the whole thing and literally saved my life. I think I paid fifteen bucks a month until it was paid off. About six months later, Warren told me he'd been pretty worried that jerk might come into the office with a shotgun or something and try to hurt me, or one of us. I think that was the only thing that scared him—at least that he ever admitted."

As it turned out there was another thing that Dr. Borgquist feared. "Warren used to say he was very proud of the fact that he didn't have to micromanage the office staff," said Monique. "That wasn't the word he used, but he never worried about how the office ran because it ran itself, and that was important to him. He didn't want to mess with all that crap. He didn't want to know if somebody hadn't paid a bill. I remember one lady—she was an old battleax—and she would not pay her bill. It wasn't big, but it would go unpaid for months and months. Finally I told Warren. He said, 'You can't turn it over to collections. I'll never hear the end of it.' I told him 'You can't afford to let stuff like this go.' Finally, he relented. 'Go ahead. Turn it over to collections.' Big mistake! I guess she saw him on the street and ripped him from one end to the other. He came back to the office and said, 'We're not turning anybody over to collections ever again.' He was just floored."

The front office and the back office were two different lands, and though Warren treated his entire staff much like a second family, he was clearly more at home in the back office, where Snuffleupagus reigned, following the wooden dowel into a zone of his own making, where a prescription of humor seemed to be on his side, not like what happened when he turned a bill over to collections. Warren was in his element in the back office treating patients.

"We felt like we were his family," said patient BZ Smith. "Every time any of us went into his office, we felt like we were connected on a very personal level. One of the ways he secured that was by always asking about our extended family. My brother had introduced me to Warren and then moved out of the county, but Dr. B always maintained a genuine interest in him and his family. He had been their doctor too, and they all loved him dearly. One of the most critical moments in my life occurred with Warren just after I started seeing Rick Thorpe. Our relationship was getting serious when I went to Warren for my routine physical exam. We started talking about Rick's diabetes. I vividly remember Warren looking at me with great love and compassion, and saying, 'I want you to know this is a very grim disease.' He opened a window on the reality of who I was falling in love with and the idea that I might need to give myself permission to leave the relationship. Nobody had said that to me before, and probably if they had, I wouldn't have taken it very seriously, but with this man whom I respected so much, who was so incredibly attentive to my health—much more so than I'd ever been—I knew he was genuinely concerned not just about Rick but also about me and how I would hold up through all that might come. And of course after that, he stood by us every inch of the way."

Pat Valkenberg witnessed many times in which Dr. Borgquist was there for patients in difficult circumstances. "Warren had a spiel for people who had cancer," said Pat. "There was a speech he gave when nothing else could be done. I listened to it so many times I could anticipate his words. 'With what we know now, with what we have now, we *can't* treat this.' There would be a huge silence. They had to take that in. You knew they were trying as hard as they could to understand. He would maintain eye contact and say, 'I promise I will keep you comfortable until the end.' He knew everyone worried about suffering.

"It was always the same. He'd look at a scan of 20-year-old woman and see hot spots in every bone in her body, and he had to tell her she was dying. She'd say, 'Isn't there something we can do? I have kids.' And the answer was: 'Nothing.' It was insane. It was horrible. Patients think that doctors can fix everything. No one thinks they are going to get a death warrant from their doctor. But that's not true. It hurts. No one gets it. Not even us. I remember when Billie called—stunned—the decapitation accident had just happened at the mine. And she was on the phone saying she didn't know how to start CPR. She was standing there looking at the chest and head of a once-breathing man, and there was nothing she could do. Warren dealt with many hard things like that, but he had a way of accepting. He would walk out of the exam room after a difficult conversation and close the door. He would look at me and I would look at him. Then he would follow the stick. There was nothing else to do."

"I was lucky enough to marry into his practice," said Amy Nilson, another patient who was touched by Dr. Borgquist's compassion. "My husband was one of his first patients in Tuolumne County, so when we got married, Warren became my doctor. I had interviewed him when I was a reporter for the *Union Democrat*. I remember taking his picture a time or two, and he used to call me his favorite reporter. I'm sure he said this to all the reporters, but I interviewed him about some pretty complicated topics—like malpractice. However, to have him as a doctor—that was when I got to see what kind of person he truly was."

"The first thing that happened was I had a miscarriage. I can't imagine a better person to guide me through that. Losing the baby was hard, but he put it into perspective in such a beautiful way. He explained how common it was for a first pregnancy to end in miscarriage. He said women, especially women who are happy to be pregnant, don't know about this possibility. He was so gentle about helping me through the disappointment. He said, 'Just take a little time.' It didn't take too long for us to get pregnant again."

"One time during my pregnancy when I went in for a checkup, it was the end of the day, so we walked out to the parking lot together. I asked him how he was doing, and he said, 'Well, this was a really hard day.'

"'What happened?' I asked.

"'I had to tell a man with young children that he had a terminal diagnosis. That's just the hardest thing.'

"'How do you deal with that as a doctor?'

"'Because I get to do this,' he said gesturing to my big pregnant belly."

Amy and I were sitting on a bench in front of the Columbia College library when she told me this story. We stared out at the pond, reflecting for a moment. "He did both sides," said Amy after a minute. "Birth and death. How could you not love somebody who had that as his passion? Having him at my birth ..." She hesitated, and then said, "You probably have plenty of birth stories."

"I love birth stories," I said.

"It was a great experience," Amy said, launching into her story. "He said I was a model patient. At 7:30 in the morning, I called him to say that my water had broken. It was four weeks early, so I was still working. I hadn't even had a day off. 'I'm coming home with a baby, right?' I said, 'Yes you are,' he confirmed. He came by the Birth Center a time or two during his regular workday. He was even able to go home, have dinner, come back, and deliver the baby at 8:00 p.m. After the delivery, he lifted the baby from my chest and said, 'Welcome to the world.' It felt like we were part of a tradition when he said that."

# Chapter 16

## ALTERNATIVE BIRTH CENTER

The mom delivers the baby; we have the honor of participating.

-Sally Arnold, OB Nurse

"Jan Dunn and I started the Alternative Birth Center at the old Sierra Hospital," said Dr. Chris Mills. "A birth center had to be licensed by the state," continued Chris, "and there were lots of rules about who could deliver there. Mothers had to be low risk and if things turned sour, they had to be moved to a hospital setting. The first center in the state was at San Francisco County General, so Jan went down and scouted it out. Then she came back, and we started setting things up at Sierra. Half of the building, which Community had just purchased, was going to be our birth center, and the other half was going to be long-term care. We applied for and got the license. It was real popular." Twenty-seven births in Warren's office in under two years attested to the interest Tuolumne County women had in an alternative to the hospital delivery room. My first experience at the Alternative Birth Center was attending a labor and delivery by my friend Julia.

"My second baby was born at the Birth Center," said Julia, "with Warren attending. I had one of those classic experiences you see in the movies. It was about ten o'clock at night when I went into labor. We'd called Warren, who told us to go to the Center. We jumped in the car, and took off, and the cops pulled us over, and Rod hollered, 'She's in labor. We're on our way to the hospital.' The cop said, 'Follow me,' and led us with his red light flashing. It was pretty hilarious because the Center wasn't that far. Joe's birth was a little more difficult than Sean's. I remember Warren arrived in boots, looking kind of like a woodsman. He was his friendly, jolly self. I immediately felt like everything was going to be fine. It wasn't his office, and when I got pregnant, I really wished he still had the birth chair, but this was OK. The room even had a couch for visitors."

"This second birth took a lot longer," continued Julia.,"because the baby's head would not turn. Warren suggested I do things like walk in the halls or squat. He was trying to get the baby to move."

"You squatted and just hung onto the end of the bed," I said. "I recall thinking your legs had to be incredibly strong to stay in the position for so long. Then at one point, Warren actually checked your dilation while you were squatting."

"Yeah, it was like the baby kept hitting the back of his head against my cervix instead of moving down. Actually, it was right after he checked me that things began to change."

"When the head crowned, Warren had us help you get on the bed, and Joe was born immediately after."

"All this goes back to the birth chair and how gravity works to make it easier. I'm not sure anyone should have a baby while lying on her back. But people get into these situations where no one is thinking about the things Warren thought about. I remember my daughter-in-law having her baby in a hospital. That night there were seven babies born and two sets of twins, so they kept giving her drugs to push her off because they were so busy. All I could think was that this is so unfair. They kept giving her epidurals, and I wanted to get her up and walking."

"I worked at the Birth Center for fifteen years," said Sally Arnold. We were sitting at one of the round metal tables on the sidewalk outside of Schnoogs, the coffee shop she and her husband owned, the place to which she had exited when she left nursing. Before she started her story, Sally had said, "This was his table. Warren's table." For this was the place to which Warren and his doctor buddies eventually migrated for their weekly meetings. I was not sure if Sally had purposely guided us to the table, but it felt apropos.

"My background was in pediatric oncology," said Sally, "so OB was a new field for me when I arrived. I'd done training at Stanford and some clinical work in Modesto. When I started, I was the new kid. The next newest person had been there for five years. I came into a line of people who had done beautiful birthing. We all had different relationships with the doctors, but working with Warren was unique. It wasn't like here's the doctor and here's us. It was more of a team. There were other doctors who had to be in charge. You had to make them think an idea was theirs when it was actually yours. Then you told them what a great idea it was. That's how we learned to get what we wanted. But there were a couple doctors—Warren Borgquist and Chris Mills, in my humble opinion—to whom you could say directly what you needed. They'd say, 'OK,' or if you did what you needed to do, and they arrived later, they'd say, 'I've got you covered.'

"Once, when I was very new, we had this woman all set up. She was getting ready to push, and Warren looked at me and very quietly said, 'You're going to deliver this baby.' I was like *holy shit*. I'd never delivered a baby and the adrenaline started coursing through me. All the other nurses had precept deliveries, so everybody had delivered but me. A precept delivery is a spontaneous delivery, like women who have their babies in the car on the way to the hospital or the gals who get to the Birth Center at three centimeters and BOOP, suddenly there's the head, and you don't have time to call back-up, so you need to know what to do."

"Warren said gently, 'You need to deliver a baby when I'm here, so when you're on your own, you'll know what to do. I'm going to talk you through this, so sit down on the stool.' I was so nervous, but he said: 'OK Sally, now feel for this. That's it. You got it. OK, what do you need to do next? Feel for the cord. No cord? OK. Now what? You've got this. Trust yourself, trust yourself.' The delivery ended up being beautiful.

"Of course, I don't think we ever deliver babies. The mom delivers the baby. We have the honor of participating as a support person along the journey. But there was Warren right there next to me. He made it look like he was delivering *with* me. The family never had the sense that a new nurse was doing the delivery. The thing is I wasn't licensed. I wasn't a midwife, and I'm not a doctor, but I was licensed to be the first person on the scene. And you're supposed to do whatever you need to do when you're first responder. But if you don't know how to do it, how in the world are you going to get there? That was a pivotal moment in my career because I learned in that moment to trust myself.

"Not long after that—and this not a Warren story specifically—but I had a mom come in. I put the baby on the monitor, and it passed a non-stress test, but something didn't feel right, so I said, 'Can you come back on Sunday and let me check you again?' They lived out past Murphys—in the next county over. I didn't want to alarm them, but I said, 'I'm working all weekend, and if you guys could come back tomorrow, I'd sleep better.' They came back the next day. They trusted me, and we put the baby on the monitor, and it was dying, so the doctor came and performed and emergency C-section. Afterwards, Dr. Davis the pediatrician said, 'Had they waited until their appointment on Monday, the baby would've been dead.' So when I think of gifts from Warren, I think of my first delivery. After that when I got scared, I could always hear Warren over my shoulder going, "Trust yourself. You've got this.'

"Many of the other doctors were more traditional. I remember caring for one woman. She had a C-section scheduled. It was actually a doctor's wife, and nothing was going well. With Warren, we'd be saying, 'Do you want to be on floor, sideways, backwards, squatting.' We'd just put pads down, and whatever their body called them to do was OK. So I said to this C-section lady, 'Do you want to get in the shower?' And the doctor was mad at me. 'Why would you get her in the shower right now?' he said.

"'Because she wants to,' I said.

"'We're preparing for a C-Section."

"'Well, it'll be a clean one. What's the worst-case scenario? She'll deliver.' Sure enough, what do you think she did?

"There are so many times as a nurse that I had to drop down into trusting myself. So much of that had to do with watching how Warren was—how I felt like he trusted us to do what we did, so that mamas could do what they do. One time, Warren had me cut an episiotomy. I still remember the crunch, and I didn't like that, but he believed we needed to have certain skills and autonomy. We're up here in the mountains, and what if it's snowing and a doctor can't get in? What are we going to do?

Birth can be wild and crazy. It can be fast or terribly slow. I'm old school. We nurses always talked about the full moon, two days before and two days after. If you ever work ER, psych, or OB, you know it's not a myth that things start popping then. There is the word lunar. And there is lunatic. We could have five women in labor with two nurses. Then what? We're calling doctors and getting people in. Our unit was set up to do deliveries, postpartum, and nursery. It was a busy place, especially on a full moon, and we needed to be able to take care of it all."

"I remember another incident. I had finished my holistic nursing program, and I was really excited about the brain science and how breathing and relaxing interface with the birthing process. This lady came in, no support, no family, a significant drug history. She was three centimeters, totally alone, and filthy dirty, so I admitted her and put her in room 203. She was writhing and screaming f-bombs, just totally panicked. I mean nobody wanted to take her. She was really a handful, and I thought, "OK. I've got this." So slowly, we established rapport. It took a little time and space and then, with permission, a little bit of touch. And then I asked her if I could do some breathing with her. And gradually, she was able to step out of her fear— to climb out of her medulla and go into her whole brain, which allowed her to go back into her body. So this not-Warren-doctor who'd already seen her when she was a mess, came in. She was seven centimeters and in her bed almost dozing, and then a contraction arose, and she did her breathing and then tucked herself back in. And we're just doing our thing, right? This doctor was pissed, and he called me out in the hall, and with a red face and pointing finger, he spit out: 'You did not have an order to give her a spinal. I write the orders around here.' At first I felt reactive, but I took a deep breath and said, 'She didn't have a spinal.' And he said, "I didn't even write an order for Stadol, and there's no standing order for it either. You have no right to just do whatever you want.' He's just going on and his face is red and now I'm enjoying this, and I said. 'She didn't have Stadol.' He goes, 'What's going on in there?" And I said, 'She did that herself. She has had no medication. She's doing it all herself. Now I'd like to go back to my patient if you don't mind.' So after the delivery, which went beautifully, he wrote his charts and then grumbled past me with no eye contact and said, 'I don't know what you did in there, but that was a good job.' We never discussed it, but from that day on he didn't challenge me the same way.

"As nurses we were working two planets in the same universe at the Birth Center. You'd have a shift with the not-Warren doctors and then you'd have Warren, who trusted us and trusted his patients. Christopher Mills would go to bat for his patients too. He had a bedside manner of a toad, but he would go to bat for patients. As a clinician, there was nobody better. I can tell you the room number for that not-Warren doctor delivery. It was 203. I remember probably 80 percent of the babies I delivered. I've had people come into Schnoogs, and I'll look at them and say, "202, thirteen years ago." I think I remember because it's such a sacred moment."

Because Warren enjoyed birth, he wanted to share it with people he cared about. Several people told of him inviting them to witness a birth. He'd invited Nicolas to a birth when he was just a young man of 17. Gail Bonavia told about being invited before the birth chair or the Birth Center were even conceived. "He asked me if I wanted to watch a birth," said Gail. "I said I'd love to, so I went with him to the hospital. I never thought I'd want to get pregnant again, but if I did, I sure wanted him to deliver. He was so good with those mothers— just incredible. He delivered my granddaughter. I got to cut the cord."

Pat Valkenburg, Warren's nurse following Billie, told a story about the time Warren invited her to the Birth Center. "It had to be up to the woman whether or not she would allow me to be there," said Pat. "He had asked her, and she was OK with it, but he wanted me to go in and get to know her by doing a little nursing—get the baby's heart rate and stuff like that. I was nervous. It was my first birth. I had the stethoscope, and I was listening for the heart rate, but I couldn't find it. She was a beautiful Tahitian woman, golden skin with this huge belly. I was moving the stethoscope all over her belly, and she tapped me on the arm. I thought she was going to say she didn't want me to be there, but she smiled and pointed. My stethoscope was not in my ears. She let me stay to observe the birth, and that was because of him. Of course after that, she and I were great friends whenever she came to the office."

Don Andrews described the incredible joy he saw in Warren not only at the birth of his son but during the pregnancy appointments. Shelley fleshed out that story with more about Warren's humor and his honesty. "Don was 35 and I was 30 when we got married. I could hear that biological clock ticking even though I had never wanted kids. I gave so much to my teaching, and I just didn't think I could give that much and have a family. There wasn't enough of me to go around. Then I met Don, and suddenly I couldn't wait to have kids. So we went in and said we wanted to start a family. And Warren in his ancient way—which is actually pretty funny because he's Don's age and only four years older than I—guided us through that whole thing.

"Mr. Old Guy was ever the Wise Guy. He said, 'Now you two need to be married for at least a year before you decide to have a baby. You've got to let this marriage settle.' We followed his advice. But then I was ready. I had an IUD, so I went in, and he said I needed to have a measles shot before I got pregnant because I hadn't been inoculated. So he gave me the shot, and then I think he got excited— he so loved delivering babies—so he yanked my IUD. Then he said 'Oh shit' because you cannot get pregnant for six weeks after you have been inoculated with measles virus because the baby can be born with birth defects. There is a very high correlation. He couldn't believe he'd yanked the IUD right after he gave me the shot. So he said, 'You're going to have to use condoms.' I'd never used a condom before, but I said 'That's fine.' I went home from the appointment and told Don we were going to have to use condoms, and he just looked at me and said, 'You're kidding. For six weeks! I don't think so.' Warren felt terrible, so he went down to Stockton—maybe he went for Visiting Nurses which was in Stockton—anyway he was down there for some reason, and he went to an adult store where they had all kinds of condoms, and he bought a whole bunch of them. And then he and Judy had us over dinner, and he presented us with all of these condoms— French ticklers, sheepskins—it was hilarious.

"Eventually we got pregnant. And then we had a bit of scare that he managed rather well. My baby's heartbeat was all out of whack in utero. I was at an appointment, and the nurse was listening to the heartbeat with the little wand, and she let me listen. I could hear the ba baba. Then Warren came in and took a listen. He said, 'I want you to go across the street to Community and have an ultrasound.' Suddenly I was petrified, thinking there was something wrong with my baby. When I did the ultrasound, they could hear an arrhythmic heartbeat, so Warren got on the phone—there were no computers then—and he called all over the country, talking to heart specialists and pediatric heart specialists about this arrhythmia in utero. I believe I was four or five months along when this happened. Anyway, he came back and told Don and me what he'd learned. He had talked to people who had dealt with babies with serious heart problems, and this was not an indicator. So he said, 'I don't think you should worry. Let's just go on and see what happens.' I had Christopher completely naturally. It was long and drawn out and totally wonderful and my baby was fine."

One day while I was on my way to conduct an interview about Dr. Borgquist, I made a stop and ran into a friend of my daughter's. We exchanged pleasantries, and then she asked where I was headed. When I briefly explained the project I was working on, she said, "Let me tell you my Borgquist story," which is an opening line I heard again and again. "I was Dr. Stolp's patient, but when I went into labor, he was out of town, and Dr. Borgquist was on call. And this is the thing. I hardly remember seeing him there. My friend, who was a midwife, took care of me. Borgquist stayed in the background, completely unobtrusive. The only time I saw him was right at the end when the baby got stuck. He and my friend did something to turn him, and the midwife basically caught the baby, which I'm sure is totally illegal. I hardly remember Dr. Borgquist, except I know he was there because his name is on the paperwork."

The headline of a *Sonora Union Democrat* article published on October 29, 1987 reads: "Obstetricians Laboring to Survive." The accompanying picture is of a swaddled newborn, in the crook of his mother's elbow. Only her hands and a bit of her hospital gown are visible. Linda Locklin, author of the article, writes: "In a dimly lit room in the Sierra Birth Center, a joyous scene is played out. A new mother, heavy with fatigue holds an hour-old baby to her breast. She kisses his wrinkled head. The baby intermittently bawls and yawns. The youthful father reclines on a nearby bed, broadcasting the news via telephone. 'Yeah, I think he looks like me.' The grandparents snap photo after photo."

Locklin captured in words the scene that Warren Borgquist and Sally Arnold witnessed over and over at the Birth Center. But that joyful scene was not the focus of the article. Rather it goes on to discuss the depressing state of affairs that had turned delivering babies into a high-risk profession resulting in skyrocketing malpractice insurance rates. Locklin reported the following statistic released by the California Medical Association: "11 percent of OB-GYNS and one third of FP have stopped deliveries although rural areas look to the latter to provide obstetrics." FP stood for Family Practice doctor, and not all FP docs who came to Sonora included obstetrics in their practices. Drs. Retherford, Renwick, and Foster were among those who did not; but Borgquist, Waldman, and Stolp did. These three doctors, looking young and enthusiastic, are pictured on the second page of the article. "We're dinosaurs," Warren is quoted as saying in the article. "I'd like to protect us from becoming extinct." Locklin named fifteen rural California counties in which there were no physicians who were delivering babies in 1987. Two of them were Calaveras and Mariposa counties, both of which neighbored Tuolumne County. As Locklin pointed out, women who live in those places have to cross county lines for care. This called to mind the woman from Murphys in Calaveras County, whom Sally Arnold cared for. Her baby would have died if not for the intuition of an obstetrical nurse at the Birth Center. The irony is that intuition had trumped technology in saving that baby's life, turning the whole issue of malpractice cattywampus.

In a sidebar of the main article, six doctors speak their thoughts on malpractice. Warren said, "In America, you're guaranteed the perfect life. It's a golden age—no war, we're economically sound. If you don't get it, somebody must be responsible. People say, 'I know you're not perfect and you're only human, but if you screw up, I'm going to assault your insurance company.'" Todd Stolp was even more blunt. "There is a profound change in society's ability to take responsibility for health care and tragedies that occur in life. It seems we're constantly looking for someone to blame." Locklin spoke with two Family Practice doctors who quit delivering babies, and then she quoted Borgquist as saying, "I've thought of quitting. My accountant tells me I'm an idiot for doing obstetrics." His malpractice insurance in 1987 was $21,500 annually but would have been $9,000-$12,000 without obstetrics. Warren confirmed what many people knew to be true: "Without deliveries in my practice, I'd be an unbalanced person."

# Chapter 17

# MIDWIVES

One way to measure a particular doctor's openness and attitude
toward women in general is simply to ask about
the doctor's opinion of midwifery.

-Marsden Wagner, *Born in the USA*

While the majority of women worldwide birth their babies in non-hospital settings, the advent of obstetrics had a tremendous influence on childbirth customs in this country, so that hospital birth is now the norm. In the 1960s and 1970s, women began to question and challenge the way they were being treated by obstetricians and the hospitals where they gave birth. These particular women wanted to return pregnancy and birth to a more family-centered position. Dr. Borgquist heard their appeal as he was beginning to practice medicine, and his response was to build a birth chair and deliver babies in his office. That approach was eventually thwarted, but around the same time, several lay midwives began to practice in Tuolumne County. Lay midwives are a special breed of health care providers, who help women deliver their babies at home. Given that out-of-hospital births accounted for 1.36 percent of births in 2012 in the United States, lay midwives and the moms who make this choice are outliers. Not surprisingly, each of the local midwives developed a relationship with Dr. Borgquist—a man who'd been called maverick and renegade, if not outlier.

"My earliest memory of Dr. Borgquist is your birth pictures at his office,'" said my daughter, Jennie Lou Tippett. "I never saw the birth chair, but hearing about it when I was so young planted the seed for me to have a home birth when I got pregnant. After my first home birth, we took our son, August, to see Dr. Borgquist when he was two days old because the midwife liked to have her babies seen by a doctor within the first three days. We went in that morning, and Dr. Borgquist said, 'He's a beautiful baby, Mom, and you look great too.' By that afternoon, August had a 104 fever. I may have been a first-time mom, but I knew that newborns don't get high fevers. We took him to Tuolumne General Hospital. I later learned that Dr. Borgquist preferred the other hospital, maybe because it was closer to his office.

"We were very frightened and holding a very sick newborn, but they left us sitting in the hallway. It was confusing because it didn't look like the ER was crowded. I got more and more worried because it felt like they weren't taking us seriously, so I called Dr. Borgquist's office and said my baby had 104 degree fever, and I was at TGH. Even though he'd seen our healthy baby that morning, he dropped everything—probably lots of appointments—and came across town to the less convenient hospital. As soon as he walked in, he said it was cord stump infection or omphalitis. That's when he became our superhero. He knew within seconds of examining August what the problem was and what to do. He directed us with respect. We never felt like he talked down to us because we were young and inexperienced and didn't know what we're dealing with or because we went to the wrong hospital or had a home birth. He handled everything gracefully.

"He transferred us to Sonora Community, where we stayed for several hours. There was a forest fire, so August could not be airlifted to Oakland Children' Hospital. They eventually sent him by ambulance, but there was no room for a parent in the ambulance, so we drove behind. August was at Children's for seven days while they administered massive does of antibiotics because it was a staph infection. After we were back home and August was fine, I learned that a local baby had recently died of the condition, which was why Dr. Borgquist was so on top of it. I don't know if the child was his patient. That wasn't part of the story—just that a baby had died."

As August's grandmother, I knew this Warren Borgquist story well because I lived it. Three days before this trip to the hospital, I'd witnessed this baby's delivery by a midwife in a tiny one-room cabin as rays of morning sun slanted through the windows. Later, I learned that this kind of infection happens in 1 in 200 newborns, but at the time, it was a condition unknown to me. In our family lore, it is the brilliant diagnosis by Dr. Borgquist that saved the life of the first of fifteen grandchildren to come, eight of whom would be born at home with Warren poised somewhere in the background as a white knight who could step in should transport be necessary.

For this reason, I was well acquainted with the three local midwives: Ellie Jasmer, Dody Rogers, and Andrea Ferroni. Ellie and Dody had delivered my brother's two children, and Dody delivered Jennie Lou's first-born and five subsequent babies. Andrea Ferroni was my daughter-in-law and was in attendance at four of Jennie Lou's births. I asked the midwives if they would meet with me to talk about their relationships with Dr. Borgquist, who was one of the few physicians who was willing to back them. We met one chilly winter evening in the waiting room of Andrea's downtown office where a wood stove glowed, emanating the kind of warmth I associated with home birth.

"The first time I met Warren Borgquist," said Ellie Jasmer, "was in the clinic at Tuolumne General." The clinic was next door to the hospital and served low-income patients who had health issues that were not emergencies. "I went in as a patient, and he diagnosed a severe IUD infection. I had PID (Pelvic Inflammatory Disease) from a Dalkon Shield. This was 1971, before I was a midwife. I said, 'I want this thing out of me.' And he said, "I don't want you to get pregnant with this infection.' And I said, 'I won't; I just want it out.' He took it out, and unfortunately, I did get pregnant."

"Did you remain his patient," I asked, "or were you only a clinic patient?"

"No, I moved to San Francisco to do my midwifery training," said Ellie. Most lay midwives either apprentice with an experienced midwife or go to midwifery schools. "Then I moved back to the county in 1977, and Dr. Borgquist was doing office births and getting a lot of flack from the OBs in town, so he started referring people who wanted out-of-hospital birth to me. When we first reconnected, he asked about my training. I told him I did thirty-five births during training at San Francisco General. 'That's about right,' he said, 'that's what we did in medical school, between thirty and forty births. You know a trained baboon can catch a baby, but one percent of births are a nightmare.' I didn't take offense to being compared to a trained baboon. He and I did a lot of co-care: women would see him and me. I would deliver their babies at home, and if I had trouble I would call him."

"Was Earlene one of those births?" I asked, referring to the woman who had been in the Lamaze class with Julia Rhodes and me. "She was pregnant when I had an office delivery, and I understand you delivered her."

"I met Earlene in labor. I was still living in San Francisco and happened to be in town, and someone told her I was here, so she called me. I went to her trailer off Peaceful Valley Road, and stayed to help deliver little Jamiel, who was the smallest baby I've ever delivered—four pounds-twelve ounces."

Ellie was holding a worn blue ledger in her lap, open to the first page. She explained that the ledger contained her notes from every delivery she'd ever done. "Let's see. Her labor was … did I record the hours? No I guess not. She had a bicornuate uterus and a small placenta. I called it a do-it-yourself home birth," said Ellie, looking at the final notation on the entry for Earlene.

"Let's hear from you, Dody. What was your first encounter with Warren?"

"My first encounter with Warren was when I was a senior in high school. He had just come from Panama. I was doing a term project on abortion, and I went to interview him, but he was not available. He was attending a birth, so I ended up talking to him on the phone. He talked to me for half an hour, but I didn't personally meet him until after I gave birth to my son. It was 1972. Patty Coombes delivered the baby, but then she had to leave town. He walked into the hospital room the next morning, wearing jeans, a flannel shirt, and hiking boots and said, 'I need to check you.'

"'Who are you?' I asked

"'I'm sorry,' he said. 'I'm Dr. Borgquist, and I'm filling in for Dr.

Coombes.' He checked me and the baby and said everything was fine, and I could be released. But I thought, "Who is this guy— this young man with long hair who didn't look like a doctor?"

"And you Andrea?"

"I feel like my first encounter was your family stories. His was a name I heard over and over again before I ever met him. He was part of every birth discussion. I didn't actually meet him until Mary Autumn's birth," she said referring to Jennie Lou's fifth baby, a home birth that ended as a transport to the hospital. "But I had talked to him on the phone. I was trying to do labs for one of my clients and either Dody or Ellie said to ask Warren. So I called him and said, 'I'm part of the Harrelson family, and I'm having a hard time getting labs.' He said, 'Here, use my labs.' My credentials were that I was part of your family."

"Didn't he help you get oxygen too?" I asked.

"Yeah, he wrote me a prescription for oxygen. Thank you for remembering that. He gave me that and permission to use his labs before I ever met him."

"That's a great segue for my next question, which is … How did he work with midwives?"

"He was a wonderful support," said Ellie.

"We called him a male midwife," said Dody, "because he was so interested in learning and experimenting. He wasn't afraid of letting women labor in different positions. He was one of the only doctors who got the emotional part—he was there for the whole thing. One time, I said, 'I have a stupid question.'

"'No question concerning birth is stupid,' he said and added, 'Birth is about the woman. I don't know what it feels like. You have to ask her.'"

"He was so teachable," said Ellie. 'One time, I was at the Birth Center, and he was with a woman down the hall from where I was working. He came and said, 'This woman always gets little tears in the birth canal. I don't know what to do about it.' I told him a few tricks, like holding the perineum with my little finger and the second finger as the head comes out slowly. After he delivered the baby, he came back and said, 'She didn't tear! She didn't tear!' He was so excited. Not only did he recognize that we knew things he didn't, he was totally willing to teach us. He was the one who taught me how to stitch the deep part of the vagina with interrupted sutures."

"So there were things he taught and questions he asked. I'm wondering if there were ways he didn't understand midwives?"

"The thing I remember about my first encounter with Dr. Borgquist," said Andrea, "was that he thought we were absurd for not breaking the water during Mary Autumn's birth. That didn't make any sense to him whatsoever. We're saying this woman shoots babies out. She's been at eight centimeters for twelve hours. The baby is sky high and super wobbly. We don't know what's going to come down with the baby if we break that water, so we don't want to."

"I was just looking at those notes today," said Dody, who also tended the birth. The two midwives continued discussing this difference of opinion with Dr. Borgquist about how to manage the birth of Jennie Lou's fifth child, which seemed unusual to them after four unremarkable and relatively quick labors.

"We called him several times," said Andrea, "and I remember saying the labor was in a holding pattern, which made me fear there were cord issues. He thought that was a crazy idea because in no way would that change the labor pattern. I kept saying, 'I think so.' And he said, 'Just break the water.'

"'I'm not going to,' I said. 'This is weirding us out, and we don't want to.'

"This would be speculating," said Dody, "but, even though he did office births, most of his births took place where the next thing needed was available. We cannot offer someone an immediate C-Section for a cord prolapse. So if he was to break Jennie Lou's water and got a cord prolapse, everything he needed for the next step was there. We did not have that. He had worked in a low-tech situation in his office, so it must have crossed his mind." Dody was trying to penetrate Dr. Borgquist's thoughts for where he both understood and diverged from midwife thinking.

"He supported Patty Coombes" added Dody. " He was the only physician who did." Dr. Coombes was one of the doctors that Chris Mills had labeled a renegade. According to a 1992 article entitled "The Home-birth Controversy" by Hannah Lapp published in *The Freeman*, Dr. Coombes "was forced out of practice when the executive committee at Sonora Community Hospital declared her incompetent and revoked her hospital privileges. The committee was unable to find a single patient who would testify against her, and no wonder: Dr. Coombes' record reflects two decades of exceptionally humane and responsible medical and birth services. Among 3,000 deliveries, there were no infant or maternal deaths, no malpractice suits, and less than one-tenth the national rate of Caesarean deliveries."

"After Dr. Coombes was blackballed, it freaked me out," said Ellie. "I called Warren, and said 'If they are after her, am I next?' He said, 'No, you don't have anything to worry about. There are different issues in her case.' According to him, Dr. Coombes would stay home longer than we did because she was a doctor. Maybe she would pop the water when we wouldn't, so when she transported it was more of a mess, and that really upset the OB-GYNs. Because I brought them in earlier, he said I didn't have a mess."

"My experience," said Dody, "is they think all of our transports are messes."

"That's right," said Ellie, "but in a few cases, I've earned respect in the sense that when I transport it is not emergency craziness. I remember transporting a case similar to Jennie Lou's. I can't remember how long the woman pushed, but the bag of water was like an inner tube or trampoline that sucked that baby right back up ever time she pushed. We finally transported because I was not comfortable popping the water, but Warren did so, and her baby came immediately. That's all she needed."

"That's the difference," said Andrea. "To us, breaking the water is an intervention— not just a run-of-the-mill procedure. It's a possibility, but not something we're going to do without really thinking about it."

"Right," said Ellie, "There's a time and place for any intervention. I remember a case during the Stanislaus Complex Fire. It was one of those huge atom bomb type fires. This family lived by the river canyon and was sleeping outside, and the woman was at the end of her pregnancy. The smoke was so bad they even closed the schools. It was terribly toxic. Afterward, I talked to a goat herder who lived on the river canyon, and he said all the goats born during the fire were premature, deformed, or stillborn. Our patient went into labor shortly after the fire was controlled. Her water broke, and it was clear—the way you want it to be—but sometimes if the head corks off the water, there can be meconium in the water that you can't see. Her water broke, but there were no contractions. I went over in the evening to check her, and I thought that there might be a little bit of meconium in the water that was leaking out, but the baby sounded great—strong heart rate with no variability in the heartbeat. But in the morning, when I checked again, the baby did not sound OK. The heart rate was flat with no variability. So I called Warren. He said to meet him at the hospital at noon. I said, 'No, I'm coming now. This baby is not doing well.'

"The nurses assessed the baby with their external monitor and said there was variability. They couldn't hear what I heard. This was before training and certifications for electronic fetal monitoring. The nurse kept telling me I could not hear variability with an external monitor. I insisted, 'Yes, I can.' Dr. Borgquist came in, and he basically agreed with the nurse. I wasn't sure how they were interpreting the information, but he went back to work. When he came back later in the afternoon, she still wasn't having contractions, and was only one centimeter dilated, so he got an electronic probe on the baby's head for internal monitoring, and it looked worse. Now he believed there was a problem, so he ordered a C-Section, and when the baby came the Apgars were horrible—at one and two— and she had extremely low respiration, so they flew her to Oakland Children's. Before she left, I met Dr. Borgquist at the Nurse's Desk, and I said, 'I should have been more assertive. I'm sorry.'

"'No, you were trying to tell me, and I wouldn't listen,' he said. Warren was so humble. We all felt bad for this baby, but I don't know if there would have been any difference in outcome if she'd delivered four or five hours earlier because the compromise with the baby's placenta probably happened because of the fire. The point is with Warren there was real humility in that moment."

Ellie's record book was in her lap, her finger traveling down the page. She stopped at a name—which happened to be her seventy-second birth—and said, "You should talk to BZ Smith about Wren's birth. That was another transport that had a better outcome."

"By the time Rick and I decided to have a baby," said BZ, "Warren had been pressured by the powers that be to no longer do office deliveries, so women were going to the Birth Center. But at the same time, Ellie had begun practicing midwifery in Tuolumne County. Warren knew there were women who wanted a birth alternative, so he took the risk to back Ellie. He took a lot of flack for that, yet he stood by his beliefs and his respect for women who wanted to do it their own way. He trusted Ellie enough to put his whole career at risk.

"After witnessing my friend Kaia's delivery, I planned a home birth with Ellie. The day came—April 18, 1980, a beautiful spring day on which the lilacs were just opening. Ellie arrived along with some of our friends. When she checked me, I was hopeful she was going to say it was time to push. Instead, she said, "We have a little butt here." The baby was breach—something we hadn't thought about. Ellie said, 'I'm going to call Warren.'

"When she called, she learned he was in Stockton at the vasectomy clinic, but they patched the call through, and he took it. He said, 'Take her to the hospital, and I will be there as soon as I can.' Ellie turned to us and explained he was in Stockton, so we could go in or we could stay home for a while longer. We decided to stay home because there was no problem. She was just breach. So we stayed home at least another hour, and then finally, the guys loaded me in the van. Rick sat with me. Ellie was in the back with the oxygen and my brother-in-law. I remember seeing Sonora going by while I was on my back with my legs up in the air looking through these fuzzy windows. We got to the hospital, and immediately thereafter, Warren arrived. I had progressed a little, but he nevertheless said, 'Let's get her into the delivery room,' and he called the OB-GYN. We were all in the operating room, Rick and I, and two of my best friends, and Ellie, and another friend was there to do sketches. The nurses were freaked out because there were so many of us. Warren just looked at them, and he said, 'Let her have whatever she wants.'

"I was on the table, and the OB-GYN came in and said, 'I think we should do a Cesarean.' I didn't want to do that. He was a relatively new doctor, and it was the first time Warren had worked with him. The OB was standing at my side, and Warren was looking at my vagina and then into my face, and I knew from his eyes that we could get the baby out. I turned to the other doctor and said, 'No, we're going to do a vaginal birth.'

"'If your baby comes out retarded, it's not my fault,' he said and left the room.

"'Let's get this baby out,' said Warren. He performed an episiotomy and BAM! Out came the baby in a minute-and-a-half. He put her on my chest, and we were all in heaven. She was a little baby with a very little head. I don't know if Warren realized that from examining me or if he just had faith in my body, but because he had faith, I did. And baby Wren was wonderful and glorious. By then, we had like ten people in the delivery room. There is a really cute picture of me and Wren with Warren, beaming his great smile."

"Sifu Bertchold was one of those scary transports," said Ellie. "And also one of those strange births that happened around the time of the Stanislaus Complex fire."

"When we got pregnant," said Sifu, "I wanted to have a home birth. I'd been at a birth Ellie attended for a close friend, and I wanted that. We were building our house, so we were living in a trailer. I didn't want to deliver in the trailer, so we went to a friend's cabin in Ponderosa Hills. That was the year of the big fire, '87. So many people in our birth group had complications.

"Stephan was born in the cabin, but the placenta wouldn't let go, so I kept bleeding. The midwives called an ambulance after trying all the things they knew. The cabin was really hard to find, so it took the ambulance awhile to get there. By the time it arrived, I'd lost quite a bit of blood, and the medics had a hard time getting an IV in because my veins were collapsed. It was just one thing on top of another. Ellie went with me to the hospital in the ambulance and Steve stayed back with the baby. What a way to start life. Everything had been so sweet and quiet, so calm and amazing, and then Boom! We entered this other world.

"Back then Warren was the only doctor in the county who would back up the lay midwives, so that's who they called. He met us at the hospital. I was barely lucid when we got there, and they put me under really fast. He had to do a D&C. Apparently he had to peel away the placenta because it was very hard and firmly attached. He came to see me at the Birth Center the next day, and he said, 'Your hemoglobin is so low, I recommend you get a blood transfusion.' That was right at the beginning of all the stuff about AIDS and transfusions, and they weren't testing yet, so it was very scary. He said, 'As a new mom, you'll be tired for a long time while your body rebuilds blood cells.' I decided it was a good recommendation, but I had to do tests later to check for HIV.

"That's how he became our family doctor. We had no insurance, and so he charged us only what he would've gotten from Medi-Cal, which was really great because we had this huge Birth Center bill. We just kept chipping away at it, and at some point my parents helped us because they didn't want us to have that on top of everything else. The Birth Center bill actually went into collections, and we paid them. What I remember most was Warren saying, 'I hope nobody in your family says you shouldn't have had a home birth.' I really needed to hear that because my brother-in-law was a family physician in Switzerland, and I wasn't sure what he was going to say.

"On the other hand, Warren also said, 'NO, NO, NO more home births. I cannot with good conscience advise you to have a home birth again.' So when I got pregnant with Micah, we went round and round with him about that. I didn't want to have all the stuff the Birth Center normally does. I said, 'I don't want an internal monitor; I don't want the eye drops, I don't want … I don't want …' We waited so long laboring at home that Micah was almost born in the car. The only reason Warren made it was because he was at the Birth Center delivering another baby.

"One of the things I appreciated about Warren was how he fed you information that would make it easier. Our first child was a hard child to parent. Warren used to say how cool it would be if we could take this kid's massive amounts of energy and put it in a bottle. When Micah was born, it was even harder because now I had two kids. I remember he said, 'One and one, when it comes to kids, does not make two. One and one makes five.' When I talked to him, it didn't feel like I was talking to a doctor. I felt like I was talking to somebody who really knew what I was dealing with. He's the one who recommended we take a parenting class. When I took my kids to see him, he always asked me how I was doing. It wasn't only about taking care of the child. He took care of all of us."

"Another person you should talk to is Dolora Dossi," said Ellie. "Warren often encouraged us to stay home for a while longer when we called him, believing that given time, many problems resolve themselves. That was the case when Dolora was in labor, but little Liam was just stuck."

"When I got pregnant," said Dolora, "Warren was my doc, and Ellie was my midwife. Throughout pregnancy, I only saw him twice because he gave his blessing to Ellie. 'She knows what she's doing, and you know what you're doing, so you don't need advice from me.' It's really hard being a 40-year-old-first-time-pregnant woman because Western medicine immediately throws all kinds of things your way. There's a lot of shaming you into tests because you are a 'high risk pregnancy.' I never felt I was a high-risk pregnancy, and Warren supported that instinct. 'You're healthy. You're in good shape. Go have a great birth.'

"Everything went swimmingly. I was having my home birth. Liam crowned, but then his head turned ever so slightly, so he wouldn't come out. Ellie did everything she knew how to do, but I was fully dilated and already pushing hard. I had to breathe through an oxygen mask to get my heart rate back to normal. Liam's heart rate would go down until I breathed the oxygen, then his would go back up. I was exhausted after pushing for several hours when it should've only been an hour and a half for that stage of labor. Ellie had been talking to Warren all along, giving him updates, and finally he said, 'It's time to come in. I'll meet you there.' Jim was driving the van. Ellie was in the back seat reaching around with the fetal heart monitor. I had my legs up on the dashboard, groaning with full-on contractions.

"As soon as I got to the hospital, the nurses started putting all sorts of contraptions on me. They have their protocols even when the mother is saying, 'I'll sign anything. Just stay away from me.' One nurse put a scalp monitor on the baby's head to measure his heart rate, so they'd have a running paper trail. 'I don't want that on him,' I said, 'Please do not put that on him,' She leaned right into my face—mind you I'm still having intense pushing contractions—and she said, 'Look honey, I'm trying to save yours and your baby's lives.' I looked at Ellie, and she shrugged, indicating 'It's out of my hands now.' In walked Warren. 'Who put this heart monitor on this baby's head?' The nurse began stammering, and he ordered, 'Get it off!' He was super protective. 'There's no need for that because Ellie is monitoring this baby,' he added.

"Then he explained he wanted to try an extractor device. 'It's our last ditch effort to get this kid out,' he said, 'but you only have three pushes. I was so tired for the first push that I didn't have much to give.

248

I looked at Ellie and Jim, and their faces said he didn't budge. So the next push came, and Warren was saying, 'Come on baby. Come on baby.' And Ellie was cheering. 'Turn your little head.' I swallowed the third contraction because I didn't have the strength even though I knew it was the last chance. Warren said, 'I'm going to have to get the on-call OB for a C-section.' So he left to prep for surgery, and I was still in full-on labor. The OB brought the paperwork, and I said, 'Before I sign this, I want you to look in my eyes, and I want you to know that I trust you, and you're going to do right by me.' But he couldn't look at me. He just mumbled something. So I said, 'I want to shake your hand." He put a limp hand in mine.

"I was huge, because Liam was sixteen days late, and he was stuck in my pelvic bones. I couldn't walk, so they had to lift me onto a gurney. I was naked and so exposed, and Warren picked me up in his arms. I remember feeling like this protective papa bear was holding me as I had a contraction in his arms. He got me on the gurney, and then I was rolling down the hallway into the OR which was freezing and everyone—nurses, anesthesiologist—were in my face, and I had another contraction. Warren said, 'Get out of her face. She's still trying to have this baby. Leave her alone when she's pushing, please.' His voice was very gentle, like hot cocoa. He wasn't mean, so that was really lovely, and the anesthesiologist was great, and then Jim came in, and he was holding my hand. Warren lifted Liam out. He had to put his hand underneath Liam's head and pop him out of my bones. Later, he told us that Liam bit him on the finger. And then they whisked my baby away while the docs worked on me. I remember, as a vegetarian, asking, 'What is that smell?' And Warren said, 'We're cauterizing some things.' So the smell was my burning flesh."

"The next day, Warren came to see us, and he was so enamored by Liam. 'Look at this guy,' he said, cooing as he sat right on the edge of my bed holding my baby. 'Can you believe how healthy he is? You know he bit me.' The OB came in while he was there and poked my belly and said, 'Bet you thought that'd be gone today?' That was what he said—not one thing more except he pushed me to take antibiotics because I had a high white count. I was supposed to follow-up with him a couple weeks later, but I was so done. I called his office when I got home and said, 'I need to talk to the doctor. I'm not taking the antibiotics. I don't want them in my milk.' So they got him on the phone right away, and when I told him I wasn't taking the medication, he said, 'All right, don't.'"

"Dolora felt like Warren was her hero," said Ellie, "and the other doctor was awful. He ordered us to leave the room. Dolora was still having contractions, and he was telling us to get out. But Warren was the primary, so he let us stay."

The story of transporting Jennie Lou Tippett came up several times during the session with the midwives. "I'd had pretty straight forward home births," said Jennie, "but my fifth delivery was different. The baby wasn't moving down, and we didn't really know why. It had been twenty hours, which was double the length of my other births. I don't recall exactly how it all happened, but after Dody and Andrea tried a lot of different things to get the baby to drop into the birth canal, they called Dr. Borgquist directly. The way I understood it, he couldn't officially or legally back up home birthing. But there was this thing called the Samaritan clause—that is, if he didn't do any of my prenatal care, he would be willing to meet us at the hospital if we needed it. So when they called, he told them to break the water at home."

"I kept reiterating," said Andrea, "that here's no way I was going to break water at minus three station with a woman who's never been in labor this long."

"It was about 9:30 on a Sunday night," said Jennie Lou, "a time when his family expected him to be with them. I always think about that, of my husband Michael being called away from us, and I just cringe. I know Dr. Borgquist was called away plenty. But I cringed to think of taking him away from Judy and everyone else in his family."

"We transported Jennie Lou to the hospital in the back of their van," said Andrea, "and Warren met us there. He popped the water, and Mary Autumn fell plunk on the bed five seconds later. That was the first time I ever laid eyes on Dr. Borgquist."

"Mary Autumn's arm was over her head," said Jennie Lou, "We feel she was too shy to be born. She's kind of an introvert and still socially shy. Obviously, I didn't see what happened, but everyone said her arm was over her head as she was born. I don't remember much. I was in my own childbirth experience, but one thing I do remember was the third stage of birth—the placenta delivery—which always comes late for me, up to forty-five minutes after the baby comes. I also like to wait to cut the cord until it quits pulsating because I'm RH negative, and Dr. B was willing to wait for those things. He actually asked me at one point, 'How much longer do you want to wait?' It was his Sunday night, and he was respecting how long I thought I needed to wait. So at his memorial when the moderator—his son I think— said to stand up if Dr. Borgquist delivered your baby, I was proud to be one of the ones who stood. Looking back, I wouldn't do it any other way. I'm glad I got to have him deliver one of my babies."

# Chapter 18

# PAVOROTTI STAYING

"Golde, do you love me?"

-Tevye, *Fiddler on the Roof*

"**W**arren took me through a pregnancy," said Susan Russel, "which was really difficult because I had a ruptured disc. The sciatica pain was so bad he actually put me in the hospital in my second trimester, so he could administer a low dose of morphine. I had to have a Caesarean because of my back. When it was all over he said, 'If you ever get pregnant again, I'm going to jump off the Archie B. Stevenot Bridge, and the only thing that will keep me from jumping is if you do it first.' It was his way of saying, 'I get how hard this was, and I'm right beside you.'

"During the auditions for *Fiddler*," continued Susan, heading in another direction, "I actually got to sing opposite Warren, but I didn't get the part. Months later, maybe even a year after the production, Judith Weldon and I organized a fundraiser called "Lovers of Love Songs." I can't remember where the money was going—something charitable. We asked people from the community to perform at the event, which was held at the Sonora High Auditorium. I asked Warren to sing something from *Fiddler on the Roof.*

"'I'll do it if you do it with me,' he said.

253

"So we did the duet 'Do You Love Me?' I was very nervous. I walked out on stage as Golde doing some kind of handiwork, and as I sat down on the stool, I released a big sigh. That settled me down, and I thought, 'OK, this is going to work.' Warren came on stage after me, and his opening line was, 'Golde, do you love me?'"

Even beloved physicians question if and how well they are loved. Judy Borgquist said that one of the reasons Warren enjoyed doing *Fiddler* was because he "loved being admired." Rejection is tough. Susan Russel didn't get the part of Golde in the production of *Fiddler on the Roof*, but later she enjoyed assuming a bit of the role on stage opposite Warren. The college drama program—under the direction of Dave Purdy and Ellen Stewart—had produced *Fiddler* a second time, in 1992, at Columbia Actors Repertory Theater, and again Warren played Tevye. When Sierra Repertory Theater produced the play, he auditioned but did not get the part. "He was deeply hurt," said Judy. "He wanted that part like crazy. I was always critical of his performance as Tevye. I saw him as an amateurish Papa, but when I saw the SRT production, I thought he was much better than the guy they cast. Warren gave his heart and soul to the role, so that was a big disappointment in his life."

On the memory cards guests completed at Warren Borgquist's memorial, his performance in *Fiddler* tops the list of recollections in frequency. The casting of a local doctor—as well as teachers, real estate agents, bookstore owners, and school kids—was emblematic of the community theater that Dave and Ellen envisioned. "Heart and soul" was what they sought and what they gave theatergoers, so much so that someone like Warren Borgquist could play the role of a lifetime. "He didn't really have theater aspirations," said Judy. "He played one part after *Fiddler*—the doctor in *One Flew Over the Cuckoo's Nest*—but he never felt excited about that part. He only wanted to be the Papa." The role and the musical lyrics embodied the man. "Do You Love me?" "If I Were a Rich Man." "To Life." These are songs that reflected truths about Warren Borgquist.

Warren may not have had theater aspirations, but the illumination of stage lighting—the heat and brilliance of the limelight—is seductive. He enjoyed performing, basking in the recognition and admiration that accompanied such occasions. "Has anyone told you how after *Fiddler* we had to endure his singing at every holiday ever after?" asked Kathleen Lorimer. "I think he sang at some of the kids' weddings. You've got to love him," she said.

"He was always the speech-a-fier," said Karma Borgquist as we studied pictures of her parents' fortieth wedding anniversary. In one picture, a three-tiered wedding cake sits on a table below a sparkling numeral forty hung from the ceiling. Warren, dressed in black slacks, black vest, and white shirt with sleeves rolled up to his elbows, stands on one side of the table. Ruth and Cliff sit on the other side looking at him.

Warren has one foot upon a stool, and his arms are crossed at the wrists and resting on his knee. He is speaking directly to his parents, whose amused smiles confirm that his speech is funny while his posture intimates not only confidence, but also showmanship.

"Warren and I took Speech class the same semester at MJC," continued Karma. "His class was at 8:00 a.m. and mine was at 10:00. I was so focused on my fear that I could barely speak. But Warren gave all these wonderful speeches and had fun doing it. The students, the teacher, everyone thought he was great. It was his exuberance. Nobody could laugh like him, and the silliest things would get him going.

"He got so excited by presents. Here's a picture of him on one of his birthdays when everybody gave him socks." In the photo, three pairs of socks are draped across Warren's bald head. He peers owl-eyed through round, gold-rimmed lenses, one side of his mouth curved in an endearingly shy half smile. More socks dangle from his shoulders, and a woman's hand reaches across his chest to hold the toe of the pair of socks between thumb and forefinger. "Even if it was the thousandth pair of socks he'd received, he acted like it was the first ever," said Karma.

Photos frequently revealed the performer side of Warren Borgquist, such as one that accompanies a newspaper announcement of the first annual Sierra Repertory Theater's Lip Sync Competition in 1984. On the left, in dark glasses and fedoras are Sonora Elementary teachers: Tom Aitken and Jeff Juhl as the Blues Brothers and Linda Child as Liza Minelli, each looking directly into the camera, staid and serious. Warren is on the right depicting a fervent Luciano Pavarotti—head thrown back, chest expanded, arms at his sides but extended so that he fully occupies his space. His eyes are closed, and his mouth open in an operatic croon. While all the performers are expertly costumed to represent their respective roles, Warren displays more enthusiasm than the others. A follow-up article, reporting the success of the Lip Sync as a fundraising activity, adds an interesting detail. While Warren didn't win the contest as a star-imitator, Doug Lorimer accompanied his performance "on a candelabra-adorned grand piano," revealing how their friendship extended beyond Death Valley.

Patricia Harrelson

Warren's geeky retention of facts, love of history, and pleasure in performance fused when he created a monologue called "Doctors of the Mother Lode" for the tenth anniversary celebration of the Visiting Nurses Association. Using Carlo DeFerrari's extensive research, Warren created and performed the monologue to entertain guests with anecdotes about physicians in the rough and tumble days of the Gold Rush. Old time doctors treated mining accidents as gruesome as the ones Billie faced when she went to work at Beardsley Reservoir, which meant Warren had great material for a dramatic presentation. In a thank-you note after the event, Executive Director, Joan Strothers, suggested the performance opened up a new avocation for him. "I'm ready for the road tour," she said. Strothers complimented Borgquist and DeFerrari for assembling a fascinating presentation with artifacts that demonstrated "just how far medicine had progressed."

The event also commemorated the alliance of Hospice of the Sierra and VNA, a collaboration Warren nourished emotionally and financially. Warren commemorated history as he was making history, salting our rural scene with personal flair and big ideals—for the hospice movement was taking off nationwide in the '80s, and he was one of the leaders bringing compassionate care for the dying to Tuolumne County.

As the Young Turks converged on the foothills, they found it inconvenient to be members of the San Joaquin Chapter of the California Medical Association, situated in Stockton sixty miles away. They needed continuing education opportunities as well as the necessary record keeping to be closer at hand as they managed their burgeoning practices. To accomplish this, physicians formed a local chapter of the state professional organization on July 1, 1978 with the signing of a charter. Warren Borgquist's signature is on the initial charter. By the 1980s, the Tuolumne County Medical Society (TCMS) was busy fulfilling the purpose of providing Continuing Medical Education to local doctors who needed to accumulate 150 hours of credit every three years to maintain their California licenses.

Mary Ellinger, Executive Director of the TCMS, preserves the organization's history. Not only did local physicians need easier, more convenient ways to accrue continuing education hours, they also needed an efficient means to page on-call doctors, something the rolling foothills

257

made nearly impossible when using the systems in place in the central Valley towns of Stockton and Modesto. "The need for a paging system had a lot to do with the formation of the local society," said Mary.

Society—in the camaraderie sense—was actually a by-product of forming the local chapter, which held meetings throughout the year at the City Hotel. The doctors convened to discuss the business of the chapter and also to enjoy a convivial dinner. Mary Ellinger recalled her fondest memory of Warren Borgquist at one of these meetings when he rose from his chair at dinner because he had to leave early for a performance of *Fiddler on the Roof* at the Fallon House down the street. "He stood and sang 'If I were a Rich Man' without accompaniment," said Mary.

Chris Mills told a story that suggested that Warren was not the only doctor with dramatic flair. "Fitzpatrick and I teamed up to start the journal club," Mills explained. "We met once a month at the City Hotel in the Morgan Room. The physicians took turns being presenters—specialists in radiology, pathology, OB-GYN. We told them to pick something that would be of interest to everybody, like a journal article that reported a break-through in their specialty or something new they thought was going to take hold. We'd tell them to bring copies of the article for everyone. I had this boat hook, and I put it up against the wall, and if somebody got too long winded or was carrying on in a manner I didn't approve, I'd say, 'Get the hook.' You know, as a way to tell them to shut up. We didn't want presentations that were self-serving, things that were aimed at generating referrals. We wanted them to pick something the other doctors needed to know.

"At the end of every presentation, Fitzpatrick, the pathologist, would present a case with slides. They were pretty bizarre sometimes. A guy who was found dead in a boat with a burn on his chest from a medal he been wearing when he was struck by lightning. A lady who ended up head down in her washing machine. Another was a woman who died out in the snow, because she was feeling hot from hyperthermia, so she took off all her clothes. The highlight of the night was the things Fitzy brought—very unusual pathology cases. I mean they were off the wall. We called them mondo bizarros."

From the way, Dr. Mills described the journal club, it was easy to see that Warren wasn't alone when it came to performing. Even Dr. Mills got into the act with his boat hook. But the journal club was also a much-needed resource for these doctors who were far from the maddening crowd. Bob Fisher, the Sonora pharmacist who went to MJC with Warren, extolled the value of the club. "They'd go over medical information and keep in touch. I think Fitzpatrick was the instigator of that one. Fitzy was the real genius of the group. The other guys worked hard to get what they got. I know Warren was a tough worker. He spent his time on the books, and it paid off because what he read and learned he never forgot. If he had a challenging patient, he would go out of his way to find out what he could. He always looked for answers."

Marjorie Borgquist described a time when she was driving with Warren pulling a trailer to help a family member move from Santa Cruz. "He was listening to CDs about myocardial infarction. I had to listen with him all the way home. It was actually kind of interesting," she added fondly.

"Warren always drew pictures and told stories about whatever you were dealing with. He'd pull a story from his life or something he'd read. I think he got the knack of drawing pictures from taking science classes—all those cells you have draw in Biology 1A. His office staff had to order packages of colored pens and make sure they were in the exam rooms. Being married to a first-grade teacher probably figured into his drawing too. And, of course, he was a fabulous storyteller. That was his gift. People need to hear things in different ways to understand and to learn, and Warren was able to create that for patients. I think my parents inadvertently helped him because growing up in our house, humor was the best way to see a divergent reality."

Karma recalled a time when Warren was in pre-med. "He was taking anatomy, and he'd just learned about the hand. I remember him describing how the hand worked. He was so excited. He had every detail down, and the way he told it was fascinating. He did that with everything. He would read something, and he could tell it back and bring it alive. He just loved to tell a story."

Imagination infused Warren's presentations—be it on stage, in the office, or simply relating a newly acquired fact to his family or colleagues. There was, however, a downside to his fertile imaginations. "Warren would go off in la la land," said Marjorie. "For instance, he'd be driving along, and he'd slow down to ten miles an hour because he was lost in thought."

"He was such an animal— physically, I mean," said Judy. "He was so big, and yet he could do anything. He practically pushed me up the slope of the Great Wall of China. We didn't go on the touristy trip. We went on some other one, and it was hard going. It was hot, and I finally said, "I can't go any further." But there was another segment of the wall to climb, and he rallied us all and made everyone go the distance. He always pushed us."

"My dad was a plugger," said Greg. "He graduated in the bottom half of his class from medical school, and it bothered him greatly, but when he did his board certification exams in the mid '80s, he finished in the top ten percent of all family practice doctors. It was a nation-wide exam taken by graduates from Stanford, UCSF, Davis, Harvard, and Princeton, and my father was in the top tenth percentile. I remember going, 'Wow, you moved from the bottom half of your class to the top ten percent of all these physicians nationwide.' That's when he told me about brain plasticity and how it's a muscle. 'You use it; you grow it. You don't; you won't.' That taught me a lot," said Greg.

The plugger, the giraffe, the encourager were roles played by Warren Borgquist. Karma recalled several instances of the encourager. "Warren and I always did bike rides or hikes when we got together," continued Karma. "One time we rode to Groveland and then back via Old Wards Ferry Road. There was this one hill that went down into a dip and then up the other side. Warren said, 'You need to pedal down as fast as you can, keeping plenty of speed, and then go like a bat out of hell up the hill on the other side because there's a mean dog at that house.' One of his patients had been attacked by the dog, and it took extensive repair work to sew her up. Another time we were hiking at Kennedy Meadows. We wanted to go up this mountain. When we found a trail, it only went around the base, which wasn't getting us anywhere, so we looked at each other and said, 'Let's go straight up.' We had to pull ourselves up by pine trees because it was so steep and then push though the brush. We got all scratched up, so we found a creek bed to follow for the trip back."

"He always made me try new things," said Scott, "the damn giraffe producer."

"Like what for instance?"

"Being out there more, communicating, being more interactive. I'm not assertive. I don't want to make waves or embarrass myself. I'm the opposite of Warren. I can't imagine ever wanting to be in a play or do anything where I had to put myself before the public. One time, I was traveling for work in China. I had the day off, so I walked up the Great Wall. I was way up on top, and I called Warren to wish him Happy Father's Day. That felt like a neat thing to do," said Scott Purdy, Warren's step-son, "to call him from atop the Great Wall. He was such a role model on how to be a parent, how to father people, and how to be in a family."

*Chapter 19*

# THE SCHOOL OF LIFE

Religion is our creative and concrete response
to the mysteries that permeate our lives.

-Thomas Moore, *A Religion of One's Own*

In 1982, Warren attended the 20th reunion of his Sonora High School graduating class. Per the organizing committee's request, he completed a questionnaire that asked about each guest's life since graduation. To the question "What have you learned?" Warren wrote, "to appreciate what I have, to accept a little chronic depression. It means I understand the situation better. To remember to always have a little chronic joy, another sign that I'm in touch with the situation."

I asked Judy what she thought he meant by a little chronic depression?

"I think he means that life is hard. There are ups and downs. I mean, he was never depressed."

"I wonder why he used that term?" I asked, thinking about Chuck Waldman's reference to the "plain old depression" family doctors saw in their practices.

"Because he saw all of the pain in people's lives—the ups and downs of everybody's life. He saw what people have to endure. I think he was using the term loosely."

Chuck had talked about family physicians dealing with "obstetrics and terminal medicine" as well as mental health issues. Dealing with all three certainly put Warren in touch with the pain in people's lives, and Judy thought that's what he meant by a little chronic depression. Rather than clinical depression, he was referring to an augmented sense of melancholy that came with the job. On the other side, "chronic joy" was apparent in Warren's huge smile. For those who had the opportunity to be at one of the births he attended, Warren's joy was in great evidence. Don Andrews put it like this. "The thing I remember most about Warren during the birth of our son was that he shared our joy. He was as excited for us to have a baby as we were. Even before the birth, he had this magical empathy at every appointment. I'm sure he had it with everybody. Throughout the labor and delivery, he had a big smile on his face. He loved hearing the baby cry at birth, and then he stuck around. We have a wonderful photo of him, Shelley, and the baby right after the birth. You could tell from his expression that he was enjoying the whole thing. Some doctors would think, 'Enough of this. I've got to go back to the office.' Or 'I wonder if the other baby is ready to arrive down the hall.' But Warren took his time finding pleasure in every detail."

When Don talked about the expression on Warren's face in the photograph, I recalled the awe captured in a photograph of my birth team's faces as they watched Warren deliver my son. I've been at over twenty births, both at the Birth Center and in homes, and it is as if time stops, everything gets still and solemn while everyone absorbs the miracle. The parents and attendants appear drenched in a moment of grace. Sally Arnold, who was OB Nurse at the Birth Center for twenty years, described the birthing process as "this beautiful thing we were doing together." Having been present at six births for which Warren was the doctor, I witnessed his faith in the process while staying vigilant for a wrong turn. He just opened up to the moment and let it be. For me, being in the delivery room felt as reverent as standing in the nave of a cathedral.

If someone had asked me in the '80s, if I thought Warren was religious, I would have said he was a humanist—a term I'd learned in a college philosophy course. A humanist, as I understood it, was someone with an ethical stance motivated by compassion and a belief that human beings have a right and responsibility to give meaning and shape to their own lives. But no one asked me that question, and even if they had, I'm pretty sure my perspective was more of a projection than any specific knowledge I had about my doctor's religious beliefs. My true curiosity about Dr. Warren Borgquist's religious views surfaced slowly as I interviewed his colleagues and family.

Janet Waldman had said the doctors who called themselves the Young Turks were "the non-religious"—distinguishing them from the many Seventh-day Adventist doctors in the community. I didn't purposefully choose a non-Adventist doctor, but I did notice, when referred to one of these doctors, that I had an aversion to the religious materials scattered everywhere in their waiting rooms and offices. Eventually, Tuolumne County would see the rise of the Adventist Health System as a major force in health-care, one that would change the lives of private practice physicians—like Warren, Chuck, and Todd—and come to define our medical community. But I didn't realize my doctor's personal and world-view regarding religion was a salient concern until after Warren Borgquist was no longer my doctor. Apparently, my lack of discomfort made it a non-issue.

Digging into his life, however, I found I wanted to know something about his religious views and if indeed he was the humanist I made him out to be. Jennifer told of the time Warren and Judy had taken them to an Easter Service at the Unitarian Church as they sought to provide the kids some religious training. She said she and her siblings had been more interested in the animals that were part of the service than in whatever was being said about the resurrection.

"Warren wasn't a Christian," Judy said. "He believed there was something, but it wasn't Jesus."

Warren, of course, worked the Alcoholics Anonymous program of twelve steps that deferred to a higher power in the first step, which was perhaps the "something" Judy said he believed in. I thought about him playing the role of a Jewish milkman who talked to God in *Fiddler on the Roof.* Tevye was a character with whom he identified. I wondered if he personally talked to God, or at least to a higher power. As a picture of Warren's rather patchwork religious stance took shape, Judy mentioned in passing that she had converted to Catholicism in the '80s. A window slid open revealing another room in this couple's life, and I wanted to see more.

One morning at Judy's, as her great-grandson Logan stood at the coffee table drawing furiously, I said, "I have a note here about you becoming a Catholic. Why?" I asked with perhaps more incredulity than I intended.

"What possessed me?" Judy repeated, shaking her head. "I don't know, especially now since I can't force myself to go to church. I can't really explain it because it was a mystical experience. We went to Rome with Jennifer in 1981—to the Sistine Chapel and all these other places where Michaelangelo had done his thing. Walking through the Forum, I imagined all the lowly people who had grown the vegetables and cleaned up after the great masters, like the stonemasons, who built things. In my mind, I saw all these people who were dedicated to the Church and the idea of Christianity." In the recording of this interview with Judy, the scratching of Logan's pencil on paper is energetic and insistent as if he was tuned into the emotional heart of her story.

"I started to wonder if I should explore something. I didn't have a religious upbringing. My parents had taken us to whatever church was closest, so they could enjoy each other's company on Sunday mornings. When I found out I was pregnant with Scott, I went to St Brigid's Catholic Church and fell down on my knees and said, 'I can't do this.' And I was told in some unfathomable way, 'Get up off your knees. You can handle it!' That was kind of mystical. And then during the pregnancy, I used to sit in Old St. Mary's on my lunch hour. When I was an adult and working at Sonora El, a colleague, Kathy Brandi, said to me one Ash Wednesday, 'Come on. We're going to church.' So we did, and it felt good.

"The next September, after that Ash Wednesday, a class started: "Do you want to become a Catholic?" I went to that class every Monday until the next Easter when I went through Confirmation. We had a fabulous priest, Father Sylva, who was very liberal. I was taught there are certain tenets of the Catholic Church you might not agree with, like birth control. If you don't agree, you just pray, and if it's OK with you and God, then it's OK. It was the opposite of what Pope Benedict was trying to foist down people's throats. The priest was brilliant, very intellectual—spiritual but also intellectual. You could ask him questions and talk about stuff."

"What did Warren think about all of this?" I asked

"He was like, 'What?'" Judy exclaimed, with a force that emphasized her husband's dismay. "Warren was a deist—his term—as were Jefferson and Franklin and all the right-thinkers of the world. He believed in God but not in the divinity of Christ, nor in any organized religion. He relied on God for his sobriety. At the end of the process to be confirmed, the leader said would you like to get remarried? So I came home and said, 'Would you like to get remarried?' And he said, 'What?'" Judy exclaimed again. "Then he said, 'If it would make you happy, of course I will.' So we had a nice little marriage ceremony."

"Who came to that?" I asked, while making a note about Warren's astonishment followed by acquiescence.

"Nobody," said Judy. "But at the Confirmation ceremony, I had to read a verse from the Old Testament as part of the ceremony. It was about Moses parting the Red Sea. That was in 1986, so Jennifer was 23. Jennifer has a louder voice than me. Speaking from her seat in the church, she said, 'You don't believe that shit, do you Mom?'" Judy laughed at this memory as she mimed shushing her daughter in church.

Judy went to confirmation class to become a Catholic on Monday nights. And there was a time when Warren spent Monday nights going to a community chorus class offered by the college. According to Don Andrews, Warren became so fond of singing during the *Fiddler* production that he decided he wanted to take part in the annual Christmas performance of Handel's "Messiah" at the Seventh-day Adventist Church. For many years, "Messiah" was a fixture of the Christmas season in our rural community as it was across the United States and Great Britain, so it sold out almost as soon as tickets went on sale. To capitalize on excellent acoustics, the program took place at the Church, which sat between Warren's office and his home.

"Warren set a goal," said Don. "He did not want or need to be a soloist, but he did want to sing all the way through the Christmas portion. I knew he loved sticking his neck out, but who would've thought he'd want to do it rehearsing 'Messiah.' I don't know how he carved out Monday nights for every rehearsal, but he did—September, October, November. I found it remarkable that a guy who was really an untrained singer would decide to take part in this performance. It blew my mind. He proudly sang in the bass section."

Don not only admired Warren's determination to attempt the challenging music, he also commended his unending solicitude regarding the aches and pains of fellow chorus members. "During breaks at rehearsal, people would ask him about a growth on their arm or a sore knee. He didn't put them off, but he also didn't doctor on the spot. He found a reasonable compromise. He might say, 'Call first thing in the morning, and we'll make room for you.' If someone needed a specialist, he'd say, 'I'll help arrange that tomorrow.' Or he might say, 'I'll give you prescription for this pain killer because you obviously need it to sleep tonight.' But he knew when to draw the line. He was very wise about those things and always appropriate. They all loved him because he would listen, and he would offer a solution. I found it remarkable."

Don was a fan of Warren Borgquist, for the man had displayed traits that Don admired: joy, patience, perseverance, solicitude—all in highly charged emotionally contexts. Warren wasn't into organized religion, but he found plenty of ways to lift his spirit. Listening and communing with others—especially his family—topped the list. I couldn't help but think of the Dali Lama who said, "My religion is simple. My religion is kindness."

In the 1980s, Judy and Warren had adult children whom they had encouraged to be outspoken and free-thinking. Their progressive parenting sent these young people hurtling forth into life with the permission to make widely diverse choices—each of which ricocheted back to touch Judy and Warren with unanticipated emotions and experiences, and an insistent call for kindness.

Daughter Jennifer's adult choices most resembled Judy's. "Jennifer went to Santa Barbara," said her mother, "where she met and married Michael and converted to Judaism. She went through all the classes and had a Bat Mitzvah. And you know how converts are. She's quite enthusiastic. They go to temple every week, and the kids have all had Bar or Bat Mitzvahs. It's been really fun for me and Warren to participate in their Jewishness. We always had Hanukkah with them."

In one picture, Warren, sitting beside an attractive elderly woman, wears a yarmulke, snugly hugging his bald head. The Jewish custom of wearing the yarmulke was meant as a reminder of God's constant presence—much like a wedding ring, it was a prompt not to stray into inappropriate thoughts and activities.

"Mom paved the way," said Jennifer, "by becoming a Catholic before I converted. Warren thought whatever you wanted to do was great. He liked the diversity in the family."

Parenting was one of those things Warren put his heart into trying to get right, and for him, getting it right had to do with being encouraging. Jennifer said, "He always thought it was good to do what made you happy." Kris Scott, Jennifer's friend, said that Warren and Judy had the attitude that "the world was your oyster." Each of Judy and Warren's children, plus their exchange student Nicolas told stories about how Warren guided and encouraged them as they matured into adults in a wide array of decision-making moments—from health concerns to professional choices to heartbreak.

"Warren diagnosed my appendicitis over the phone," said Scott Purdy. "I was working in Los Angeles, and I went to the Harriman Jones Clinic at Long Beach. It was kind of in a shady neighborhood, and I think they thought I was trying to get drugs. The doctor examined me and said, 'You have indigestion" and sent me home. I didn't think I had indigestion, so I called Warren, but he and my mom were out. I finally reached him at eleven o'clock and said, 'I've been having stomach pain. It's killing me.' Warren said, 'Push in and let go real fast." Arrghh, I groaned because it hurt. He said, 'You have appendicitis. Get to the hospital right away.' So instead of going to Long Beach, I drove down to Orange County to the hospital, and they operated that night."

Scott was 24 when Warren diagnosed his appendicitis over the phone, having apparently learned from the mishap with Mimi when he'd ignored her complaint of a bellyache. "My dad and Judy saved me in so many ways," said Mimi. "Dad always made us do things outside our comfort zone because he believed you have to conquer your fears. Like this one time he made me hop across the rocks down at Knights Ferry. Dean Colli was with us. I was freaking out, screaming 'I can't do it. I can't do it.' He kept saying, 'You can do it! Take a chance. You might get wet. So what?' I was screaming at him, throwing a temper tantrum. 'I can't do it. You're mean! Why are you making me?' Finally, I went for it. I fell in, and he jumped in after me. The water was only about waist high. When we got to the other side, he said, 'You survived! Hello.' His whole lesson about life was right there. You have to try. If you don't try, you'll never know." Dean Colli had told this story, and now Mimi was explaining the message she took away.

Nicolas told a story with a similar message. "Everyone in my family is a pharmacist," he explained. "My grandfather was a pharmacist, my uncle, my dad, my mom, my brother, my cousin, my sister-in-law—all of them. The family mantra was: 'It's an interesting profession and even on the weekend, you're still making money.' I was struggling between going into medicine or pharmacy. When I told Warren my family said pharmacy was a good option, he looked at me and said, 'Nicolas, that's crap.' That was the first time I understood what kind of thinker he was. He did not consider other's options; he made up his own mind. I'm 53, and I still sometimes wake up in the morning and say, 'Maybe I should've became a pharmacist. But this is not an argument. You should do something you are interested in, not something that's convenient."

"It was hard for Nicolas," said Judy, "when he went home. With us, he learned he could speak his mind, and that was not acceptable in his family. I think his parents were upset the first year or so after he went home. I'm quite close to his parents now and as our friendship grew, they explained: 'With our friends, we don't talk about our children. How they're doing or our feelings. We just don't.' Our openness was strange to them."

"How do you think Warren influenced Nicolas to be a doctor?" I asked

"By loving what he did. By showing Nicolas how intellectually interesting it was—how it was a puzzle in which you have some of the parts but you have to figure out the rest. Nicolas is very bright, so he liked that, but he did not want to be a family practice doctor after watching Warren and the hours he worked, especially during the year when he was living with us. Warren was always away birthing a baby or going to the ER. Nicolas eventually became an anesthesiologist," said Judy. "We went to Lausanne for his graduation from medical school. Warren gave him a stethoscope with his name engraved on it."

Warren had less direct influence on his son Greg's choices. After his arrest in South Korea, Greg spent a year in the military correctional system. "My last year in the military was the easiest I had. I was in Fort Riley, Kansas, and I worked as a chaplain's assistant, a lifeguard, and a gardener. When I got out, I was going to go to Cabrillo College in Santa Cruz, but my sister Jennifer convinced me to go to Santa Barbara City College, and that's how I met the belle of Santa Barbara County—Kati. I was very fortunate to attract one of the most sought after young ladies. I was 27. We waited two years before we got married. I was a kid and totally naïve. I'd been too prideful to ask for help after the South Korea thing. My dad wanted to hire a lawyer for me, but I turned him down. However, that's the thing that got me aligned to meet my wife and taught me lessons I now share with my students. When Kati came into my life, my dad said, 'Boy, I must've done a better job of raising you than I thought because if you can get a girl like Kati, you've definitely got something going.' He was really impressed with her. My grandparents fell in love with her too. St. Katherine—they anointed her. Aside from my parents bringing me into this world, she's the greatest thing that ever happened to me."

As with Greg, Warren and Judy had to stand on the sidelines heartsick while they watched the challenges Scott faced. "Scott went to Cuesta first and then Colorado School of Mines," explained Judy. "He didn't have it easy. At Cuesta he met Alice. She was beautiful … and bipolar and alcoholic. They were so in love. They got married, and for a while she was OK, and they had Evan and then Sean. But then she just kept getting sicker and sicker. One day I got a phone call from Scott saying Alice was missing. 'What do you mean missing?' I said. She had gone the store, and he didn't find her for two weeks. That happened during one of her manic periods. After this disappearance and getting her back, Scott sent her to a rehab, and she tried to get better, but it didn't take, so he sent her to another rehab. Finally, they divorced. Scott had the boys every other week for about five years—much longer than it should have been, but split custody was court ordered. Alcoholism is just a terrible disease. Couple that with bipolar, and it's just tragic. Eventually, she overdosed on pain medication and died."

Judy told this story while we were once again in the company of great-grandson Logan, who was sitting in the next room watching something called Bubble Guppies. He interrupted the telling of the story of Scott and Alice—his grandparents— several times when something wasn't working right in the video program. The interruptions gave me time to think about how the difficulties in Scott's life must have interrupted Judy and Warren's life with worry and concern. Once again I was reminded that the doctor I saw in the examination room—the man who attentively listened to my physical complaints and adroitly inquired about my life—was a human being with his own personal disquiet. The last time Judy went to help Logan, I thought of a story his Uncle Evan had told, several days earlier on the phone, when I asked about his first memory of Gramps.

"When I was about 3, before my brother Sean was born, I remember Gramps put me on his shoulders. Mom was really protective of me back then, and she didn't want me to go anywhere. He assured her that we were just going around the block, but I guess it was a pretty big step. I was getting to know Gramps, and he was acting crazy all along the way. He crawled under a bush, and I started hitting the bush, and he started bellowing, 'What are you doing, you 3-year-old kid?' And then he clamored, "Telephone pole, Telephone pole,' and he bumped into the pole and bounced off. He did stuff like that for the entire walk, and by the time we got back, I was laughing and totally in love with Gramps."

When Judy and I reviewed the pictures from the pasteboards at Warren's memorial, she pointed to several of him carrying grandchildren. "He always took the kids on his shoulders," she explained, "and then as they walked along, he'd say, 'Uh oh!' and pretend he was going to bash into something."

As Warren moved into his 40s, he bumped into a bunch of new experiences. He became the parent of adult children. His wife converted to Catholicism. His daughter converted to Judaism. He sang Handel's "Messiah." He gave an engraved stethoscope to a young Swiss doctor he had influenced linguistically and professionally. He jumped in a river to build a daughter's confidence, and he watched a daughter-in-law fail to avoid the tragic grip of alcoholism and mental illness. His son refused his offer of financial assistance after he had screwed up yet another time. But the young man believed this led him toward a saint of sorts in the woman he married. Researching the specialty of Family Medicine, I learned these doctors are trained to focus upon the whole person who lives in a complex setting. They are aware of the varied social, emotional, and environmental factors that influence the health of their patient and the family. Warren Borgquist didn't get this training in a three-year residency; he got it in the school of life. Many a patient will see in these stories the source of his empathy.

If pressed back in the '80s, I would have labeled Dr. Warren Borgquist a humanist. His empathy and compassion were the indicators. I had also read that humanism is the philosophy of those in love with life, and that too was my experience of Dr. Borgquist. Judy called him a deist, saying that it was his term. When I researched the word, I learned a deist believes in God based on rational terms rather than on the revelations prophets receive from God. One source said deism is a natural religion—a "bottom-up" faith—while revealed religion is "top-down." Warren, I thought, would have seized the term "bottom-up faith" with good humor. For me, his faith was visibly apparent when he was sitting patiently with a birthing woman or a terminal patient, for I'd been touched by his quiet repose in both situations. At a time that is at once holy and terrifying, Warren Borgquist radiated peaceful composure.

Best-selling author and spiritual advisor, Thomas Moore, wrote a book on the subject of personal religion in which he describes how one can find mystical experiences in life, art, nature, and service that provide a sense of purpose that satisfies spiritual needs. Moore goes so far as to say, "I suspect that the stethoscopes [doctors] wear around their necks are vestiges of the former religious nature of their position." Perhaps Warren tapped into the sacred in every day living, as well as in his professional life, as a means of finding a "secular religion." French philosopher and Jesuit Priest, Pierre Teillhard de Chardin, said, "We are not human beings having a spiritual experience. We are spiritual beings having a human experience." I don't know if Warren consciously envisioned a personal religion or saw himself as a spiritual being, but it is easy to discern his deep appreciation for the human experience in his parenting, his doctoring, and his willingness to entertain both "chronic depression" and "chronic joy."

# *Chapter 20*

# A BEAUTIFUL DAY
# IN THE NEIGHBORHOOD

"Successful people … love what they are doing
and they love it in front of other people."

-Mr. Rogers

"Warren was our doctor when Peggy had a miscarriage," said Ross Carkeet, "but he wasn't on call that day, so we were directed to Dr. Mills. On the way to his office, we stopped at the pharmacy to pick up some medication they told us to get. I went in while Peggy waited in the car because she was in throes of the miscarriage. When I came out, she told me Dr. Borgquist had come out of the grocery store with a half-gallon of ice cream. 'I ducked down,' she said, 'so he wouldn't see me, because if he did, he'd want to know how I was doing. I didn't want to ruin his day. His whole family was in the car waiting for him.'"

Practicing medicine in a small town was like that. An odd mix of proximity and intimacy resulting in a unique set of circumstance for doctor and patient alike. Warren had spent his high school years in Sonora, and his parents owned a dime store on Washington Street. His wife was a teacher and eventually principal at Sonora Elementary School. They had neighbors and friends, and they took part in service organizations.

They went to local theater productions, and they ate at local restaurants. And of course, Warren shopped at local markets, hardware stores, and pharmacies. He was a resident of the community as well as a practicing physician.

"We had 'blow job' competitions out on the street—his blower against my blower," said Karen Sinclair, daughter of the Borgquist's neighbors Betty Lou and Denny Sinclair. I talked to Karen and Betty Lou in their front room, where they reminisced about their long-time neighbor.

"I'm telling you, out on the street, it was who was the biggest slob—me or Warren," said Karen. "He'd get on me for the way I dressed, but I think he was sloppier. What was nice was that we were all there for each other as neighbors. He was a doctor, Judy was a principal, and I was a teacher who worked at her school. We didn't bother each other, but if someone needed something—medical emergency or whatever—Warren would be there."

By way of example, Betty Lou explained that it was Denny Sinclair who alerted Warren to the ash can blazing at the end of his driveway after Greg set it there.

"One day I was out in the yard messing with the vacuum cleaner," said Karen. "I had the filter out, and I was trying to clear it by hand, and here comes Warren.

"'What are you doing?'

"'Clearing my damn filter. What does it look like?'

"'Come on,' he said, "I've got an air compressor.'

"I followed him to his shop. 'Jesus Christ, Warren,' I said. 'Where did you get all these tools?'

"'She doesn't know everything I do,' he said smiling that silly grin as he referred to Judy. 'You can borrow anything you want,' he said as he blew out my filter."

"He was always building something," said Betty Lou. "When he got into something that was over his head, he'd hire someone to work with him. Warren and Judy bought that house more than thirty-five years ago. It's like the Winchester Mystery house. They just kept adding on and adding on."

"Mom used to do Warren's ironing," said Karen. "He wasn't a slob when he went to work. He wore nice khakis and pressed shirts."

"About every ten days, he'd bring a great big tote full of shirts and slacks," said Betty Lou. "At that time, he was a great big guy, so there was a lot to iron. When he paid me, he wrote cute little sayings on the corner of the check—little compliments: 'Fast & Smooth' or 'Smooth as silk.' Or 'The best ironer ever.'"

"One was 'Betty Lou's lunacy,'" said Karen. "I remember that one. He used to put the tote out in the side room. Then Mom told him it was too heavy. He either had to bring it into the laundry room or bring it when I was here, so I could get it in."

"Sometimes he'd wait three weeks to bring the stuff," said Betty Lou.

"Mom chewed him out when it was that long."

"One time, I took the ironing up to his house. Judy was writing me a check, and the phone rang. Judy yelled, 'Warren somebody wants to talk to you.' That's when I realized he was skinny dipping in the hot tub. When he started getting up, Judy said, 'Sit back down.' I turned my head and said, 'I'll see you later, Judy.'"

"She came home in shock," said Karen. "She couldn't handle it— old school, you know," added Karen, who everyone at Sonora Elementary fondly called, "Coach Sinclair."

"I also cleaned their house sometimes," said Betty Lou. "There were little yellow duckies in the bathtub. I asked Judy about them, and she said, 'He plays with them when he takes a bubble bath.' He was such a kid at heart. I always loved that this grown man had little yellow duckies all around his bathtub."

"He always wore those weird socks," said Karen. "So when I saw an off-the-wall pair, I'd get 'em. I got him Christmas socks that had a button you pushed to make them sing. They were hard to find because they don't make a lot funny socks for men."

"Every once in a while when something would happen over there," said Betty Lou, "like somebody'd get sick or there would be a funeral. I'd cook a big pot of chili. He absolutely loved my chili."

Neighborly ways and acts of friendship rippled from the Borgquist household. "I was involved in planning a women's symposium," said

Shelley Andrews, Judy's friend from student-teaching days. "We held the symposium at Columbia College, and Warren was a major resource, helping with stuff related to women's health. He hooked us up with John Dorman, who was a neurologist, and John did some kind of presentation. Dorman's wife Sandy was involved in all kinds of stuff related to women's issues. That's where the Tuolumne County chapter of NOW [National Organization for Women] began—during that first women's symposium. It was an incredible event. There were 80-year-old women and there were 18 year olds. Nothing like that had ever happened before, and I don't think has happened since. This was not a gathering of professional women. It was all about women who didn't work."

"John and Sandy Dorman were our close friends," said Judy. "John was a neurologist who came here in the seventies, and he was Warren's running partner. We did all sorts of things with them. Then when John went to some doctor conference, he met Della and that was the end of that. After John and Sandy split up, Sandy fell in love with a woman. Then she headed off to Berkeley and got her PhD. When we did the cross-country trip, we visited her in New York City. Then after having female partners, she shocked us all by marrying–what was his name? Oh crud, I forget. But then he died, and she met David online. Warren and I married them. We both had Universal Life Minister certificates. So we married David and Sandy. I've done eight marriages. Warren and I performed two of those together."

"I met Judy Borgquist because of my friend Judy Wilson," said Kathleen Lorimer. "Warren was welcoming all these new doctors, and they had a party, and Judy and Jim Wilson dragged us along. Judy B and I had an immediate connection. I remember Doug was a little funny about Warren because he remembered him in high school when he was kind of a dork, but as we got to know them, our families got connected forever. Here's a funny story. Doug, the kids, and I were out hiking. Jason had my hand, and we were going along this snow bank and he pulled me off balance. I went shooting off the bank and hit the scree and landed right at the edge where there was a waterfall. I didn't go over, but I ripped open my leg.

"'Call a helicopter,' I said.

"'No we've got to walk out,' said Doug. 'I'll call Warren.'

"In those days you had to stop at a pay phone, so we did, and Warren said he'd meet us at the hospital. Judy came with him. He was working on me, and she said, 'Oh thank god, you wore your good underpants.' That was like the third time we'd met, and I thought, we're going to be friends for life. We've been through a lot with our kids and our marriages. All of it."

"Warren and Jim and Doug had their thing. They'd go off for a week in the desert or they'd go climbing. Doug and Jim were very lean and kind of show offs, and there was Warren, the little tractor—always keeping up, never giving up. I so admired him for that. One time when they went off on their desert trip, Judy and I decided to go to Guadalajara. We had a fabulous time. I would say as far friendships go, it was Judy and I and Doug and Warren because I always irritated Warren.

"How so?"

"I would call him on things, and we would go back and forth. But there was this deep caring for each other. He just didn't want me to get away with anything, and I didn't want him to get away with anything. Sometimes, I felt like we were jealous of the time the other one had with Judy. We were young. It was definitely a love-hate relationship because I totally respected him as a doctor, but he could be very braggadocious.

"Our families got together on Christmas Eve," said Kathleen. "Each year we alternated houses. The tradition in my family was everyone brought something to read. Sometimes we would sing, and at the very end, Warren always read those paragraphs in the Bible about Jesus' birth. After the readings, we'd have a great meal. Their kids were a little bit older than mine, so my kids were in awe."

"Valentine's Day was another big holiday for us. We always made Valentine cards. Oh, the creativity that came out in those Valentines! They were a great way of connecting with each other. It was really fun to watch the kids try to find the right poem for the certain person. I have a picture from one Valentine's Day where we're trying to balance a spoon on our noses. Warren did it perfectly."

"Was he your family doctor?"

"Yeah, but we never went to the office. I'd be there for a dinner party and say, 'Hey Warren would you look at this?' When Doug and I would go away, our daughter Brynn always stayed with them. She was close to

Warren. He taught her how to drive because I tried, and it wasn't a good match. I'm sure he told her about sex and contraceptives, too. I had a strict Catholic up bringing, so we didn't talk about stuff like that. Warren didn't just see us as family friends. He saw each of us as individuals. For instance, my son Jason had his own relationship with Warren as did Brynn."

"Judy told me her story about converting to Catholicism. Why do you think she did that?"

"I went to Mass with her a few times. I was raised a Catholic. Doug was totally anti-anything, so we never did anything with the kids. Judy was in Italy and had some profound experience and when she came back she went to Mass, and then BOOM, she said, 'I'm going to become a Catholic,' and she went right into it. She was totally devout and was on this and that board and taught classes. I said, 'You can have it.' Judy stayed involved for quite a few years. Then one time, she said you ought to come hear this new priest. So I did, and he was fabulous, and that's why I started going again. I had this childhood friend who had breast cancer and went through all the treatments and then it came back in her bones, so for eight months I took care of her. Father Kraft would come visit her. He didn't do any actual Catholic stuff, but he sang with us, and he was there at the end when we were washing her body. And he spoke at the celebration of life. He was very open. He blessed the labyrinth I made in my yard. Warren and Doug were both anti-religion, so it was nice that Judy had somebody to go with. Judy and I used to walk every morning up by the college where Chuck Waldman lives. One time we were walking along, and suddenly Judy wasn't there. She had gone right down the embankment."

Over and over, I was struck by the subtle metaphors, like the story of Judy sliding down the embankment during a walk. This tiny tale followed Kathleen's version of Judy's conversion to Catholicism—the Judy she'd known suddenly gone in some way. People tell stories in ways that reveal much more than what's on the surface. Betty Lou Sinclair told of the rubber duckies around the doctor's bathtub and the sweet, almost sexy notes he wrote on checks. Karen Sinclair could tweak a Borgquist encounter in a lecherous direction with a turn of phrase. Peggy Carkeet slid out of sight so as to not ruin Warren's time with family. Details reoccurred; dinners and celebrations, tools and teachers spiraled around and within Warren's world.

"They invited us to get-together at their house," said Bill Boyd. He turned to his wife Celeste and asked, "What year was that? '91?"

Celeste nodded.

"Was the invitation related to your professional connection?" I asked Celeste.

"Probably," she answered. "Judy was on the committee that hired me for a position at the County Schools Office."

"We didn't have a doctor," continued Bill, "So while we were there, I asked him if he could be our doctor. At the time, he wasn't taking any new patients, but he said, 'We can do that.'"

"That was the start of long friendship,' said Celeste. "You used to work with him in his shop," she prompted Bill, encouraging him to say more about his friend.

"When we first met, I offered to help him, but he said he liked to work alone. Finally, he was building these big doors to his workshop, and he asked me to come help. That's when he told me, 'I don't measure twice and cut once. I measure four times and cut twice.'" Jim Andrasko, who spent considerable time helping Warren remodel the house, would soon confirm that the man made errors that needed correcting.

"I used to pick up stuff for him at the hardware store," said Bill. " I'd say we needed six of something, and he'd say, 'Get a dozen.' I was on his account at Andy's, and when I walked in, the gal who worked there would say, 'What does he want now?' I'd say, 'We need this and that.' And she'd say, 'Don't you want few extra?' And I'd say, 'That's already factored in.'" Bill chuckled at the memory. "Warren always had the grandkids do things in the shop. For instance, he'd say, 'Run this through the saw. It won't cut your finger off.' He was very safety conscious."

"And he was a great teacher," said Celeste.

"Like when he and Judy took the kids on a trip, he always had a bit of history to share. Or he'd ask them questions: 'Do you know how the plane flies?' And then he'd explain aerodynamics—the passage of air over and under the wings." Bill had heard such conversations first hand, for over the years, he and Celeste accompanied Warren and Judy and a grandkid or two on long flights to Europe and China.

Gill McKee also met Judy because they were educators, administrators in the county school system. "Of course, she's a dynamo. And then I met Warren, and he was a dynamo too," said Gill.

"Gill and Judy were friends," said Jim McKee, "but I met Warren as my doctor. It was so nice to be comfortable with a doctor right out of the chute. None of my previous doctors—or subsequent for that matter—have come close to providing the feeling he gave of being seen and heard. He assisted in an operation on my knee. He actually asked if he could assist the orthopedist. I thought it was pretty nice that my doctor wanted to be there for this relatively minor surgery. He did my yearly physicals, and when more serious stuff came up, like cholesterol and high blood pressure, I felt like I was in the best hands. Where other people wanted to talk to a specialist for issues like that, my feeling was: We've got Warren."

"I used to call him the one-stop-shop doctor," said Gill, "because he took care of everything. You didn't have to run around to all these different specialists because he did it all."

"Over the years we became close friends," said Jim. "They used to have this Christmas party we went to. Between his position in the community and Judy's, they knew so many people. It was quite the party. We'd have them up to our home in Twain Harte for lunch. Warren loved to walk on the West Side railroad grade in the spring when the lupine were blooming, so that was something we did with them. Sometimes the lupine bushes were so high they were bending down over us off the mountain side."

"One cute thing he said was 'I'm going to retire on April 1, 2013. Don't you think that's a good date?'" Gill called the remark cute, but the April Fools' irony hit disquietingly as did Jim's next comment.

"I remember something he said during one of our visits," said Jim. "Judy was about to retire, and Gill had already retired. Warren said, 'Jim, your cholesterol is good. Your blood pressure is good. You and I both have to stay in good health because we have to take care of our ladies.' Judy had been going through some stressful stuff and had been relying on him, so I thought that comment expressed his worries about Judy.

"I could always count on laughing when we had a dinner date

with Judy and Warren," Jim continued. "Other friends and co-workers weren't exactly boring, but nothing was like dinner with the Borgquists. It was never a downer. We'd make jokes about our government, the administration, never dwelling on the negative or downside. We had a regular night out for sushi after he got off work, so it was a little later than we usually ate, but it was always a fun time. Warren would get that half grin on his face, and you knew he was about to set you up with a good belly laugh.

"We belong to Sierra Bible Church," said Jim, "so sometimes I would talk to Warren about the Lord, and Judy wanted that, so we'd talk. He believed in God though I wasn't quite sure where he stood. Still, he was a godly man and respected the truth of the Bible. Gill and Judy were in that woman's club—Delta Kappa Gamma—so they'd be at their meetings, and we'd hang out and talk. Judy would razz him about working in his shop and having a big mess out there. Every time I went to their place, he said, 'Come on, Jim. I want to show you what I've done.' Maybe that's what made him a good doctor—his inclination for wood crafting and workmanship. I remember Judy saying, 'If you don't get this kitchen done, I'm going to get someone in here to finish it.'

"'No, no,' he said. 'I'll take care of it.'

"The next time we came for dinner, he had built all the drawers and cabinets specially tailored for her. But there was always quite a scene in his shop. That was his man cave really. He had every tool imaginable."

Gill McKee and Judy Borgquist were members of Delta Kappa Gamma. The letters D and G in this women's organization stood for the motto "Do Good" which was the aim of the group. Delta Kappa Gamma was committed to making the world a better place by promoting education and cultural opportunities, but members were also interested in fostering friendship. Judy valued friendship. She had maintained close contact with a group of friends from high school who continued to meet a couple of times a year, more than fifty years after graduation. She was also a member of the American Association of University Women, participating in the AAUW book club and as a program chairperson for the AAUW Annual Home Tour. Four homes decked out in holiday glory are on the tour each year, and the money raised from ticket sales goes to scholarships for women. Warren hoped someday to showcase their home on the tour, but Judy wasn't so sure about tackling the task.

She was also a member of Omega Nu, which provided another outlet through which she and Warren socialized. "There are about thirty-five members," said Judy. "You have to be invited to join. We'd meet twice a month, have dinner and wine, and then take care of the business part. Some people think of it as a sorority and some people think of it as a charitable organization. It's both. On the nights we met, a bunch of the husbands—not all of them but about ten—go out to dinner, so Warren used to do that."

"Our big fundraiser of the year is the Omega Nu rummage sale at the fairgrounds. The hospital rents us a space in the old Community Hospital building—the part that used to be doctors' offices—and that's where we store the stuff we collect. The week before the sale, we sort and box everything. Warren's job was to load all those boxes on his truck and make a thousand trips to the fairgrounds and unload them. Books are my area, so he would make bookcases with bricks and boards. It took three days to set up, and on Saturday night, when it was over, we had to cleanup. Warren helped haul all of the stuff we were going to keep back to the storeroom. He did a ton of heavy lifting and worked long hours on that rummage sale. But it was worth it. We raise almost six thousand dollars to provide clothes for kids at Christmas plus a bunch of scholarships."

"Judy and I met when we were both teaching at Sonora Elementary," said Ann Leonard, "but after a year, I moved up to Curtis Creek School, so we drifted apart. Then I got into administration and so did she. Judy was really struggling because you do as an administrator. I ran into her downtown and after a few minutes of chatting, I suggested we meet for coffee. I gave her a book that basically said how difficult it is to be an educational administrator. If you're pleasing everyone, then you're not doing your job. And if you're not pleasing everyone, then you're going to lose your job. Basically, it's the kind of job where you're there for five years, and then you're out. She said that book saved her life—that and talking to someone who understood.

"So we started getting together. My husband Jim and I would have dinner with Judy and Warren. We did a lot of dinner parties. Judy is a wonderful hostess. They always had a dozen people at their dinner parties. Warren cleaned the house and got everything ready, and Judy did the cooking. They were a team. Warren was so unpretentious. He did what needed to be done, and he always had that million dollar smile."

"After we bought a house in downtown Sonora, it got even more convenient to socialize. One time, I was in this hammock out on our back porch. Suddenly the whole thing collapsed, and one of the metal supports landed on my knee. I couldn't move, and the pain in my knee was excruciating. Jim called Warren, who jumped in his car and came right over. The two of them got me in the house. My knee wasn't broken—just badly bruised."

A lot of friends talked about how doctoring slipped into socializing with the Borgquists, including John Burgess, one of Warren's friends from high school. "I lived overseas for ten years in Hong Kong where it gets really hot in the summer, so my wife decided to come back to Sonora to have our third child. We were at a play—*Babes in Arms*—with Warren and Judy when Val went into labor. We all left the theater to go to the hospital. Suddenly, there was Warren bringing Ursula out of the delivery room and putting her in my arms."

Sometimes, when talking about Warren, people mentioned in passing something that disclosed a distinctive facet of the man. For instance, Nicolas told about going to Death Valley with the family on one of his visits to the states. "I remember zipping through the desert with Greg in his BMW at high speed. And then we met Judy at a nearby motel. I was leaving the next morning, and after dinner, she said, 'We'll see you in the morning.' And then in the morning, she had already left because they hate good-byes. They cry at good-byes, so she just left a note. You know, Warren was the first guy I saw crying. It was during a movie in the theater."

Susan Russel told two short anecdotes that revealed charming inclinations in her friend, the doctor. "I remember when my son Evan was little," said Susan. "I don't remember exactly how old— maybe 6. We probably had him there for a sports or school check-up. Warren came in and looked right into Evan's eyes and said, 'Have you ever thought about becoming a general practitioner?' He was always looking for somebody to come to work with him and take over his practice. Somebody he had trained. Another time at a Sierra Repertory Theater function," said Susan, "Don Andrews and I were talking. Warren came walking up, and Don said, 'Look at this man. He knows our insides and outsides, and he still likes us.'"

# *Chapter 21*

# MOD PODGE

We all want to feel that our physician really likes us,
sees us as special, and is emotionally moved by our plight,
attracted not so much by the fascinating biology of our disease
but by who we are a people.

-Jerome Groopman, *How Doctors Think*

"We weren't allowed in the room while Dr. Borgquist was working to resuscitate Mom," said my sister, Anne Stock, referring to his care of our mother when she suffered congestive heart failure. "They were behind a curtain, and we were standing in a tiny hallway. He was yelling questions to us while he worked to save her. 'Has she had any surgeries?' 'Does she have cancer?' I remember your exact answer. 'She had surgery last November to remove a small contained malignant tumor on her lung.' As fast as he asked, we answered. They were intubating her—working like crazy, and he was talking to us nonstop."

My memory of that event occurred perhaps twenty-four hours later when Dr. Borgquist gathered my four siblings and me in a tiny room near the ICU. I don't know if we all happened to be there or if he summoned us. He said, 'Your mother is not dying right this minute, but you need to prepare for the end of her life.' We had guessed this was so, but for him to say it so directly was really important because then we could talk about it. He opened the way and gave us permission. Sadly, he decided to transfer her care to a specialist, and though Mom did not die for another six months, the new doctor did not discuss the fact that she was dying. But from the time Warren spoke to us, we dealt with our mother as if it was the end of her life.

"Dr. Borgquist was connected to some big events in my family," said Anne. "Not only was he there for Anastasia's birth and Mom's congestive heart failure, he also walked us through spinal meningitis, a fractured skull, and Charles' vasectomy. When we went to that appointment, Dr. B said, 'You can stay and watch. Charles watched you have your babies.' So I sat on a chair in the corner of the room while he did the procedure." For my sister, for me, for all of his patients, Dr. Warren Borgquist appeared and reappeared across the days of our lives, arriving to treat fractured femurs, dislocated elbows, retained placentas, and more ear infections and cases of pneumonia and tonsillitis than anyone can count.

Throughout the 80s, the Fairview Office was flourishing even as office staff came and went. "Something happened in Pat Valkenburg's personal life," said Monique, "So when she left, we got Cindy Smith, a little blond with a sweet voice. After Gail Bonvia and Samantha Marrs left, we hired a biller. Her name was Sandy, and she was the bomb, doing not only billing but all the bookkeeping. When Dr. Stolp came, we hired a receptionist for him, but Sandy did the billing for both doctors. Stolp also had his own nurse—Maureen Wertz. We had a gal who came over from the hospital to transcribe for us—Karen Solo. Billie's daughter worked as a go-fer. This was before FAX, so she'd go back and forth to the hospital for labs and X-rays. Somewhere in there, Warren decided he wanted me to be the office manager and take over billing and bookkeeping, and that's when we brought Judy Williams in as the receptionist. Then Cindy Smith left, and we hired Patty Patton as his nurse.

"I'd heard Warren was looking for a nurse," said Patty Patton, "so I decided to apply. He was actually in dire need, so he interviewed and hired me on the spot. While I was working for Borgquist, I was still working part time at Tuolumne General Hospital. I'm well rounded because I worked in a lot of different departments in that hospital—ER, ICU, surgery, long-term care. He would come in to see his patients at the hospital so that's how he knew me. Patients often asked him to check something, like a sore on their back or leg. Sometimes he was the one on call, so the person asking wasn't even his patient. He always made sure things got treated. He would write notes on the back of charts, such as, 'No skin break down. Excellent nursing care.' The nurses really appreciated that. None of the other doctors did that. Once he told me, 'These older patients have lost their spouses and sometimes a lot of family, so they don't get hugged or touched enough.' At the end of his visit, he would give them a hug. Every one of his patients looked forward to that.

"We handled a lot of stuff,' said Nurse Patty, who was always referred to with this title. "He took care of fractures right here in the office—he'd splint and cast. He was an all-purpose doctor. He probably handled as much stuff over the phone as he saw in the office. We had three phone lines. It was not uncommon for me to talk to one patient, put them on hold; talk to a second patient on line two and put them on hold; and talk to another patient on the third line, put them on hold, and then page him. He'd say, 'Tell number one he needs to come in; I'll take the call on two, and call in this medication for the third.' He knew his patients."

"When Anastasia was 3," said my sister Anne, "Charles was pulling her from the back seat of the car to the front seat, and he dislocated her elbow. We didn't want to go to the ER, so we called Dr. B's office, and they had us come right in. Dr. B relocated it in a minute. He knew us. That's another advantage of a doctor knowing his patients. We got to avoid excessive red tape."

Nurse Patty admitted that Warren's all-around doctoring had consequences. "By afternoon, he was always running behind," she said. "Usually an hour behind." And then there was the humorous side. "Warren had a skeleton picture hanging on the wall in one of the exam rooms," said Nurse Patty. "Patients started writing little sticky notes and putting them on the picture while they were waiting—things like 'Donner, party of fifty' and 'Anorexia.' Pretty soon the whole picture was full of sticky notes. He also had pictures on the ceilings for patients to look at. He used to go to San Francisco to a poster store. I can remember standing on the exam tables, so I could reach the ceiling and push in the thumb tacks to hold the posters."

Ross Carkeet remembered the posters. There was one in particular, with a number of interesting guidelines that Ross thought typified Warren. "The two I remember were, 'Never pass up a child's lemonade stand' and 'Be kind to animals, the elderly, and children.'" Stories about Dr. Borgquist and children were plentiful.

"He liked to teach his patients little tricks about how to do things," said Nurse Patty. "He'd teach new mothers to check if a baby with a fever could tuck her chin to her chest because if she couldn't, it was a sign of spinal meningitis. He'd say, 'Tickle her belly, and see if she can look down.' He was also always teaching us stuff. He believed you needed to listen to the parents of the small children because they know their kid better than you do.

"I had a mother call and say, 'My boy has diarrhea, so he's got an ear infection.' 'What?' I said, thinking she was a little nuts. 'Yeah,' she said, 'Every time he has diarrhea, he has an ear infection.'

"'Really,' I said, 'OK, I'll work you in.' So I arranged an appointment, and sure enough that kid had an ear infection, and diarrhea was his only symptom. He wasn't running a fever. He wasn't pulling his ears."

"It was so much fun to come for those well-baby checks with Warren," said Amy Nilson. "When he held your baby, you could see this was a master at work. There was always such wonder in his face. A few years after the birth of our son, I started wanting more children. I think that's something that happens in a women's body, the desire to have more. However, my husband wasn't all that thrilled with the idea. Warren said, 'You definitely need to have more than one, so the poor child doesn't have the laser focus of two parents on him the whole time.' We did not, however, have another child," added Amy.

"Both of my kids had been cautioned to never ride on the back of a bicycle," said Lynn Browne, a patient who shared many stories. "It was right before school started, when my daughter was entering kindergarten. The kids had gone out to play in the early evening, and suddenly I heard hollering. My son was absolutely hysterical, and a woman I didn't know had my daughter balanced on top of my car. I didn't see any blood, so I couldn't understand what was going on. Jimmy was screaming, 'I'm sorry! I'm so sorry!' While riding on the back of his bike, my daughter's foot had gotten stuck in the spokes.

"As the woman flexed my daughter's leg, her heel fell down. I thought it was bone I was looking at, but it was actually her Achilles tendon. I ran inside and called the exchange. When they put me through to Dr. Borgquist, I said, 'Please. Something really bad has happened, and I don't want anybody but you.' He told me to meet him at hospital. I was driving these two kids, one screaming how sorry he was and the other screaming, 'I don't want stitches,' while flying forty-five miles an hour down Snell Road. He met us at the ER door and took her from me. After a quick exam, he said, 'She's going to be fine.' It took thirty-seven stitches to put it right, and she started kindergarten on crutches wearing a bedroom slipper, but you can't even see a scar today."

BZ Smith recalled the time her daughter Wren was bitten by a spider. "It was looking nasty, and we were worried, so Rick decided to call Warren even though it was a weekend. This was back in the days before Prompt Care. We called thinking we could just get his advice, and he said, 'Bring her over. I'm working on some stuff at the house, but just bring her over.' We lived really close to the Borgquists, so we loaded Wren in the car and drove over. When we walked in, there was Warren wearing a tool belt. He was in the middle of a massive construction project. He sat down with our little girl and looked at her knee. He cleaned it up and said, 'Don't worry. You're going to be fine.' And she was as happy as a clam. My children absolutely loved Warren. Wren was never afraid to go to the doctor, not for one minute. He was always so genuine with her."

"Warren liked to make the medical experience a little less intimidating any way he could," said Nurse Patty. "He didn't want kids to associate pain with coming to the office, so he sent them to the Health Department for their immunizations. Then state regulations changed, and he couldn't do that anymore, but it had been good idea. I remember running into a patient at the bank in Twain Harte. Her little boy was with her, and when I said 'Hi,' he backed up against the wall. Later, she explained he was afraid I was going to give him a shot."

"Sometimes, we'd be at the office until seven or eight o'clock," said Nurse Patty. "Partly because of his time issues. But also because he needed to call patients. He made notes about people to call, and we'd kept notes about people we thought he should call. At the end of the day, he called every one of those patients. He also had emergencies that kept him late."

"About four weeks after August's birth," said my daughter Jennie Lou, beginning a story I knew well, "I was standing in a pool of blood. It was gushing. I'd had unusual bleeding since the birth, but this was out of control. I got the portable phone and the baby and went out onto the deck, so there wouldn't be blood all over the house. I was able to reach Dr. Borgquist, and he told me to come right in, so I called my husband at work, who came to get me. It was really late in the day, but Dr. Borgquist and Nurse Patty stayed to take care of me. It turned out I had a retained placenta and needed a D&C. I don't think anyone would do this in an office anymore," said Jennie Lou, referring to the procedure called dilation and curettage that removes tissue from the inside of the uterus. "But I was one of those people who avoid doctors. My son had been born at home, and I just like to do things myself. I would've been more afraid if I'd had to go to a hospital. Dr. Borgquist knew me. He always said I reminded him of his daughter Jennifer.

"He had to give me morphine, and it made me pretty silly. I knew, even in my drugged state, that it was dark outside, and they were taking care of me and not home with their families, so I kept saying over and over, 'Thank you, Nurse Patty. Thank you, Doctor Borgquist.'

"He always invited people into the geeky part of medical procedures, so he asked my husband, 'Do you want to look inside your wife's dilated cervix at the retained placenta?' Michael was like, 'No, I'm good.' There was another time when Michael was having a sebaceous cyst removed. Dr. Borgquist had a mirror so Michael could watch if he wanted. He was a little more interested in that, but he definitely did not want to look at my retained placenta. But Dr. Borgquist always offered. I liked that he was willing to explain things. He took the time to help us understand what had happened, and he made sure we knew that he did not think this had anything to do with home birth. I felt like my choice was respected."

Jennie Lou continued, describing a later discussion with Dr. Borgquist about not immunizing her children. "He said, 'If you're going to question immunization, then here are the ones I think all kids should have,' and he gave me a list. 'And these are medium ones; take 'em or leave 'em.' I think polio was on that list. When we all got pertussis, he took my call in the middle of his scheduled appointments, and he was willing to diagnose over the phone. That might have been because he didn't want to contaminate his office. Still, he was willing to trust my judgment. I described what was going on, and he listened. My son had been sick with a cold, and he was lying on the floor when I heard the whoop. I'd never heard it before, but I knew what it was. I doubt if any other doctor would handle something like this on the phone. Maybe there's a liability involved or what if it was actually something more dangerous or a baby died. We were living in a one-room out building on our property—300 square feet— while we built our home, and I had three kids, so we were all exposed. We had a 1 year old at the time, and babies under 1 are at risk for complications. She wasn't sick when I called. Because he gave me so much respect, I was willing to listen him. He said, "If it were my child, my grandchild, I would give her antibiotics.' I didn't want to give my kids antibiotics unless it was absolutely necessary. But I listened to him. It was too late though. Her cough started the next day, but she might have had a milder case because of those meds."

"I remember when we made him a new stick—the one that told him where he was supposed to go next," said Nurse Patty. "We used to paint it different colors because he liked that kind of stuff. One time, we glued wrapping paper around the stick and put Mod Podge over the top. It was quite a cool look." Mod Podge is a popular craft product used in decoupage—an all-in-one glue, sealer, and finish. When Patty mentioned making the stick colorful and securing it with Mod Podge, I saw it as an apt emblem for this colorful, slow moving doctor who patched and smoothed people on a daily basis.

"Patients loved how he explained things in simple layman's terms," said Nurse Patty. "He would draw pictures of what was going on. He had one of those pens you can push to get red, green, blue, or black ink. We had to make sure there was one in each exam rooms. If we didn't, he came unglued. 'Where's my pen?' he'd holler. One of his patients told me he had all of Dr. Borgquist's artwork on his refrigerator."

Bob Fisher, the pharmacist who was Warren's study partner at Modesto Junior College, said he and Warren used to talk on the phone. Like Warren, Bob had returned to his hometown to practice. "Our conversations were probably way too long, but we enjoyed talking about the drug of the day and what was going on with pharmaceuticals. Warren would call to ask what they were using to treat this or that. If I didn't have an answer, I would try and find it. Conversely, he would always have something to share. He was never afraid to ask for advice and never afraid to take it.

"I remember all the docs up here were under-treating Giardia. We have these open canals across the county that supply drinking water, so they were seeing plenty of it, but they were simply treating the symptoms. There are two phases of Giardia. An active form that causes the symptoms, and inactive cysts that exist for a long time. Because he'd trained in the Canal Zone, he was well aware of that disease. He precipitated a breakthrough for a lot of local docs with regard to Giardia."

"The skin check was beyond what anybody had ever done before or has done since," said Nurse Patty. "We didn't have a dermatologist in town, so he took off a lot of skin lesions. He used to say, 'I want Tuolumne County to have the best looking elderly population possible.' He'd even look in patients' ears. He was so thorough. I can hear him saying, 'OK, this one's got irregular borders. It needs to be biopsied.' If it turned out to be melanoma, he sent them to San Francisco because that's where the best clinic was. He said, 'They take a blow dryer and go through your hair at the Melanoma Clinic.' He knew people couldn't see stuff on their backs, and no one looks between their toes. Lesions can hide in all kinds of places, and all of a sudden you have a bad diagnosis, which could have been prevented. So he checked everywhere."

"The liquid nitrogen was always pretty interesting, "said Dr. Todd Stolp. He used it on everyone. I heard it all day long—ZZZHHH-ZZZHHH. A real outbreak of skin stuff," said Todd with amusement, recalling his days of sharing an office with Warren.

"Each of us had our own little pet projects," said Dr. Stolp. "Warren consistently picked up stuff because of his generosity. One was the Primary Care Clinic. The Emergency Room was being used for management of hypertension and diabetes. Diabetics were coming in to refill their insulin. They couldn't find a doctor, which was just crazy for a chronic disease like that. So we decided to launch a Primary Care Clinic next door to TGH, adjacent to the Public Health Department. The physicians had been tearing their hair out because they didn't want to see these patients because it actually cost them money. It was a nightmare to figure out all the convolutions required to bill for services. But the county had direct billing capabilities, so it made sense to open a general medical clinic operated by the county for the safety of that population. At the same time, the doctors were happy to get this problem out of their offices, so they were willing to donate their time. We got eight local primary care physicians to review charts and see patients once or twice a week, and Warren was one of them. That's how the Primary Care Clinic started in the county. It qualified as a rural health clinic, so reimbursement went up significantly. It became a safety net system for the Tuolumne County poor.

"Warren also did medical legal exams for victims of sexual assault. When I came to the county, I discovered that they had no way of getting a medical legal exam done properly. Prosecutions were really impossible without the required exams, so we set up rotating physicians to do them correctly. The hospital had a list of doctors. The calls typically came at 2:00 a.m. The victims came in with a rep from the DA's office—the Victim Witness Program—and the hospital called us to come in and do the exam.

"We'd see these gaps in health care that frustrated us. You could either stomp your feet or you could do something. That was one of the beauties of this county and still is. The many ways doctors rose to fill the gaps were never very obvious. Warren and I got involved in a variety of things that got people necessary care," concluded Todd.

"I remember when the Hmong came into the community," said Monique. "I don't know how many came, but of course they couldn't speak any English. So who agreed to be their doctor? ' Oh, my god,' I said when Warren told me, 'What the hell are you doing?'

'They can't talk to me, and I can't talk to them,' he said, 'but they can point to where it hurts.' When their kids had a fever, they would bring them in all limp in their arms, which scared the hell out of me. They'd be rubbing a lemon or a lime on their heads. That's how I knew the kid had a fever. He delivered babies for them. He did a whole lot for basically nothing. No pay."

There was the doctoring Warren did for which he received minimal or no pay, and there was the office staff that he needed to pay. "Warren always wanted people in the office who fit in and worked nicely together," said Monique. "He inherited Marge and Gail and the woman who preceded me, but after he hired me, we all got a say in hiring. He'd say, 'We need such and so in the office. Who do you think would work?' Then we'd toss around ideas of people we knew, and sometimes we'd steal the right person from wherever they were working. We stole Samantha Marrs from the hospital. She handled billing and insurance for years. When Todd came, we stole for him too. We got his receptionist Carol from the hospital. And we stole his nurse Maureen Wertz from TGH. We stole our transcriber, Karen Solo, from Dr. Whitney."

"I worked as a transcriber for Warren and Todd, and a few other doctors in that complex," said Karen Solo. "I was born and raised here, so I remember Warren's folks when they had the dime store, and I remember when he came back to Sonora in the '70s. But then my husband and I moved to Washington State for a few years. We tried to adopt while we were there, but it was painstakingly slow, so when we moved back here, I talked to Warren because I knew he handled some private adoptions. We talked, and then I went on my way. I'd see him occasionally at the hospital, and eventually he hired me to do transcription. He was fun because he always spoke directly to me on the recordings. He'd tell stories, and add a little levity. He'd be dictating along and all of sudden say, "Oh guess what? And then he'd tell about something funny. It made transcribing less boring. He was also very appreciative, which was refreshing. One afternoon, when I was working for Dr. Burn, one of the orthopedists, Warren called. 'Are you still interested in adopting?' he asked.

"'Sure.'

"'Come over after work. I want to talk to you.' So I stopped by after work. I hadn't even bothered to pick up my husband. Warren said, 'One of my patients had a baby last night.'

"'Last night? You mean she's not pregnant?'

"'No the baby is here,' he said with his big smile.

"I was so excited I didn't even ask if it was a boy or a girl. I just left to get my husband. One of the nurses I worked with made a list of what I needed, and I ran to Thrifty to pick up the essentials. By seven o' clock, we picked her up and were on our way home. She was 22 hours old. Most people have nine months to get ready, but I only had a couple of hours.

Warren's office staff threw a baby shower for us two weeks later. We got an attorney, and he took care of everything, and in eight months it was all done."

"We had a good time together," said Monique. "We always dressed up for Halloween, and we exchanged gifts at Christmas. Warren loved spring, and every year when things were blooming and the hills were green, he took us on a picnic. We'd hike up to Table Mountain or to Peppermint Falls or go to Red Hills or out in Columbia beyond the airport. In the summer, he and Judy always had us over for a swim party.

One year, the City Hotel sponsored a Secretary's Day Luncheon. We cut the ad from the paper and made copies and put them in his office and in the break room, hinting that he should take us. When he didn't respond, someone said we should put it in the bathroom where he was always reading. So we put the toilet seat up—like a man would leave it— and taped it to the seat. He went into the restroom between patients and came out with the toilet seat around his neck and the ad still taped to it. He went into every room and said, 'See how my staff reminds me to do things?'"

"Did Monique tell you about the time he was upset—what we called 'on the rag'?" asked Nurse Patty. "He'd been cranky all morning. So she went into his office and taped a Tampax to his desk. He came out holding it in the air and said, 'Who put this on my desk?' Monique said, 'Do you think you need it?' He immediately apologized to everybody."

"Every once in a while he'd be missing in action," said Monique. "One day at about 9:30, he called the office and said, 'Mo, I'm stuck. Can you come get me?'

"'Where the hell are you? You're supposed to be here.'

"'I rode my bike to Groveland to see Dr. Thompson.'

"'Where are you now?'

"'I'm about to go down Priest grade. Can pick me up? I'm going to be late.'

"'No kidding.'

"'Go to the house and get my pickup, so we can haul my bike.'

"Dr. Thompson was the orthopedic surgeon. He had an office below ours on Fairview, and years earlier he'd been the Borgquist family doctor. He and Warren were good friends, and they often visited back and forth in each other's offices. And some mornings, Warren would ride his bike over to visit Dr. T. Three or four times, he visited too long and called me to pick him up. It was just another delay in the office schedule we weren't expecting."

"I remember taking my son to the pediatrician," said Charlene Ingalls. "He was over six feet tall, and he was so embarrassed. After the appointment, he said, 'I'm not going back there. Find somebody else.' So I took him to Warren. In retrospect, I wish I'd stuck with Warren for my kids after they were born instead of going to a pediatrician. I remember him telling my son, 'When I was a teenager, I wasn't smart, but I wanted to be a doctor. I'm a perfect example that you can be anything you want, because I was not doctor material.' It was incredible that he could say that to a kid."

"He had no problem telling me or my husband Guy if he didn't know much about what ailed us, but he'd find out and get us where we needed to be. One time when he referred me to another doctor, I said, 'Is this who you'd send your wife to?' And he said, 'Absolutely.' Oh, and I remember he was so good with that spray gun for things on skin problems. He told me, 'You're blue eyed, blond haired, and fair skinned. You're in big trouble.'

"One time Guy was having prostate problems. It was toward the end of the day, and he went in all dirty from work, and the nurse said, 'It will be awhile, but you can wait.' And Guy said, 'I'll make an appointment.' As he was getting in his truck to leave, she came out and said, 'Warren wants to see you.' Warren loved to talk heavy equipment with Guy. He'd say 'I'm going to own a tractor someday. I'm going to do what you do.' Guy could not believe what he was hearing. He was filthy dirty, and Warren, who was nice and clean, was saying, 'I'm going to retire when I'm fifty and buy a tractor and build a house.'"

# PART IV

# GRAMPS

# Chapter 22

# HEAVEN FOR KIDS

A person's a person, no matter how small.

-Dr. Suess, *Horton Hears a Who*

"Like many people in Tuolumne County, Warren delivered me," said Sarah Purdy, "but he was also married to my father's first wife, so in a strange way, we were somehow related. That was always difficult to define. What do you call your former wife's new husband's relation to your child? I think everyone was probably confused about how to classify this additional person who was neither child nor grandchild, niece nor nephew. Eventually, as I got older, I came up with something. Judy and Warren became my fairy godparents."

"How did this extended family work?" I asked.

"Probably as dysfunctionally as any other extended, blended family. My older half-brother and sister, Scott and Jennifer, are seventeen and fifteen years older than I am. They were exciting older creatures who fascinated me. I spent time at Judy and Warren's house, mostly in the context of hanging out with them. They went off to college fairly soon, so it was never like a real sibling relationship. Also, Warren came into the relationship with Greg and Mimi, so for me that meant I had these four semi-step-half-siblings. Then as they grew up and married, each of them had three children—so twelve grandchildren all together. It was a big, weird family."

On the day after Thanksgiving, Jennifer and I sat on the couch in the Borgquist front room. Judy had invited me to come talk with family who were visiting for the holiday. Two of Jennifer's children—Jake and Emma—were sitting at the counter with Jennifer's friend Kris Scott, talking with Judy who was in the kitchen. The scene was no doubt similar to many around the county—grandparents chatting with visiting grandkids, high school friends reconnecting during the long weekend spent in one's hometown.

"Tell me about the family tradition of a pregnant mom coming to Warren to hear her baby's heartbeat for the first time," I said.

"When we were putting together the photo board for the memorial," said Jennifer, "I was amazed at the number of pictures of bellies and Gramps with the Doppler, right here," she said, patting the couch on which we sat.

In one of those photos, Mimi lies back, her dark hair splayed across a couch pillow, her legs draped over her husband Patrick's lap. Her brown eyes big with amazement are trained on Patrick who is looking earnestly at Warren, holding the Doppler to Mimi's belly. The device consists of a black box with an amplifier and a coiled extension cord connected to a transducer that detects the heart tones. Warren is grinning, and it is easy to imagine what he hears: the swift paced lub-dub, lub-dub of his grandchild's heartbeat.

"Who doesn't want to hear that sound?" said Jennifer. "My friend Kris over there is in one of those pictures too. Warren was an equal-opportunity belly guy. He delivered several of my friend's babies, and that was fun for me."

During subsequent conversations with Warren's children, I asked each of them if they recalled hearing their babies' heartbeats in utero. When I asked Scott, he said, "You mean the Doppler thing? Yeah, we did that with Evan and Sean."

"All through the generations, even with Logan," added Judy, referring to the great-grandchild who was in utero when Warren died. It

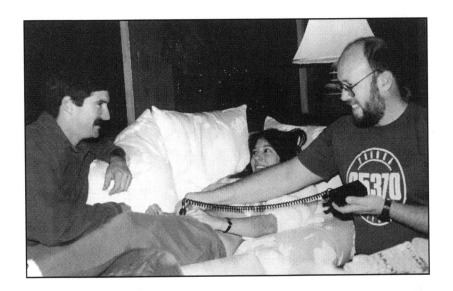

wasn't surprising that the sound of Logan's heartbeat coming so close to Warren's death quickened in Judy's memory.

"We heard Jessica's heart on the couch at Warren's," said Kati, Greg's wife. "That's when he named her Thumper Fox."

"All the grandkids have Indian names," said Greg, "My dad gave them the names and used them when he made up stories."

"I can't remember if he was curious or concerned," added Kati, "but we got special treatment because he knew Jim Wilson, so we had a private sonogram with Jim. We got to see her before she was born."

"I was premature," said Jessica, "but I had a really loud heartbeat for how tiny I was, so that's why Gramps called me Thumper Fox."

At Warren Borgquist's memorial, twelve grandchildren wowed the assembly, as one after another they spoke with sweet affection about time spent with Gramps. Many of them told funny tales about Cousins Week, another family tradition.

"Cousins Week started with Evan, Sean, and Jake," said Judy, referring to her three oldest grandkids. "We had Scott's boys here for a week, and Jennifer came with Jake. I'll show you a picture." Judy fetched a framed photo from her hallway gallery. Three youngsters lay on their bellies in the grass facing the camera. Dark-haired Evan is on the left, his chin lifted, presenting one of those for-the-camera smiles, this one featuring a mouthful of baby teeth. Sean poses in the center, wearing a brown cowboy hat that is tilted back. A shock of bangs hangs above a keen, intense gaze. His closed mouth is pursed as if to say don't-mess-with me. "Sean was always a little trickster with a quirky sense of humor," said Judy, "And look at Jake. He's just a baby but looks as if he can hardly wait to start. He is always interested in everything, very inquisitive."

"We spent the week playing with the kids," said Judy as she set the photo on the ottoman, "and when it was time for them to leave, I said, 'We're going to do this every year,' so that was the birth of Cousins Week. The next year, we had three more grandkids: Kacey, Jessica, and Christopher. The second Cousin's Week was at Jennifer's. After that we always went camping. By then, the grandkids were coming fast and furious. The third Cousins Week was in Pinecrest, and the next year, we went to a campground out of Tuolumne City toward Cherry Lake. Then we started having their parents pick where we went.

"Cousins Week was always a full week, and everyone was supposed to go for the whole week. Making them commit those first years was tough. They gave me a lot of flack. 'Mom! A whole week!' Judy mimicked her children's reaction to obligatory attendance, her voice pitched high and indignant. 'We hardly have any time off, and you're saying we have to be together. You're so controlling! It's our only vacation.' Scott was really pissed. Warren didn't even support me. 'Honey, I know you want them to get together and be best friends, but they're all different, and it's never going to work.' He thought it was a crazy idea. Of course, after it got going, I got a lot of strokes. The grandkids used to say, 'We'll always have Cousins Week—even if you're dead and gone.'

"Warren bought a trailer just for Cousins Week. He only used it once a year, but it had an elaborate kitchen set up with shelves and pipes, so we could have hot water. He rigged this huge pot to a propane tank to heat water. He labeled all these boxes with weird spellings, like 'Con da mints.' At first, we brought all the food, but after a while, we gave everyone a day to cook. We camped in tents, and he bought a little porta-potty, so I didn't have to go a mile to the bathroom in the middle of the night. I'm a very private bathroom person, so I made him put it outside with a curtain around it, but eventually, he said, 'This is ridiculous. It's the middle of the night. It's me. We've been married for years. I'm probably asleep. Pee in the tent.' He emptied it every morning, and he told the boys, 'If you're a real husband, you'll get one of these for your wife and happily empty it for her.'

"I made up all these customs for Cousins Week, like the talent show. Nobody in our family has talent—well, a couple of the younger girls can sing—so it's hilarious. Once, I brought my autoharp, and they booed me off the stage. One year, I told a story. 'When I was a little girl, I took ballet lessons. I was so excited, and I tried to do an arabesque, but my dad said the reason they closed the ballet studio was because of me. Then I described all the other ways I was without talent. I finished by saying, 'But I guess I must have one talent, which is love, because look what I have done by bringing you all to Cousins Week.'"

"We had special evenings," said Jennifer, elaborating on Cousins Week. "Boys night to cook. Girls night to cook. We also had Margaritaville. Kati is also an alcoholic—so she and Warren would go to an AA meeting while we had Margaritaville. We always had crafts and games. And we hiked. The reason we're the Giraffe Clan originated during Cousins Week because Warren always made us try new things. We tried kayaking when we went to Jedediah Smith State Park on the north coast. We kayaked down the river, and he ran along the riverbank yelling, 'You can do it! You can do it!' while we were running through these piddly little rapids. After that, we always had kayaks at Cousins Week. Then he bought a sailboat—a little one that we could put in the Cousins Week trailer. And we always had to hike to the highest mountain around.

"The talent show was traumatic," continued Jennifer. "There was a lot of angst. One year we made up a song to the tune of 'Partridge in a Pear Tree.' We rewrote it. 'The first night of Cousin's Week /my family gave to me/ a potty behind the tree.' One time three of the cousins fell and scrapped their faces, so we had a line about 'Three scraped faces.' Emma was really into singing opera when she was 5. She'd belt out these operatic arias, and the one she sang the most was 'My beautiful donkey balls.' I don't know why that statement came to her, but she sang it frequently and loudly, so instead of 'Five gold-en rings' we sang, 'Five don-key balls.' Every tent had intense snorers, so the next line was 'Six snor-ing tents.' We sang about all of the follies, fun, and tragedies that were part of Cousins Week," said Jennifer. Then she belted out, "Five don-key balls," drawing out the syllables to replicate the talent night performance, after which we both dissolved in giggles.

"Gramps was the glue that kept Cousins Week going, making sure everyone got along and everyone came. No excuses," said Evan Purdy. "One of the early traditions, when we were younger, was eating stone soup. We'd read the book, and then we'd make the soup, put the stone in, and eat it. That was pretty cool. For talent show night, my talent was playing the guitar. I'm the artist in the family." A print of Evan's art hangs in my home. The canvas is awash with honey-colored water behind a charcoal drawing of a Native American standing on a boulder in the middle of a river. Pine-covered mountains create the perspective of a gently flowing river.

"After my mom passed away, Gramps and I went kayaking on a lake during Cousins Week," continued Evan. "It was just the two of us. He understood what I was going through. I wanted to experiment with drinking and partying. It bothered him, but he understood. I looked up to Gramps. His advice was always good. Even if you didn't ask for it, you ended up thinking, 'Yeah, that helps.'

"When we were kids, he gave us nicknames—kind of like tribe names—our Giraffe Clan names. I was the first, and I was Turkey Feathers—the worst name you could give anyone. Sean had a good name, like Dancing Wolf. Kacey was Cat's Claw, and I was Turkey Feathers. I hated it, and he always called us by our clan names when he told stories. Finally, when I was about 7, I said. 'Would it be okay if you didn't call me Turkey Feathers anymore?' He said okay, and he never called me that again."

"How did Warren come up with the name Turkey Feathers for Evan," I asked Judy.

"He was walking with him one day, and said, 'C'mon, Turkey Feathers,' in that goofy way he had of just blurting something out. That's the way every name came. It just popped out. After that, when he told Evan stories, he was Turkey Feathers, and we got him a stuffed turkey. And then we got each of them a stuffed animal that they had to leave at our house, so they wouldn't lose them."

"What are some of the other names?" I asked

"Sean is Coyote Foot. Jake's name is Road Runner. And Kacey is Cat's Meow, which I hated because it sounded sexist."

I couldn't help but notice that Evan had romanticized his siblings' animal names. Rather than Dancing Wolf, Sean was Coyote Foot, not exactly a flattering sobriquet, and Judy saw Kacey's name—which Evan remembered differently—as unflattering, though the expression generally refers to something that is outstanding. The tribe names seemed to emanate from Warren's playful spontaneity, a term of endearment that erupted to express pleasure with the child in the moment.

"He always made up stories on the fly," said Sean, "and they were very detailed." At first, you didn't know where a story was going, but then he'd thicken it up and throw in other cousins by using their names, and it would become an elaborate, magical tale. We live in Nevada City, so when we went to Sonora, the thing we looked forward to was Gramps' stories at night on the big couch bed. I remember a couple times we had pillow fights, and Gramps was right in there with us. Or we'd decide we were going to build a fort in the living room, and he'd help us. Imagine that room covered in pillows and blankets and sheets. He'd get in the fort with us and tell stories.

"When I was in seventh or eighth grade, Gramps invited me to come to Sonora and build a soap box derby car with him. Of course, I said yes. I was into cars and building and tinkering. Gramps was instructive, but at the same time he wanted me to do things by myself. He wanted me to learn." As Sean related this story, I remembered Marjorie talking about Warren building his own soap box car in Escalon when he was a kid. I also recalled a picture of Warren working with Sean in the shop. The picture probably predated the soap box building, for he appears to be a keenly focused 7 year old using an electric drill under Gramps' watchful eye. Warren wears a royal blue T-shirt, hand painted in red with the words "Circle of Joy."

"Before the race," Sean said, continuing his story, "we took the car for a test drive out on this piece of property he owned that had a really big hill, probably two-hundred yards up and fairly steep—enough to build pretty good speed. The bottom of the hill leveled out toward an embankment with a telephone pole standing at its peak. I jumped in the soap box derby car, and off I went. I was picking up speed—15, 20, 25 miles an hour— and when I got to the bottom of the hill, I hit the brake. Nothing happened. So I went flying up the embankment and flew four or five feet in the air. Gramps came screaming down the hill in the truck.

"'Are you ok? Are you ok?'

"'Yeah,' I said. 'I don't know what happened.'

"We took the car back to the house, where we discovered we had put the weight directly under the brake pedal so that when I hit the pedal, it hit the weight instead of going all the way down to engage the cable. We just busted up laughing. The night before the race, there was the place where you showed your car, and the judges gave awards. I got the award for originality."

I wondered if Sean knew the story about Warren injuring his foot as boy when he was test-driving his own soap box derby car, but since he was recalling another incident, I didn't ask. "I remember the first time I rode my bike without training wheels. Gramps was running behind, holding the back of the seat and telling me that I could do it. He said, 'Go at your own pace and just focus.' And suddenly I was riding my bike.

"I also remember a sad day for me at Cousins Week. I think I was 7 or 8. Usually when we visited Gramps, he'd put us up on his shoulders. If there was a low hanging branch on a tree or something like that, he'd head for it, pretending to run us into the branch. It was fun, but that year, he turned to me and said, 'Sean, you're too big.' I was devastated." Sean went on to explain that he knew he was too heavy to ride atop his grandfather's shoulders, but it wasn't easy to be excluded from the pleasure of such rides.

Rare was the recollection in which a grandchild felt dismayed by Gramps. The norm was stories in which Warren was encouraging, inspiring, or understanding. "When I was little," said Jake, "I had this phase when I didn't like saying hi to people. Once, we were on this walk down by the old train near the fairgrounds, and Gramps saw a friend across the street. He told me to wave, but I said, 'No!' I just didn't want to. So instead of making me do it, he said, 'Do this: The wipers on the bus go swish; swish; swish.'" Jake waved his arms as when singing the children's song from which the line came. "I just did it with him. Gramps was like that. He didn't fight you on weird little stuff. He just did what helped you be a good person."

"I forget the name of the music," said Jake, "but Gramps played this big dramatic classical piece when we drove in his truck. It was about the War of 1812. He made up a story to go with the music, about how all the men were kissing their girlfriends and wives goodbye and going to war. I was in first grade, and we had an assignment to write our own books. I wrote mine on the War of 1812, based on the story Gramps told me."

Kacey arrived in the family via Scott's marriage to Cyndie. She doesn't recall much about the early days as a Borgquist grandchild, but others do.

"We came here for dinner," said Cyndi. "Kacey was 3."

"I remember them standing at the door," said Judy, "and she was hiding behind her mom."

"This family was so different. They weren't like my family," continued Cyndi. "Warren and Judy greeted us with open arms. Warren always said, 'There are no step grandchildren,' referring to Kacey."

"We were all just his family," said Scott, "Layer upon layer upon layer of family. You could see when he came into a room how he cared for everyone. For him, it was family first, and then he was a doctor."

Kacey found herself sandwiched between two brothers in the Purdy family. "I distinctly remember Gramps saying, 'You can do anything that your brothers can do. He was big on treating boys and girls equally. The boys had to do the cleaning, and I had to do yard work when we were at Grammie and Gramps'. Whether you were a boy or girl, he was going to teach you how to change the oil in the car. Gender roles are learned when we're young, and Gramps did his best to make it a less male-dominant world.

"Gramps was the big outdoor man, so we went on hikes with him. He was always raring to go. I remember a specific hike when I was little. I was terrified of heights. We came to a railroad trestle that was ten feet off the ground—a good height for someone who was young, and I remember Gramps was so encouraging. 'Just do it,' he said. I really learned a lot from him about overcoming my fears. He was a big guy, so you wouldn't think he was athletic. You wouldn't think he'd hike or get on a bike, but he never limited himself. He was always on the go, always ready for an adventure."

Christopher, Mimi's son, was born in Santa Cruz. "I think that's why my name—Surfer Seal— popped into his head," said Chris, who was born shortly before the second Cousins Week. "We used to have a lot of squirt-gun fights," he said when asked about a memory from Cousins Week.

"One of my cousins was super into guns and the military, so he always brought a bunch of squirt guns. I also remember when we went kayaking on the ocean and Gramps led us into these caves. Aunty Jen was freaking out as we started bumping around on the rocks. That was real exciting—definitely one of the most memorable Cousins Weeks."

"I was Thumper Fox, Jake was Road-Runner, and my brother was Buckhorn," said Jessica, launching into a story about the clan names. "We would gather on this huge bed at Gramps. We'd be lying all over the place, so excited, and Gramps would tell a story. Right in the middle, he'd ROAR," said Jessica, mimicking the huge noise Gramps made. "Or he'd do something else extreme. He was a super-good storyteller.

"I remember one time he explained buoyancy to Jake and me. We were pretty young, and we said, 'Why are you telling us this?' He said, 'You have to endure these talks,' and we'd be like, "OK, go ahead." He would get so excited and walk in front of us, gesturing with his hands. His mannerisms were so exuberant that he made whatever he was telling much more exciting than it probably was.

"One of my favorites memories was getting ready for Cousins Week. Someone probably told you about his crazy kitchen in the trailer. When I was only 7 or 8, Gramps gave me a clipboard and said, 'OK, make sure that we have everything.'

"'Do we have the Cheetos,' I'd ask, all official like, and if he said, 'Yes,' I'd say, 'Check.' And mark it off. He'd be like, 'You're doing such a good job.' I felt so helpful.

"My favorite Cousins Week was Sequoia Kings Canyon about ten years ago. Gramps was directionally challenged, and so am I. My mom says I got it from him. We were going on this hike, and for some reason, Gramps headed out behind the group, but he ended up following some other family with a bunch of kids. We got back from the hike as it was getting dark, and everyone asked, 'Where's Gramps?' Then we started hollering, 'Gramps! Gramps!'" Jessica bellowed just like she probably did when seeking her grandfather in the woods. "He'd been gone probably four or five hours by then. Suddenly, he came strolling down the trail, smiling. 'I followed these people,' he said. 'It turned out it wasn't you guys, but it was a beautiful hike, just phenomenal.' He kept talking about the gorgeous view and how we all ought to do that hike next time. He was lost, but he was so calm about it," she concluded, her laughter gurgling merrily with the memory.

Emily's clan name was Dolphin Fin, "because when I was a baby I would make little noises that sounded like a dolphin squeaking. Gramps always made us the heroes of the stories he told. In the story, there'd be a big problem, fight, or conflict, and we were always the ones who resolved it or solved the mystery. They weren't short stories either. They were twenty minutes long, night after night, and every one was different."

While the clan stories in which the grandkids were heroes were cherished, Emily also recalls how Gramps could spout boring, useless information too. Once during Cousins Week, Gramps gathered all the grandkids and took them for a walk. "We were about five minutes into our walk," said Emily, "and he stopped and picked up a pinecone, a tiny little pinecone, and started explaining what tree it came from. Then he put it down and walked a little farther and grabbed another pinecone—a different one. He did that for the entire walk. We were like, 'We don't care.' No matter how many times we said, 'Let's turn around. We want to go back. We're bored,' he would say, 'No, we have to keep going. You have to learn about this. It's important.'"

"All four of our kids are very different, so it was good for them to be together at Cousin's Week," said Judy. "And it was important for the cousins to be together. They're going to need each other in life," she said with a hint of wistfulness, emotion that grew perceptibly when I asked her about one of the cards from Warren's memorial that read, "When he helped me climb Moro Rock," signed by Alex Woodruff.

"Who is Alex? " I asked.

Judy started crying. "Whoa," she said grabbing a tissue to wipe her eyes. "You never know what's going to set you off. That's my cousin's son. Alex didn't write that. His mom probably did. He was born without a corpus callosum," she said, naming the broad band of nerve fibers that join the two hemispheres of the brain. "They always came to Cousins Week. Always!" said Judy, emphatically. "It's Alex's favorite week of the year. He can walk but not well. In Sequoia National Park, there's this granite dome called Moro Rock. It's a hell of a climb—a steep narrow trail with switchbacks and ledges. Warren knew how powerful it would be for Alex if he could do it. It was no easy feat. He should have been helping me get up to the top," said Judy with a wry smile. "But I made it. Warren pushed all of us to do stuff, even Alex."

"Burney Falls was my favorite Cousins Week," said Scott. "For one thing, we chose it, but also because we hiked to the top of Mt. Lassen. Warren led the charge. We got to the very top, and it was pretty special. Then we went into some of the lava tubes. There were signs that said 'No trespassing,' but we went in anyway." Most people think certain warnings don't apply to them, and perhaps Scott was revealing the Borgquist version, that is, when it came to adventure, certain restrictions could be ignored.

"Then there was the time in Eureka when we all went on a fishing trip and came back with piles of crab," added Scott. "When we landed, they had the pots boiling, and we ate crab and fish. Eating was always part of the adventure," added Scott. Greg and his son Gabe also recalled deep-sea fishing. Greg said that he, Gabe, and his dad were the only ones who didn't get seasick. Gabe remembered that Gramps caught the most fish, and he let each of his grandkids pull in a fish. Like Scott, they remember the feast after the fishing.

"We kayaked in the ocean caves on that trip," said Cyndie. "Kacey thought Grandpa was killing her." Indeed, Kacey described this experience with fear animating her face. "She was really mad," said Cyndie, but in her own telling Kacey couldn't hide the pride she also felt at having fought the waves in her kayak. "The first Yuba River trip was fun, and the last one at Shasta was good too," continued Cyndie.

"They were all good," said Scott.

"We were a tight family," said Greg, "especially when the grandkids came into the fold. I own every one of them, my nieces and nephews, my stepbrother and stepsister. Cousins Week was very powerful in making our family a family." Then Greg took one of those leaps he was prone too. "I remember my pops had this theory that we're automatically going to love our offspring, but if we want to make extended family work, there needs to be resemblances that jump across generations, so we'll love them too. It's something that happens biologically to preserve the larger extended family."

When Greg related this theory, I recalled my first encounter with Zac Garmin, Warren's nephew. Others, including Zac's mom Marjorie, had told me how much he resembled Warren, but I was nevertheless unprepared when introduced to Zac. Standing before me was a man who totally resembled the young Dr. Borgquist I'd met in 1977. Not only did he look like Warren, his mannerism reminded me of him. And his smile—the same broad beaming smile, swift and friendly. Eventually, I would talk with Zac and learn about his relationship with his uncle, but in that brief encounter, I simply marveled at the uncanny resemblance.

"He loved to play with his grandkids," said Judy. "He would get down on the floor and roll around. He'd carry them piggyback and get into the pool and have them jump off his shoulders. I know they loved me, but he was the fun grandparent—the playful one. Every story he told included the kids with the names he'd given them. They were the heroes, and there was always a terrible villain. The content of the story depended on who was here and the season. One that I recall was the pumpkin-glop story, obviously around Halloween. There was a bad guy, and he was stealing all the kids' Halloween candy. They decided they were going to get him. I think he was on top of a hill, and they threw pumpkins at him, and as he rolled down the hill, they were chanting 'Pumpkin Glop.' I didn't always listen because he was in his glory with the kids, and sometimes he would get embarrassed about how dumb the stories were. It was just his special time."

"For Warren's 50th birthday, we all went on a cruise to Mexico," said Scott. "The entire family."

"I got each family different colored T-shirts," said Judy.

"We went snorkeling at Cabo San Lucas," said Scott. "We drove those Unimogs—big four wheel drive things—in Puerta Vallarta."

"And we went to Mismaloya Beach," added Judy.

"After that, 50th birthday cruises became a tradition," said Cyndie. "Whose idea do you suppose it was?"

"Mine," said Judy. "He just got on board. He loved it though, because his whole family was there, every single one."

Among the photos displayed at Warren's memorial, many picture him with a grandchild or two. There is one of him on the beach in Mexico during the 50th birthday cruise with Jake on his back as he crawls on all fours in the sand, palm trees waving in the background. In another, baby Jessica rides on his shoulders as he walks down a wooded path. In yet another, Jake stands atop Gramps' head in the swimming pool. Warren's arms reach up so that Chris can grab his thumbs as he prepares to leap into the water. Five youngsters—Gabe, Moriah, Ryan, Chris and Jessica—are pictured sitting on the big bed in rapt attention around Gramps as he tells a story. There's an adorable shot of Jessica in a pink flowered dress holding a toy phone to her ear, across from Warren who is speaking into the portable house phone, the two engaging in an earnest conversation. In that photo, Warren is wearing a T-shirt with the photo of Evan, Sean, and Jake from the first Cousins Week emblazoned on the front.

"He was a good communicator," said Scott, continuing to reminisce about his step-father. "Every time he was with any of the kids, he'd sit down and have a good conversation, which I'm not very good at."

"He could see into you, " said Cyndie. "If there was something bothering anyone, he'd say, 'Let's go for a hike' or 'Let's go for a walk.' Then once he got you by yourself, he'd get you to talk, and he'd listen."

"And he could put up with Mom's strong personality," he said, gesturing toward his mom. "He mellowed her. He acted as a buffer between her and everyone else. That was his special power— to be able to do that."

"What power did he lack?"

"Hmm," said Scott as he considered. "One comes to mind. He built a tree fort at each of our houses for the grandkids. He'd arrive ready to build, but he always forgot some tool he needed. We'd say 'You can go home and get it.'

'Oh no,' he'd say, 'I'll just go to the hardware store and buy it.'"

"If you went down to his shop," said Judy, "he had five drills—one

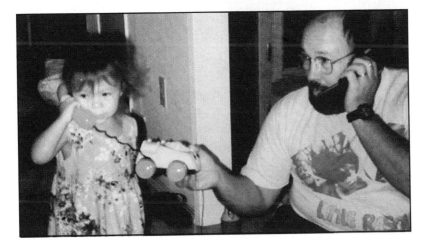

for each of the houses. He just loved building, especially for the kids."

"When he built our tree house," said Jennifer, "I was only thinking about how much fun it was going to be. He asked where we wanted it, and I pointed up in a tree. Later, when my cousin came over, he said, 'What were you guys thinking? They're all going to die.' It was quite high. But it was too late because we'd already put it there."

"When they built Heaven for Kids," said Judy referring to the park adjacent to the Tuolumne County Library, "Warren took three days off work to volunteer. Omega Nu raised ten thousand dollars for the project, and members volunteered to take part in building the structures. That's how he learned about it. He used to say: 'It's the richness of community-ship that enhances your life. You go to meetings, you work on projects together, and then, when you go downtown, you run into these people and say, 'Hello, how are the kids?' That's the reason he wanted to be a part of making Heaven for Kids. He singlehandedly built the towers—the pointy things at the center of the structure. He spent hours working on them after everybody else had gone home. He just had to make the two towers different from what the plans called for. I have a picture of us all standing on the rope bridge that swings between them." In the photo, Warren stands at one end of the bridge and Judy at the other with a huge contingency of family between them. The smiling family is flanked by the two towers Warren built. The bridge on which they stand bears a sign etched in gold letters: "Heaven For Kids."

# *Chapter 23*

## PLAN B

Blunt tools are sometimes found of use
Where sharper instruments would fail.

-Charles Dickens, *Barnaby Rudge*

"God dammit, Warren!"
Judy Borgquist was cursing her husband and frankly it didn't surprise me. We were sitting in her front room on a January morning. Our chairs faced the fireplace, but Judy gestured behind us toward the rest of the room. "He left me with all this fading furniture. I thought he had tinted the windows," she said, looking sadly at the wall of glass that faced east. Clear winter light shone on a large sectional that was the focal point of the room. "Now I have this faded furniture."

"What color was it?" I asked

"Yellow—a buttery yellow. It's almost white now."

"Hmmm," I sympathized.

"Oh, well," said Judy turning back to the fire. "Who cares?"

"You do."

"This has been awful."

With this admission, Judy was turning from the faded furniture to the plumbing fiasco she'd dealt with all morning. I'd arrived at the Borgquist home to find two Roberson plumbing trucks at the foot of the steep cement driveway and Judy standing in the doorway in a purple leisure suit, one hand on her hip, the other holding a mobile phone to her ear. Tape marked the driveway in a trail of Xs, and the doors to both the laundry room and the storage room stood open, revealing parts of the home that were usually concealed to guests. One of the plumbers was winding up a long plumber's snake with a camera on the end used to probe the interior of pipelines.

When I reached the short flight of stone steps leading to the front door, I realized Judy was speaking with an insurance company. I felt like an intruder. Two plumbers, the camera, and an insurance call told me this was not a good time to talk about Warren. I also knew Judy was leaving later that day for a vacation in Maui. As soon as she got off the phone, I suggested we postpone our meeting, but she said, "No, let's do it!"

I was getting used to Judy's confusing stance when it came to Warren. When she said, "This has been awful" or when she cursed Warren, I knew it was as much about missing him as it was about plumbing and faded furniture.

"Thank God, it happened a few days ago instead of this morning," said Judy trying to make the plumbing fiasco tolerable. "It would have been really awful if my granddaughter had to deal with this while I was gone."

I had a list of prepared questions on my tablet, but they seemed irrelevant now. I suddenly realized I wanted to know more about this home that Judy and Warren had made. "Tell me about this house," I said to the woman whose children's handprints—his and hers—were pressed forever in the driveway that I climbed to get to the Borgquist's front door.

"I already told you about buying it in the rain when we were living in the rental over on the Cassinetto's property. First, Warren spent a couple of years remodeling and fixing up the bedrooms for the kids. Oh, let me tell you about our bathroom because that was really fun. I painted it white and accented it with red and black towels and shower curtain. There was a cup in the bathroom with red and black pens, and whenever people came over, they would write quotes on the wall—things like the ones on the refrigerator."

I'd noticed a refrigerator magnet before we sat by the fire, commenting that the words seemed apropos for the day. *Life might not*

*be the party we'd hoped for, but while we are here, we might as well dance.*
"Everyone—all of our friends and family and the kids and their friends—wrote stuff on that wall. It was wonderful. I pasted all this self-help stuff on the wall behind the toilet. It was the '70s, and you had to improve yourself and meditate and stuff like that. So I cut all these quotes out of magazines and glued them to the bathroom wall around a poster of a poem by Judith Viorst, called 'Self-Improvement Program.' It's all about doing yoga and pottery and organic gardening. All the stuff that was the rage back then. The poem was really funny with a Viorst-kind of twist about trying too hard to improve."

The plumbers knocked, interrupting Judy's story.

"We aren't going to dig up the kitchen too, are we?" quipped Judy, making light of what was marring her day.

"Not yet," said one, who then asked permission to check something in the master bathroom.

Judy agreed, sighed, and continued in what seemed like a new direction. "In 1975, we did the cross country trip that made us a real family. During the trip, the kids told us they didn't want to move. Once we decided to stay here, we started remodeling. Warren's dream was to build his own house, but he had to settle for rebuilding the kitchen in this house." Judy left her chair by the fireplace and headed to the kitchen. I followed.

"For three years, I was without a kitchen. By then we had made a kind of sunroom out there." She pointed toward a large bright room off the kitchen. "It was a screened porch, but one year I just couldn't bear the thought of not having the space available year round, so while Warren was in Death Valley, I had someone put in some hokey windows. Then we started remodeling the kitchen. I had a card table with a microwave oven, an electric fry pan, and a toaster oven. Somehow I made food out there in the sunroom. We even entertained—actually had parties, believe it or not. To wash dishes, he ran a hose from the backyard through the open door into one of those old white metal sinks. But no hot water. I had to heat water to wash dishes. It was very primitive, but he got to do his dream. He designed and built every cupboard, but you can see that he never finished the phone cupboard. A friend was going to do it for me, but he hasn't, so I finally just called a contractor, and supposedly in a month or so he's going to come and do it.

"Anyway, Warren did everything except that last little bit. And he planned everything according to my wishes. He measured how high I could lift a Pyrex pan. 'This is where the refrigerator is going to go,' he said. 'Can you lift a Pyrex dish that high?' And then he put in a cupboard that worked for me over the refrigerator. He said, 'The sink is going to be here and the stove here, so what do you want by the stove?' I have hot pads and stirring things right where I want them. He measured every bowl I had and used the measurements to determine how deep the drawers would be. He believed that only drawers should go down below—and I agreed. Cupboards are useless. So only drawers, and do you see how close this is?" Judy pulled out a drawer to show how the tops of the bowls were mere millimeters from the top of the drawer. "'And where do you want your knives and your silverware?' he asked. I wanted them right by the dishwasher." Judy pulled out a drawer full of cutlery.

"This is beautiful," I say rubbing my hand over the counter top.

"Oh, my god, that's the most ridiculous part of the whole kitchen. It weighs three tons. Getting that in here was a nightmare."

The plumbers traipsed in again. "We haven't put any numbers on this yet," said one of the men, whose name, William, was lettered on his shirt.

"You put one on it a little while ago that made me cry," said Judy.

"I was just throwing out a number," William said, bantering with Judy. "You aren't going to be out of service for more than a day," he continued, "but there is going to be a lot of jackhammering."

Judy wanted them to do the work while she was in Hawaii, but the plumbers wanted her here. "OK, do it when I come back. I'll move out for a few days," she conceded.

"You won't have to. You'll just have to put up with jackhammering."

"If you can live without a kitchen for three years . . . " I interjected.

"This will be nothing compared to that," said William.

"Thank you, Patricia," Judy said, allowing a bit of sarcasm to seep into the plumbing mess. After the plumbers left, she continued where she'd left off. "So anyway, he built this kitchen."

"Tell me about this," I said stepping across a short hallway from the kitchen into a space that could have been a breakfast room but was occupied by the huge bed where Warren had once told stories to the grandkids.

"Warren came up with the idea to make a bed here. We had the two small bedrooms the kids were in, but now there are twenty-five people in our family. So this bed is for guests, and we watched TV here. I picked this fabric because I love palm trees. This poor old upholsterer covered the bed all by himself. A king-sized Tempur-Pedic mattress weighs a lot. I don't know how he did it. I used to sit over there on that side, so I could put my wine on that shelf." She pointed to a narrow shelf running the length of the wall along one side of the bed. "And Warren would be here." She patted the other side of the bed. "Now I just sit on his side and pull that little table over. The mattress is all bumpy from where we sat."

"Warren designed all the remodeling in the house. Jim Andrasko was the carpenter who did a lot of the work."

At the mention of Jim's name, I had made a quick note in the pad I was carrying, "Jim working on Borgquists' house same time as JL's." Jim Andrasko had helped build my daughter's home, and I remembered her husband's frustration when Jim canceled work on their place because of something going on at the Borgquist's. The fact that the delays benefitted the doctor who had saved his son's and wife's lives only a few years before mitigated his annoyance.

There is a picture of Warren and Jim Andrasko in the early stages of remodeling the kitchen. The two stand side-by-side, each with a straight arm resting amiably on the other's shoulder—a stance that is comradely but also creates a peculiar, arms-length distance between them. Both sport dark beards, with Jim's being the longer of the two. Warren holds a screwdriver in his free hand and a tape measure is attached to his belt loop. The counter tops are strewn with tools and kitchen paraphernalia, and behind them, the piping under the kitchen sink is exposed where cupboard doors have been removed. Warren's smile is broader than Jim's, who looks as if he knows something Warren doesn't.

I was eager to talk with Jim to hear his take on the mammoth remodeling project. After leaving multiple phone messages on his voice mail requesting an interview, I eventually received a fat manila envelope in the mail with Jim's return address marked in the corner. I opened the envelope to find six pages of neat writing on both sides of lined yellow tablet paper.

Hi Patricia,

Sorry I haven't gotten back to ya about Warnie...I'm not good at personal interviews, so I thought I'd just scribble a few reminiscences for you.

We all loved Doctor Warnie. He was always so kind and conscientious in the dealings I had with him. He used to fondly refer to me as "the resident carpenter" (I worked there for 15 years, off and on) and the residence became affectionately known as the Borgquist mystery house. I told him we really ought to start charging admission for tours. He was quite proud of the "project" that became a life-long passion. He was bound and determined to make that house a masterpiece. Especially since originally it was just a modest "Hatler-built house" that he felt lacked the quality of a doctor's residence. He eventually succeeded even though it wasn't without trials & tribulations. He probably spent way too much money on the project, but it was really a Sistine Chapel kind of creation that started as a "therapeutic hobby" and became an obsession.

Once we spent a whole week trying to drill a couple of holes that were almost three feet long through the concrete foundation of the fireplace so we could run wires and a gas line to the fireplace insert. The problem was that we worked from underneath the house, which became a maze of belly crawling pathways and lights like a mine. I had to beg off and leave on Friday. I felt like I was abandoning the attempt, but he had totally lost track of time and space...After the weekend, I honestly thought he would abandon it as a futile attempt and try a new approach but to my amazement on Monday, he had achieved the impossible by actually cramming bodily into the fireplace and drilling from the top to make the two holes meet like the transcontinental railroad. Of course, it wasn't without failures which only served to make him all the more earnest in his endeavor. He actually had Trotter's weld an extension onto the bit, but it broke off in one of the holes, so he had to abandon that hole and start another. The fact that he had figured out the angle just by guessing and a strong hunch and his perseverance to boot, made it happen. That was Warnie—bound and determined. Amazing really. And between the two of us the fireplace turned out beautiful. Fitting for the Borgquist residence!"

Pretty much everything followed this pattern. Another time he ordered the front door from a company in Indiana. The thing had to be trucked clear across country. The trucker called from the bypass and said his truck was a fifty-three foot semi, so I should bring my truck to pick up the door. That's when I began to suspect something was wrong. Sure enough, it was in this huge ten-foot crate that hung out the back of my little Toyota by three feet. I got it to the house and dismantled the crate to discover Warnie had not noticed that the door, which was arched by the way, was eight feet tall—not the usual 6' 8". I called Warnie and told him the news, wondering what to do? Eight feet wasn't going to work, and also, it was four feet wide. But lo and behold, Warnie once again prevailed. He spent all weekend rebuilding that door. It was a massive project that required rearranging the shop, buying more tools, appeasing Judy, who was ready to kill him, and of course, getting me involved to finish and get it hung. So once again he pulled it out of the fire. Life is all about Plan B, I guess.

Warnie loved a challenge. He could dissect a problem, examine every angle, every approach, mull over every possible outcome or direction like a mad scientist. I was constantly astounded at the complexity a job could take and the thoroughness he wanted in the finished product. Like sanding for instance. I would be covered in sanding dust from getting a cabinet "smooth as a baby's ass" as he liked to phrase it. I'd spray a coat of paint on it, only to come back the next day to find he'd come home from the office and RE-sanded all the paint down to the wood again. I squawked about it and pointed out how much it was costing him, but he didn't care about the money. He just said, "Smooth as a baby's ass."

Many a time we had some big elaborate project going on, like the giant sun-room windows on a track to slide open with screens for the summer, and I'd work all week to his master plan specifications only to arrive the next Monday to have him tell me he had scrapped the plan because he "just couldn't live with it"— one of his reoccurring expressions—and he now wanted it done differently. Everybody told him, "Warnie, you spend a dollar trying to save a dime," and he knew it, but he didn't care. It was a point of pride with him. Great qualities for a doctor, I might add, but kind of costly to the creed of contractors. Still everybody expected this behavior from him. It was his nature.

Another expression he liked to bandy about was he wanted it "bullet proof" which morphed into wanting it "bomb proof." I couldn't believe the magnitude of the overkill we constructed into every project. It often had Judy in tears of frustration, like when I was sanding and painting and re-sanding and re-painting the interior of the house for weeks. Then one Monday, I got there to find Warnie skulking off to work with his tail between his legs, pleading to me to "wrap it up and get her done." A complete reversal of baby's ass smoothness, of which he considered himself to be the expert judge—and rightfully so. He claimed with utter dismay that "Judy had a meltdown" and the "job was good enough." Man, I wanted to hug Judy. I was getting pretty tired of remodeling the remodel. Besides, "I had broken the bank" as he told it, and Judy wanted her house back. But I knew the pattern: Warnie would set you on a task, like pushing boulders up hill in purgatory, and he'd skip off to work. The castle became this ginormous bastion that came with a price. Oh well! It made a fabulous showpiece. I used to joke it was good enough to feature in Fine Homebuilding magazine, and he'd counter with "at least Pretty Good Homebuilding magazine."

And it wasn't just me, the resident carpenter (who actually was there at times more waking hours per day than Warnie), who worked on the place. There were armies of guys working over the years. I'll never forget this one guy, Jose, from the stucco crew. He was from El Salvador and bilingual and so happy to be in the U.S. He must have impressed Warnie, who put Jose to digging out the dirt from the basement, which had to be wheelbarrowed about a mile from the sub area to the driveway where the five-yard dump trailer was to be filled. Apparently, everyone forgot about poor Jose, who worked until dark like a hard-rock miner. He needed a ride home, but Warnie was working late, so Jose kept plodding along until the trailer was mounded so high with dirt that it broke the tongue. When Warnie finally got home, Jose was still diligently picking away at the clay that resembled an ancient Mayan temple all perfectly stepped. Needless to say, Warnie had to have him empty half the trailer to fix the broken tongue. I was so impressed with the ancient Mayan temple look of the sub area that I said, 'This has to be part of the tour of the Borgquist mystery house.' Warnie laughed and then called the welder to fix the tongue.

Another feature of the house that hardly anyone ever sees is the roof, which took many weeks of blistering work to fit with fiber-mesh and a painted-on-latex snow roof. It had to be "bomb proof." It turned out looking like a skateboard park. Warnie didn't want any sharp angles, especially over by the pool, where I learned everybody liked to cannonball off, trying to make the biggest splash. Of course, I had to give that a try. What I thought was a fairly new tradition turned out to have been going on for years. Everybody in Sonora had jumped of the roof into the pool or heard of it. I'm pretty sure Warnie had major apprehension and anxiety about the pool, wondering if the concrete sides would crumble, like in an earthquake, causing water to gush out and go who-knew- where. Something you'd rather not dwell on too much, but also validated his overkill-bomb-proof approach.

But chaos seemed to have its day, regardless. There was the incident I like to refer to as 'Borgquist Creek.' We were always battling plumbing, and one time, there was a pretty good break on one of the irrigation lines. I could not locate the leak because it was so confusing and over-engineered—something Warnie put together—so he insisted he had to fix it himself, while I worked on other tasks in the shop. At any given time, this great flood of biblical proportion would start in the back yard when the timer clicked on, causing a little creek to flow down the hill into the street, meandering toward the Adventist church, forming several small lakes on the way. People just went about their day-to-day business, too busy to do anything other than think "There must be a leak somewhere."

But one day, I was happily wrestling with some small project in the nether regions of the shop, with saws and compressors blaring away, when I looked up to see this irate stranger gesturing angrily at me to take off my ear protection. He was mad as hell because water had gotten into his meter box that was on the ground and shorted out the wires to his irrigation system. I was kind of dumbfounded, not realizing the water had come from Warnie's backyard, but a little investigation revealed the source. Of course, I apologized all over the place and turned off the valve to stop the flow. The guy was still hopping mad and he stalked off saying, "Tell your dad that he better get the goddam thing fixed."

When I told Warnie the guy mistook me for his son, he said, "Oh, you poor man."

The whole metamorphosis of the house was amazing. Just when I thought we'd done every possible re-model, we'd roll around to another. We probably could have completed a couple houses in the time spent. It was quite the challenge and went past the point of no return again and again, but Warnie was very proud of it. A man's home is his castle, which I believe is the rough translation for Borgquist, which in Swedish means something like 'wall of the castle.'

Once Warnie paid me the highest compliment. He said he thought he should quit his doctor job, and we could partner up and build houses together. He wasn't serious, but it gave me a warm feeling that he thought that much of my ability. It gives me great pride to know I was part of the whole epic journey. When I drive toward that corner and see the contoured walls up high like a citadel and the shimmering wall of glass from the sunroom, I shiver with admiration.

"Jim is the contractor I called to finish the phone cupboard," said Judy on the day of the plumbing fiasco. "He is the one who refaced the original crappy paneling with fiber board, and he built the fireplace and cabinets. Warren did the kitchen by himself, but Jim was here all of the time working on the other stuff. I bet he made a whole year's wages off this project. He did all the wood working and built the cabinets out there in the sunroom.

"Warren took great pride in this house. We always said, 'It's a good house for two people because it's not big, but it's big enough to entertain.' We loved to entertain. This house is him. My older son Scott says, 'Mom, you can't take care of the house by yourself without a man. Something always goes wrong.' And of course he's right. It would be a lot cheaper if I sold this house and moved to Sonora Hills, but I can't. This place is him. His spirit is everywhere."

# Chapter 24

# THE BIGGER PICTURE

Children see magic because they look for it.

-Christopher Moore, *Lamb*

As I interviewed family and friends about Warren, many asked if I'd spoken to Brynn Lorimer Hart. However, each time she and I tried to make a date, circumstances intervened to prevent our meeting. I wasn't bothered though. By this time, I trusted that something was guiding the project, bringing me to people who could shed light on Warren Borgquist exactly when I was prepared to understand how their stories fit into the bigger picture.

Brynn and I finally met in the toddler classroom at Sierra Waldorf School where she worked. The March day was mild after a wet El Nino winter, and the door to her classroom sat open to bird song and the smell of new grass outside. Tiny benches rested upside down atop tiny tables in the room, signaling that class was over. I sat on a dainty love seat, and Brynn sat in a large rocker with her two-year old daughter Mielle in her lap. She introduced me to the child, who stared at me with big brown eyes. Mielle stayed silent and watchful during our conversation.

"Tell me about the Lorimer and Borgquist families when you were younger," I began. "What do you remember?"

"We got together quite often at my parents' or at the Borgquists' for dinner parties, social events, Christmas gatherings. On Christmas Eve, or a couple of days before, we always had a time where we each read something aloud. Later while the other grown-ups gathered to visit, Warren told us stories. I'm really sad that I can't remember the content of those stories. They were very imaginative. I only remember being engaged, and that they took place faraway with creatures and beings. His voice in particular kept us mesmerized.

"His presence was always so big to me. He had a way of making me feel invited in a snuggly way. I've been trying to remember how I saw him when I was little because our relationship changed over the years. When I was little and sitting on his lap, I remember feeling safe. From early on, he was a father-like presence. I wasn't as close with my father. I mean my father was there, but he's not cuddly. He's more prickly," said Brynn as she smoothed the top of Mielle's head. "As a little kid, I sat in my dad's lap, but it had a different feel. Warren was softer, more gentle—a more approachable male figure in my life. I loved to go over there because he always had something silly to say or some way of making me laugh. He also had a way of engaging with my brother, who was very introverted. Now that I'm here at Waldorf, I understand more about individual make-up. I see that my brother was melancholic. He was very quiet and reserved, and it was OK with Warren that he was that way."

"You're awfully snugly today," said Brynn to Mielle, who had adjusted her position several times trying out various nestling options.

"Though I couldn't really see it as a child, I now realize that my mom and Warren had a complex relationship. I hate to call it a love-hate relationship. That's so cliché, but it was a something like that. Warren could embrace my mother and all her craziness, but sometimes he was thoroughly irritated by how emotional she could be or how she misinterpreted things or turned something small into something huge. I can see that Warren embraced my mom in certain ways, but as a kid I didn't really see that because my mom and Judy were usually talking in the kitchen with their glasses of wine, and my dad was outside with Warren."

"Talk about how your relationship with Warren evolved."

"During elementary school, I enjoyed being at their house and being part of the celebrations, but it wasn't until high school that he became somebody I turned to—either about things that were going on with my friends or my parents. My mom was a total source of irritation to me when I was a teenager, and Warren and I kind of connected around that. He became somebody I felt comfortable talking to. Sometimes I'd walk over to their house after school. Or I'd meet him there for lunch. He had perspective—because he wasn't my parent. He had a way of listening and talking to me about the world, so I turned to him, especially when I was a junior in high school and my parents divorced. That was very impactful on my life because it was hard on my mom. There was a lot of sadness, a lot of grief every day for a long time, so I spent time with Warren and Judy because they could lift my spirit. They understood because they were my parents' friends, but they also had some distance. Theirs was a house of warmth, a place I could talk and be.

"Even after high school, Warren and Judy figured in my life. I went away to school but came back after a couple of years. I didn't really know what I wanted to do. I did childcare for Trish Rowe and Ken Renwick, because they had the twins and needed help. Then Judy suggested I do AmeriCorp, which I did. We were placed in elementary schools around town, and I requested Tenaya because Judy was the principal there. We received what was called a living stipend, which was nothing of the sort. I was 20 years old, receiving this miserable wage, so the Borgquists invited me to move in with them. They had a big house, and their kids were off on their own, so they gave me a room while I was working at Tenaya in exchange for helping out around their place. Warren didn't think there was women's work or men's work. That was not how he operated. He would say, 'OK Brynn, this weekend we're digging trenches to lay some pipe. We're going to use the power auger and dig some big holes.' I remember working when it was 100 degrees—dirty and dripping with sweat.

"Warren thought it was important for me to get my hands dirty—to do heavy lifting, to clear, move, and load brush on the truck. And I had to drive it to the slash pile. He also taught me how to drive because my mom freaked out and stuck her hand on the roof like this," said Brynn holding her palm up and flat, as if to the car header for balance. "And she made these faces, and I got so riled. 'I can't go with you, Mom,' I said. 'It's stressing me out.' Every one was adamant that I learn to drive a stick shift. Warren took me in his little pickup. He was so patient.

"So Judy and Warren gave me a place to live, and I went on a trip

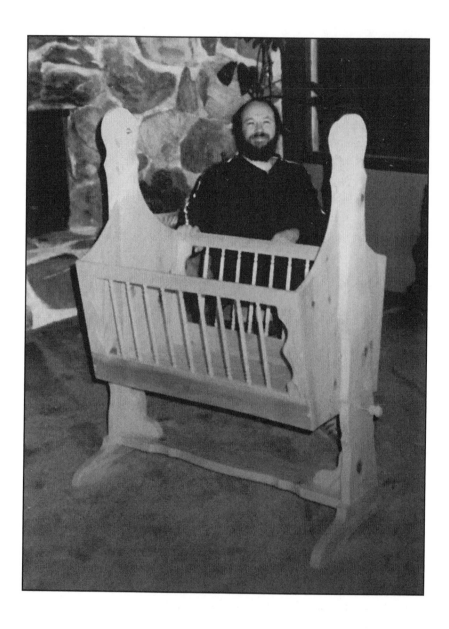

with them to Burney Falls, camping for Cousins Week, to help out because there was a bunch of little cousins around by then. It was a lot of fun, traveling with Warren and Judy as a 20-year-old. Again Warren had stories, but now they were about big-people topics like history. He could talk about any subject in full detail and make it magical and interesting. He might launch into a story about the Roman gods, and he was captivating, with a sense of humor that put a twist on things. Living with them was huge for me."

"Do you have any stories of him as a doctor? Your dad said he took care of you kids."

"Oh yes, I mean throughout my whole life. When we were little, we didn't go to the office. We just drove to his house. All the way through high school, we went to him. I remember talking to him about birth control because my mom was like, 'Ah sex. No, we're not going talk about that.' But with Warren, he'd sit you down and say, 'You're not going off into the world naïve. This is what you have to know.' So yeah, he talked to me about all kinds of stuff. I remember being at Cuesta College and calling him because I thought I had a strep infection, and he called something in for me. When I was living in San Diego, I called saying, 'I think I have a yeast infection.' Another time in San Diego, I was walking down the stairs, and I missed a step and landed funny on my foot. I heard this little grrrich. Pretty soon, I couldn't stand or put any pressure on it. The next morning, I was sitting on the couch when Judy and Warren showed up unexpectedly. They were visiting friends in San Diego. He examined it and said, 'You've broken a bone in your foot.' They took me to get a boot and crutches, and for the next couple of days, they took care of me.

"When I got pregnant with Bennett, I saw an OB up until about six months, and then suddenly I knew I didn't want to have the baby in the hospital. I called Trish Rowe, who said to call Ellie. I called, but she was going to be out of town for the month of December, so she said, to call Andrea. I remember meeting with Andrea and thinking, 'Yes, you're exactly what I want.' So my husband and I invited Warren to dinner to tell him. I was so excited, but he went, 'You're crazy!' That made me a little nervous, but I think he was coming from the protective father place. After he sat with it a little bit, he said, 'OK, that's what you're going do, and I'm only a phone call away.' Everything suddenly shifted because he would be there for me, and I knew nothing was going to go wrong. After Bennett was born, Judy and Warren came over."

When I interviewed the midwives, they had talked about Warren coming to meet Bennett after he was born. "Warren wanted to help," said Dody. "Brynn had some tearing from the birth, so Andrea said, 'You can stitch her up.' And Brynn said, 'I'm comfortable with that.' He talked his way through the whole thing, describing everything he was doing. I learned a lot from watching him," Dody said. "It took him a really long time, and it was not a super bad tear, so I thought, if it takes Dr. Borgquist forty minutes to stitch her up, I feel better about myself. It was really lovely. He just wanted to participate in the birth. He was so excited to be there."

"I was so happy that night," said Brynn, as she rocked her second child during our visit in her classroom. "We passed Bennett around. Warren held him and said, 'He's only a few minutes old, and he is so loved.' That was a sweet moment. That's one of the things that kills me. That my kids won't . . ." Tears spilled from Brynn's eyes. She was too choked up to continue, so we sat in the quiet as she rocked her daughter who had fallen asleep in her lap. I surveyed the room, a lovely space, created to nurture toddlers, and I realized how sweetly it was holding us as Brynn told her story.

"Warren came over a few days after Bennett was born with a wooden cradle he'd made—the one all of his grandkids used. He'd burned each of their names into its sides. I put it right by our sliding glass door in the best light. I would sit there rocking my baby, full of the peace that was passed down in that cradle, and feeling like I was part of Warren's family. I think Bennett experienced that too."

There is a picture of Warren with this cradle in the living room of his own home, shortly after he finished making it in 1986 for Evan, his first grandchild. The pine glows a warm amber hue, and the gently curving lines of the end pieces promise an airy swing. Sitting behind the cradle next to a statue of a laughing Buddha, the cradle builder—Gramps— beams a squint-eyed, closed-mouth smile of contentment.

"He comes to me in my dreams," said Brynn. "I remember one

very specific dream when he told me he was okay. And I said 'You're not gone,' and he said 'No, I'm not gone. I'm here.' I remember waking up and feeling like, yeah, he's here. Of course, not having him here physically is hard, especially now that I have my own kids. He was going to be that guy down all fours carrying them around on his back."

Sitting in the toddler classroom with Brynn, I felt Warren's presence in a very big way. The room was purposely designed to be serene and congenial, and I realized we'd been speaking in hushed voices the whole time. I left that interview in a peculiar state—tearful and fragile. This wasn't the first time I was emotionally moved after an interview, but I'd never experienced Warren as a felt presence as I did when talking with Brynn.

That afternoon I came to understand more fully how Warren took to the role of parenting. Be it his own children or a family friend's, be they youngsters, teens, or adults—he approached the task with the amiability, directness, and absorption that he did everything. In the '90s, he may have been remodeling his castle—working for three years on the mammoth project with Jim Andrasko— but he'd been engaged in building his concept of family for most of his adult life.

"My dad rode my ass until I quit being a carpenter in Humboldt County," said Greg, describing how Warren's concern reached into his adulthood. "I came down to Modesto to go back to college to become a teacher because my dad rode me like a jockey. He told me that I was a great husband and a great father, a great neighbor to whomever might be my neighbor, but I was a failure as a provider. He told me that I needed to provide for his grandchildren what he had provided for me in health care, sustainability, and dependability—a house, medical care, food, shelter.

"During my first year of teaching, he frequently wrapped me in his big hug. I had fallen into the job ass backwards—through a series of crazy coincidences. When I first came back to Modesto, my dad told me to call this woman he knew. She had me do some handyman work at a school in Turlock called John B. Allard. I spent three hours working, and she paid me for eight hours at a wage that was like a whole week's worth of work in Humboldt County. Three years later, I was doing a pre-intern class, kind of student-child psychology class, and we had to do mandatory observation. We drew slips of paper with the name of the school where we were to go observe. When I grabbed a slip, it was John B. Allard. I ended up getting hired there for my first teaching job.

"Now I teach alternative education in Stanislaus County," said Greg. "When kids get expelled, it's our job to provide a place for them to get their education. Half of my population is there because there is too much trauma-drama in mainstream high school. We provide a much smaller setting, which works better for them. I've worked in a self-contained classroom for eleven years now. I've had some kids stay with me from seventh to twelfth grade—for six full years. I treat all my kids like I treat my own, except I'm probably a little harsher with my own because they are not coming from these rough backgrounds. I deal with a lot of broken kids. My father gave me the gift of empathy. I can feel somebody's pain. I'm an emotional guy and so was my dad. We cry much more quickly than the average person."

Warren's daughter, Mimi talked about when her dad "rode" her, to use Greg's word. "One time at Cousins Week," said Mimi, "we were camping as usual. I had three kids, and my youngest, Emily, was eight months old. I was stressed out and probably going through postpartum blues. I was giving my husband a hard time about going off and fishing and having fun while I was at the camp with the kids. Dad came into my tent and said, 'You are acting like a bitch.' He had never talked to me like that, and I was in my thirties. His voice was very stern, and it really threw me.

"'Excuse me,' I said.

"'Your husband is a great husband,' Dad said 'and he's just trying to enjoy this vacation. You're treating him horribly. You're acting like a bitch.' I was shocked. My dad didn't say that kind of thing. That Cousins Week is now jokingly known as 'the year Mimi was the bitch.'"

With Mimi and Greg, Warren sometimes took a stern parental stance. With Brynn Lorimer and his nephews, he had the luxury of being more of a pal. "We often had dinner at Uncle Warren's," said Zac Garmin, "like for holidays or just random times when we'd go over for Sunday dinner. Or we'd see them at my grandparents' house for Thanksgiving or Christmas. We went to swim at their house, too. They had older kids, so we chased the kids who were in high school in this or that game. We were always on the run.

"It was kind of funny because when I was a kid I was frustrated or mad at my mom because she had kept her maiden name, but it had this cool aspect too because when people asked, 'Who's your mom?' and I said, 'Marjorie Borgquist,' they'd connect the dots with Warren, and that was a proud thing, 'Yeah, that's my uncle,' I said. I was in second grade when we moved here from Santa Cruz, and he had delivered like ten percent of the kids in my class. And that was cool, too.

"I remember him telling stories, not the specific story but the feeling I got from the story. I have a vivid memory of being with a group of my cousins in Big Sur with the waves crashing and the story of a magical adventure. I remember the smell of the ocean, but we were actually sitting on his living room couch, only I had gone to the place he described in the story. So now I have two kids who are 7 and 8. I have a captive audience for twenty-five minutes on the way to the Waldorf School three days a week. And there's a third child who rides with us. I've been telling them stories on this drive since they were in first grade, about flying dragons or whatever, and they are based on stories Uncle Warren told. Each time, we head down into the Rawhide Valley, I end the story when we pass the house on the right with the palm trees. To me, palm trees represent paradise, so my story always ends in paradise. Now when I come to the end, all three kids say, 'It must be paradise.'"

"That's your Warren legacy," I said, "to tell those stories."

"It is," Zac said. "Here's another funny story about Uncle Warren. My daughter's teacher at Waldorf is Julie Orth. One time, we went to her house on Racetrack about four or five years ago, before she was Kaylee's teacher. It's up on top of the hill, and as we were walking around the property, I had the feeling I'd been there before. I mentioned this to Julie, and she said, "Word is that a doctor used to own this property." And I knew immediately it was Uncle Warren's property because I'd been there with him. And the thing is, at that point, we had no idea Julie would end up being Kaylee's teacher."

As Zac told this story, I realized he was talking about one of the properties Warren had purchased when he dreamed of building his own house. It was the place he'd taken Sean to try out his soap box derby car. Now, years later it was owned by a woman who was Warren's grand-niece's teacher. Talking about storytelling on the way to Waldorf School had shaken loose this tidbit in Zac's memory, another example of how connections meander and criss-cross in small town life—and through the tales about Warren Borgquist. For instance, when I'd sat with Brynn in her Waldorf classroom, she'd mentioned Zac, and two days later, I was sitting with Zac hearing his tales about Warren. Jim Andrasko had worked at the Borgquist house while building my daughter's home. Warren knew a woman who offered Greg a temp job at the school where he'd later get his first teaching position. This was not the kind of structure a carpenter builds. It was the village noted in the ancient African proverb and made widely known in a book written by Hillary Clinton—the description of a community in which people care for one another, help raise one another's children, and weather all kinds of issues together.

"When I got older," said Zac, "I worked for him. Mostly yard work, but he would pay me more money than I was worth and take me out for lunch and teach me how to drive a stick shift. He'd work me really hard for a while, and then we'd do fun stuff, and all the while he would fill me full of amazing facts about the most random things. Of course, Uncle Warren was spread thin. He had all kinds of stuff going on with his kids and grandkids, and being a doctor and traveling with his wife and doing everything that they did, but when I got to steal a few minutes with him, it was awesome.

"I like to say I'm blessed with natural immaturity," said Zac, apparently thinking about working and playing with his uncle. "Actually there is a lot of that in my family. We have a lot of fun, and I think it originates with my grandparents' unconditional love—no judgment and no guilt."

"Are you talking about your Borgquist grandparents?"

"Yes, well actually Grandma B. There were times when I hadn't seen her for six months, but when I came in the door, she never said, 'Where have you been?' No, she always said, 'I've missed you. It's good to see you.' Those words make you want to be with your family." Zac smiled, and I marveled at the subtlety in the distinction he was making between these two greetings, for I'd never realized that one could evoke guilt while the other might produce longing.

"What was it like having a doctor in the family?" I asked.

"The thing I remember was he always gave it to you straight if there was an issue. He'd say, 'You broke this bone' or 'This is what's wrong.' And sometimes he said, 'Toughen up, kid.' I think about that all the time, 'Toughen up, kid.' He was saying, 'It's not that bad' or 'It's not that big of a deal.' But he would also tell you when there was something to worry about.

"One time based on some preliminary tests, he thought that I had a heart condition. His initial reaction was to tell me to go get life insurance and come back. So I went and got all my ducks in a row, got life insurance and set up a trust, and then I went back to see him, and he ordered more tests, and it turned out I was fine. But now I'd taken care of all this stuff you should do anyway but most of us procrastinate doing.

"Back when we were kids though, if we needed stitches on a Sunday, we didn't go to the emergency room. We went to see Uncle Warren. Whenever we had something screwy, he would come take care of us, or sometimes he met us at the emergency room. Then when Grandpa got sick and then Grandma, he was there. He was a sap, just like the rest of us. We're all saps, who cry at sad commercials, and he was totally solid with that. Having a big a heart, he could handle it. He could take it all on his shoulders."

# Chapter 25

# BIG-HEARTED DOCTORING

Life is very inefficient and not cost-effective at all,
from a health-care efficiency point of view.

-Victoria Sweet, *God's Hotel*

"Dr. Borgquist always told us about a scene from a Monty Python movie when we brought a new baby to his office for a check up," said Jennie Lou Tippett. My daughter was the mother of nine children, and Dr. Borgquist was describing a scene from *The Meaning of Life* in which the characters sing the song "Every Sperm is Sacred."

"I was offended," said my daughter about Warren's allusion to Python's satire about the Catholic teachings on reproduction. "It took me years to appreciate his sense of humor," continued Jennie Lou. "I eventually asked if he told all his big families this story. 'Do they get the same treatment or do you save it for us?' He assured me everyone heard it, the Catholic families, the German Baptist families."

My daughter's struggle with Dr. Borgquist's particular sense of humor made me want to mediate the issue, to soothe her ruffled feathers and swab her personal choices with appreciation At the same time, I wanted to defend our family physician's personal style, his unbridled storytelling and references to obscure pop culture that were not within the frame of reference of his audience. Just as when he'd explained buoyancy to Jess and Jake, I'm sure his Catholic and German Baptist families wondered why he was connecting Monty Python trivia to their lives. Gramps told his grandchildren that they had to endure these talks, and they complied because he was so exuberant in the telling. My daughter eventually came to terms with the storytelling too, which was evident in the chuckle she emitted as she told this story. I knew her acceptance came in part because Dr. Borgquist "got her."

"I had the impression that there was more to his thinking about me—that he was more patient with me—because of his daughter Jennifer," said Jennie Lou, who leaned steeply in the direction of alternative and natural practices and remedies, such as home birth and herbal medicine, cautious use of antibiotics and liberal employment of chiropractics.

Warren and I often had conversations about our daughters, Jennifer and Jennie Lou, who were coincidentally both married to Michaels, had converted as young adults to Judaism and Catholicism respectively, and migrated to the fringe when it came to medical decisions. We laughed a bit smugly and joked about their far-fetched thinking. However, we did not shrug off their well-researched and thoughtful approach to medical decisions for themselves and their families. I was grateful Warren was a good listener and willing to learn because that's the kind of doctor my daughter needed.

Other family practice physicians in Sonora—Chuck Waldman, Todd Stolp, and Eric Runte—talked about the particular brand of doctoring they and Warren offered the community. I had a chance to talk with Dr. Runte—who arrived in Tuolumne County in 1994—at Schnoogs coffee shop, early one morning before he went to work at his downtown practice. Eric and I sat at a tall, round bar table in a wash of morning sun streaming through the shop's plate glass windows. The tall, handsome doctor, neatly dressed in slacks and a blue shirt, sipped coffee and talked amiably about practicing in Sonora.

"I came to Sonora because it fit the parameters of where I wanted to work," said Dr. Runte. "It had nothing to do with Warren. My wife wanted to be close to her sister who lived in Davis at the time, so we drew a two-hour circle around Davis, into which Sonora fell. I always liked the mountains and remembered coming through here when I was a kid, so I came to see what was available in the foothills. I met Warren the first day I came to interview for a job. He was part of the family doctors who formed a call group—Dr. Stolp, Chuck Waldman, Ed Clinite, and Warren.

"I was a new graduate, just out of residency, and Warren was the fatherly-type who would come in and put his arm around me and say, 'Hey, you're doing great.' I questioned myself in the beginning. There's so much going on, and he was very supportive. When I had serious things to deal with in ICU, I sometimes needed someone to tell me it was OK to do this or that. He was always available, whether on the phone or in person. He knew the kind of stress we faced because he had more experience than any of us.

"Family practice is a specialty where you spend a lot of time getting to know people and trying to understand what their needs are as you put them into the context of their medical problems. That's what attracted me. For the patient, this is unique in medicine because specialists delve deeply into a specific problem, whereas a family doctor needs to look at the whole picture. It becomes kind of a friendship, but at the same time the doctor is the expert. It's a broader spectrum of medicine that requires pulling it all together. That is what drew me to the specialty and just being important to people and taking care of them.

"We had a unique group of family doctors who did full-spectrum family care," said Dr. Runte. "There really wasn't anything we weren't doing other than surgery—though we did certain forms of surgery. Our entire group worked the ER and ICU, using Maquet ventilators, putting in deep lines, very aggressive therapies that are done in an ICU setting. We all delivered babies, took care of newborns, and had outpatient practices. The volume of work when you have such a broad set of responsibility is overwhelming. I remember some of my colleagues, and actually even some of my teachers telling me, 'Eric you can't do it all.' Even though that's what they were training me to do. For fifteen years, I didn't know that was true. Then I realized I'd better decide what I was going to do because you really can't do it all."

"How did you decide?" I asked. "I mean if you're trained to do all of that, how did you figure it out?"

"You figure out how you can get more sleep. That's your number one priority, so you cut out things that keep you up all night. That was my most important issue. And that's the underlying cause of most burn-outs—doctors not getting enough sleep because they're up at night."

Dr. Ken Renwick told a story about Warren admitting that sleep was a priority. "Back when I started working at TGH in '86 or '87, I was work-ing the Emergency Department (ED), and Warren was providing admis-sions coverage. If I saw someone in the ED who had chest pain or pneu-monia, I would call Warren and give him a thirty second summary of the case. Then I'd suggest what we could do next, and he'd say fine and that was it. Then one day Warren took me aside and said, 'I want you to know that when you wake me up in the middle of the night, I can't get back to sleep, and I'm really dysfunctional the next day, so what I'd like you to do is admit everybody in my name, and then call me in the morning around seven and tell me who I've got. My deal with you is I'll accept anybody you admit.' He had to say this last part because there were a few docs who were famous for disputing admissions. But Warren never played that kind of game. Part of the deal he made was practical too because occasionally after he got a call at two in the morning, he would totally space out and not remember because he wasn't really awake. He'd agree to the admission and then go back to sleep, and by morning, he'd forgotten all about it."

Dr. Renwick elaborated on issues faced by family practice doctors. "Some programs are more popular: ophthalmology, anesthesia, and der-matology. Basically the ones that have easy practices where you're not up all night and you make lots of money. Most doctors won't go into family practice because they want to make money. In Tuolumne County, there were family practice docs who did OB and those who didn't. Warren was in the group who did. If you did OB, you not only were wakened in the night, you were yanked out during the day and you lost all that prac-tice revenue. No one makes money off OB. You're always losing mon-ey."

Claire Mills also spoke of the money issues related to medical prac-tice. "The reason doctors hire nurse practitioners and PAs is because we make the money for practices. We move the patients through. In my situ-ation, I'm paid a percent. I don't like being paid a percent. I would much rather be on a salary, but being paid a percent means that if I want more money, I have to see more patients. And that doesn't work for me. It's so ingrained in me to take care of the patient that I can't say, 'Oh I'm so sorry, your five minutes are up. Come back next week.' Warren and Chris, those early pioneers, they didn't train Jan, Ann, and me so they could make more money. They were doing it to broaden care and to bring desperately needed primary care services to the community. Their reasoning was more altruistic. These were not well-paying jobs. I mean doctors have always made a lot of money but not so much in a rural community. Nobody came to Tuolumne County to get rich."

The call group was another way a family practice doctor could get much needed rest, so I asked Dr. Runte how their group worked. "Each week, one of us took over call on Thursday afternoon and was responsible for patients through the weekend—Friday, Saturday, Sunday. We covered everyone else's practice during that time. Some of us would do our own deliveries if we weren't out of town, or we'd come in if we had a special patient in the ICU. Warren spent a lot of time creating a colored chart of the call schedule. It was very involved because nobody wanted to be on call every Christmas or Thanksgiving, so he had all the holidays set so we each rotated through. He made it very equitable. He had little sticky notes all over the chart as he pulled it together. It took him a couple weeks to do it each year."

"We actually met once a week in cafes and coffee shops. We met here for a time," said Dr. Runte, gesturing to the lightly occupied tables at Schnoogs. "We did a little business, like planning the call schedule, but mostly we talked quietly about cases and socialized and reconnected because we were pretty much on the run most of the time. There was like a force-field around us. It's kind of intimidating to walk up to a group of doctors. Not that it should be. It just was, so we never got interrupted. People might say 'Hello,' but they could see we were busy. We were able to interact for a second with them without interrupting our conversation. That was nice. We had a very strong bond and a lot of respect for each other. We felt comfortable with each other's medicine. We trusted each other. We had to because we took over each other's patients. Good communication and trust were essential to a call group because you had to rely on your colleagues to come deliver a baby or take care of a very sick patient. The camaraderie was awesome, and that energized us and allowed us to continue for so many years."

Todd Stolp had also talked about the camaraderie of the call group when he and I met at the old Tuolumne General Hospital. "We were a very tight-knit community of doctors. We'd run into each other at two o' clock in the morning in this very building. You'd come in because you were on call or because you were the only one who knew the situation regarding a particular patient. Your hair was all mussed up, and you were standing side-by-side with your friend, another doctor doing the same thing. We talked about stuff—about our kids or our relationships with our wives or things that we valued or whether this was the life we antici-pated. So we got real close."

"Warren and I had a big heart and empathy for our patients" con-tinued Erick Runte. "A lot of family docs do, but he drew that out a little bit more than I. He expanded work further into his life than I did into mine. He spent even more time with patients and took his work home at night. Both of us probably spent too much of our personal time on our work, but it seemed like he did a lot more."

It was true. Warren did devote a lot of personal time to his professional life, and he was married to someone who operated the same way. "The worst thing I ever did," said Judy Borgquist, "happened shortly after I became a Principal at Sonora Elementary. I asked the Board for permis-sion to miss a meeting because Warren was going to have surgery the next morning, and I wanted to go to the hospital with him the night before when he checked in. The Board President said, 'No.' Today, I would have said, 'Forget it. I'm going.' But I was new, and they were really hassling me, and I almost didn't get the job in the first place. I was scared of them, so I didn't go with Warren. Jim Wilson went. Warren said, 'No problem. I understand.' But later he told me it hurt his feelings. I have always felt terrible about that."

It's easy to see both sides of this incident, that is Warren squelching his wish to have Judy with him before surgery because of the challenges she was facing at work, and Judy ignoring her heart as a new and unsure school administrator. Also, given what Eric Runte said, Judy had likely extended Warren plenty of latitude when it came to his professional life intruding on her needs. For example, she had mentioned the intrusion of calls in the middle of the night. But Warren had organized a way for them to deal with stuff like this, so I imagined them revisiting this incident during one of their early morning coffee check-ins and getting to the truth of how each of them felt, just like the docs talking to each other when they met in the quiet early morning hours at the hospital or at local coffee shops. Warren's communication style was frequently cited not only by family, friends, and colleagues but also by patients.

Dr. Borgquist was known to push the edge of convention. His patient Jill Southard related a sweet instance in an anecdote on one of the memory cards collected at his memorial. " I loved how he doctored with heart— sometimes ignoring policy. Our family benefited from this approach several times, but he also touched the life of a dear friend. My friend was traveling to California from Florida to visit her beloved Sierra Nevada, but because she had a rare disease (which caused significant pain), she needed a California doc to prescribe morphine for her arrival and throughout her stay. Warren agreed to be that doctor. He even passed her 'doctor test.' Very few docs would admit they didn't know anything about her disease, but Dr. Borgquist admitted his ignorance. No one could foresee that the catheter that went into my friend's heart to deliver the morphine would come out during the visit. When that happened, he had to arrange surgery for her. This normally unstoppable woman was a bit rattled, but everything went okay. My friend died about five months later, but before that happened, she got to return to the mountains in California because of Warren Borgquist."

The Borgquist's Swiss exchange student Nicolas Millet described another instance in which Dr. Borgquist went against or at least side-stepped policy. "After I graduated medical school, I started an intern-residence, but after two years, I decided to take six months off to travel. First, I worked as a GP in the Swiss House, and then I came to Sonora to work with Warren for three months—from October to January. Well, not actually working. I'd passed what was called the ECFMG for medical graduates in my country, but to do things correctly here would've taken months to go through all the paper work, so Warren said, 'Why don't you come to my office and do some basic stuff, things like taking histories and managing physicals? It was very nice to see how Warren could do all these different things. He was a GP, a psychologist, a gynecologist. He was doing some surgery. He was pretty amazing."

Dolora Dossi recalled an amusing incident when Warren cared for her in the Emergency Room. "One morning, I was getting ready to go work," said Dolora, "putting a comforter on a very high bed, a sleigh bed, and I lost my footing. I landed full force on my wrist, trying to break my fall. I looked down and knew it was a bad break. I was alone, so I had to pick myself up off the floor with my arm dangling. I wrapped a robe tie around it and called my elderly mother to come and get me. She got lost trying to find my house. While I was waiting, the shock wore off, and I started getting woozy. At the time, I was dating a radiologist, Matt Nesper, so I called him too and asked him to meet me at the hospital. He was helpful, but he was also into showing the techs the break. 'Come here you guys,' he said. 'You need to see what a really bad break looks like.' Then Warren showed up and took one look and said, 'Yeah, this is really bad. I'm going to need to set it.' He turned to my mom and said, 'Peggy you don't want to be here when I do this.' That was fine because she didn't want to be there anyway.

"After Warren looked at the films, he said, 'You need surgery." But the radiologists couldn't agree. Jim Wilson didn't think I needed surgery. Matt was on the fence. Meanwhile, I was on Sodium Pentathol and started telling everybody about being at the Borgquist home when I was a teen and seeing pictures on the fridge of Warren and Judy in varying degrees of undress because they were trying to diet." Dolora laughed as she remembered blabbing away while on a drug that is called the truth serum. Who knows what the assembled health care professionals thought, but given Dr. Borgquist's usual candor and the fact that one of the doctors was his best friend, and the patient was dating the other radiologist, it's likely such a story was not an isolated occurrence in the small town emergency room.

Dr. Warren Borgquist was like a walking urgent care, whether stumbling upon one of his patients in the ER like he did with Dolora, examining a jaundiced baby at the end of his driveway, or responding to a call on the weekend about a spider bite. On one occasion, Warren helped a family with the confusing changes an elder was experiencing. According to Beth Palmer, Warren and Judy invited her mom to an impromptu lunch when she wouldn't go to a doctor about the memory problems she was having. "Judy set lunch for us at the kitchen bar, and Warren came in from working outside. Mom thought he was the gardener. He compassionately chatted with Mom over lunch to help diagnose her Alzheimer's. It was a turning point for our family."

Sarah Purdy told about burning her eyeball with a curling iron just before she was to go on stage in a performance of *Arcadia* at Columbia Actor's Repertory. "The plastic tip of the curling iron scratched my cornea ten minutes before the curtain went up. Even though my eye was gushing tears and all red, puffy, and painful, I was determined to go on. My mom called Warren as I headed on stage with my squinty, leaky eye for the first scene. After the scene, Warren was backstage with his doctor's kit, having hustled his butt over on a moment's notice. He gave me some eye drops that numbed the pain, so I could get through the show. The thing is, regardless of the inevitable difficulties in our extended family, Warren was always there when we needed him."

Warren was there for many families with the big heart and empathy Eric Runte described as characteristic of family practice doctors. That he let doctoring spill into his personal life was pretty apparent but not necessarily unusual. Some people are simply always there when needed, and Warren was one of those. Generosity doesn't, however, pay the bills. Even at the office, Warren's generous allotment of time with each patient had drawbacks with greater consequence than a considerable back-up of patients in the waiting room. If it takes a long time to manage a single appointment, then that means fewer appointments in a day and consequently less billing. It's a simple economic principle, but not one Warren, or other family doctors for that matter, were inclined, or even trained, to heed.

"By the '90s MSOs were in full swing," said Dr. Chuck Waldman, using the abbreviation for Management Service Organizations. "The idea of a family practice where you paid cash was history. The $20 office visit was done. That's when insurance started calling the shots. I'd see patients out on the streets and ask, 'How are you doing?' and they'd say, 'Sorry we can't see you anymore. We got reassigned to another doctor.'

"No more paying $10 a month on the bill for your baby's delivery," I said, remembering how I'd done just that in 1977.

"Yeah, that was actually doable not that long ago," said Chuck.

"Sadly things change rapidly. The MSOs decided on this business model with efficiency experts and time motion studies. That's how they were going to run medicine, but that was not how we practiced. I've spent hours on a patient who was ill trying to figure out what was going on. The main ailment is related to how life is affecting them. That doesn't come out right away. It takes time to discern."

Chuck was talking about "slow medicine," something I knew personally as Dr. Borgquist's patient but heard named by Dr. Victoria Sweet in her book *God's Hotel: A Doctor, a Hospital, and a Pilgrimage to the Heart of Medicine.* Dr. Sweet worked at Laguna Honda Hospital in San Francisco from the 1970s into the 1990s. An almshouse—the last in the country—Laguna Honda welcomed patients who had fallen on hard times and needed extended medical care. Early in her tenure at Laguna Honda, Dr. Sweet encountered Dr. Curtis, who was treating a stroke patient who had been waiting three months for Medicare to approve a pair of shoes. Dr. Curtis left the hospital, drove to Walmart, and bought the shoes. Dr. Sweet wrote, "It was a simple thing, but it never would have occurred to me to do it."

I think such a thing would have occurred to Dr. Borgquist, for he was like Dr. Curtis in that both men were motivated by pragmatic, common sense impulses. Reflecting on this incident, Dr. Sweet identified something she called time-costly caring and treating patients with the "tincture of time." Drs. Waldman and Runte chose family practice because they enjoyed the puzzles patients presented, and they knew it took time to piece together a puzzle. What Dr. Borgquist's patients witnessed was the plugger who listened and investigated, and they were willing to wait for a long time to be served by him.

"For a while we had a wonderful community," Chuck Waldman had declared. "It was very special. We had a lot of things going for us: hot, new drugs and a lot of confidence. It was the golden way. You assume it's going to last forever, but nothing lasts forever, does it? We didn't survive private practice," said Chuck, "and Warren didn't survive period." With the privilege of hindsight, Chuck's pronouncement rang with finality.

# *Chapter 26*

# HOLY SHIT

A rill in a barnyard and the Grand Canyon represent, in the main,
stages of valley erosion that began millions of years apart.

-George Gaylord Simpson, "Uniformitarianism"

"At that point, I was paying the bills," said Monique, referring to her responsibilities in Dr. Borgquist's practice in 1993. "The overhead was huge. I was keeping his private checkbook for him too. Gail used to hide money, and I tried that, but he got really mad. 'I don't want you to do that anymore,' he said. 'I need to take responsibility. I need you to tell me what's happening.' So I took everything to him and explained. 'This is what we have in the bank. These are the payroll taxes that are due tomorrow, which is payday.'

"'Pay all the employees first,' he said.

"'If I do, there will be nothing for you,' I said. I can't tell you how many months we went on like that. I kept saying, 'You can't afford to stay in practice.'

"'Why not?' he asked.

"'Because the money is not coming in.'

"The insurance companies were cutting everybody," continued Monique. "You had to join and be a provider, and that cut what you got paid. Medi-Cal was getting worse and worse. And Medicare was not too good to begin with. Crazy stuff like that. But he took everybody on his shoulders. He was that way as a boss. He worried about all of us. Did we have enough to be okay? It was very hard on him. I kept saying, 'You've got to sell your practice. You've got to do it.'"

"There was a real sense of anxiety on the part of the physicians," said Dr. Stolp. "We sensed a threat to what we believed, and for me—for many of us—our vision wasn't practical. We had an idealistic vision of what we wanted for our practice and our families and our futures. Part of the problem was that there were very few checks and balances on how you made a lot of money in medicine. That was the chorus from the system—they said we needed to put in checks and balances. When physicians tried to one-up their efforts to bill, the system would put in a balance, trying to prevent things from being overly costly. Then docs would overcome a balance with another technique.

"I remember Warren once saying, 'You know, if you remove something from the skin, if you excise it, then you can bill separately—with a different code—for the closure.' You're not supposed to do that," said Todd, shaking his head dubiously.

Nurse Patty, Dr. Stolp, and several patients had mentioned Warren's skin checks—the thoroughness with which he examined the skin and the sound of the liquid nitrogen canister all day long: ZZZHHH-ZZZHHH. The office lore regarding his obsession with careful skin checks was that he'd once missed a melanoma, which had subsequent dire consequences, and he was never going to let that happen again. But Eric Runte had expanded this view by adding a financial slant. "The thing about using liquid nitrogen to treat a lesion on the skin is that it might take thirty seconds, and you can charge thirty-five bucks. Warren was a bit loose, shall we say, with his billing on that. People would walk out of his office with their whole body treated."

"Treating skin lesions could spill in the cash," said Dr. Stolp.

"On the other hand, there were certain things you couldn't bill for," said Dr. Runte, who was probably thinking of the time spent to sort through the puzzle of a particular ailment—the psycho-social elements of illness that a doctor can only discern thorough conversation and the effort invested in putting together a viable treatment plan.

"For family practice doctors" said Dr. Stolp, "the financial incentives were not properly aligned with quality health care preventive practices, knowledge about dietary habits, family planning, sticking to screening procedures, that sort of thing. If good practices were what a doctor was getting paid for, rather than something like freezing a skin lesion, then there could be an excellent outcome in the health care system. But that's not what was happening."

"As we saw it," continued Dr. Stolp, "we were spinning our wheels with all the insurance requirements and spending more and more time trying to juggle the business end. Medicine was changing. The managed-care renaissance had arrived and the initial model was one in which the primary care givers were gatekeepers. So with family practice as the most solid primary care specialty, it suddenly became a desired entity. If you were a primary care person, you became the gatekeeper, and you had value with the insurance companies. That was the initial model, and so we were getting busier and busier, managing both outpatients and inpatients in the hospital, rarely seeing our families. At that point, I had kids in soccer and other activities, and I never got to any of their events. At the same time, we were getting calls from large corporations and insurance companies wanting to buy our practices.

"We used to have meetings on Fridays. You've probably heard about how Warren got those started. We ate greasy omelets, first at the Country Kitchen and then Woods Creek Café. They always knew when we were coming, and they knew our orders. We discussed the changes in the health care system. Those discussions revolved around the fact that we were spending too much time on business decisions, and the insurance companies were putting out more and more requirements, more forms, more updates. There wasn't time to do everything we envisioned. The rest of the world, or the country anyway, was building a structure to deal with the insurance demands—things that would improve our efficiency and allow us to focus on the things we cared about, which was our patients. So we started asking: Are we interested in selling? Who would we be interested in selling to? Both Sonora Community and Tuolumne General were interested in buying our practices. And so was Gould Medical Clinic down in Modesto."

"What happened," said Jim Wilson, "was back in the '80s there was a push to turn hospitals and physicians into insurers. I remember when they came out of the valley to get the physicians together to talk about this idea. Some of the private physicians, and especially some of the hospitals, moved that way, and when the hospitals did, they decided it would be to their advantage to make physicians their employees. So they bought their practices. They gave them X amount of money for their practice and brought them in to the hospital situation even if they stayed in their former offices. They basically hired them and in return paid them a salary and did their billing. They might have paid their malpractice insurance too, but since the radiologists didn't go that way, I can't remember for sure. This sounded pretty good to a lot of local clinicians, so they went ahead and did it. It took the headache out of their practices, but from my way of thinking," added Dr. Wilson, "they made a pact with the devil."

"We each had different economic interests," said Dr. Stolp. "For instance, Warren owned a portion of his building. The hospitals were exerting leverage on him. He said they wouldn't buy his building unless he went with them, so he had that economic concern. Chuck and I didn't want to pick sides in the local war between the hospitals. We didn't want to be sandwiched in that battle, so we were leaning towards Gould. They had the most money at the time and were a large system. There was an offer from them, and they said, 'Not only would we like to buy your practice, but we will build you a brand new clinic to your liking in Tuolumne County, and we have other local doctors interested in being in that clinic, like Dr. Hongola. We'll send up oncologists because we think there's a need for oncology up there.' This was managed care, and they envisioned that these satellite clinics would be feeding sources for their facilities. Gould was owned and operated by physicians, not by administrators or other non-physician entities. All of these things were pluses," said Dr. Stolp. "We needed help with our billing. A brand new clinic run by a reputable, physician-managed group was attractive. They really wanted us, so Chuck and I said, 'We can't turn it down.' We officially sold in 1995. Warren couldn't afford to go with us because he needed that investment in the building to work out, so he sold to the hospital."

"Warren got two offers," said Monique Tomasovich, who had worked with Warren since 1972. "The first one was from Community

Hospital, and it was the better one. 'I can't do it,' he said. 'I can't sleep with the enemy.' He'd always been the spokesman for Tuolumne General, so he was reluctant to go with Community. 'You can't think that way,' I said. 'You have to do what's going to work for you.' So he thought and thought and finally, almost in tears, he said 'I'm signing.' So Community took over everything in '94, and things changed. We became hospital employees."

On Jan 6, 1994, the *Sonora Union Democrat* published an article announcing the purchase of Dr. Borgquist's practice by Sonora Community Hospital. Borgquist is quoted as saying, "After 23 years in private practice I'm ready to do something else . . . I am a horrible business person. I have no ability or interest in it. The move won't change anything for patients except the name on the bill."

According to Paul Tharp, the hospital spokesman, "Health networks such as the one Sonora Community is building are the trend in health care today. . . Such networks allow doctors, clinics, hospitals and home health care providers to team up and negotiate more effectively with insurance companies. . . By taking the business aspects away from the physician, it will give him or her more time to spend with patients and focus on health care," concluded Tharp.

"One night, after Warren sold the practice," said Charlene Ingalls, "he was walking out to the parking lot with my husband Guy after his appointment. Warren told Guy that things weren't like they used to be. 'I just couldn't do it by myself anymore,' he said. 'I had to join because of the insurance.' He was bummed. Where before he was his own man who'd see how ever many patients he could, now he was under somebody who was telling him what he had to do. And that was hard for him. 'I'm not good at being told what to do,' he said, 'but the insurance was killing me.'"

"When Warren went with Sonora Regional, I didn't stay much longer," said Patty Patton, using the new name for Sonora Community Hospital, which since 2004 has been Sonora Regional Medical Center, part of the Adventist Health System—a faith-based, not-for profit health care delivery system in California, Hawaii, Oregon, and Washington. The hospital built a beautiful new 152-bed facility and changed its name. It took a while for locals to use the new name automatically, but by the time I interviewed Patty in 2013, she had internalized the change. "Warren had six weeks of vacation coming," said Patty, "but I only had two. They said they'd move me to another spot, so I could work while he was off, but that did not happen. I had a family and had to work. I ended up getting a full-time job at Tuolumne General Hospital, so I gave my notice.'

"In August of that year," said Monique, "they sent me to Lolly Lane to do billing. I'll never forget the lady telling me they were moving me up there. I was devastated and started crying. She let me go home. After work, Warren drove out to my place, and we cried together. He was so sad. 'It's not your fault,' I said. 'You had to do this or you wouldn't have been able to stay in business.' He knew I was right."

Warren sold the business and took a vacation. He knew how to take vacations, a practice that started when he was a child and his family drove to Nebraska each summer. He and Judy had established a tradition of long summer vacations at the start of their marriage. They'd also created three family customs: taking a big trip with each of their children at the conclusion of high school, Cousins Week each summer, and the practice of a 50th birthday cruise, which started with Warren—actually the same year he sold the business. In another example, Dr. Renwick described a river trip with Warren and a cadre of other medical professionals through the Grand Canyon.

"Steve Hall and Jim Wilson were the two who coordinated the Grand Canyon trip," explained Ken Renwick. "They were the main organizers, and Warren was the doctor for the expedition. He gathered all the meds, suture kits, and other stuff. At the beginning of the video footage of the trip, there's a scene with him organizing it all. Because he was a family practice doctor, he got stuff for free. Wilson and Hall, because they were radiologists, didn't get anything. Besides they aren't real doctors," added Renwick with a chuckle that suggested this was an inside joke among the doctors. "Warren was definitely a real doctor."

"How many people were on the trip?" I asked.

"Somewhere in the high teens. Most of the people who went were from the hospital. And there was a friend of Warren's—a guy named Bill Boyd—who did all the videography. There were people from radiology, nurses, PAs, and some respiratory therapists. More people from TGH than Sonora Regional, but there were people from both."

"Warren and I were working in his garage one day," said Bill Boyd.

"when he asked me, 'You ever been down the Grand Canyon?' When I said, 'No' he said 'How'd you like to go?' They had fifteen people, and the permit required exactly sixteen—four in each boat with four boats. At the beginning of the trip, a Ranger gave us a forty-minute talk, so we wouldn't kill ourselves in the canyon. He said there are very few drownings. Most people get hurt because they get bit by rattlesnakes or fall off rocks. Then he added that a helicopter costs $1000 an hour to pull you out if you get hurt. After that, he gave us this thing like a Triple-A Triptik that noted where every rapid was. I brought my video camera and an extra battery, totally sure everyone else would also bring video cameras, but not one person did. Everyone had a chore on the trip. Warren was the garbage man, and I got the chore of being the videographer."

The first frame on the video lists the people on the trip: Steve Hall as the Leader; followed by the Boat Captains, Ryan and Sacha Hall, Ken Renwick and Jim Wilson, and then eleven rafters. The second frame reads: "Rafting the Colorado River in the Grand Canyon - August 1-16, 1999. In the opening scene, Warren stands talking with Jim Wilson and another rafter. Four deflated yellow rafts lie on the beach as they walk among them making preparations. Soon the camera pans in on Warren holding a hand-held generator. As he begins to blow up one of the rafts, Ken Renwick steps over to offer guidance. After the rafts are inflated, there are several scenes of packing, including the one Ken mentioned in which Warren has all his gear, including the medical supplies, spread out on a blue tarp. He gives a thumbs up as Bill says, "Talk about organization!"

Much of the footage was taken on beaches when the party pulled out for lunch or to camp for the night, though there are some shots from inside the rafts traveling the spectacular corridor of the river on calm, tea-colored water. There are plenty of shots of scrumptious spreads of food. They ate well: wildly varied sandwich options, huge fruit salads, smoked oysters and crackers for appetizers, curried rice or spinach lasagna for dinner. The rafters—dressed in shorts, T-shirts, and floppy sun hats—range from rail thin Ken Renwick to rotund Warren to the athletically muscled likes of Jim and Judy Wilson. The campsites are beautiful, with splashes of sun bouncing off red canyon walls and patches of blue sky with fluffy white clouds appearing in clefts between cliffs.

"Warren rigged it so that he and I shared a tent," said Bill. "Every

night, we would solve the world's problems. Night came early because we were so tired, and by 4:00 p.m., one side of the canyon was in the dark."

Occasionally, Bill filmed from the bank. "They dropped me off ahead of the rapid," said Bill, "and I'd make my way down, so I could video as they went through." At the Mile 24-1/2 Rapid, Bill filmed three raucous rafters hooting and hollering, one of whom stands at the front of the raft, a single hand raised while his other hand holds the ropes like the reins of bucking bronco.

"That worked really great until we got to Lava Rapid," said Bill, "where it appeared I could get on the bank and, with no difficulty, make my way down. Wrong! I could not get through because the razor grass was ten feet high. So I decided to get up above it. I climbed up the cliff on an old animal trail and made my way to this gorgeous, pristine cactus desert with rattlesnake trails all through the white sand, At this point, I was about one hundred feet above the river, and I could actually see them below. We had whistles, but they couldn't hear mine because of the rushing water. I kept going until I came around a corner in the trail, and there were Ralph Retherford and Warren, who'd come in search of me. Warren's first words were, 'I didn't really give a shit about you, but what was I going to tell Celeste?' That little side trip took about an hour and twenty minutes."

"We had a system," sad Ken Renwick, "or at least I did. I rowed all the big rapids, but then I had other people row the others, and I helped them learn how to do it because quite a few had never rowed before. It was good practice for them to do small rapids, and some of the smaller rapids were pretty big. One time when Warren was in my boat rowing, he got off the main channel and into what could be called a whirlpool, which was potentially dangerous. It wasn't a spill-over but a recirculating area below a rock, and the boat started to get pulled into an area where it might have flipped backwards. So Warren and I switched off. I took over and got us out of that bind. Jim's Judy was in the boat with us, so he was on the sidelines, a little worried. It's tricky, especially with a big raft, to get it out of an area like that.

"But the whole trip went fine," continued Ken. "We didn't have any catastrophes. The closest was one instance with Christine Elder, who's the PA for Dr. Cooper now. She was on the US Olympic rowing team. A very powerful rower. The boat she was in flipped, and she disappeared. When the boat came down, we thought she was trapped underneath. We were looking for her, but she wasn't there. As it turned out, she was such a good swimmer that she was on shore way up ahead. She handled herself quite well."

There is a ceremonial scene in the video, during which Warren offers a tribute to Christine Elder as she prepares to leave the trip at Mile 72. She and Warren stand at the entrance to an arc created by the party holding their oars aloft. Warren puts one arm around her, and the other rests on his hip as he recites a corny poem he obviously wrote for the occasion: "Chris got thrown out with us/ The rapid sort of got her/ But we all know//That when she swam out,/ She still had both her oars/ in the water." With that, he hugs Christine and whipping off his hat and placing it on his heart, he gestures for her to walk through the arc to initiate her departure.

"Warren had a ball," said Jim Wilson. "I remember coming to Granite Rapid, and it was pretty horrendous. The rapids change with different water levels, and on the day we did Granite, it was pretty high. You scout rapids from above before you do them, and I didn't see a great way through. I can read rapids pretty well from my kayak, but with a raft, it's different. You can't really slow it down, so you have to choose your entry point and make sure that you hit the point right-on. I told Warren and Judy, 'I'd run this alone, but I need weight in the boat, so I need you two with me.' And they said, 'OK.' We made it through without flipping, but the raft completely filled with water, and I was glad it did because that water and their weight got us through some pretty big holes."

"Once," said Bill Boyd, "we stopped at this place with a narrow canyon and a waterfall. Supposedly there was an oasis at the top of the falls. Warren said, 'We're going up there,' and I was thinking, 'Go ahead. Enjoy!' because I'm not big on heights. But he and Jim Wilson conned me into stove-piping up the sixty-foot climb, and sure enough there was paradise up there."

One of the most joyous scenes in the video is the entire group standing beneath a giant rock overhang, singing "Amen" in harmony. The acoustics in the natural chamber are incredible. Warren grins with delight. After the "Amen" chorus, Judy Wilson and Ken Renwick perform a yodeling duo. On one sandy beach, Ralph Retherford leads the group in Tai Chi beneath a pink cloud floating on high. At another point, Bill captures Warren, Judy, and Jim swimming among tadpoles in a narrow canyon where the water is rusty red. In still another scene, the group relaxes in a natural sulfur spring. Warren floats on his belly, his bald head glistening. Time spent floating, rowing, laughing, eating, and relaxing on the Colorado River—the life blood of the arid southwest—sure seemed to suit these medicine men and women.

"I worked at Lolly Lane for about two years," said Monique. "Working at that business office was unbearable. It wasn't like working with Warren who gave and gave and gave. They gave nothing. They were so stringent. I hated telling patients 'You have 90 days to pay this bill.' I knew they couldn't do it. I knew they worked seasonal jobs and paid their bill when their taxes came. But for the hospital, that was a no-no. I'd say, 'They've been patients for twenty years; you can't send them to collections.' There was no kindness, no consideration. Warren knew I was miserable.

"When he signed the contract with the hospital, they agreed to keep his employees at the same rate of pay and benefits. I can't remember the term, but it was something like we were vested for that. Everything rolled over fine and worked great for a while. Then all of a sudden, they told him that wasn't the contract anymore. He blew a gasket. He came up to the business office and hauled me out the door, saying 'Those dirty sons-of-a-bitches.' He just went nuts.

"'Warren, you can't worry about this,' I said. 'You have to know you've done the right thing for you, your life, and your family.'

"After two years, a friend of mine opened a home health agency. She called saying she needed an office manager. Would I be interested? I was glad to leave that situation. I was as happy working for Warren on the last day as I'd been on the first, but it all changed when I went to Lolly Lane."

The changes implemented in the interest of efficiency were Monique's un-doing, but there were other changes implemented to improve the business of medicine that forced difficult adjustments and resulted in significant career changes for some of the family-practice doctors. Chuck Waldman left the profession and devoted his time to art. Todd Stolp got excited about making a difference in the world through public health rather than individual health. He wasn't sure how or if these changes affected Warren Borgquist, but he told an interesting side story that seemed to speak to how these physicians handled the stress of professional life.

In 1992, Todd Stolp met Neil Shulman, who wrote the novel on which the movie Doc Hollywood is based. "He's a real crazy guy," said Todd, "and he wanted to work with me on some children's books, which we did with the CDC. The first one was *What's in a Doctor's Bag?* Then we did *Germ Patrol,* followed by *How to Have a Habit.* They did quite well in the east coast," said Todd. "Sold a couple hundred thousand copies."

"So Warren did the theater thing as Tevye," I interjected, "and Chuck painted, and you're talking about illustrating and consulting on children's books. I see a spark of creative energy that you all shared. Is that accurate?"

"I think there is a commonality among individuals who were inter-ested in living in a rural setting and providing prenatal to death-bed care. We shared that vision, and that was what drove us together and kept us as friends, so I don't think the creative thing is surprising. I've known a lot of physicians who have a creative outlet. I think we have a certain ob-sessive-compulsive focusing. You want your health care provider to have that, so they are attentive to detail, but that also drives us to funny little habits and pastimes."

"We bought Holy Shit during Cousins Week," said Judy Borgquist, launching into the story behind one of their favorite pastimes, vacationing in their RV. "We were headed for Lake Oroville, and whoever made the reservation screwed it up. We got there and didn't have the reservation until the next day. They said we could pitch a tent in a grassy area and then move later. It was a nightmare. Warren and I decided to go into Marysville or Yuba City and get a hotel. We couldn't find a vacant room, so we ended up in Sacramento, right beside an RV sales lot. We were always going to buy an RV, and since we couldn't get into the camp site until noon the next day, we decided to go look at RVs."

"I opened the door of one, and it was decorated in a giraffe motif—the valances around the windows were covered in giraffes. There were giraffe pillows. I didn't even go in, I just said, 'Warren, this is it. We have to buy it.' It turned out it had everything he wanted—Cummings engine, diesel, blah-blah-blah. So we bought it on the spot. He had the pickup truck, so he put me in the RV all by myself to drive to Cousins Week in a 40-foot motor home. I'd never driven anything like it before. When you're first driving a big RV, you should never make a right turn. You should do all lefts. I was trying to turn right, and there was this lady who was all bug-eyed. I waited until she got out of the way, so I could make the turn. When I drove into the campground, every single person said, 'Holy shit.' So that's what we called our motor home, Holy Shit. And Holy served us well."

Neighbor Karen Sinclair recalled the arrival of the RV on Calaveras Way. "We went out one day, and the god-damned thing had cut off half the street. They had to park it a certain way, so traffic could get by, but nobody cared. It was just so funny."

While Judy and Warren purchased the motor home initially during Cousins Week, they found many opportunities to enjoy traveling with friends. "I went to Las Vegas with Warren and Judy in their motorhome after Jon passed away," said Ruth Hagstrom. "What a kick. Riding in that motor home, you were up high. It was huge—like a house—and Warren loved it."

"We have a motor home," said Ann Leonard. "And they had Holy Shit. We went quite a few places with them, for instance up to Bend Oregon near the Rogue River. We camped up near the Sonora Pass at a place called Mill Creek, where we took a day trip to see these rock formations. It's off the beaten path and not easy to find, so we took several different roads before finding the right way. Warren was always so relaxed. My husband gets uptight, but I remember Warren saying, 'It's a great day. We're having fun. We'll get there when we get there.' When we camped with them in Palm Springs, Warren backed his car into a tree and wrecked it. That didn't even bother him."

Friends Jim and Gill McKee also traveled with the Borgquists in their respective motor homes. On one trip Warren said to Jim, 'Come here, I want to show you what I bought. I got tired of going out in the dark and holding the flashlight in my mouth, so I bought this.' It was headlamp." Among the many pictures of Warren, there are several in which he is wearing this headlamp. He looks like a doctor wearing a head mirror in an old-time kid's picture book, back when such devices were as emblematic of physicians as stethoscopes.

"We used to joke," said Eric Runte, "that Warren paid for his RV with his liquid nitrogen gun."

# Chapter 27

# HOSPICE

*When we finally know we are dying,*
*and all other sentient beings are dying with us,*
*we can start to have a burning, almost heartbreaking sense of the fragility*
*and preciousness of each being, and from this can grow a deep, clear,*
*limitless compassion for all beings.*

-Sogyal Rinpoche, *The Tibetan Book of Living and Dying*

"It was clear that Warren was particularly good at end-of-life care," said Eric Runte. Many people told stories about Warren's care of the terminally ill. Most were poignant and some included elements of humor, like one told by Billie Hammer, his nurse at the Mono Way office. "There was this guy who was terminal," said Billie. "He had some neural muscular thing. He was married, but he and his wife broke up—probably over his ailment. He kept conning Warren. He just wanted to go to the Mustang Ranch. So finally, Warren said, 'Let's go.' When they came home, they had T-shirts. 'Did he get some?' I asked. 'Yeah,' Warren said. It was pretty funny that he helped this guy get laid before he died. That's the kind of doc he was."

"Initially, Warren worked hospice in its capacity as a satellite of Stockton VNA," said Gail Bonavia. "He used to say our VNA was the bastard child of Stockton. He thought VNA and hospice were necessary services in this county. Because he could see we were the bottom of the totem pole for Stockton, he decided to take over VNA, which included hospice. That meant that he had to borrow $50,000 to support the services until they were able to get some billing going. He sent me to the VNA office, and I set up the billing, so we could get his money back. The interest rate was almost 25 percent, which is pretty hefty. There was a story that he and Judy needed a new roof on their house at one point, and he couldn't afford it because he was paying for VNA."

Susan Schlindwein, a hospice nurse, wrote one of the memory cards collected at Warren's memorial, which prompted me to call her to learn more about Hospice of the Sierra. Susan lives in Twain Harte in a quaint cabin with cedar siding. When I arrived on a chilly, November morning, the wood stove was stoked and generating warmth. Susan had piled a number of reference books on the coffee table, probably because I'd mention that I not only wanted to hear about Warren and hospice, I also wanted to know about hospice in general and the Tuolumne County incarnation of this service.

By way of introduction, I asked Susan how she came to be a hospice nurse. "We always say you don't wake up one day and think: I'll be a hospice nurse," she answered. "It's more of a calling." She went on to explain that she had worked several jobs before landing with VNA. "I was a home health nurse first, but after a few years, one of the hospice nurses left, so I took that job. It was scary, but I took to it like a fish to water. And I never wanted to do anything else after that.

"Warren was the hospice medical director. I knew him from around the community, pictures in the paper, stories about the birth chair. His reputation kind of preceded him. We formally met when I was introduced as the new hospice nurse at a meeting.

"I remember telling one of my daughters he was really amazing. I thought I was a pretty good nurse, and I think I was a darned good hospice nurse because of the all the things he taught me. Early on, I called him about this little old lady in a nursing home. She was barely seventy-five pounds and lying in her bed moaning in despair. She wasn't dying right that moment, but she was clearly distressed, and I didn't think I could do anything to help her. I called Warren, and he said, 'Slap a patch on her.' I was new, so even putting a patch on a patient was a big deal. It's not strong medicine because it's time released in small quantities, but I said, 'Can I do that?'

"'Hell yeah,' he said.

"Yes, of course, I thought. It will be just enough medication to take the edge off, make her comfortable, and let her have some peace. I was learning how to handle such situations. Shortly after, I remember reading a newsletter from a national hospice organization that said even if giving somebody pain medicine should hasten their death, we are morally bound to treat the pain. I came in thinking the nurse and the doctor were supposed to fix what was wrong with a patient, so this was a different mindset.

"It was quite a learning curve that took probably six months. In the beginning, I was handing out sheets on nutrition, but when I got back to the office, the more experienced nurses said, 'Why are you trying to get them to eat?' It took me a while to get that what nurses usually did wasn't needed here. There was no need to take a patient's blood pressure, for instance. You come at it from a different perspective. This person is dying. What can I do to make him comfortable? Warren was so compassionate in this regard. I learned from him that if a patient said, 'I can't have any salt,' I could say, 'Yes, you can.' What difference was a little salt going to make at that point? I learned to say, 'You can have whatever you want. You can have ice cream for breakfast, lunch, and dinner.'

"You could see Dr. B's outrage when there was an injustice, but he was also extremely calm when things weren't going well. I remember one time this gal called. I knew her from church, and she lived near me here in Twain Harte. Her husband was on hospice, and she'd been cleaning the catheter to his medication port and accidentally pulled it out. She panicked. It's not like you can just put it back, especially if you're an amateur. I'd never even put one back in. It was Friday night in the middle of a snowstorm. I told her to hang on, and I called Warren. He said, 'I'll come up. Can you meet me there?'

"'I'm not sure.' I said. 'The roads aren't plowed, and it's getting dark.'

"'Where are you?' he asked. 'I'll come get you.'

"'I'll walk to the cross street to meet you and show you where they live.' As I hung up, the phone rang again. The woman had found a neighbor with a Jeep who was going to take them to the hospital, so I quickly called Warren and told him to meet them at Tuolumne General. So that all worked out, but he was willing to come do a home visit in a snow storm."

According to Dr. Chuck Waldman, Warren had a big influence on family-practice doctors regarding house calls. "He was all about taking care of people," said Dr. Waldman. "Warren set the stage for that, and it became the way we practiced. When you're in our town, this is how the tribe works—the Tribe of Turks. Not so much a mandate, but it was modeled by action, by example. We were all independent enough to not like rules. We follow them, but we admired the example Warren set. We'd go out and see people even when told not to. It was crazy and hard, but I loved making house calls. One time, my nurse and I went to see the grumpy old father of one our patients. The guy wouldn't go to the ER, and he had this horrible rotting ear that the family was trying to deal with. We went to his apartment, and his ear was a funky mess. There we were with the windows open and the flies buzzing. The old guy was demented, so he wasn't cooperative, and we had to take a big wedge out of his ear. We got in trouble for that one."

Dr. Waldman didn't explain what kind of trouble, but he'd made his point about the dedication to caregiving that he and Dr. Borgquist shared, which Susan Schlindwein witnessed on a snowy night.

"The hospital kept my neighbor overnight," Susan continued, "because of the snow. The next day, I was alone with him in the room. He said he wanted to talk to the doctor. When Warren came, the man asked, 'How will I die?' We were used to getting this question. After a brief pause, Dr. Borgquist quietly told him how it was likely to go and assured him that we would be there. He wouldn't die alone.

"Warren always made one particular point about the patient and the family," continued Susan. "The family follows you around with a bazillion questions they won't ask in front of the patient. Frequently, they ask the big questions while walking you out to the car. Warren said, 'Say what you have to say in front of the patient.' He did it all the time. I could see how this cleared the air. He'd come in, and a patient would say 'You guys were talking about me, right?' and Warren would say, 'Your wife had some questions,' and then he'd proceed to relate the conversation he'd had with the wife. The premise of hospice is to be honest. Warren was very good at that."

Susan moved on to another story about a nurse who ended up in hospice care. "She was my patient, and all the people she worked with planned a birthday party for her. 'I have to go to the party,' she said. 'We'll get you there,' I said. When you work hospice you see people set goals—things they want to do before they die—places they want to go or events they want to attend. I called Warren and told him what was going on, and he prescribed an amphetamine. He told me exactly how much to give her and how often she could take it. This gal was young and pretty. She dressed to the nines and danced and ate and socialized. The party was at the Opera Hall and much of the medical community was there to celebrate. I had the medication in my purse, and at one point she asked, 'Can I have another one?'

"'You sure can. Warren said you could have one every two hours.'

"That's how Warren did it. If grandma wanted to go to her grandson's graduation, he'd get her there, and he'd get her there feeling good because there was a medication she could take to make that happen. It wasn't just for the patient. It was good for everybody."

Patty Patton told this same story, adding, "He learned to do this because of something that happened with a patient who wanted to get to his son's graduation. They got him to the graduation, but the man slept through the whole thing. After that, Warren did what he could to help patients enjoy what might be the last big event of their lives."

Billie Hammer told a similar story about Warren understanding what a patient needed. "Leah was our insurance gal's best friend, but we were all friends with her and her husband. One day, Warren said, 'Leah's terminal. She's got astrocytoma.'

"'But she's pregnant,' I said. We'd just confirmed her pregnancy a few weeks before. I couldn't believe she had a terrible spinal tumor. I felt so sad watching her little baby bump grow when she came for appointments.

"'The main thing,' said Warren, 'is be calm and treat her like you would the rest of the pregnant moms.' It was her first baby. Leah decided on no chemo, no nothing. She didn't want to hurt the baby. Eventually things got really bad—terrible headaches and paralysis. Warren built her an apparatus, so she could talk into a recorder and make tapes for her baby. Finally, she decided to go to a lake on the East Side of the Sierra with her parents and her husband to die. Warren used to drive over the Sonora Pass every week to see her. He was her doctor until the end. I think she was there for about five or six weeks. She had a healthy baby boy, and then she died. It was heartbreaking."

A few months later, I met with Susan and three fellow hospice nurses at a local restaurant. As we ate, I asked them to tell me about their experiences in hospice with Dr. Borgquist.

"We saw him mostly at IDT," said Dawn Leibold.

"What is IDT?" I asked.

"Inner Disciplinary Team," she answered. "Weekly meetings with the medical director, nurses, social workers, and the chaplain. Warren always offered tidbits or helpful facts. We'd be working through the agenda, and an issue would come up, and his memory would be jogged because he was always reading. You could tell he paid attention to anything new. He would tell us about what he'd learned. I still use a lot of those things."

"For example?" I asked.

"Some of it is kind of mundane," said Dawn. "For instance, many terminal patients deal with constipation. We use stool softeners as the standard maintenance, but he suggested switching to milk of magnesia or mineral oil. I still use those every day, and it works much better." Though I found talk of constipation during a meal a bit unusual, to these nurses who faced it on a daily basis, it was merely another feature of their work.

"One of the things that was so great about Dr. Borgquist was you always felt like he respected you. He was so gentle, and it always felt like we were a team," said Dawn.

"You could count on him," interjected Susan.

"Yeah, because we would call him . . ."

"Out of the blue," said Janet Murphy, finishing Dawn's sentence

"He would always be there. Even when he was with a patient, he would still take our calls, which most doctors don't do," continued Dawn.

"He'd take the call because he knew we weren't calling to pass time," said Susan. "These were hard problems—people in pain—and he always had an answer."

"Things to try," said Dawn. "He wanted us to use compazine for nausea, but I almost never do that. He never made it sound like: 'This is what you have to do.' It was more of a suggestion, just an idea, something to try."

"Trish, do you want to jump in here?" I said to Trish Romero, the one nurse who had yet to speak.

"I didn't know him as well as the others, but my impression was pretty much what Dawn has said, especially the part about him never talking down to me. He'd offer a suggestion, like, 'I just read this article, and I think this might work.' He seemed willing to . . . not experiment. That's not the right word, but to try things to make it better for his patient. His last hospice patient was my patient. I was the case manager. It got to be a real struggle at the end. That's when I got to know him because he was her physician, not just the hospice medical director. He was her doctor. I relied on the fact that I could get ahold of him. That was nice because one day we hit a wall. The woman's pain was out of control. I was literally chasing her around the house to give her what she needed. I was on the phone with him constantly. 'The meds aren't working anymore. Now what do I do?'

He'd say, 'Trish, let me think about this.' The woman was taking Dilaudid, so that's what she had on hand, but all of a sudden she was in a crisis. So after Warren thought for a while, he said, 'Give them to her rectally. Start with one and then give her two or even three, and see what happens. Call me back in fifteen minutes. We were on the phone back and forth for more than an hour. I felt like I was talking to a friend, getting advice from a smart friend instead of bothering the doctor."

"And he never complained, did he?" asked Susan.

"Nope, he never even got an attitude. 'Just keep calling,' he said. 'Call me at home. If you can't get me there, call my cell phone.' He made himself completely available. Finally, she went to sleep. I had to leave, but I came back later, and she was sitting on the front porch smoking a cigarette, all better. I felt like I got to know him fairly well in that short time," said Trish. "I didn't know him for years like these two, but you kind of get to know a person's character in an intense situation like that. I felt like I had a lifeline through the telephone. He never got excited, never raised his voice, and he never sounded like he was in doubt. He just said, 'Do this and call me back. Do that and call me back.'"

"I want to emphasize that physician accessibility is big in hospice care," said Janet. "The thing is Dr. Borgquist was not of the generation who'd been trained to be accessible. The younger doctors have cell phones, so it's much easier now. Dr. Borgquist was incredibly accessible and responsive for his generation."

"We could relax and be ourselves," said Dawn. "It was nice to be able to say what we were thinking."

"We knew we wouldn't get blindsided with 'I'm the doctor and you're the nurse,'" said Susan.

"Yes," said Dawn. "It was always collaborative. I remember one time Susan and I were walking in Relay for Life, and we spotted him walking hand-in-hand with Judy."

"I can see it in my mind's eye," said Susan. "We smiled because we saw them coming. Warren said to Judy, 'I want you to meet two of my very favorite hospice nurses.' I'm sure had it had been Janet and Trish, he would have said the exact same thing."

"I remember his red shirt, his socks, and Birkenstocks," said Janet. "There was something about the red shirt. I remember him being really up on the days when he wore that red shirt."

"On those days, said Susan, "he was on top of the world."

Tammie Little spent fifteen years working intermittently in various capacities with Hospice of the Sierra. "In '95 or '96, I was a student at Columbia College," said Tammie, "and I took the VNA Hospice volunteer orientation, and that's when I first met Dr. Borgquist. I was struck by his compassion, his approachability, and his matter-of-factness. I knew this man was as genuine as they come. It was inspiring to know I was going to be on his team providing care for end-of-life patients. Of course, back then in my late 20s, I didn't have that language.

"There's a large gap between when I first met Dr. Borgquist to more than ten years later when I came back to hospice as an RN. During that time, I lost my sister. She was on hospice for less than a week. My sister died from alcoholism. There was a lot of denial, so she wouldn't allow hospice to come until she was too weak to refuse anymore. If you know Dr. Borgquist, you know he had a history with alcoholism. It's not a secret. So when I say my sister was an alcoholic, that's not who she ultimately was. Just like that's not ultimately who Dr. Borgquist was, but it made him a real human being. Anyway, a lot of people and circumstances inspired my return to hospice."

Hospice of the Sierra stayed busy doing the best job possible for those in the community who were at the end of their lives. "One time," said Susan Schlindwein, "we were doing a training— a national conference— through speaker phone. We were connected with hospices all over the country. Lloyd Schneider was our chaplain, and he was brand new. We listened to other hospice groups talk about various problems and how they solved them. When it was over, I remember Lloyd saying, 'They're doing the same thing in the big city hospices that we do here.' He couldn't believe that this tiny handful of people in Tuolumne County was doing the same caliber of work as a big city hospice. Warren looked at him and he said, 'We're small, but we're good,' and then he grinned."

I met Lloyd Schneider at the Tuolumne County Library. We sat in comfortable easy chairs in a corner of the library under big windows that showered us with light as he talked about his time with hospice, beginning with meeting Kathy Beck, a hospice nurse. "For years, Kathy pestered me: 'We need a chaplain,' she'd say, and I'd say, 'I'm doing other things.' Then she got promoted to supervisor, and said, 'We're required to have a chaplain, and we can't get anybody to take this on.' To make a long story short, I finally agreed in part because I'd been running into Warren for years. After I had prostate cancer, a bunch of us started a prostate-cancer support group. Warren was one of our monthly guest speakers. Someone asked him, 'What if all this medical stuff doesn't work?'

"'We have hospice,' he said, 'and in truth, more people die *with* prostate cancer than *from* prostate cancer. We're going to keep working with you for as long as it takes.' Those words told me about his heart. He was looking at quality of life and going on. That excited me, so when Kathy bent my arm again, I jumped on board."

"How and when does the chaplain fit in to the hospice team work?"

"The basic four members of the team are the social worker, nurse, medical director, and chaplain. The team gets embellished with others too—specialists, home health aides, volunteers. At our weekly meetings, everyone was free to talk. Our parameters were to discuss every patient who had changes during the previous week. The chaplain basically listened to everybody."

"Is there anything specific you learned from Warren?"

"The big one has to do with the fear family members have about the use of narcotics. Warren repeatedly said, 'When a patient is in pain, the medicine works on the pain. The person is not having a fun trip.' I learned how silly it was to worry about a person becoming an addict when he only has a few months to live. It was Warren's on-going insistence to teach people that opiate drugs allow a person to maintain some kind of normal function without pain, which I see as the most humane and godly thing we can do. Of course, there were times when someone in the house couldn't or shouldn't have been around those kinds of meds, so we had to intervene because meds were disappearing at too rapid a rate. Warren was the one who usually had to work that out. Sometimes it was the social worker. The thing is, for seven years, we assembled as a team to work out stuff like that, and I was part of it. It was about all of us looking at each situation—daily, weekly, and monthly— making our best decisions to care for the patients. Another thing I appreciated about Warren was how he brought his personal life to the meetings. It was cool that he talked about his kids, his grandkids, soap box derby constructions. These were things he wove into a meeting."

"What did that do for the team?"

"I think when you share something of yourself, it's much easier to have an honest connection. It helped us see him as another human at the table. While a lot of weight fell on him as the medical director, the rest of us had to do our part with integrity. The whole hospice team worked hard to make honest connections and really listen. We had cases where a person declared, 'I'm a life-long atheist,' but I saw some of these people come to a place where they were now rethinking that life-long belief. So, if the team wanted to know if I'd go see a person who claimed to be an atheist, I said, 'Absolutely.'"

"My uncle was raised Catholic," I told Lloyd, "but he hadn't practiced for years. All of a sudden when he was in hospice he wanted to see a priest. When the priest came, he didn't ask if my uncle wanted to confess or receive Communion, which is what I thought he would do. No, he just came to chat with an elderly man who decided he ought to talk to a priest before he died."

"That reminds me of something I noticed," said Lloyd, "from being with different families and their faith practices. Roman Catholic families seemed more comfortable with the dying process. So I asked Father John, up in Twain Harte, what was up with that. He said, 'Every week we celebrate the cycle of life.'"

Sitting there in the sunlit library with this former hospice chaplain, I felt Father John's explanation shone a beam of understanding on Dr. Borgquist. Every week, he spent time witnessing the cycle of life, and though I wasn't sure if the word "celebrate" described how he came to the birth-to-death experience of a family physician, he appeared much more comfortable with the process than many of us.

"Warren brought modern, new ways of looking at and dealing with death and dying to the mountains," said Shelley Andrews, who was an early hospice volunteer. "With my current perspective of many years and three different hospices in three different places and two different states, I understand it was his compassion that was particularly unique. He played a major role in starting Hospice of the Sierra. Sonora would have been the last place you'd expect something like this to happen. It took vision to create. And it was amazing the way the community took to it.

"I was what's called a lay volunteer," continued Shelley. "Warren was the first person I heard talk about death and dying and about pain control. It was so new to allow people to continue to take morphine to control pain so that their quality of life was such that they didn't die suffering. It was radical. Back then people might have thought we had a Kevorkian on the loose, so it was a public-relations issue as well as a health and quality of life issue. It took a very powerful, compassionate person like Warren to make people feel okay about new ways."

Hospice Nurse Dawn Leibold had said Warren let nurses "shoot from the hip." From the stories several people told, it was apparent that he too shot from the hip when the situation demanded. "This is a story I love about Dr. Borgquist," said my sister Anne. "He went to Steve and Debbie Peters' house as Steve was coming to the end of his life with a brain tumor. They told Warren about their wish for Steve's heart to go to a mutual friend, who happened to be another of Dr. Borgquist's patients—a child, a pretty grown up child with leukemia who needed a heart. Now whether Dr. Borgquist could make something like that happen or not, he nevertheless provided a grieving family the joy and satisfaction of expressing their last desire without negating the possibility. Steve and Debbie talked about that visit because it gave them a purpose—a way to give when facing Steve's death. In the end, there was no heart transplant, but they were able to speak to Dr. Borgquist and feel like he would do it if he could."

"When Rick had his stroke," said BZ Smith, "Warren was away, and Todd Stolp was on call. Todd knew he was stepping into big shoes to be there for us, and he was wonderful. Of course, as soon as Warren got back, he was right there for us in every conceivable way. Eventually, Warren felt that Rick needed to see a specialist, so he sent us to Dr. Austin, but he stayed on top of all that was happening. I remember the day he talked to me about putting Rick in a nursing facility because he was worried about how I was doing. Right after that talk, Dr. Austin had the same conversation with me. By then, we knew that Rick was on his way, so that was a tough decision. I made it with Warren's very keen support.

"Near the end, we brought Rick home, and Warren helped me set up hospice care and guided me in getting everything ready. Rick was home for about a week before he died. On the day that he died, the first person I called was Warren. He and Judy were leaving on a trip to Europe. They were actually getting in the car to go to the airport, and he told Judy, 'I have to go over there first.' So he came over and sat with our family. Rick's body was there, and he talked to Wren, and to Rick's brother, and to me. He sat with us until the mortuary came to take Rick. He never left our side. When the body was gone, Warren said his goodbyes and left. He stopped his world to be in our world."

That was the effect Warren had on his patients—that he had stopped his world to be in theirs. His calm, unhurried presence created that effect. He leaned back with calm composure as my youngest child was born and then shortly after the birth, he left to climb Half Dome in Yosemite with friends. He sat attentively with BZ and her family in the wake of Rick Thorpe's death when scheduled to leave on a trip with Judy. But he didn't miss his plane because somehow he had the capacity to move to the next moment with unhurried aplomb—a trait that was called all kinds of things depending on who was looking.

Warren was away on a trip when his friend Jon Hagstrom died, but to hear Ruth Hagstrom tell the story, Warren was there when she needed him. "Jon's cancer diagnosis came after he went in the hospital because he thought he was having a heart attack," said Ruth. "They did all these tests, including a biopsy, but we didn't know what was going on. Warren called and said, 'We're going to have a meeting at your house.' The kids were there, and Warren explained that Jon had lung cancer.

"'How much time do I have?' asked Jon.

"'Six months to a year,' said Warren.

"He was so honest, and his demeanor made it easier. But Jon was only 67, and the kids were devastated. He went to one chemo appointment. He didn't want to do it, but he went to placate the family. When the next appointment was scheduled, I remember getting up that morning and saying, 'You don't have to do this,' and he said 'Thank you.' He was pretty sick for about six months. One time, he decided he was going to have an omelet, and he went out to clip some chives and fell off the deck. He knocked his head and started talking weird. Who did I call? Warren! He came over to the house during his lunch hour to check on Jon."

Karen Sinclair, who lives across the street from the Borgquists, tells a story that surpasses all expectations for a good neighbor let alone doctor. "Dad never went to the doctor," Karen explained, "but Mom started seeing Borgquist because she had bronchial asthma. When things started happening with Dad, Mom got him to see Borgquist. He sent him to the hospital for tests, and before we even left the hospital, Mom and I knew it was bad. We just didn't know how bad. We were waiting for the follow-up appointment with Borgquist, when he called and said, 'Get everybody over to the house.' Warren told us Dad had esophageal cancer. Dad looked at Warren and said, 'But Doc, I quit smoking.' Sadly, he'd only quit a few months before when he had pneumonia. 'How long does he have?' I asked.

"'You've got two months, maybe three,' Warren said directly to Dad. Every single person in the room heard a different amount of time. We were in shock. After Warren left, we had to go ask him again."

"It was two months to the day," said Betty Lou, Karen's mom.

"Dad started doing the treatments," said Karen. "And Warren saw him every single week. At one point, we talked about an operation to put a shunt in, but Dad said, 'I am not doing it.' And Warren said, 'I don't blame you. It might not do a damn thing to help.' After Dad made that decision, Warren said, 'You have to get hospice in.' So Mom, Dad, and I met with hospice. I'd never seen my dad have a meltdown, but when we went to that meeting, he fell apart. 'I'm not ready for this,' he said. We had to explain how this was going to allow us do the things we needed to do for him. Warren picked our hospice nurse, and she came twice a week. Dad said, 'I don't feel sick. And she said, 'Good! You don't look sick.' She was great. They'd just sit and talk because there was nothing happening except she had gotten us some morphine. And then one night, he had this severe attack. After that, Mom and I started front loading—giving him his medication before he ate, and after that there were no attacks. We told Warren what we were doing. 'Oh my god,' he said. 'I'm taking that back to the hospice team. Just keep doing whatever works.'

"Dad was still doing everything. He would go gamble. He was driving and golfing. Then one day, he quit on the course. I said, 'Dad, do you want to go home? And he said, 'No, I want to watch you.' But that was his last time out. On Thanksgiving, we thought things were going real well. He asked me, 'Do you think I'll make it till Christmas?' The other kids said he was really getting pale, but apparently Mom and I couldn't see it. The day after Thanksgiving, Mom and I had to go out. We were at my sister's when he called. 'Where are you guys?' I could tell something was wrong, so I drove like a bat out of hell to get home."

"We started him on the morphine, and I called hospice. They were telling me what to do, but Mom said, 'I'm going to call Warren.' His house was full of family, but he came over and looked at Dad and said, 'Jesus, you haven't given him enough to do anything.' And then he told me how to mix the meds to get him out of pain. After Warren left, I had to go out for awhile, and Dad called me while I was gone and said he wanted a chocolate pie, which he never got to eat."

"That night, he suddenly looked at us and said, 'I think it's time for meds. I mixed the dose and, and he said, 'You're a shitty bartender.' He put some chocolate in the mix, and then he and Mom went to bed."

"We all fell asleep," said Betty Lou picking up the story line. "Well, I don't know if he fell asleep. I didn't hear a thing, but something woke me up. I was afraid, but I knew I had to get up and see what was going on. I turned on the light, and he was so cold. I got Karen. 'Something's wrong . . . I think Daddy's . . .' Karen went to check, and she could see the blood, so she called Warren, and he came over at three in the morning."

Karen resumed telling the story. "Warren walked in. He looked at Dad and then at Mom and said, "Isn't this absolutely beautiful. Denny went in Betty Lou's arms.' Then he said, 'Don't let them take him out of the house. Wait till everybody gets here to see him and say good-bye.' And then he just sat there and talked with us. He stayed for a long time. He kept saying, 'Oh my god wasn't that great. How peaceful. In Betty Lou's arms. Because they were in love. They had a hell of a love affair.'"

Warren, who had seen more passings than most of us witness in a life time, could see the wonder in a man leaving life from the security of his own bed with his wife near at hand.

# PART V

# BALD GUY FOR PEACE

# Chapter 28

# CIRCLE OF LIFE

Will the circle be unbroken
By and by, lord, by and by
There's a better home a-waiting
In the sky, lord, in the sky

-Ada R. Habershon, Christian Hymn

When I met Cliff Borgquist, Warren's father, he was a custodian/ bus driver at Twain Harte Elementary where my children went to school. His wife, Ruth Borgquist, ran a child-care business from their home in Ranchos Poquitos, a subdivision east of Sonora. I asked Karma how her parents got to East Sonora from the Upper Dime downtown.

"After they sold the dime store," said Karma, "they raised turkeys for a while on Chicken Ranch Road, and Dad drove truck for a food distribution place. Mom made drapes for people. She had great number sense and could figure things out in her head so she was right on the money. Then they bought the house on Ranchos Poquitos in 1971. Or rather Warren bought it for them. Shortly after they moved in, Louise Garrison, who used to work for them at the dime store, needed a baby sitter for her granddaughter. And then there was a baby brother, and Mom took care of him too, and it kind of snowballed from there into a thriving child-care service. I'm not sure when Dad started working at Twain Harte School."

My children thought Cliff was cool mostly because he was funny, a characteristic atypical in bus drivers. He was also kind. One time, when my 5-year-old son, Culley, was riding his bike after school on the playground with some older neighbor kids, he hit a curb and flipped over the handlebars. Cliff, who witnessed the accident, put Culley in the cab of his truck, threw his bike in the bed, and drove him home. I looked up from cooking dinner to see Cliff and my bloody son standing at the sliding-glass door. Culley had a broken arm and had knocked loose two front teeth, which were hanging from his mouth. I hardly remember thanking Cliff, but I do remember the bald man with a kindly smile who stood at my door. Not until I saw pictures of Warren with his father many years later would I note the resemblance between the two men.

Ruth Borgquist also figured into my life when I went back to college after having three children. One summer, I needed someone to watch my 3-year-old while I continued to take classes. Dr. Borgquist suggested his mom—or Grandma B as everyone called her. My son, Raleigh, went to Grandma B's that summer. I remember Ruth as a very large woman who sat in the middle of a room full of children, radiating warmth with laughing brown eyes. Again and again while talking to people about Dr. Borgquist, they mentioned that Grandma B had cared for them or their children.

In one picture of Ruth and Warren, she sits before a birthday cake, smiling into the camera with her beloved son behind her, his hands resting on her shoulders. They both wear large, round spectacles, and while Warren is fully bald, Ruth wears a wig styled in a curly do. "We have female pattern baldness, so Mom wore a wig the last fifteen years of her life," Karma once told me.

Around the time Dr. Borgquist moved his practice to a spacious office on Covey Circle, he and his sisters also began the process of caring for their aging and declining parents. "I think we were in denial about Dad," said Marjorie Borgquist. "He changed, in that he would ask for explanations about things he should have understood, and then when we explained, you could see he didn't get it. He'd say, 'Oh yeah. OK. Now I get it.' But he didn't. At first it was intermittent, and then it happened more and more. Then we had to take the car away from him because he started getting lost. He did the shopping at John's Sierra Market or Safeway—a few miles from home—but he wouldn't come back for hours, and Mom worried. He wouldn't admit that he'd been lost. Mom told me about these lapses when he'd be gone. She wasn't quite sure what he was up to, but she thought he might be drinking. Actually, he had stopped drinking in bars because he would get too disoriented, so he adjusted for that. Then one time, they went to Alfredo's Restaurant in downtown Sonora with a bunch of their friends, and he went around the block to get the car to pull up front, so Mom wouldn't have to walk far, and he got lost. His friends went looking for him, and they found him up by the Red Church. That was probably 2002.

"Was that the point when he got evaluated?"

"Warren evaluated him and told us. Of course, we didn't believe him."

"Because he was your brother?" I asked.

"That and he always over-reacted. We had a family meeting, and Warren told Dad that he had Alzheimer's. Everybody was crying and all upset, and Dad said, 'Guess I better pay the bills.' Mom and Dad had a role reversal after that. Dad became the passive one. Mom had always been mellow, easy going, nothing bothered her. Now she was upset, so she yelled and fussed at him because she wanted him to step up to the plate. She was upset but also sad. She had to have someone come to work around the house and keep an eye on him. He was wandering or he'd hide from her. I had a friend come and stay with him for a while. He really liked her. She was kind of a loopy gal. He always said she was as crazy as a peach orchard bore. You know when the peaches fall, they ferment and the bores get drunk. He liked Laurie, so he stuck around. He didn't run away from her."

"But there were times when he'd be angry, and we would have to medicate him because he got violent. Finally, we had to get somebody to live with them—that was probably 2003. We brought in a gal who had worked for someone Mom knew, but she turned out to be a real weirdo. Her reference was on vacation, so Mom did talk to her right away. 'We fired her,' the lady told Mom when she finally got ahold of her. 'She was crazy. She set fire to the pasture behind our house.' When we heard that, Joaquin went and moved the gal out.

"After she left, Mom and Dad felt that she was in cahoots with the people who robbed them. They didn't even know they'd been robbed until Dad went to get in the car one morning to drive down to get the newspaper, and it wasn't there. So then they started looking around, and discovered someone had been in every room of the house taking random things. Even out in the shop. Who knows if they went into their bedroom while they were asleep? Then Dad was diagnosed with bladder cancer."

Lisa Garmin, Marjorie's daughter-in-law, remembers being at Zac's grandparents when they got the news. "I remember Warren telling them they needed to talk. He sat with them and said, 'Dad, you have cancer.' I don't remember if he told him how bad it was, but Grandpa said, 'I guess I need to pay my bills.'

"He was such a character," continued Lisa. "I remember when Zac and I went to tell him and Grandma B that we were engaged. After we told them, Grandpa didn't say a word. He just got up and walked out of the room. I was thinking, oh my god, what's the matter? And then he came back with a heavy ball attached to a long chain and a handcuff, and he said, 'Here you go Zac.' He made everything into a joke," said Lisa, laughing fondly.

"Dad was pretty sick by the time Zac and Lisa got married in Watsonville," said Marjorie. "Warren and Judy officiated at their wedding."

"I never went to my nieces' and nephews' weddings," said Karma, "but for some reason I went to that one. I think it was related to Dad, so we could get a family photo with him, which was awful because he looked horrible."

"That wedding is a total blur to me," said Marjorie. "We had the Garmin family get-away at the same time because they were all here for the wedding. And Dad was so sick."

"It took a long time for us to drive to Watsonville from Sonora," said Karma. "We had to stop a lot. By then, the cancer had moved to his bones, and he was in pain. We'd stop, and he'd get out of the car and lean on the hood. The bone cancer was in his pelvis. It was too bad he had to travel all that way."

"Mom wanted him there," said Marjorie. "And then Craig and I got stuck after the rehearsal dinner cleaning up. Dad had wet his pants, and he was furious and was yelling and wanted to leave."

"He was in such pain," said Karma. "I left with him and Mom. I can't remember who drove us. It might have been Greg."

"All weekend, we couldn't let Dad out of our sight because he would get lost," said Marjorie, "and Mom was so heavy she couldn't walk, so they were both isolated. The place we stayed was a series of cabins, and Dad was furious. 'It's a *jail*,' he kept saying. 'You're keeping me in *jail*.' Marjorie accentuated the word with a bitter shape. "Karma slept in their cabin in a closet," continued Marjorie. "That was very sweet." Marjorie and Karma giggled in a schoolgirl way about Karma sleeping in the closet, but the burden of getting Cliff and Ruth to this wedding sounded huge.

"Dad smoked till the end," said Marjorie. "Warren stayed with him the night before he died." Marjorie teared up at the recollection. "Dad was out of his mind with pain, and Warren gave him morphine. Dad wanted to smoke, but he couldn't hold his cigarette, so Warren had to help him. Warren could see he was nicotine deprived because that's how powerful nicotine is. At six in the morning, when Walmart opened, Warren went and got a nicotine patch to put on Dad. That night, Warren came with Greg and his family, and everybody visited with him and held his hand. It was lovely, really beautiful."

"He was on morphine and was in and out," said Karma. "I remember making jokes with him, and he would shrug and smile."

"When he got ready to leave, Warren said, 'I've been with a lot of people when they die. He'll make it through the night.' But of course he didn't."

"Marjorie, Mom, and I went into the living room to decompress," said Karma. "Mom couldn't sit in his room. The chair wasn't comfortable. For some reason, I went to check on Dad just as he was spitting up. I remember grabbing some tissues and hollering for them to come."

"When Karma yelled, 'You need to come now. I think it's Dad's time,' Mom didn't get it," said Marjorie. "She didn't want to. She started talking about sewing, and we had to say, 'Mom, Dad's leaving now. It's time to say goodbye.'"

"He just relaxed and died," said Karma. "And we just sat there for a long time."

"And then we called Warren, and he came back with Greg's family. Warren's grandson Gabe said, 'I see angels around his bed.' And Moriah said, 'I see angels too.' And then the oldest, Jessica, said, 'Well, I saw them first.' It was perfect. Just perfect."

"We didn't call the mortuary. We just kept him that night. We covered him with a blanket, and we put flowers around him. He was a very handsome older man. He kept his good looks."

"He died of pneumonia," said Karma. "He didn't die of cancer, but of pneumonia, three days before their sixty-third wedding anniversary on July 30, 2004.

"He died on Lisa's birthday, two weeks after the wedding," said Marjorie.

"The most painful thing was that Warren could never please Dad," said Karma recalling another certitude of the Borgquist family. "It was even harder after he became a doctor because Dad was not educated, and there was always an awkwardness."

The building on Covey Circle to which Dr. Borgquist moved his medical practice in 2000 had a huge waiting room that felt cold and impersonal, especially to those of us who had been with him since the cozy little office on Mono Way. Nor did it have the warm, fuzzy feel of the Fairview office, but once you got back to the examining rooms, Warren was there with the same slow-paced attention and sense of humor that had always made the wait worthwhile.

"I was 20 when I graduated as a Medical Assistant," said Suzanne Njirich, Dr. Borquist's nurse at Covey Circle. "First, I went to work for Chuck Waldman. Warren came over to meet me—because they worked right next to each other back then—and he said, 'Can I give you some advice?' I was scared to death, so I stammered, 'Yeah' and he said, 'It's really hard to kill someone.' That's what he told me."

"How did you get from working for Waldman to working for Borgquist?" I asked.

"I'd moved with Waldman to the Covey Circle building. It was Gould Medical Clinic. Chuck Waldman and Todd Stolp had gone with Gould, and that's where the clinic was. Then Gould sold out, and Sonora Regional bought the building and took over. I worked for Julie Gustafson for a while. When Warren's nurse moved away, I took her place. She had been slow moving. I was the exact opposite. I came in and was like Boom! Boom! Let's go. And you know Warren was like la-de-da."

"You're stepping right into a question I've ask everyone. How did you deal with his time issues?"

"I was patient. You know why? Because he took a long time with everyone. I'd tell people who were waiting, 'When it's you, he'll take that long too. And none of them cared. They brought their books, their knitting. Teachers brought papers to grade."

"What was a day in the office with Warren Borgquist like?"

"He'd get there late, so he'd be immediately behind, but we had him blocked off from twelve to two, so he could get caught up a little bit."

"Except, from what I hear, he liked his lunch time too."

"He did like his lunch time. He always left at lunch. He'd usually go home and of course, he came back late. He didn't care how far behind he was. I could do all my work in between patients because I had a lot of time."

"That didn't necessarily mean you got to leave early, right?"

"I never left early, but honestly I didn't care. He was so good to his patients. I remember him saying he was doing his third generation of vasectomies and circumcisions. Isn't that crazy? He loved doing both of those procedures because he could talk the whole time. He didn't have to think. I remember one time Judy had changed the ring tone on his phone to 'Hallelujah, Hallelujah.' He was doing a vasectomy and had just finished the last stitch and his phone went off, 'Hallelujah, Hallelujah.' Oh my god, we laughed so hard. He was very good at both procedures. He didn't usually like the parents in the room for circumcisions, but once in a while, if he knew the parents and knew they could handle it, he'd have them hold the baby and talk to him because that helped."

When I met with Dolora Dossi—Jennifer's friend and Warren's patient— she brought along a DVD with a video of Warren caring for her infant son. We sat on the floor in front of an old Mac she'd brought for the purpose. When she popped the DVD into the player, the menu came up, and among the list was one called "Warren Video." She clicked the icon and a window opened revealing a chubby baby, lying on a blue Chux pad atop an examining table. The baby was naked from the waist down, and his legs were flailing in the way an unwrapped newborn does—a discomfiting bicycling motion in search of balance and stability. The baby was Liam, Dolora's son, who had been delivered by Caesarean section after a lengthy labor. In the video, Liam's upper half is clothed in a red onesie, and he is turning his head toward the camera, mouth searching for the comfort of the breast. A little flurry of activity obscures Liam from view. I catch a glimpse of Suzanne Njirich, and then suddenly there is Warren leaning over Liam, tucking the Chux around his flailing legs—a gesture that is automatic and natural. Liam stills and looks directly at the man who has just steadied him with the simple gesture of wrapping him snugly in paper.

"What a vigorous little guy," says Warren, holding Liam's gaze.

Dolora speaks off camera about family coming to see him on Thanksgiving. Only her thumb and forefinger are visible stroking Liam's foot, which is peeking from the Chux that is around his body.

The bearded doctor talks quietly to Dolora, his eyes never leaving the baby. He is studying the child, running a practiced eye over him, his scrutiny swathed in wonder.

"He was such a family guy," said Suzanne. He used to tell me, 'Wait until you have grandkids.' Now I know what he was talking about. I want to start doing Cousins Week like he used to do. It was a big thing for him. My grandkids are two, and I'm going to start doing it with them next year. You have to say 'We're doing this.' That's what Judy and Warren said, and it always worked. That's something that I learned from him." "That's a good legacy to carry forward," I said, noticing that Suzanne was describing what she'd learn from Warren's personal life rather than his professional life.

During the time Dr. Borgquist was at Covey Circle, he cared for some of my grandchildren. We were one of those third-generation families, fourth really because Dr. Borgquist had also doctored my mother. My daughter, Jennie Lou, was among those who were reluctant to immunize, and both she and I had discussed her thinking with Dr. Borgquist.

"We didn't do anything until our fourth child," said Jennie Lou. "We'd gone through whooping cough and chicken pox with the older three. But then we had Athan, who had asthma, and I shuddered to imagine whooping cough on top of that, and also pneumonia is sometimes a side effect of chicken pox. So I said, 'OK we need to get him some vaccinations. I went to see Dr. Borgquist at the Covey Circle office. I was completely off any well-baby schedule for immunization, so I said something like, "I want this, this, and this.' It was perfect timing because he was in this office with a lab. It was after he joined with the other doctors, and it was called Sierra Practices. I was able to go in and custom-order our vaccines. We did something with the DPT—Diphtheria, pertussis and tetanus. I don't think I wanted him to add the diphtheria. I think he was probably just glad that we were doing some of them."

"Talk about Dr. Borgquist caring for Athan when he had pneumonia."

"I was the kind of person who was hesitant to run to the doctor for every little thing. But I'd noticed a pattern with Athan. When the family had a cold, he would get it too. We would all get better, but he wouldn't. When he was about eight months old, this happened. Only, he got worse to a point where I was afraid to lay him down because his breathing was so bad. I got on the phone with Dr. Borgquist's office, and they took it very seriously, telling me to bring him right in. I don't know how often they told someone to come right now, but a baby with breathing problems must have been a red flag. These days, I think they tell people to go to the ER because they have to maintain the schedule for the people in the doctor's office. But we were able to get right in, and I could see by the look on Dr. Borgquist's face he was worried. He later said Athan was in the worst condition of any baby he'd ever seen with pneumonia—lethargic and just laying in my arms. He gave him oxygen for a little while and sent us to the hospital. At the hospital, there was a conflict with the doctors. We didn't realize what was going on, though we did consider the pediatrician abrasive. I don't think we talked to her that much. We were just thinking about our baby. Dr. Borgquist sat with us until Athan was medi-flighted to Valley Children's Hospital in Fresno.

"It took us five hours to make arrangements for our other children and drive to Fresno. When we finally got there, Athan was sitting up in the crib, smiling at us. He had marks on his face from where he ripped the tape trying to pull the oxygen mask off. He was doing so well that they decided not to put the oxygen back on. When we'd last seen him, he was lying lethargically on the gurney, but by the time we got to Fresno he was as happy as could be. When I later told Dr. Borgquist, he said 'Oh, that's so embarrassing.' That's when he explained he wouldn't have sent him to Fresno, but that the pediatrician insisted that was the protocol for a baby with Athan's oxygen levels.

"The second time Athan had pneumonia, he was fifteen months old. We saw someone else at Covey Circle because Dr. Borgquist wasn't available. Even after boosts of oxygen, Athan was just under the lowest oxygen level that the hospital gauged safe, so the doctor said he had to admit him. Later Dr. Borgquist came by on rounds and said, 'He doesn't need to be here. We'll figure a way to get him out.'"

Then Jennie Lou made a connection between her experience with Athan and my own with her brother Raleigh. "Here's where our story is similar to yours," said Jennie Lou. "They wanted to put Athan in a crib. However, like you, I was still nursing my son. Dr. Borgquist requested a bed, so that I could nurse him during the night."

Some twenty-five years earlier, my 3-year-old son Raleigh had broken his femur and had to be hospitalized and in traction. Hospital policy stated that a patient under the age of 4 had to be in a crib, but Raleigh was a nursing toddler. In my mind, allowing my child to suckle at the breast well past infancy was as much about nurturing as it was about nourishment, and it was going to be impossible for me to nurse him if he were immobilized in a crib. I was adamant that when my child was in pain and frightened, I needed to be able to nurse him. Dr. Borgquist heard my anguished plea and made the necessary arrangements with the hospital administration for him to be placed in a regular bed.

"Warren loved the babies," said Suzanne Njirich. "He loved the teenagers; he loved the parents, but he was really, really good with hospice. One thing I always admired was when somebody was diagnosed with cancer, he would bring the whole family in and talk to them all at once, so everybody knew what was going on."

Kristin Fulton told a story about her family and the role Dr. Borgquist played in a really tough life-and-death decision. "Back in the '90s," said Kristin, "my brother, Joel, had an accident one windy night. He suffered a profound head injury. At the time, he was taken to Memorial North Hospital in Modesto, and they said he was going be a vegetable. Some of my family thought we should take him off life support, but my mother and my brother said no because growing up he had been a nine-lives kind of boy. So he lived through the trauma, and eventually we brought him back to Sonora to a long-term care unit over by the Wonder Bread place. Joel was in a persistent vegetative state for fourteen years.

"It was crazy," said Kristin. "He could press his thumb to indicate yes and no. He'd press once or twice, and he could also blink with his eyes to say yes or no. But that wasn't always the case. He would go in and out of being able to do that. Sometimes he'd pull out his feeding tube, and they'd put it back in. It seemed deliberate, and he had complications. It was painful to watch, but my mother wanted to keep him going even though he couldn't move, and he had to sit in one of these chairs and drool on himself. It was just terrible.

"When My mom died, the rest of us got together and talked about it. Finally we said, 'Let's ask him.' So we did. 'Joel, if you want to be taken off life-support, close your eyes and hold them shut.' And that's what he did. So we told Dr. Personius, who was his doctor, and he said, 'I will bring it before the Ethics Committee.' Warren Borgquist was in charge of the Ethics Committee. There were about fifteen doctors who filled the conference room at the old hospital. I was nervous as a cat for some reason. Warren came in and the other doctors followed. He sat first. It was very formal. Dr. Borgquist smiled at me reassuringly across the room. My older brother, Michael, was very collected, and he presented, and they listened. And then Dr. Personius reported his assessment of Joel. The whole thing lasted probably half an hour, after which they asked Michael and me to step out. In a while, Warren came out, and he said, 'We'll let him go.' Thinking back it was really amazing because it was during the time when Terry Schiavo was in the news and other kinds of cases were to going before courts of law," Kristin concluded.

More than ten years after her brother died, while telling this story, Kristin was fidgety and clearly less comfortable than the normally composed woman I knew, perhaps displaying the nervousness she'd reported feeling at the meeting, which seemed fitting as I imagined how hard making such a decision would be. After she and I talked, I did a little online research to better understand what she, her family, and the Ethics Committee were dealing with. The first thing I learned was that a diagnosis of persistent vegetative state is not always easy to discern because "there is a spectrum from the vegetative state to full awareness." The state can be intermittent, and it's possible in some cases, like Joel's, to establish a form of rudimentary communication. Medical professionals are uncertain if these patients have a day-to-day memory or appreciation of their situation or whether they can experience physical or emotional pain or pleasure. One legal case in Great Britain summed it up this way, "The question is not whether it is in the best interests of the patient that he should die. The question is whether it is in the best interests of the patient that his life should be prolonged by the continuance ... of medical treatment or care" (Airedale NHS Trust *v* Bland. AC 1993:789, 868). What a hard decision for all involved. I often wished I could ask Warren to explain his perspective, and this was definitely one of those times.

However, I had to rely on the stories of others to garner knowledge about Warren Borgquist's ethics and discernment. For instance, Suzanne Njirich told a story that revealed something about Dr. Brogquist's particular approach to unusual situations. "Warren would do anything for his patients. He had this one patient—a woman with a very bad heart. The woman was in San Francisco—she must've either just had surgery or her heart was acting up—and she had a court date for her divorce in Sonora. He went at the appointed time and stood in for her."

Kati Borgquist talked about her father-in-law's kind regard for others. "When I was going through the counseling program for a certificate," said Kati, "we learned about unconditional positive regard for other humans and what they are going through. Warren had that. He never saw people as an addict or any other label. I think his mother influenced the way he saw people. We lived with Cliff and Ruth for a while," said Kati "Ruth knew everybody, and it always amazed me that she had the privilege of knowing all kinds of information about people but never bad-mouthed anybody. I mean she could tell you about somebody—even a very sad story—but it would come out in a positive way that wouldn't hurt the person if they were right there next to her." Ruth exhibited her brand of positivity right until the end of her life.

"Dad died in July," said Marjorie Borgquist. "And then Mom decided in September that she wanted to move into Skyline." Marjorie was referring to a local assisted-living facility. "All of us were working, and she was lonely even though someone came by at least once a day to visit. Also Mom and Dad had never locked their doors, but they started locking them after the weirdo cleaned them out, so she was nervous being all alone."

"Her style was to have everybody around her," said Karma. "She liked it when the room was full."

"Then she was diagnosed with colon cancer," said Marjorie "and she was ready to go. She didn't even want to sew anymore. She had sewn all her life for everybody. When she met someone new, she'd ask, 'Do you have a granddaughter? I'll make her a dress.'"

"She was in a one bedroom place at Skyline," said Karma, "and everyone thought it would be a good idea if somebody was with her all the time. I spent a month with her. It was so hard to talk directly about death. We couldn't get to it. There was one time when she said, 'I feel like everybody is waiting on me.' That would have been a good opportunity to say something, but I just froze."

"Wasn't Warren the one who was forthright about that kind of thing? Was he less direct with his mom?"

"No, he was direct," said Marjorie.

"But I couldn't," said Karma. "There was a kind of a block between Mom and me. But we actually had fun during those last four weeks at Skyline. Remember that guy who came on Sunday mornings?" asked Karma.

"He was so obtuse," said Marjorie

"He was the father of one of the kids she'd had at day care," explained Karma. "This guy just felt like it was his duty to come and visit Mom. He'd come early Sunday morning. He was boring and dull, and we'd all sit around trying to be polite. Most of the time we hadn't had even had coffee or breakfast yet. I swear he stayed for half an hour to forty-five minutes. I think it happened three Sundays. Finally, it dawned on me that we could lock the doors. At least on Sunday mornings. Why the heck didn't we do something sooner?" finished Karma.

By way of answering Karma's question, I reminded her of another story she and Marjorie had told. "When you were little kids and company came, you had to sit in the front room, and no matter how boring they were, your Mom said you had to sit quietly and be polite."

"That's right," said Marjorie, "we had to endure it. So that's how she was—totally herself until the end. It used to irritate the crap out of us, but now I'm thinking it served her fine—like at the dime store and in her childcare.

"Ruth was so happy when she was at Skyline," said Judy Borgquist. "She had no worries, didn't have to take care of anybody. She would just entertain everybody. She had such a social life. It was adorable watching her. I think that was the happiest year of her life. Zac and Lisa were expecting their baby in early December," said Judy, "Ruth wanted to see the baby."

"I planned a home delivery with Kaylee," said Lisa Garman. "Ellie was our midwife and Warren was our back-up. I went into labor at two in the morning on the fifth. We watched the sun come up and I labored all day ... and then all night. My water broke at one in the morning on the sixth. Warren showed up at our house at six in the morning, and I was only two and a half centimeters dilated. 'Lisa,' he said, 'if you're not progressing you need to go to the hospital.' So we went to the hospital, and I remember Warren asking me, 'Do you want drugs?' And I looked at Zac. Warren said, 'No, I'm asking you. Don't you dare look at anybody else. Do you want an epidural?' And I said 'Yes!' He knew how much I wanted to do a vaginal delivery, so we pushed for four-and-half hours. He even put suction on her head, but she was just not budging. So at eleven o'clock, he said 'You have to have a C-section.' I was crying, but he stuck with me. He was there all the way even though Dr. Mills technically did the delivery. Warren said when they cut through the uterus, Kaylee's middle finger popped out.

"She came out feisty,' he said. He just loved telling that story."

As feisty Kaylee came into the world, feisty Grandma B was leaving.

"We played a lot of cards," said Marjorie. "Mom was such a good sport. She kept saying nothing hurt.""But she wasn't playing well," said Karma. "We played… god what was that game called?"

"Hand and foot," said Marjorie. "And we played canasta. Her card playing ability diminished, so we had to make it so she didn't lose so abysmally. But she played cards until the day before she died. I remember the visiting nurse came and asked about her pain level on the scale of one to ten. Mom said it was about a seven or eight. 'Really?' I asked, and she said, 'Yeah, I think I'm ready to take the morphine now. So she did, and she died a day later."

"At her funeral, Warren sang 'Sunrise, Sunset,'" said Judy. "He didn't have a great voice, and of all the songs from *Fiddler* that was not his best, but he belted it out."

# *Chapter 29*

# THE WORLD

The authentic watermark running through the background
of a life's work is an arrival at generosity,
and as a mark of that generosity, delight in the hopes of the young.

-David Whyte, *Consolations*

In 2003 Dolora Dossi's husband, Jim Toner, was a major organizer of the local Peace March to protest President George W. Bush's promotion of war in Iraq. Similar marches were held in hundreds of cities around the country on the same day. About three hundred and fifty demonstrators showed up to march in Sonora, and Warren Borgquist was among them. People gathered at Woods Creek Park, mingling under sycamore trees and settling on the play apparatus. The mood was buoyant in anticipation of marching to Washington Street and then up to Court House Park for a rally. Two images stand out from that day. One occurred as I sat atop a slide with my grandson while we waited to march. I saw Warren walking below me. The words "Bald Guy for Peace" were lettered in black ink on his hairless head. Years later, at his memorial, I saw a picture of that head again, Warren's bald pate with those words, and Kathleen Lorimer sitting beside him, holding the pen that wrote the words. Warren's head rested on a big Valentine heart—a comical allusion to the Viet Nam War protest, "Make Love, Not War." The other image I

recall is Jim Toner speaking at the rally from the steps of the courthouse with his son Liam—a child delivered by Warren—nestled on his chest in a front pack. Jim's speech centered on his concern for the innocent families in Iraq who might suffer from the imminent invasion.

Warren's aversion to war was evident when he claimed conscientious objector status as a potential draftee to the Viet Nam War. At the time, he was launching a medical career and father to two young children. By the time Dolora Dossi and Jim Toner were welcoming their son, Warren Borgquist was grandparent to twelve children, and he and Judy had initiated the practice of taking each grandchildren on a long trip somewhere in the world. When I asked Judy why the trips for the grandkids took place after eighth grade rather than after high school, she said, "After high school was awkward. Our relationships with the kids when they were younger was easier. They enjoyed talking with us."

"I was the first to go on a grandkid trip," said Evan Purdy, Scott's son. "We went to England, Ireland, and Scotland. Then we went to Paris, and finally to Switzerland."

"Did you choose those places?"

"Originally I wanted to go to Italy because I love pasta. I thought that was all we would do—eat pasta or pizza. When I got older, my thinking changed. My mother is Irish, which made me want to see that part of the world.

"Since you were the first, I imagine they learned something about how to do these trips from you."

"There's a good story about that. Gramps actually learned a valuable lesson: Secure your wallet and your belongings, especially your wallet. In Paris, he got pick-pocketed. It was toward the end of the trip. He had his cards and everything in that wallet. I was only 13, so I don't know the logistics of how it got solved, but we got a good picture of him in front of a sign that said 'Stay clear of this area; pickpockets are rampant.' He stood there with his finger on his chin looking at the sign with an I'm-oblivious look. In truth, his attitude was shit happens."

"What was the best part of the trip?"

"Going to Switzerland. My adopted Uncle Nicolas lives in Switzerland. His family owns this amazing castle-like building. We hiked to this little castle with a tower looking out toward all these different peaks. Long ago, they would light a fire in the tower when they saw invaders coming and send the troops that way. So that was really cool. We sat up there with Nicolas and his family, and they made a home-cooked meal right out of the old kitchen of the castle."

"Another major moment was kissing the Blarney Stone. And in Edinburgh, they have this big ordeal where all these people get together in kilts and play the bagpipes, and there were fireworks. That was in a castle too. Culturally that was cool—seeing the old structures and learning the history and how things change hands.

"The worst part was that I got sick in Ireland. Also, it was hard to adjust to the time difference. I was so tired, but it was great to spend time with my grandparents. They've always been a major part of my life, and to actually spend that kind of time with them was pretty special."

"Did Gramps have the sex talk with you?" I asked, diverting to a question I would ask each of the grandkids after I learned Warren sometimes had this discussion with the grandkids during their trip.

"Yes, but it was later. He brought it up when my girlfriend came with me to visit them. He sat us down and worked through it with models of the organs. As you can imagine, my girlfriend was freaked out. She was very embarrassed. I don't think she ever forgave me for that."

"We went to Thailand, Cambodia, and Bali," said Kacey, Cyndie and Scott's daughter. "I picked Bali and Thailand, and Gramps wanted to go Angkor Wat, so he incorporated Cambodia. The whole trip was amazing, but Gramps in particular made it unique. There was this mountain we were going to climb, but I was still in my teenage stage of being stubborn about certain things. Gramps kept bugging me to climb this mountain. I believe it was in Thailand, and I said no, so we never climbed it. Then Grammie and Gramps bought a painting with that mountain in the background, so after we got home, he would always point to it and say, 'That's the mountain we could've climbed.' They also bought these beautifully handcrafted chairs that Grammie put in the dining room with the big table. The chairs each have animals carved on the back." The blond wood chairs, graceful rather than ornate, are visible in pictures of large dinner parties in the sunroom at the Borgquists.

"That trip did a lot of things for me. It opened my eyes to seeing different cultures and appreciating where I came from. Cambodia, for instance, was probably the most difficult place to visit from a privileged-American standpoint. People were still getting killed by landmines. We saw children with no arms or legs, begging for money. We did the poverty scene and the night scene on that trip, so I got a very real sense that people could be dying while tourists sat at the Ritz Carlton drinking a martini. It was an experience that made an impact on me, especially at that age when I was starting to realize that terrible things were going on in the world. That trip inspired my love for travel and also made me feel lucky to live in a safe country."

"Did he have the sex talk with you?"

"He did. I got my birth control from Gramps. I'm sure he provided his children with birth control, but I was the oldest granddaughter. I brought my boyfriend, and we had the sex talk. Gramps taught me all these interesting things that I'd pass on to my friends, and they'd ask, 'How do you know that?'

"'My grandpa told me.' I'd say.

"'Eww,' they'd say, 'You talk to your grandpa about stuff like that?'

"I think he was used to having uncomfortable discussions because he was a doctor, so for him it was the norm, and he brought that with him when he talked to his grandkids. The pair of them—Gramps and Grammie—were perfect because you could talk to Grammie about anything, but then if there was a medical question, Gramps would be able to give his expertise."

"We went to the Galapagos Islands," said Sean Purdy, Scott's son. "And then we went to Machu Picchu and the Amazon. I don't think I picked Machu Picchu. That was Gramps."

"Why were you interested in that part of the world?"

"I loved the rain forest. I love bugs and spiders and …"

"Seriously!" I interjected.

"Yeah. In the Amazon, you see spiders that are nine inches in diameter. When we first got to the Amazon, we got off the boat and were heading to the front door of our lodge. Between the lodges were two trees with a five-foot web spread between them. There was a huge spider, about as big as your hand, sitting right in the middle of the web. It was pretty crazy.

"In the Peruvian Amazon, we were on a hiking trail with our guide. Being the bug guy, I was looking around, and I saw this giant armored millipede that was probably five or six inches long. I picked it up and threw it at Grammie, and Gramps really went off on me because she was freaking out. But it turned into a fond memory because later he came to me and said, 'You just can't do that kind of thing.' That really stuck with me. I got that it was a mean thing to do, which I regretted.

"That trip made us a lot closer," said Sean. "I had a lot of issues in my childhood. My mom passed away when I was 12, so I was a little pissed off at that point. I was mad at the world and kind of a little shit. Spending that much time continuously with Gramps and Grammie and having so much fun made a difference. Gramps even said, 'I had a great time with you.' They probably weren't too sure coming into the trip whether I was going to be good or not."

"Did he ever have the sex talk with you?"

"Yeah. He brought out his gigantic model of the female anatomy and proceeded to go over every part it. I don't think he had a male model—just the female—but he went over every part describing how it worked. It wasn't that bad because it was just me, but I remember being there with my brother and one of his girlfriends. That was bad—probably the longest sex lecture I ever witnessed—looking over and seeing this terrified look on the girl's face. I believe he did it the first time I took Czernia to Sonora to meet them too. He pulled out his model. I know he prescribed birth control for her."

"I went to China," said Chris Gallagher, Mimi's son. "Ever since I was little I liked white rice and Chinese food, so when they said, 'Where do you want to go?' I said 'China.' It was awesome. We went to Tibet, to Bejing, and a whole bunch of other places I can't pronounce. We went on a three-day cruise down the Yangze River. We saw the terra cotta warriors. We saw martial arts. We climbed the Great Wall. Actually, Gramps and I were the only people in our group who made it the whole way. He always finished the hike, that's for sure."

"One of my favorite Gramps stories," said Emily, Chris's sister, "is one Grammie told about when they were in China with Chris. Gramps went down to the hotel lobby to get batteries for their camera. He said, 'I'll be back in ten minutes,' but he was gone for three hours. Grammie was furious. He claimed he just went exploring, like it was no big deal. He never admitted that he got lost."

Chris's trip was different from the other grandkids in that it involved a big group of Judy and Warren's friends who also had grandchildren. "We had a grandchild, who has also just graduated from eighth grade," said Celeste Boyd. "The trip just kind fell together. We made up a little party from Sonora: Ruth Hagstrom and her grandchild, Anneka. Stan Olsen and his grandson, the Borgquists and Chris, and Bill and I."

"All of us kids went exploring when we could," said Chris. "One night, we snuck out and went to the black market where they sold all these cool knives and things. I still have the one I bought that night. There was one other elderly couple with our tour group that no one knew before that trip, and they gave all the kids a package of coins that picture the different dynasties through the ages. I still have that as well."

"After that trip," said Judy, "Warren decided we weren't going to do trips with other families because he didn't have enough time alone with Chris. He always did the sex lecture on that trip, and it was getting toward the end, and Warren hadn't had a chance to talk to Chris. We were in some museum, and he said, 'Christopher, sit here now.'"

"Yes, we had the sex talk," Chris said. "It was in the middle of an art museum. It was the most awkward thing on the planet because no one else in the whole room was talking but us. He had his notebook, so he was doodling pictures the whole time."

"It used to be that each grandkid went on a separate trip," said Jessica, Greg's daughter, "but Jake and I made this pact to go together because we graduated eighth grade the same year. I was supposed to go after him because I'm actually younger, but he and I wanted to go to all the same places, so we told Grammie and Gramps we wanted to combine our trips. We said that way we won't hold up the cousins who come after, and it'll be cheaper because they wouldn't have to fly on two separate trips."

"We went to Germany, Greece, Italy, Switzerland, and France in five amazing weeks. When we were in Rome, the taxis were on strike. They say that in Italy there is always a strike going on. It's like a thing there, but that year there was also a heat wave, and there is no AC in Europe. We had to walk about thirteen miles one day when it was a hundred degrees. We were just dying because we were trying to see everything, and we couldn't ride anywhere. We wanted to see the Borghese Gallery, which is amazing and one of Grammie's favorites. When we got there, the line was really long. So Gramps went up to the attendant and lied. 'Look at my wife,' he said. 'She's got terminal cancer, and she's never coming back here, and this is one of her last goals. Look at her. Her face is as red as a tomato.' So we got in. We were so lucky. That was one of my favorite parts of the entire time, the Borghese Gallery."

"And in Santorini, we did the donkeys, but Gramps said, 'I don't want to ride on those poor donkeys,' so he marched all the way up. There were so many stairs, and he hiked all the way. I remember I cried when we left Santorini, and he said 'You've got the Borgquist sappy gene,' which is true because I'm super emotional like him. One of my favorite memories of Gramps was when we went to the movies with the cousins to see *P.S. I Love You*. I had Kleenex and was blubbering, and I looked over at Gramps and he was crying too."

"One night when we were in Paris," said Jessica, getting back to the trip, "we'd gone to the Seine and checked out the Eiffel Tower, and then we went to dinner. Grammie is much better at directions, but Gramps said, 'I'm going lead us home. I've got this.' But we got lost and went in the same circle four times. He kept making up little facts about the buildings we were passing and making us laugh. It got dark, and Grammie was saying, 'Oh, Lord,' and he kept saying 'I've got this.' And finally, we said 'Grrr, give us the map,' but he made it all so funny."

"Did Gramps have the sex talk with you?"

"Yes, he was very modern, very open minded in his views about everyone. He was a kind-hearted person and very fair about everything, like gay marriage. I feel like a lot of people his age weren't as open minded. So that was refreshing. And another thing, he didn't think younger kids should watch war movies, but sex scenes were OK because sex is natural and war isn't. He despised war." In that one sentence, Jessica revealed a whole lot about Warren Borgquist's worldview.

"We flew in to Frankfurt," said Jake. "We were there maybe a day or two, and then we went to Athens and spent a little over a week, traveling all around Greece. After that, we went on a week-long cruise in the Aegean on this boat with big beautiful sails. I think it was over a hundred years old and most of it was constructed of wood. It was a little bit annoying being 14. Grammie and Gramps were there and one other couple in their 50s and everyone else was their age or much older.

"And Jessica?" I asked.

"Yes, Jessica and me and Grammie and Gramps. We heard some of the same stories several times. They'd forget they told us. But it was fun going over all of the archaeology and history. Gramps really helped get me interested in history."

"And what about the sex talk?

"He told this story of when he was with his first wife, trying to French-kiss her, but his tongue was so short he couldn't get it out of his mouth. So he ended up cutting it, right here under his tongue," Jake opened his mouth and pointed to the frenulum, the band of tissue connecting the underside of his tongue to the floor of the mouth. "After it was cut, he could stick out his tongue more. And another story was when he was first starting out in San Francisco as a doctor. His boss was a real hard-ass and everyone tried to avoid him because he would just go off and yell and ridicule people. So one time a patient came in who had been using a vibrator that got stuck up in him, and Gramps knew he couldn't let the boss find out about this. He'd destroy this guy. So he decided to just tell him the guy had stomach pains. It had been a couple of hours and the batteries were mostly dead but there was still this little vrrrr," said Jake, imitating the quiet sound of vibration.

"So you were 14, and he was telling you these stories," I said. "That's amazing. He was no-holds-barred in that department. Totally comfortable."

"We had to promise we wouldn't tell any of the other cousins until they went on their trip," added Jake. "Another story was on the first night in Nice we were going to watch a movie, so Gramps ordered it, and he accidentally got this porno film. There was this pretty explicit scene, and he quickly turned it off and said, 'If your parents ask what you learned today, say the world sucks.' He turned everything into humor."

"My cousin Ben and I went to London for a week," said Gabe Borgquist. "We're really close in age and would have been friends even if we weren't cousins. At first, I just wanted to get on the plane and go to a different continent, but we were delayed. So we were just sitting there, and Gramps was explaining lift—how the wind goes over the wing and curls under and actually lifts the plane. It was the most boring thing you could listen to for like two hours. He did all these little diagrams. The first one was passable, but he said it wasn't good enough. So he redid it, like a surgeon going super slow, making it look perfect. Now I catch myself explaining lift to people. Every time I see an airplane take off I think of Gramps.

"After we got to London," said Gabe, "Grammie was resting in the flat, and Ben and I wanted to walk around, so Gramps decided he was going to give his own little tour. He's not the best with directions, but we were going to look for a castle that was nearby. We went to a huge park that wrapped around the castle. We were walking, and he kept pointing forward and saying 'Its right up there; I know it is.' Ben and I, we could have sworn it was to the right, so we said, 'I'm not so sure about that.' He had a map, but we spent an hour walking the wrong direction. Still, we had fun because we kept laughing. We saw these restaurants with funny names. There was a billboard with two identical bald guys, and they were holding each other with a big goofy smiles."

"Sounds like you're describing Gramps."

"Yeah, I know. That's why it was so funny. He had us take a picture, and he was smiling exactly like the guy on the sign. Eventually, he said, 'I'm going to let you boys take it,' so he followed us, and we got right back to our hotel."

When I asked about the sex talk, Gabe repeated the story Gramps had told Jake about his short tongue. "He was talking about kissing my Nana," said Gabe, closing the story. "He said that he didn't know what to do because his tongue was too short, and the way he said was to die for. But it wasn't awkward with Gramps. It was never awkward."

"What do you think kept it from being awkward?" I asked

"His smile. He would always tell you stuff like that and smile."

"We went to Kenya and Tanzania as well as London," said Ben, Jennifer's son. "My cousin Gabe and I are both into animals and adventure. A little more so than the rest of the kids. From the time we were pretty young, we talked about how cool it would be to go to Africa. Obviously Grammie and Gramps thought it was a great idea."

"We stopped in London because that's where we caught our flight to Africa, so we decided we might as well go early, so we could spend a week there. We rented this little flat on the outskirts of the city, and we took the tube everywhere. We went to a bunch of museums and walked around a lot and only got lost a few times. One day, we went to the Ritz for tea. At first, we were going to take the tube because it was cheaper. But Gramps wanted to take a taxi, so he could say, 'To the Ritz, please.' We'd finally decided to take the tube because it was more cost effective, but then the train broke down, and we got to take a cab after all, so he got to say, 'To the Ritz.'

"In Africa, we were with a tour group. We went to the Maasai Mara National Reserve in Kenya, where we saw all sorts of animals—a wildebeest migration and hundreds of giraffes and elephants. One day, we went on a hot-air-balloon ride. We had to wake up at four in the morning. Grammie was really sick. She was throwing up and didn't want to go, but Gramps made her because he knew she would regret not going. There's actually a video in the hot air balloon with Grammie throwing up over the side, but she's happy she went. It was a big balloon with maybe eight passengers. We hovered above all these animals, and they didn't notice us because we were silent, floating above them. We actually floated over a tree with a leopard in it, and we saw an elephant chasing a lion. They drove the safari truck out to where we landed and set up little tables. We had omelets out on the plains of Africa. The adults had champagne. We were in Tanzania and Kenya for three weeks. It was crazy, seeing the poverty and how they lived, the way they get food and water. It's a different world there. It makes you think. It's life- changing," said Ben.

Not all the adventures with grandkids were in foreign countries. Gabe recalled a trip to the Mojave Desert. "Gramps bought a little trailer for his Jeep, so he could take my dirt bike. It was Thanksgiving weekend, and he was really looking forward to it. We passed the turn for the road into the campground, so Gramps drove down this really narrow road in the motor home, looking for a place to do a U-turn. He finally said he would have to unhook the Jeep. We found the widest spot for a U-turn, and there were other cars waiting, so he was trying to be quick. He unhooked the Jeep, but he forgot to put it in Park. When the motorhome pulled away, the Jeep started rolling. He tried to jump in and turn the wheel, but he tripped and fell, and the Jeep rolled over on top of him—across his leg and stomach. Grammie was in the motorhome freaking out. I remember I was too shocked to say anything. The girls were yelling. The Jeep was teeter tottering on top of him. A little bit this way; a little bit that way. So he grabbed the tire and turned it off of him, and he rolled out of the way of the rear tire and got up. My favorite part was when he got to the door of the motorhome. He stood there with tire marks down his shirt, brushing himself off, and he said, 'Well, that didn't go as planned.' Later that night, he showed us the bruises, which were purple and green and terrible looking. He acted like nothing happened, but it turned out he broke a couple of ribs."

"Gramps was the guy who could motivate you," said Ben. "He could empower you to do stuff. Like if something was wrong at the house or with the car, he'd casually call you over and have you try to figure it out. He bought these vacuums, and he made his own attachments out of PVC pipe that he reshaped so he could do different things with them. I remember him trying to figure out how to keep the volume of the tube constant enough to get the same airflow through it. When I was little, he built an attachment for my skateboard to make it into a scooter. He made sure I helped. We all worked on projects with him. He built tree houses at all of the grandchildren's houses. We had this two-story tree house in our yard that was very elaborate. When we moved, we actually cut our tree house out of the tree and brought it with us. It's not in a tree anymore. It's just sitting in our driveway. Some day, we'll reassemble it in a new tree, and it will live on."

When I asked Jennifer, Ben's mom, why the trips for the grandkids took place after eighth grade rather than after high school, she said, "Because they realized they were getting old, and they wanted to be sure everyone got a trip." Everyone did get a trip, but four of the grandkids did not get to go with Warren. He died before Emma, Jennifer's daughter, got to go on her trip, so I asked her, "What do you miss the most."

"The comforting figure to talk to or just sit next to. To have a snack with. To be around.

"What kind of snack would you have with him?"

"It was fun to make things with him. When I was a kid, we made a table to put cookies on for Santa. Not that I actually believed in Santa because I'm Jewish but …"

"But you went along with him, making the Santa table. Was this a little table?"

"Actually, pretty tall. I assumed Santa would be a tall person. Either that or evil. He watches you all year and breaks into your house." That was my first taste of Emma's particular brand of humor. "Donuts in the snow were fun with Gramps."

"When did you do donuts in the snow?" I asked, knowing she lived in Santa Barbara where it rarely snowed.

"When we were driving up in the mountains. He let me drive when it was snowing, and we did doughnuts in the Jeep."

"So you were 12, driving the jeep in the snow on a mountain with your Gramps."

"It was fun. When we were little, he gave us names. I'm Otter Rock; Ben is Bear Cub. Gramps made up little stories using our animal names. He was good at telling stories on the spot. There was one where I was from Ireland, and this wave came and washed away all the little rocks, so the otters couldn't use rocks to crack open food, and these mean people had the rocks, and they wouldn't give them back." Though Emma didn't go on the traditional trip with Gramps, he took her to Ireland in this story.

"The thing about not going on the trip with Gramps is that was when he gave the sex talk," said Emma. "You had to wait until you were on the trip, probably because it had inappropriate humor. It's kind of wrong that I don't get to find out about that from him."

Ryan Gallagher, Mimi's son, was another grandchild who didn't do a trip with Gramps, but he nevertheless had stories of memorable moments with his grandfather. "During Cousins' Week, when we were out in the wilderness, Gramps would build these bathtubs for us. He'd use those storage containers, the kind with a lid that latch over the top. They're pretty good sized, and we were little kids. He rigged up a generator for a water heater. Then he'd pour the hot water into the storage containers and give us baths. We'd be all nice and warm out in the cold wilderness. That was one of the best things about Cousins Week—Gramps' bath."

"Another memory I have is kayaking when I was really young. Me and Gramps were in the same kayak. The river probably seemed bigger than it was because I was a little child. And it was raining. We flipped, and we both fell out. The water was so cold it just sucked the breath from my lungs. I didn't know what to do. I froze. The next thing I knew Gramps had me in the boat, and he was kicking his way over to a rock island. He flipped the boat onto the rock and hoisted us both up. He had a semi-dry towel in his backpack that he wrapped me in, and he put his jacket around me and rubbed my shoulders to warm me up. Then he got the kayak ready, and we set off again. I remember sitting in the kayak cold as hell and shivering but glad to be alive."

"When I was really young, probably 3 or 4," said Moriah Borgquist, Greg's younger daughter, "I made up a song about Gramps at Cousins Week. He was the fun grandpa, always ready to do silly things. The song went like this: 'I love my Gramps because he's so chubby, chubby, chubby.' Everyone worried he would find it offensive, but he loved it, and he would dance while I sang. I loved his chubbiness. He was like a big bear. He gave the best hugs. That big scruffy face and big smile. He was a big teddy bear, who always went for a hug."

Warren was the "fun grandpa," who took his grandkids on exotic trips around the world traveling in airplanes, taxicabs, hot air balloons, and kayaks. He took them to magical places where they were the heroes of their own stories. He got lost with and without them. He told them useless information and much needed facts of life.

# *Chapter 30*

# MY CRAZY PEOPLE

> Perhaps the greatest legacy we can leave from our work
> is not to instill ambition in others
> ... but the passing on of a sense of sheer privilege.
>
> -David Whyte, *Consolations*

On December 31, 2006, Dr. Warren Borgquist closed his private medical practice. When I asked Gail Witzelsteiner, the Public Relations Specialist at the Sonora Regional Hospital, about Warren's retirement, I learned she not only had a business relationship with him, but he had been her doctor since she saw him at the Clinic at Columbia College in the 1970s. "I thought he was delightful and decided to have him as my personal physician," said Gail. "A number of years later, almost a decade and half, I was pregnant, and he did my prenatal care. I have such fond memories of him coming into the exam room very slowly with this giant grin on his face. Because I had a Caesarean, he didn't deliver my baby, but he assisted with the surgery. I remember him standing behind the screen, holding Katie up for me to see, saying, 'Hi, Mama.' It was so dear.

"Our whole family—the three of us—saw him for our care. One time when Katie was 4 or 5, he asked about her. I said, 'Oh, Warren, she's perfect—absolutely perfect.' And he said, 'That's wonderful. Just don't think you had anything to do with it.' I was taken aback because as a first-time parent, you think you're working so hard to do a good job, but of course his theory was they are gifts from God, and you get what you get. We were just lucky parents who got a perfect one.

"I hope I can say this without crying," Gail continued, her voice cracking. "He helped me through the deaths of my mother, my sister, and my father. There were a lot of life-changing events in my life he was a part of. I guess that's largely the role of family practice doctor."

"It's a beautiful practice," I said.

"He talked about that—the fact that he could be with people from birth to hospice. We have much to be grateful for in terms of his contributions to those practices in this community."

"I believe you had something to do with his retirement party?"

"We did have a party for him," said Gail. "Over the years, he used to say he would retire when the children he birthed were having children of their own. He was going to stop before the next generation came, which of course he did not do. One of the things he wanted … the way he put it was, 'I want a brass band to play when I retire.' We were able to pull a pretty good-sized group of students from the Sonora High School Golden Regiment band to play at his party."

"How perfect," I said, "since he played in that band when he was in high school."

"Yes," said Gail as we sat in her home, jazz playing softly from a sound system across the room. After a moment of reflection, she continued, "Warren was my physician until he stopped practicing. He was always a step above—in birth practices, in hospice—and speaking of stepping, I always remember those colorful socks peeking out of his Birkenstocks."

"That's one of those great Warren Borgquist images that show up over and over," I said, thinking that Gail's reminiscence encapsulated the man's career rather well.

After retirement, Warren stepped aboard Holy Shit with Judy for a good, long trip. "Our trip started by going to Baja for a month with Jim and Judy Wilson," said Judy Borgquist. "They had this tiny little Casita trailer, and we had our giant motorhome. One time, Jim and Judy were in front of us, and they got a flat tire. So we had to stop the motorhome in the

middle of the busy Baja highway that had no shoulder and a steep incline on either side. We couldn't find the flares, but we had these fluorescent plastic bowls. I grabbed those and stood in back waving them until Warren found the flares. Jim frantically changed the tire with trucks whizzing by. We had to step out to look around Holy Shit, so we could tell the trucks behind us when they could go. It was very dangerous.

"And there was this one crazy dinner. We always shared dinner in our big RV because their place was too small. We were stopped at a beach, and Jim went spear fishing. He caught only one fish, which he cleaned and cooked. We thought it was the best fish we'd ever tasted. We even talked Judy—who will not eat fish under any circumstances—into having a bite. The dog had a bite too. Jim had taken a picture of the fish, so when he got home, he looked it up, and it turned out to be a deadly puffer fish. Guys in Japan go to school to learn how to skin and bone this fish because one bite of its deadly poison can kill you. It paralyzes your lungs, so we all could have died, including the dog. Jim must have done a really good job cleaning it because we didn't die. It was a miracle!

"Even with the difficulties, we had a blast. One of my favorite pictures from the trip is of Warren, Jim, and the dog all peeing together on the side of the road. It was so cute," said Judy, describing the photo I'd seen on the wall in Jim Wilson's guest bathroom. Another photo from the trip features Warren, who has climbed yet another rocky edifice, standing at the edge of a cliff on tippy toes, stretching tall with an outstretched index finger to touch a rock overhang. Something about the photo captures his indomitable spirit—forever reaching, not for the stars but to touch hard proof that he'd made it.

"We planned to explore all of Baja," said Judy, "but we only got to Loreto. After that we turned back to the States. Jim and Judy headed home, and Warren and I started across the country—the southern route. We always stopped after no more than six hours of driving. We knew people who'd visited Bisbee, Arizona, so we stopped there. We saw a lot of Texas. When we got to New Orleans, it was St. Patrick's Day. We followed the parade of bands, dancing in the street. People were kissing me and giving me gifts. I still have one—a green feather boa. I told Warren we had to go to Georgia in the spring because it was supposed to be the most beautiful place on earth, and it was perfect. We biked through the botanical gardens among the azaleas, dogwood, wisteria, and cherry blossoms. I thought we would die from happiness. We went to St. Simons Island and then drove north. When we were almost to Washington, DC, we got a call that we had to come home. Ruth was really sick, so we drove straight back across the country. But the trip was magical, the motorhome so cozy. Our own little home. We loved it so much, and we loved being together. We had so much more we wanted to do."

"He had a year when he stopped practicing" said Dr. Ken Renwick, "and traveled in the motorhome with Judy. He had a lot of fun, but he loved to practice. He loved to take care of patients, so he went back to work at Forest Road Primary Care."

"You practice in a clinic," I said. "Can you talk about the differences between what you do and what he did?"

"Mine is more like a community practice because most of my patients are insured. At Forest Road, Warren's patients had Medi-Cal or CMSP—that's County Medical Services Program—so most are low-income patients, many are unemployed and/or disabled for one reason or another. His patients were mostly under 65 with accompanying chronic problems, including drugs or alcohol. They hadn't taken care of themselves or they'd had horrible things happen, catastrophic accidents that were disabling. I covered that practice for a short while for the guy who preceded Warren. That guy left suddenly, and the hospital was desperate to replace him. Warren was ready to practice again, so it served everybody's needs. I don't think anybody could have done that job better than Warren. He served a need, and I think he felt good stepping back in."

Brittany Norwood was Warren Borgquist's Medical Assistant (MA) at the Forest Road Clinic. We talked on the phone about her experience working with him. "I came to work at the clinic on a temporary basis, to fill in for someone. I'd heard stories about what a respected doctor he was, so I was really nervous, but he put me at ease by asking questions about school and my future. 'Where are you going from here?' he wanted to know. 'I know you're not going to be a medical assistant forever.' From the first time I met him, he encouraged me to continue my education. It was pretty cool."

"So you were there as temp person," I said. "Then what happened?"

"I was supposed to be a fill-in person for all of the clinics. Forest Road was the first one I went to, and I never left. They eventually created a full-time position for me as the fifth MA. We had four providers—two doctors and two nurse practitioners, and they each had their own MA, and they hired me as an additional MA to help wherever I was needed."

"And then you became specifically his MA?" I asked.

"Right. His MA decided to continue her education in nursing, so when she left, he offered me the position. That was about a year after I started at Forest Road. He loved that I was fresh out of school. I was terrified at first, but he was a teacher. He'd pull up an x-ray and say, 'OK, what organ is this?' And then he'd explain what I was seeing. He'd be talking to a patient when I was in the room—explaining something going on in the heart, for instance—and he would point to me and ask a question. He didn't do it in a way that put me on the spot. I always felt like he was trying to help me better myself."

"Can you explain how a medical assistant fits in the hierarchy of the office?" I asked. "What were your job responsibilities?"

"I was responsible for setting up patients in the examination room. I would call a patient in from the waiting room, get their weight, their vital signs, and fill out the chart for him. Print out anything he might need—lab results, x-ray results, notes from other doctors. Then he would come in. He taught me how to do extra things like check a patient's pupils. For vasectomy procedures, he'd have me check the semen samples. He taught me things that medical assistants normally don't do. He wasn't one for following guidelines. If he felt like he could trust me with something, it didn't matter if it wasn't in my job description. Our relationship was very different from most doctors and their medical assistants."

"What you're describing sounds like what LVNs once did, so what's the difference between an MA and an LVN?"

"There really isn't a whole lot other than how we are licensed. An LVN can work under her own license, and a medical assistant works under the doctor's license. If an LVN messes up, it's her license on the line, but if an MA messes up, it's the doctor's problem. That's why a lot of doctors are very strict about what their medical assistants can and cannot do.

"At our clinic, you could only be seen if you were on Medi-Cal, so most of our patients were disabled or injured, and they couldn't work.

They had to take medication—pain medication. It is was hard for some people to understand the way he practiced—the trust that he put in patients as far as filling their prescriptions or letting them come back in three months instead of every month. Some people looked at that and thought it was bad practice. But he had been a doctor for thirty-eight years. He was still operating like an old-school doctor. He believed that you do what's best for the patient. If they couldn't get the gas money to come back every single month to get their medications, he gave them multiple prescriptions. The modern perspective says you can't put that much power in their hands because they are going to screw you over, or you are going to get sued. He wasn't worried about that. He was worried about patients having what they needed when they needed it. Of course, there are patients who ruin it for everybody, but you're going to have that in any practice."

"Dr. Renwick showed me a memo Warren wrote explaining his approach to the pain management," I said.

"I typed that paper for him," said Brittany, "from his handwritten notes."

The memo Brittany had typed from Warren was addressed to "My pharmacist colleagues, My physician, NP, and PA colleagues," and dated May 2010. The subject line read: "My difficult clinic: Forest Road Health and Wellness, A Rural Health MediCal/CMPS provider." Warren's legacy of written documents is minuscule: notes from his 20-year high school reunion, funny endearing notes to Judy, and a few poems to friends and family, so it was unique to examine a memo composed by him which recorded "my scattered thoughts that I present to the Emergency Department providers that do my night and weekend coverage (bless 'em)." Scattered is an apt descriptor, for the memo flits from one thought to another, full of assumptions that his audience will understand his references, abbreviations, and brand of humor; full of odd line breaks and unusual punctuation and capitalizations. The memo was not typical of something sent from one professional to another. The document is most certainly from his heart, mind, and hand.

Dr. Borgquist makes it clear that he is aware of the perverse behavior and manipulations of those addicted to pain medication. "I know my patients can be difficult, and please know we consider untoward behavior to you pharmacy folks the same as untoward behavior to us. So please call us." Warren Borgquist did not tolerate disrespectful or fierce behavior in his office. Monique Tomasovich told about Warren calling to task a disrespectful salesman, and Brittany would tell a similar story about a threatening patient. At the same time, he understood how driven these patients were. He dropped the following cautions throughout the memo, evidence that he'd dealt with the varied ploys of addicts:

> Getting them off short acting opioids is the adult equivalent of taking a binky from a baby.
>
> Accept that 20-30% are addicts *and* drug sellers—among the best cons.
>
> Oxycontin is the bane of my existence. It is sadly the smoothest, most easily liked, long-term, long-acting opioid. Getting people off it is like pulling a binky that's epoxied in. Its so lipophilic even long-term users get into the euphoria zone with each use. A bottle of 90 is worth $3600 on the street. If you got $850/mo social security … what would you do?
>
> If a patient has an acute pain—fractures, contusions—and is on methadone or morphine, don't give short-actings to those who say, 'I need them Norcos, Doc.'

"Borgquist didn't feel like he was something special," said Dr. Renwick. "He took a very practical approach and sought guidance, so he could do his best. He arranged for a pain management specialist to come and do an in-service for all the docs who were interested in pain meds. Warren's legacy of more liberal pain treatment at Forest Road evolved naturally from his robust support for hospice. He brought the perspective of sufficient pain relief into hospice treatment. Then he stepped into dealing with chronic-pain management at the clinic. Of course, this continues to be a highly debatable issue. The thing I find interesting is that I've never sent someone to a pain management specialist, like those in San Francisco, and had them come back on less pain medicine than when I sent them. I think it's sad that at the end of Warren's career, there were people who put him down for prescribing narcotics to these people. I don't think they really understood the situation. He was caring for people that nobody else would. I can remember him saying something like, 'A bunch of them are just crazy, but they are my crazy people.'"

"He looked beyond what patients looked like," said Brittany. "They came in filthy dirty from living on the streets. He treated these people like he treated everyone, and they didn't get that anywhere else. He would cut their toenails because he knew no one else would. He cleaned their wounds. He did so much more than a general practitioner would normally do. He could have sent some of them to specialists, but he knew they couldn't afford it, or they would have to wait a long time to get in. They were already there, and they had waited hours to see him.

"Patients got frustrated. Some got really angry. One time a patient threatened me. He was in the room yelling at me. I was terrified because the guy was talking about guns. I was acting meek, saying, 'I'm so sorry.' Dr. Borgquist heard him yelling and threw the door open and said, 'What's going on in here?' He chewed the guy out. 'Do not talk to my staff like that or you will never come back here.' It was kind of weird to see him so angry because I'd never seen that side of him. Then he calmed down and talked to the patient, and they ended up on OK terms. He was very protective of his staff. He would go to bat for every single one of us.

"He loved us. You know how you have friendships? He said we spent so much time together at work that we develop what he called workships. While I was at Forest Road, our lead medical assistant, Casey, died in a car accident. It was a horrible, traumatic time for the entire office. She was young, in her early thirties, with two or three children. He gathered the whole office together and had us hold hands. He said, 'Let's talk about Casey.' It blew me away to see this doctor worried about all of us, wanting us to express our feelings. He cared so much about her. At her funeral, he said wonderful things. I didn't even know they'd been close, but the things he said told me how he felt about all of us—his workships."

"One of the things I loved about Dr. Borgquist," said Tammie Little, who returned to work with hospice as an RN in 2009, "was that he worked with a patient population that most doctors avoided like the plague— MediCal patients, indigents, alcoholics, drug addicts, and people who were otherwise undesirable. That was endearing because I'm kind of that underdog too, and I lean toward people who are ostracized. When I came back to work hospice, I knew if I was getting one of his patients, the bad news was that the patient was going to be a train wreck, and the good news was that Dr. Borgquist was going to give me whatever I needed. It was unlike working with any other physician. The only physician who came close was Dr. Personius."

"We got this one patient in April of 2010. Let me paint a picture for you. This guy had tattoos up one side and down the other and big ol' caged ears, those holes with big spacers inserted. And he was not cooperative. He didn't like to take his meds, so every time I turned around something was happening with him, but I knew I could call Dr. Borgquist any time, and he'd always get back to me. One time when this patient had been on our service for two months, he was having a pretty tough week, and I got a call from his wife. She was hysterical. The sheriff was at the house, and they were going to arrest him on an outstanding warrant for god-knows what. So I rushed over there. He was standing on his porch, white as a ghost, puking. The law enforcement guys didn't know what to say. They felt so bad, so I called Dr. Borgquist and put him on the phone with the sheriff. I don't know what he said, but I heard the sheriff say, 'Thank you very much. Sorry to bother you. We'll take care of it.'

"I had another patient—a hard-core alcoholic and drug addict who was dying because of his lifestyle. His liver was shut down and everything else was shutting down. He lived in some hovel on Big Hill Road in a god-forsaken little trailer. His caretakers called and said, 'Things are real bad. Nothing is working.' I called Dr. Borgquist who answered immediately and gave me medication orders. I was able to call that family back in fifteen minutes and say, 'I spoke to the doctor. Do this, this, and this.' That's how effective Dr. B was. That's why it was so amazing to work with him because he treated everyone like a human being, and he was never too busy to call back."

Brittany's and Tammie's stories about Dr. Borgquist were the same stories told by staff and patients when he was in private practice and working as medical director for Hospice of the Sierra. A lot of folks appreciated his style of doctoring, so when word got out that he was practicing again at the Forest Road Clinic—in the same building where he'd once had a private practice with Chuck Waldman and Todd Stolp—some of his former patients tried to get in to see him.

My daughter, Jennie Lou Tippett, was one of his those. "We didn't have health insurance at the time," she said, "so I thought we'd qualify, but they rejected us. I remember feeling like they were holding him hostage, 'What do you mean I can't see Dr. Borgquist? I'm his patient.' In my mind, I was his patient based on relationship more than on whatever legality they were citing. I was his patient because he's the one who cared for us, and it just seemed weird that they could tell me I wasn't. I kept trying to figure out different ways to break down the door, not literally, but some way to get around what they were telling me." As Jennie Lou decried the impossibility of getting to see Dr. Borgquist once he left private practice, I thought of the William Osler story Todd Stolp told about the doctor's office door with markings from the repeated knocking of patients.

"One thing that impressed me," continued Jennie Lou, "was when he told me he hoped someday to go to work for Doctors without Borders. I don't remember exactly what country, but he was interested in a Muslim country. He said that sometimes when women gave birth there, the perineum tore and then grew back together in a manner that caused bowel movement to come out the vagina. These women were shunned. It was a tremendous shame for them. He said it was a simple surgical repair that could change a woman's life, and he wanted to do these procedures for them. Medicine was not just his practice, it was his passion—and his recreation—it put food on his table, it was his everything." And then my Catholic daughter said, "I liked to think of him as a secular Mother Theresa. For her, it was about the individual. It didn't matter whether they were Hindu or untouchables or left to die in the street of leprosy. Dr. Borgquist was personal and respectful like that regardless of who you were. I don't know if there were people he struggled to treat. I was not aware of any. I don't know that he was motivated by anything spiritual like Mother Theresa, but he shared a similar goodness."

"We were probably one of the few patients to follow him from his private practice to the clinic," said Jim McKee. "It was like a war zone in that waiting room. In fact, I couldn't stay in the waiting room. I would go outside and stretch. I told the receptionist where I was, so she could call me. There were incidents when people had to be hauled away ..."

"One day when I was there," interjected Gill McKee, "this guy came walking down the hall literally wall-banging, bouncing from to one side to the other. All of a sudden an ambulance rolled up, the medics hopped out, grabbed the guy and slapped him on the gurney and away they went."

"Warren told me his office was like the bar scene in the Star Wars movie," said Jim, "the one with all these alien creatures. 'That's my office,' he said."

"How did you get to be his patients," I asked. "I know others who tried and were rejected. Did you just call him and say, 'We want you as our doctor?'"

"Yep," said Gill.

"We both worked in special education and had dealt with his patient population in our jobs. 'You guys are special' he said, 'I know you can handle it.' Warren was down to earth. He could work with a college president or the homeless. It didn't matter."

"I remember having a conversation with his nurse," said Gill, "and she said that sometimes after work he'd walk out to the waiting room and look around and say, 'This is where I'm supposed to be. These people need me.' He wasn't frustrated. He embraced it."

Warren's colleagues who saw him go to work at the Forest Road Clinic had their own thoughts about the direction his career had taken. According to Jim Makol, "Intellectually, Warren had the point of view that there are people who need help and not necessarily just somebody to diagnose and treat their disease. Everybody's got a story. There are plenty of people who are challenged financially, who don't know how to take care of themselves, who can't pay their bills, and he took the position to accept these people with all of their twiggles, even if they weren't perhaps the most admirable people."

"It was a good for him to take a break," said Bob Fisher, the pharmacist. "When he and Judy got back, they were doing great, and he wanted to get back to practicing medicine, so he took over a difficult thing. He was dedicated enough to think he could make a difference. And he might have for some people. He used to say, 'There's a niche for me here. I can do this.' It wasn't where I would have liked to see him personally, but he was willing to do it. From TGH all the way to that clinic, he provided healthcare beyond belief. I can't say where the greater good was accomplished."

"Warren was a great dreamer," said Chuck Waldman "but he was a great actor too. I'd run into him and ask 'How are you doing?' He'd say, 'I'm doing great. I'm just so happy.' But I saw sadness in his eyes. I'd left medicine by then. Medicine is a hard job under the best of circumstances—a big responsibility, an honor, you're trusted. People expect too much, but you try to do your best."

"My sense was that he loved it," I said.

"Yeah, I loved it too," said Chuck, "but I was going to die."

"I remember Warren talking to Chuck and realizing that practicing medicine was bad for his health," said Janet Waldman. "He gave him a book called *Is This Worth Dying For?*"

"It was a good book," said Chuck.

"And after he read it, Chuck stopped practicing," said Janet.

"I was angry when I quit," said Chuck. "Anger hurts the one who carries it, and it hurt me bad. But when I saw him, he'd put on the act— 'I'm happy, and this is just so damn great.' I'd think, 'Oh, Warren, don't keep fooling yourself. You can only do that for so long.'"

"Warren wasn't the arrogant asshole some doctors are," said Judy. "He was humble and normal and natural. He could empathize."

"Why didn't he get arrogant?"

"Warren never believed he was that good," said Judy. "His father never said, 'I'm proud of you,' even when he graduated from medical school. His mother always told him he was great, but he didn't believe her because his father told him he wasn't. He was 2 when his older brother died of a brain tumor, and I think his parents were traumatized and never got over that. Warren felt that he had to be his brother *and himself*. He had to succeed and make something of himself because Phil died. The thing is, he was a natural healer, a natural listener, and so interested in medicine. He seemed like such a doofus, but he always knew what was up-to-date in medicine. He was brilliant in that respect, and he loved the puzzle of medicine."

# *Chapter 31*

# MAGIC OF THE NIGHT

The universe is full of magical things,
patiently waiting for our wits to grow sharper.

-Eden Phillpotts, playwright

After Warren started working at the Forest Road Clinic, he bought a yellow Jeep. Betty Sinclair remembers being out on the street one day when Warren drove up. "You act like a young kid in that yellow Jeep," she said.

"Yes, I am. I'm just livin' life."

The stories about Warren during the spring and summer of 2010 are frequently prefaced with the words "the last time." Over and over I heard anecdotes that began with "the last trip" ... "the last Cousins Week" ... "the last time I saw Warren" ... stories drenched with hindsight and affection. They were the stories of Warren "just livin' life" —the life he lived for 66 years.

Dean Colli described his and Sharon's last visit with Warren and Judy during Easter weekend on the Colorado River. "Warren was in charge of entertainment. We kayaked and off-roaded in the Jeep, and we guys climbed some boulders. Even though he was a bit larger than I, Warren often relished the chance to test the limits of my physical courage. He seemed to enjoy our meager feats more than I, saying that he was put on this Earth for many reasons, not the least of which was, as my good buddy, to loosen me up. The Higher Power did take charge of some adventure that weekend, tossing an earthquake our way. As we played cards in the Borgquists' motor home, we thought the desert winds were tossing us around a bit, until we began to get phone calls and e-mail from family and friends inquiring if we were OK. It made for a good laugh, which were never in short supply."

"I remember the last track meet he came to," said Jessica Borgquist. "He and my sister, Moriah, rode bikes to the meet because he had to drop his Jeep at the dealership for servicing. I was running the 400-meter race, and they barely made it in time. I was in the block, and I could hear him yelling, "Go, Jessica!" And I could see him because he was in this bright orange vest. The gun went off, and we're running. He ran down the front bleachers the whole way right next to me. I ended up winning first place. That's when he ran down the stairs and out onto the track. He was so excited, jabbering about the race. 'I was so scared,' he said, 'because all those girls were over a head taller than you, and I thought you were going to get smoked. I am so proud of you.' My coach said, 'Looks like you have a fan here.' Gramps was my biggest fan."

"The last time I saw Gramps," said Moriah, "I had the pleasure of going on a bike ride with him. First, we rode from my house to MJC to watch my sister's track meet. He was wearing his reflective orange vest over a yellow shirt and blue biking shorts, and his helmet was on sideways. His yellow Jeep was in the shop, and that was his favorite new toy, so after the meet we were going to ride our bikes to the shop. We ended up getting lost in the McHenry Orchards. He was not very good directionally, but this was Modesto, and it's very simple. There's only straight, left and right. Sadly, I knew where we needed to go, but he insisted he did too. So I just followed along. The thing was, during that whole trip I was amazed because for such a big man, he could go and go on that bicycle. He was an absolute trooper. I kept wondering how he was still going, until finally we got to his yellow Jeep."

"After he went to work at the Forest Road Clinic," said Monique Tomasovich, "the agency I worked for was down where the old Fairview Pharmacy had been, and we often met in the parking lot. The last time I saw him, he was excited because he was going on a trip with some of his kids. They were doing good, and my kids were doing good. He had helped my daughter, who had an alcohol/drug problem and was in AA. He'd recently been there for her five-year anniversary. So everything was going well. He had that smile. 'Life is good,' he said, "and Judy is wonderful.'"

"We went on a trip to France for Grammie's 70th birthday and my dad's 50th," said Evan Purdy. It was Grammie, Gramps, my dad and Cyndie, and Kacey. And I took my girlfriend Harmony along."

"Three of our kids have December birthdays," said Judy, "and Warren was November 27, so we counted him as December too. We also have several in-laws with December birthdays, so I made up this rule. If you take someone on a date, you have to ask, 'When's your birthday?' And if they have a December birthday, you can't go out with that person again. When we were in Paris, I said this in front of Harmony, and she went up to her room and cried because her birthday is December 17. When we were in Paris that last time," Judy continued, "Warren and Nicolas walked the streets for eight hours, talking about life and medicine. Nicolas is so grateful that they had that day together."

Nicolas was grateful for something else as well. "When they came to France that last summer," he said, "we met in Paris. My new girlfriend and I had dinner with Judy and Warren. In the '90s, I'd had children with another women, and then after ten years we separated. I remember, when I met my new girlfriend, I was talking on the phone with Warren, telling him how adorable she was. We'd been together about one month. He asked, "How old is she?' I said, 'She's 26.' I was 47 at the time. 'What do you think, Warren?' I asked, and he said, "Well, Nicolas." That's all he said. But then all four of us met in Paris, and they were thrilled to meet her. I remember Warren said, 'How often do you meet someone who loves you, adores you, who wants the whole package, the good and the bad?' I think he was very happy for me."

"After Paris, we went to Nicolas' parents home," said Judy. "They were away, but we stayed there, and the sewer stopped up. There was

Warren, arms deep in shit, trying to unplug the sewer lines, and the rest of us were going, 'Eww.'"

"When we were staying in Fayence in the south of France on that last trip," said Kacey, "I went on a bike ride. Gramps had done the ride the day before, and he told me the route he took. The ride was completely uphill, and it wasn't a great bike trail. In fact, it was very difficult, and I was struggling. I was pretty fit at that time, and I remember thinking, how the hell did he get up that hill? I was a fit 20 year old and could barely make it. How was it possible that such a big guy could do it? The thing is, giving up was just not in his DNA. He was simply the most resilient person I know. He told stories about being in med school where he wasn't the smartest guy. He was never the tallest. He didn't want to be buried on the tallest point but rather the second or third tallest. He didn't have an ego complex. He just worked really hard to do well. That's why he was so good at things you wouldn't expect him to be good at," Kacey concluded.

"Harmony has a fond memory of Gramps from the trip," said Evan. "We were staying at this Château in the south of France. It was a spectacular place. He was down at the pool swimming by himself, and she went down to swim with him. He stopped for a moment and said, "Isn't life great?' and then he continued swimming."

"Our last Cousin's Week was at Lake Syskiyou near Mount Shasta," said Sean Purdy. "We went on a bike ride down below the dam, and I was riding beside him. I remember he turned to me and out of the blue said, 'Sean I've never felt better in my life.' He was just so happy. I could tell that he was loving the day."

Evan recalls talking with Gramps that last Cousin Week. "I was talking to him about what I wanted to do with my life. At the time, I didn't have too much direction, but I knew I wanted to go back to school. I'd had fun working with my other grandfather in Montana. We did architectural rock landscaping, so I was telling Gramps I wanted to be landscape architect. He said, 'I don't really see you in that kind of work, but if you want to do it right now, then that's great. Pursue it.'" Then Evan underlined the fact that Gramps had simply validated that momentary possibility. "Now," said Evan, "I'm headed in the direction I really want to go— becoming a graphic artist."

Ben Lebell, Jennifer's son, also remembers the week at Mount Shasta. "One day, a few of us decided to hike up Mount Shasta. We tried to get everyone to go, but some of the others wanted to rent a boat and play on the lake, so it ended up being my dad, my brother, Gramps, and me who went on the hike. We were all runners—except for Gramps—so we started running up the trail. We were passing people with backpacks and all this gear. They were in big boots with clamps for the snow. We were just in our shorts and running shoes. Eventually the trail stopped, and it was like running up the side of the mountain with a snow pack. We got pretty high. Then we started the descent, and not too far down, we found Gramps plugging away with his walking stick. He was still coming. He made it really far. You could see the smile on his face because it was a beautiful view up there. We were above the tree line, so we could see all the lakes surrounding us."

Ben's brother Jake remembers that Gramps, "just kept slogging along." Emma Lebell said, "Gramps wasn't particularly old but he wasn't exactly young. Still he didn't stop very often. If we needed help, he would help us, but he never asked for a break."

"Gramps always described himself as a plugger," said, Ben. "He may have been slow, but he kept plugging away. That's definitely something I'll take away from having him in my life. Knowing that things may not work in the timely fashion you want, but as long as you keep plugging away, then life will be good, and you will get there"

Maryann Curmi tells the story of her friend Tammy, who had pancreatic cancer and was one of Warren's last hospice patients. "After her diagnosis, Tammy's goal was to see her son Jack graduate from high school," said Maryann. "The very first doctor she saw had given her a death sentence. 'Just take her home and get her comfortable,' he said. 'What are you talking about?' I cried. 'This is a 49-year-old woman.' So I started calling everybody I could. And somebody said to take her to UCSF, so we got her there. She amazed everyone. She lived for two-and-a-half or three more years. Her doctor said, 'You're making history, Tamara.'

"Warren came into Tammy's life after all the good stuff started wearing off when it was time to call hospice. Tammy used to say, 'I love that man,' even though she didn't see him very much. She probably only saw Warren a handful of times, but there was a connection. I remember that she appreciated the fact that he told her that when the time came, someone was going to need to administer morphine, and she knew that when that happened her days were numbered.

"I was pretty much her caregiver, and this one particular Friday, I felt like I needed to be away for an hour. I checked on how she was doing, and she said, 'Fine. I saw Dr. Borgquist today.' So I told her I was going to go to the Concert in the Park, but I'd be back because we planned to go to dinner. I was standing in the park listening to the music when I saw Warren. He was never my doctor, but he knew me through theatre, and he came up to me, arms extended, and we hugged. He asked how I was doing and then said, 'She's quite the gal.' I said, 'She thinks the world of you.' Then he said, 'She's got something important to tell you.' So at that point I thought I'd better leave because that was all I could think about.

"When I got to her house, she was putting on her make-up, but I thought something was odd. That's when I realized she was dressed only to waist, and the rest of her was in pajamas and slippers, so I asked, 'Do you want to go to dinner in your slippers?' And she said, 'Yeah.' On the drive to the Eproson House, I asked if she'd talked to Dr. Borgquist about eating because she was getting stopped up, and she said, 'I didn't tell him.' After we got to the restaurant, I asked, 'Are you keeping things from him on purpose?' By this time there were long pauses between my questions and her answers, so I said, 'Tammy, the reason I'm pestering you is because I saw Dr. Borgquist at the Concert in the Park.'

"'What did he say?' she asked

"He said you would tell me how your meeting went today. And then this woman I had only seen cry three times in seventeen years, started crying so hard I couldn't understand her. The only thing I could make out was 'the M word.'

"'Tammy I don't understand,' I said. She was weeping, and the server was standing there, looking at this woman with make-up streaming down her face—a skeleton in pajama bottoms, slippers, and a cute top. It was surreal. Finally I got it out of her.

"'Morphine time' she said.

"'Aaahhh!' I said and turned to the server and said, 'Can we box this stuff up please?'

432

"So I start administering morphine that night, and as the week progressed, she slipped into a morphine stupor. To tell you the truth, her son and I wondered how long she could go on. I was changing her diaper. She was totally out of it."

A week after Maryann Curmi saw Warren at the Concert in the Park, Dr. Meredith McBride found a note from Dr. Borgquist on the chart of a patient they shared who was being prepped for life threatening surgery. "He detailed the situation, and concluded his note with 'Good luck, Dr. McBride!' That little sincere, heart-felt statement he'd inserted into the official medical record typified what made him so real and so reachable to his patients and to the medical community."

Later that day, Brittany Norwood, his MA, said good-bye to him at the office. "It was probably 6:30 or 7:00," said Brittany. "He'd gotten a call from hospice saying that one of the patients needed a change in medication. He was on his way to take care of that. It was the last time I saw him."

That evening, Judy and Warren headed downtown for Magic of the Night, an annual summer event with sidewalk sales, restaurant specials, street vendors, and entertainment up and down Washington Street from the Red Church to the Opera Hall, the old cruising ground of Warren and his high school buddies on Friday nights in the 1950s. "I met them at Alfredo's for dinner," said Kathleen Lorimer. "We were already seated— Janet and Tom Donaldson, Jeannie and Steven Shepherd, me, Warren and Judy—when Brynn and Nick came in. Warren went over to sit with them. They had a great conversation. I know Brynn carries that evening in her heart. After dinner we walked to Coffill Park, where there was live music. I remember watching Warren and Judy dance."

On Saturday, the couple went to Pinecrest Lake. "We took our kayaks," said Ann Leonard, "Judy and Warren, Marjorie and Craig, Jim and I. We hauled them down to the water and paddled all over the Lake. Judy was the queen, and Warren was the rower."

"He was always a swimmer," said Marjorie, "but he was like Jack LaLanne that day. He tied a rope to himself and the kayak and then swam along, pulling Judy in the boat. He made jokes and waved. He must have pulled her for twenty minutes or so."

433

"It was a great day," said Ann. "We stopped on the way down the hill for lunch, and we laughed a whole lot more. On the drive home, Jim and I talked about Warren—he looked better than we'd seen him look in a long time. He'd lost weight. He was happy and smiling."

"The oddest thing is that I was not there on Saturday night when Warren came to see Tammy," said Maryann Curmi. "There was a Pretenders concert at Ironstone. I had bought tickets for both of us when they first came out in June because we thought she was going to last another summer. That Saturday, everyone convinced me to go. I had a horrible time. Dr. Borgquist stopped to check in on Tammy while I was at the concert. I don't know if the hospice nurse called Borgquist because Tammy was getting cantankerous. When she was in pain, she'd start flailing. Anyway, he came by that night to give her something. When I returned, she kept saying, 'He was like an angel, Maryann. He showed up, and there was this big moon. He looked so good, like there was a light shining on him.' She was so calm, and then she slept.

"The next morning, I asked the hospice nurse what he gave her. 'Propofol,' she said, and then explained, 'He knows her days are numbered, so why not let her get some sleep.' And then she excused herself to answer her cell phone. Tammy was sleeping, so I sat there waiting. When the nurse returned, she said, 'Dr. Borgquist is dead. Tammy was the last patient he saw.'"

# *Chapter 32*

## DAMMIT, WARREN

> You know, everybody dies.
> My parents died. Your father died. Everybody dies.
> I'm going to die too. So will you.
> The thing is, to have a life before we die.
> It can be a real adventure having a life.
>
> —John Irving, *The World According to Garp*

"The world stopped," said Judy. "It just stopped."

The entire community was stunned. Every person I talked with remembered exactly where they were when they heard the news of Warren's death—heard that he had not awoken on the morning of August 15, 2010. We were shaken with disbelief. While phones rang across the county and word spread, the family gathered around Judy. They raced from their homes, from a Bar Mitzvah, from a river trip to the dwelling he had crafted.

"It was an incredible week," said Scott Purdy. "Everyone stayed at Mom's."

The family pulled together a memorial service that would be attended by nearly five hundred people at the Family Worship Center. When Dave Purdy offered to help, he became the director. "We talked about possibilities," said Dave, "and one question kept recurring: How

435

many people were delivered by or had babies delivered by Warren?" So that became the opening.

When Scott Purdy faced the assemblage and asked the question, two thirds of the people in the huge hall stood, wiping tears from their faces. On a screen above the dais, the smiling visage of our doctor looked down upon us.

"Warren said that he wanted his ashes put in Death Valley on the third highest dune because he was always the third buffalo back," said Judy. "So the whole family—every member—including Warren's sisters and their families, plus the Wilsons, Kathleen, Nicolas, Dean Colli—we all went. We waited until at the end of March around Easter when he, Jim, and Doug usually went, and we stayed at a little motel. Not the fancy one. The first night, I arranged a barbecue in a special area just for us. Before dinner, we had a cocktail party and hors d'oeuvres. The next morning, we went out to the third highest dune. I gave everyone a baggie of his ashes, and we had a little ceremony. We each said something about him, and then we dispersed, so everyone could do their own private thing, putting his ashes where they wanted. I had a little Jeep that I put with mine. I still cry when I see motorhomes and Jeeps.

"My friend, Sandy was really helpful. She had been widowed about a year before. She told me about having a necklace made with her husband's ashes in it. At first, I thought that was weird. 'Think about it,' she said. 'I believe it will be a comfort to you because it was to me.'

"I had Warren's wedding ring in a little dish beside my bed," continued Judy. "When we were in Africa—in Tanzania—we were at souvenir shop. He insisted that I get this necklace with Tanzanite. One day, about a month after he died, I wore that necklace. When I took it off, I threw it in the dish, and it went right into the wedding ring. So I thought, now I know what to do, because Sandy had said you have to have something meaningful. I took it down to Gold Fever. They didn't think it was weird because they'd done it before. They put a gold backing on his wedding ring, and put his ashes inside the space. Then they put another gold piece on top and attached the Tanzanite piece. I wore it continuously for a long time, and I still wear it when I go on a trip.

"I can't believe how many trips I've taken since he died. The first was with Ryan and Moriah. Warren had really been looking forward to that trip because we were going to Sweden—his home country. In the middle of Stockholm, there are these little islands, and you can take a boat to one where they've recreated a village with old shops, like a candle shop and a bakery. We were walking around this village and suddenly I realized there was no one around. We saw this stone with something like hieroglyphics—some kind of etching, possibly Runes. Warren had told the kids that he needed to learn some of these symbols to be able to translate them before we traveled to Sweden. There was this beautiful tree with white flowers. I took a picture of the kids in front of the stone, and then we went behind it, and each said a little something about Gramps and left some of his ashes there."

"We went to Skansen," said Moriah, telling her version of the story, "where we found a really beautiful spot. There was a flowering tree with the sweetest smell—very entrancing—and under it was a gravestone. It had intricate engravings including a big red sun. We read some of the details on the stone and learned it was the grave of a family man—he had twelve children. It was the perfect spot, so we left some of Gramps' ashes there.

"We also went to Tivoli Gardens in Copenhagen," said Moriah, "an amusement park with gardens and lights. It was absolutely beautiful, and there was a super large swing. To get on, you have to climb stairs that are two stories high, and then it lifts you about seventy-five or eighty feet, and you're looking out over Copenhagen. I'm not good with heights, so I said 'No!' I wasn't going. My cousin Ryan kept saying, 'You're going; you're going,' but there was no way I was doing it. Then Grammie hit me with a line: 'If Gramps were here, you would be going on that swing.' Just like that there was no debating.

"There was a metal platform that rose and then dropped away. I was terrified. I was holding my breath and clinging to the chains. Ryan was swinging side to side, scaring the living daylights out of me. But it was the most spectacular view. It was nighttime, and the sun doesn't set until about twelve o'clock in the summer, so it was sunset—bright orange and dark blue and the city lights. It was astonishing. I was scared, but I knew Grammie was right. If he had been there, I would have done it, so it was definitely something I did just for him.

"Ryan had his own eye-opening time. Usually he eats very plain, very American— hotdogs, corndogs, chicken nuggets. That's pretty much his diet. Grammie and I were open to trying everything. We wanted to try all the wild, weird food they have, and Ryan refused to eat those things. So after a while, Grammie and I said we're here, so we're going to eat their food. Sorry, you're going to have to find something. Finally, when we were in Talon, Estonia, Ryan tried wild boar and ostrich, and he absolutely loved it."

"Wherever I go, I take him," said Judy. "It makes me feel good. I told you the story of the poop overflowing when we visited in the South of France shortly before he died. When I returned to Nicolas' parents house, I put some of his ashes right on the sewer hole where the mess came up. And I put ashes where he'd made a little toilet for me out in back behind a shed. Warren always wanted to go to Cappadocia in Turkey, especially to the underground city. So when I was there and the guide was lecturing, I hung back when I saw a little niche. I said a few things and then put him in the niche. I recently went to Delphi. We'd had so much fun with Jake and Jessica when we were there. In the amphitheater you can stand at the top and whisper down at the bottom and hear every word. We ran up and down and testing what we heard. We had a fabulous time. This last time, when I saw a rock with a crevasse facing the amphitheater, I whipped him out—I always carry him in baggies—and put him in the crevasse and reminded him how much fun we had."

"At first, it was creepier than heck—especially this," said Judy, holding up the necklace. "But I had to dig out so many of his ashes to put in baggies for Death Valley that I just got used to it. Now I get a spoon and put them in the bags when I travel. I always advise people not to disperse all the ashes. I tell them you might want to do something like this because it's a comfort to me. There will always be a hole," she admitted. "I wake up sad every morning. We had some good times and some bad times. No one escapes. Once I said to Warren, 'Maybe when I'm eighty it will be smooth going.' And he said, 'No! My mother always wanted a still pond of life. There is no still pond.' There are definitely still moments, but not much coasting. Mostly uphill. Dammit Warren, I still have to stick my neck out! I hate that. I'd rather have it be easy. But no."

An auditorium full of people had attended Dr. Warren Borgquist's memorial, numb and bewildered, listening to his colleagues, friends, and family reminisce and celebrate the man's life. Afterward, while Judy traveled and spread Warren's ashes, we patients sought a worthy replacement. "Dr. Borgquist was connected to some big events in my family," said my sister Anne. Having known his largess, we were at a loss.

"I keep forgetting he's dead," said Kris Scott. "Because I can't picture a world without him."

"He sounds bigger than life," said Charlene Ingalls, "but to anyone who knew him that wasn't an exaggeration. He was bigger than life. I still don't have a doctor. I've tried five different physicians. They don't know me. How do you start over?"

Like Charlene, I had never given a doctor my history because I had gone to the same doctor for thirty years. I was unhinged the first time I tried. It can't be done. You can't give a medical history with all its permutations. It's impossible.

"I have to quit searching for a repeat," said Charlene. "No one's going to talk to me like he did. They take your vitals and tell you that because you're over 60 you need all these inoculations: pneumonia, shingles, flu. I wish Warren were here to ask. Dang it, Warren! You left us!"

Judy wasn't alone in cursing Warren. "I was ready to make an effort to stop saying god dammit, Warren," said Jennifer, "but it's hard because he isn't here to take my boys off to college, god damn him."

"Mimi says if I'd quit cursing him, he might come to me in a dream or something," said Judy. She was sitting on the faded yellow couch with sunlight reflecting off the pool in a play of light behind her. Across the room, sitting cattywampus on an end table, was one of many giraffes.

# ACKNOWLEDGEMENTS

To Judy—thank you for trusting me.

To Warren's family—especially his sisters, Karma and Marjorie—and to his friends, patients, and colleagues, thank you for your stories. You gave me so much more than has arrived here on the page. I hope what I've chosen to include feels right.

To two extraordinary transcribers—Suzanne DeCaccia and DeeAnn Horn—thank you for your patient attention to noting every word of each recording.

To the Kickstarter donors—especially Culley Harrelson, Scott Purdy, and Liz Swiertz Newman—who invested in the project, thank you. Your contributions paid for hours of transcription.

To my indomitable editor—Liz Swiertz Newman—thanks for your eagle eye and many years of friendship.

To the Word Project Press team—Melody Baker, Sy Baldwin, Gillian Herbert and Sally McCllelan—thanks for your artistry and intelligence.

To my writing group—Blanche Abrams, Carol Beiderman, Kristen Fulton, Sally McClellan, Shelley Muniz, Ellen Stewart, Ann St. James, and Suzan Still—you are midwives extraordinaire, coaching me wisely and enthusiastically.

To my family—I know you feel as fortunate as I in having had Dr. Borgquist as our physician. This book was conceived during the time we spent in his care. Thanks for your endearing recollections.

To Cindy—your constancy and devotion exceeds all expectations.

# BIBLIOGRAPHY

Gawande, Atul. *Complications: A Surgeon's Notes on an Imperfect Science.* Henry Holt and Company, New York, 2002.

Groopman, Jerome. *How Doctors Think.* Houghton Mifflin Company, New York. 2007.

Marion, Robert. *The Intern Blues: The Timeless Classic About the Making of a Doctor.* Harper, New York, 1989.

Moore, Thomas. *A Religion of One's Own: A Guide to Creating a Personal Spirituality in a Secular World.* Gotham Books, New York, 2014.

Sweet, Victoria. *God's Hotel: A Doctor, A Hospital, and a Pilgrimage to the Heart of Medicine.* Riverhead Books, New York, 2012.

Whyte, David. *Consolations: The Solace, Nourishment and Underlying Meaning of Everyday Words.* Many Rivers Press, Langley WA, 2014.

Zink, Therese (Ed). *The Country Doctor Revisited: A Twenty-First Century Reader.* University Press, Kent, Ohio, 2010.

Made in the USA
San Bernardino, CA
05 October 2017